BATTLE DRUMS AND GEYSERS

Lt. Gustavus Cheyney Doane, 1875. W. E. Strong's account of the Secretary of War W. W. Belknap tour of Yellowstone was published in 1876 as
*A Trip to the Yellowstone National Park in July, August, and September
1875.* All copies of the 1876 edition had a photograph of each member of
the party pasted into the books. The above reproduction is from the copy
at the Library of Congress.

BATTLE DRUMS AND GEYSERS

The Life and Journals of
Lt. Gustavus Cheyney Doane,
Soldier and Explorer of the
Yellowstone and Snake River Regions

Orrin H. and Lorraine Bonney

Foreword by George B. Hartzog, Jr.

SAGE BOOKS

THE **SWALLOW PRESS** INC.
CHICAGO

First Edition

Sage Books are published by

The Swallow Press Incorporated
1139 South Wabash Avenue
Chicago, Illinois 60605

LIBRARY OF CONGRESS CATALOG CARD NUMBER 70-91169

Dedicated to

all those who have worked to preserve for all time and for all people a portion of our land in its natural and wonderful state, without thought of commercial gain or the vandalism of improvements. These individuals have enriched our environment and made our National Park system possible.

One cannot explore the earth's surface from an observatory, nor by mathematics nor by the power of logic; it must be done physically. . . .

Caution might prevent, but with caution no results will be obtained. Risks must be taken, and there is an element in human affairs as fortune, good or bad.

Gustavus Cheyney Doane

CONTENTS

PART II

The Yellowstone Exploration of 1870

PART III

The Snake River Exploration of 1876-1877

ILLUSTRATIONS

PART II

PART III

MAPS

FOREWORD

About noon, on a clear day in September 1870, a party of explorers followed the course of the Firehole River in Wyoming Territory. Abruptly, they broke through the dense lodgepole forest into an open, treeless valley. Directly ahead, no more than 200 yards away, a column of water was spurting 150 feet into the sky. Bright sunlight glittered through clouds of steam, which drifted slowly across the silent landscape. And so the geyser, which the explorers named "Old Faithful," emerged from the era of fable and romance, ultimately to become the most famous natural phenomenon in this country, if not the world.

Of several early parties who visited and explored the Yellowstone country, by far the most important was the Washburn-Langford-Doane group, the "Yellowstone Expedition of 1870." Made up of nine prominent citizens of Montana, it was escorted by a small cavalry detail under the leadership of Lt. Gustavus C. Doane. General Henry D. Washburn, surveyor-general of Montana, headed the expedition; Nathaniel P. ("National Park") Langford, whose later articles in *Scribner's Monthly* gave wide publicity to the discovery, became the first superintendent of the Park.

The 1870 expedition grew out of widespread curiosity over the true nature of the Yellowstone region; tales of some early explorers — Jim Bridger in particular — had created a certain amount of disbelief as to the existence of mountains of glass and streams so saturated with alum they had the power to pucker distance itself. One expedition member declared: "A more confirmed set of skeptics never went out into the wilderness than those who composed our party, and never was a party more completely surprised and captivated with the wonders of nature."

The selection of Lt. Doane to head the military escort was a fortunate choice. General Hiram M. Chittenden, historian of Yellowstone, said of Doane that "no member of the expedition holds a more honorable place in its history." One of the valuable contributions of this book is the biographical account of the life of Gustavus C. Doane. He was one of that special breed of American explorers who ever yearned to see the yonder side. But the heart of the book deals with Doane's journal account of the famous 1870 expedition. It is a story of great historical interest.

In itself, the exploration was one of the remarkable adventures of the American frontier. From Helena the route covered some 300 miles of uncharted wilderness, into an area extremely difficult of access, at a time when the danger from hostile Indian attack had somewhat reduced the civilian contingent of the party.

The most significant achievement of the expedition, certainly a landmark in the history of the National Park Service, was that it led directly to the establishment, two years later, of Yellowstone National Park. Lt. Doane's superb account, submitted to Congress, was the first official report on the resources of the Yellowstone region, and helped prepare the way for the Yellowstone Act.

The Doane journals rightfully belong on the shelf with those of Lewis and Clark and other great explorers of the American West. I am personally grateful to Lorraine and Orrin Bonney for their carefully researched and skillfully edited book, and I know them to be intimately acquainted with the country through which Doane led the 1870 expedition. The National Park Service — and National Park visitors — have already profited from the excellent guide books prepared by the Bonneys.

Readers of the Doane journal will follow with high pleasure the route of the explorers. I was particularly moved by Doane's account as the party, upon reaching its objective, ascended a mountain, later named Mount Washburn, and looked down upon the vast panorama of Yellowstone. There indeed were the grand canyon and falls and lake, just as had been reported. There were the columns of steam, evidence enough of boiling springs and geysers.

At long last, Jim Bridger was vindicated – if a few of his most bizarre tales could be excused as exploration oratory.

The book is a timely one: this year is the 100th anniversary of the expedition, and in 1972 we will celebrate the 100th anniversary of the establishment of Yellowstone.

Now precious to all Americans as a National Park, Yellowstone today is even more valuable as an idea. Yellowstone's children, some 1,200 national parks and preserves in nearly a hundred countries throughout the world, are testimony to the importance of that far-sighted Act of Congress which President Grant signed on March 1, 1872, dedicating and setting apart "as a public park or pleasuring ground for the benefit and enjoyment of the people" that tract of land lying at the headwaters of the Yellowstone River.

Looking back on his exploration of the Yellowstone, Doane observed, "It is probably the greatest laboratory that nature furnishes on the surface of the globe."

His prediction was wholly accurate, but the nineteen-man party of explorers in 1870 could scarcely have imagined that one hundred years later, in 1970, 2,000,000 people would be viewing Old Faithful. Nor could the party have anticipated that within a century the seeming vast wilderness of Yellowstone would, with the other National Parks, comprise the last remaining tracts of unspoiled America, invaluable sanctuaries from a technology which seems destined to engulf the human spirit.

GEORGE B. HARTZOG, JR.
Director
National Park Service
Washington, D. C.

PREFACE

Trekking to Oregon over the old covered wagon trail when he was five years old, racing with his parents to California during the gold rush, growing up among the Forty-Niners, putting himself through college, rising from private to first lieutenant in the battles and skirmishes of the Civil War, serving as mayor of a Mississippi city during Reconstruction, commanding the tough troopers of the Second Cavalry in the Indian battles, exploring from the Arctic to the Rockies, Gustavus Cheyney Doane and his life story are the West and its story — exploration, adventure, toil, frustration, conquest.

Doane himself penned an interesting self-consciousness about the role of a pioneer:

> It is something to march under the guidance of the star of empire, and feel that a mighty nation follows on your trail. Frontier celebrity is cheap and lasting, as compared with other, and explorations furnish a source of reputation wherein the rewards are, and ever have been, more than commensurate with the efforts put forth. The fame of the pioneers of this country is as brilliant today as that of her statesmen, and so will continue till the end of time.[1]

[1] T. F. Rodenbough, *From Everglade to Cañon with the Second Dragoons 1836-1875*, 405.

Lieutenant Doane, an outstanding and capable soldier, typified the finest men of the western frontier. With war drums beating out the westward advance of America, Doane was there, participating in the major Indian campaigns which followed the Civil War — from Sitting Bull and the Sioux through the Nez Perce campaign and the strategy of Chief Joseph to the pursuit of Geronimo and the Apaches.

During the lull between battles, while others dulled their boredom in drink and play, Doane was the student and the explorer. He contributed to the world the first scientific account of the wonders of the region now known as Yellowstone National Park.

Doane stood above his fellow army officers as much in his unusual desire for exploration as in his military skill and in his commanding appearance — six foot one inch tall, 190 pounds of strength. General W. E. Strong reports:

> Lieutenant Doane is a striking officer. Tall, straight as an arrow, very dark complexion with black hair and a long, sweeping, dark moustache, he would certainly attract attention in any company. He is a superb horseman, a keen and daring hunter, and a dead shot.[2]

Major General Hugh L. Scott, who was to become chief of staff of the U.S. Army in 1917, served under Doane in the Nez Perce campaign of 1877. Scott, then a second lieutenant just graduated from West Point, says:

> I modeled myself on him as a soldier, watched him carefully. . . . He was a thorough plainsman, able to do everything anybody else could do on the prairie except interpret. . . . [I] learned from him how to set

---

[2] W. E. Strong, *Trip to the Yellowstone National Park in July, August and September 1875*, 39. Doane's height and weight figures come, respectively, from the Army Records of G. C. Doane, Record Group No. 94 and from Doane's own Snake River journal, December 18 entry. (See Part III of this book)

up an aparejo[3] and to throw the diamond so that, if
the packing should be delayed, we two would pitch in
to help pack ourselves and get the command out of
camp in a hurry. There was no delay, for no one
loitered where we were in the train, and we could put
our hands to anything and show others how it was
done.[4]

Doane deserves more credit than he has received from historians for his contribution to the Indian campaigns themselves
and to developing friendly relations with the Indians. For
example, his first contacts with the Crows kept them as peaceful neighbors to the military at Fort Ellis. In 1876, when the
Sioux and Cheyennes wiped out Custer, the Crows did not join
with them Doane's efforts had helped. However, when battle
was called for, Doane and his troops were there. Perhaps the
outstanding monument to Doane's military skill and leadership
is the fact that he never lost a man under his command to the
Indians.

Fred Munn, reminiscing in 1939 about his days with the
Second Cavalry in Montana, remembered Doane well and still
after more than sixty years selected him out for special notice:

One of the officers at Fort Ellis who was well thought
of by the men was Lieutenant Doane of the second
cavalry. He was a thorough cavalryman, often requesting scouting duty with one of our four companies at Ellis. He was a big stalwart man. . . . He
appeared to have no fear under any conditions, consequently we welcomed detached duty with the
Lieutenant, more than with any other officer.[5]

[3] The aparejo (from the Mexicans) consisted fundamentally of two straw-filled
pads, one on each side of the animal. The packer would pound and shape them to fit
the animal. In the hands of an expert they protected the pack animal better than any
other arrangement. Poorly done, sores, lameness, and other pack disabilities would
soon put the animal out of service.
[4] Hugh L. Scott, *Some Memories of a Soldier,* 59.
[5] "The Punitive Aftermath with Miles, Howard, Brisbin and Doane . . . " *Montana
the Magazine of Western History,* Spring 1966, 64.

Doane never held rank above company commander, but he was a trusted and sought-after adviser to the top field commanders and he was often singled out for mention in their reports and memoirs.

If the army and military skill were his profession, knowledge and exploration were Doane's passion. He himself stated the philosophy which shaped his career:

> Army service on the frontier is a life of peculiar characteristics, and no occupation is so generally misunderstood. Its idle hours, which are numerous, are an enforced idleness, arising from a necessity to be present in case of an ever-possible emergency. Yet it is an attractive life. Its monotonous round of duties may often be greatly varied through personal effort, and a fair field of ambition is always open to those who, in the absence of *greater* opportunities, have the energy to grapple with those lesser ones which the lapse of time and procession of events invariably cast to the surface.
>
> It is something also to break down the barriers of the unknown; to behold the mists of darkness fade; to marshal the videttes of the vanguard of progress; to form the crest of that wave of civilization which sweeps onward, invincible and without ceasing, through the breadth of a great continent, until it meets the reflux tide from the broad Pacific's slope. . . .
>
> A single exploration by a junior officer [Fremont] in 1846 carried him afterward successively to a spot in the United States Senate, the possession of a princely estate, a candidature for the presidency, and the command of the Western army at the commencement of a great war. The field is open still. Its invasion does not require exalted rank. A poor subaltern, yet unknown, while traversing with weary steps the barren wilderness, or scaling the mighty

summits from which the waters part and flow, may stumble, under fortune's favor, upon some new discovery, the merit of which will secure to him all that history vouchsafes to greatness – a paragraph in the encyclopaedia of the human race.[6]

Doane's drive for exploration did not always fit neatly into the framework of his military career. He once took leave of the army in order to lead an expedition from which the government had suddenly withdrawn its support. At least twice he went over the head of his reluctant post commander in order to get approval for his expeditions. One such was the notable Yellowstone exploration in 1870. The expedition, without Doane's military escort, might never have gotten underway and the results certainly would not have been so successful without Doane's observations and his journals.

With a scholarly college background embracing the scientific knowledge of his day, Doane the explorer was able to observe carefully and, more importantly, to write – of the land, its energy, and its activity.

His career is a real saga of an American officer of the last half of the nineteenth century. In appreciation for Doane's part in winning the West and his part in making Yellowstone known, the editors bring to life his journals and his adventurous story and give this scholarly soldier his due: "a paragraph in the encyclopaedia of the human race."

O.H.B. and L.B.

---

[6] Rodenbough, *From Everglade to Cañon*, 405.

PART I

THE LIFE OF GUSTAVUS CHEYNEY DOANE

Carlisle Barracks July 2nd 1875

G.C. Doane. of California
      Born in the State of Illinois. Town of
Galesburg. County of Knox, August 29th 1840.
Crossed the Plains in 1846. to Oregon; Emigrated
thence to California in 1849. Graduated, with first
honors at the Pacific University. A.D. 1861, Enlisted
in the Cal. Vol. Dec 10th 1862, Co. assigned to 2d Mass
Cav. Jan 5th of the following year. Was present
at the Capture of the South Anna Bridge in May
1863, by Col Spears Command., subsequently
participated in several skirmishes with Mosby
Men on the Defences of Washington. Was promoted to a 1st Lty of Cavalry in the Miss Marine
Brigade Mar 4th 1864, was in action ten times
during the succeeding six months. including the
Battles of Chicot Lake. and Port-Gibson. Had the
honor to be assigned to Command either the
advance, or rear guard. in eight actions. Had
been recommended for a Colcy of Vol. in 1865
when the Close of the war. Cut-short the field
of promotion
                    Respectfully Submitted
                    Your Obdt Servt —
                    G.C. Doane —

Doane's letter, in his own hand, briefly summarizing his life and his Civil War army career, supporting his application for a commission in the regular army. *Courtesy National Archives.*

CHAPTER 1

EARLY LIFE THROUGH THE CIVIL WAR: 1840 - 1868

CHILDHOOD AND EDUCATION

Gustavus C. Doane was born May 29, 1840, in Galesburg, Knox County, Illinois. His farming parents were Solomon Doane and Nancy Davis Doane.[1] Little is known of Doane's early boyhood.[2] In 1844, when he was four years old, the family moved to St. Louis. For two years the Doanes resisted the beckoning excitements of the Far West, alluring stories of

[1] Doane and the army, after some correspondence, agreed on the May 29 birth date for retirement-age purposes, although Doane once wrote the army giving it as August 29, 1840.

According to Gilbert H. Doane, historian of the Doane Family Association of America, Inc., Gustavus Cheyney Doane was a lineal descendant of John Done, who settled in Plymouth Colony about 1630, the progenitor of the Doane family in America. G. C. Doane's great grandfather, Solomon Doane, a farmer, was born in Eastham, Cape Cod, Massachusetts in 1705. His grandfather, Joshua Doane, also a farmer, was born in Eastham in 1745; he had ten children. G. C. Doane's father, Solomon Doane, was born in Royalston, Massachusetts, September 4, 1813 and died of lockjaw in Alamo, California, August 5, 1866.

G. C. Doane was the first of six children born to Solomon and Nancy (Davis) Doane. The other children's names were James H., Anna G., George E., Charles J., and John E. Born in 1851, George E. Doane settled in San Diego County, California and gave his name to Doane's Valley on the side of Mount Palomar. He was reputed to be a skilled hunter and a highly unskilled writer of poetry. His colorful career and eccentricities during the time he lived in Doane's Valley are amusingly described in Catherine M. Wood's *Palomar from Tepee to Telescope*.

[2] On June 16, 1892, after Doane's death, his widow, Mary Lee Doane, wrote the Society of California Pioneers stating that even she was "not as familiar with his childhood as I should like to be." She noted that "part of his early life was spent at Benicia, [California] and later his father moved to Santa Clara, or near there . . ."

which were drifting back to St. Louis. But in April, 1846, the family packed its belongings and wagontrekked along the deepening ruts and through the choking dust of the old trail to Oregon. Five-year-old Gus trudged along, rode horseback, or sat in the ox-drawn wagon, watching and learning. There were many pioneers of strong character for a small boy to hero-worship.

He heard the creaking wheels, cracking bull whips, and bawling oxen which had formed a loose traffic pattern for 300 miles. He saw strings of wagons pass, fall behind, repass. Inconspicuous in the evening shadows, the small boy could sense tragedy in the tones of his elders as they discussed emigrants who died of hardship. Grass was scarce, the season dry. Indian night raiders drove off oxen and horses — the sole means of transport. About 2,500 persons left the Missouri frontier that year for the Pacific coast; 1,700 of them went to Oregon.

In this year of 1846, the Oregon boundary dispute was ended and the Mexican War begun, events that were to give the United States clear title to the vast territory between the Rocky Mountains and the Pacific Ocean. Young Doane was one of those destined to play an important part in its exploration, conquest, and settlement.

After three years in Oregon the boy saw his parents caught again in a gilded dream of promise, this time the magic delirium of the California Gold Rush. In May, the nine-year-old boy was skipping up the gangplank of the British ship *Janet,* sailing with his parents, and watching the high breakers roll in from the Pacific. Crowding the ship's rails with the Doanes at their arrival in San Francisco was an advance guard of gold hunters pushing to disembark and get on their way to the mines. The glittering flakes of gold discovered by James Wilson Marshall January 24, 1848, in Sutter's Mill race were emptying half of Oregon's white population of 10,000 into California.

Placer sands and hopes drained away in the waters of the Sacramento River. The small boy began to realize that success in life meant work and study rather than running after fortune. For a young boy as naturally studious and curious as Doane, the schools of the day were mostly failures and of little help to him. Bancroft says of four poorly attended shanty classrooms in San Francisco, "The gold excitement carried all off to the mines."[3] Doane taught himself when tutors were unavailable. With the energy and perseverance that characterized his life, he gained enough education to enter, in 1857, the University of the Pacific at Santa Clara, California.[4]

Here the seventeen-year-old Doane worked his own way through college. Even then his mind was set on a military career. The frustrations and disappointment of not obtaining his vigorously sought appointment to West Point did not stop him. He was a good student.

He first enrolled as a science major, then changed to classics. In his well-rounded curriculum he studied the math courses – algebra, geometry, trigonometry, calculus, analytical geometry. He took four years of Greek with all its classics, and some Latin courses. His practical education was to help him considerably in his chosen career and ambitious explorations, especially his studies in surveying, astronomy, navigation, and the sciences of botany, zoology, geology, minerology, physical geography, physics, and mechanics. General subjects were logic, rhetoric, history, political economy, Constitution of the United States, mental philosophy, evidence of Christianity, and moral science.[5]

Doane joined the Archania Literary Society, a local fraternity which later became Gamma Upsilon Chapter of Phi Kappa Tau. He graduated as a classics major, with first honors, on June 13, 1861, receiving a B.A. degree.[6]

[3] H. H. Bancroft, *History of California,* VII, 717.
[4] Now located (since 1924) at Stockton, California. From 1911 until 1961 it was called College of the Pacific.
[5] University of the Pacific letter of June 1, 1964. O. H. Bonney Collection.
[6] Alumni records at the University state that Doane received an M.A. degree in 1869, but do not state from where or in what manner earned. In early 1869, Doane was quartermaster at Fort Russell, Wyoming, and left there in May for Fort Ellis. It can be assumed that his master's degree was awarded by the University of the Pacific under their standard provisions, which were similar to those of other American universities during the eighteenth century and well into the nineteenth century, such provisions being basically copied from British practice – e.g., Oxford University still today provides for M.A. degrees in similar fashion. The regulations under which

BILLY YANK

After a year at home Doane decided that enlistment in the Civil War would be the best way to start his military career. On October 30, 1862, the twenty-two-year-old Doane signed up at San Francisco in "The California One-Hundred," on the Union side. He gave his occupation as farmer.

In December these volunteers, all expert horsemen, but still not a part of the U.S. Army, paid their own expenses east, going by ship from San Francisco to Panama, across the Isthmus by land, and by ship again to New York and then to Boston.

Doane's group was accepted into the U.S. Army on January 8, 1863, and was assigned to Company I, Second Regiment, Massachusetts Cavalry, under the command of Colonel Charles R. Lowell. The men were paid from October 30, 1862. Doane enrolled for a three-year enlistment. A month later, at Camp Meigs, Reidville, he was transferred to Company H, Second Cavalry, and appointed sergeant. Combat action was immediate.

"[We] participated in several skirmishes with Mosby's men on the defenses of Washington," Doane wrote concerning the great Confederate guerrilla fighter who proved to be a nagging problem to Colonel Lowell's cavalry.

In the spring of 1863, Colonel John S. Mosby and his Partisan Rangers had made two great coups: capturing Brigadier General Charles B. Stoughton from Union headquarters twenty miles behind the lines, and taking Sheridan's complete supply train. On June 11 of that year, Doane's entire regiment crossed the Potomac at White's Ford to pursue Mosby. "Go where you please in pursuit of Mosby," were the orders. The regiment patrolled the left bank of the Potomac, watching the fords from

Doane would have received his M.A. were as follows (though "literary occupation" likely was loosely interpreted, it is not known how he qualified at this point):

> The degree of Master of Arts may be conferred, in course, on every Bachelor of Arts of three years' standing, or more, who has been engaged, since his graduation, in some literary occupation, and has sustained a good moral character. It will be conferred only on those who apply for it at least a week before commencement, and provide for the payment of the customary fee. (University of the Pacific catalog 1863-64)

Poolesville to Harper's Ferry.

On July 30, 1863, Doane's outfit nearly captured Mosby. Spies located Mosby and sixty to eighty men moving along a road two or three miles from Aldie, Virginia. Two hundred Second Cavalry men galloped out to surround them. But Mosby's men took flight, leaving behind wagons, twenty horses, and prisoners they had captured earlier.

Beginning August 6, 1863, Lowell's regiment became the cavalry arm of the forces defending Washington. Scouting in Maryland followed. Doane was in the thick of the South Anna Bridge fight near Ashland, Virginia, from June 23 to 28, 1863, under Colonel Sam P. Spear. In this engagement the Federals slipped across the river on a single floating log boom, charged the Confederate breastworks, won their skirmish, burned the bridge, then countermarched to Hanover Ferry before Rebel reinforcements could counterattack.

Though Doane never told it, the War Department records disclose that the Rebels once captured him — to his shame, court martial, and loss of rank.

Colonel Lowell's cavalry brigade was marching from Louisville to Centreville, Virginia, October 2, 1863, on a four-day raid. Doane, returning from another skirmish, had to start on the march to Centreville without rations or rest. His horse, losing a shoe, gave out the second night, forcing Doane to trail behind. He lost his company but fell in the next day with the Thirteenth New York Cavalry. At a 10:00 A.M. halt, Doane and a lieutenant from the Thirteenth slipped off to commandeer breakfast at a nearby house. Leaving the lieutenant, Doane returned to find the column had gone on, taking their horses. He found himself afoot with two others — a corporal and Sergeant Mandeson of Company E. They slogged ahead, overtaking another soldier with an extra horse, sending the corporal forward on it for more horses.

A little farther on and twenty yards away, a man rose at the edge of the woods. "Don't shoot," Sergeant Mandeson told Doane. "He's one of our men." Doane holstered his pistol. Then the man, who wore what appeared to be a Federal hat and overcoat, whipped around and pointed a pistol straight at Doane. At the same time another soldier in Rebel uniform, whom they had not seen before, covered the sergeant.

The two Rebels, probably Mosby's men, had circled around the column through the forest and back to the road about 300 yards behind the column. They had barely missed capturing the corporal too. The chivalrous Rebels took Doane's and Mandeson's weapons, pointed out the road the column had taken, and let them go.

On October 16, before a regimental court martial at Vienna, Virginia, Doane was "busted" from sergeant to private over the "capture" incident. He was pronounced guilty:

   I. Of leaving his company without permission because his horse was unable to keep up with him;

   II. Of leaving the column to procure food without permission;

   III. Of surrendering without resistance to an equal force.

Doane also had to pay for the pistol the Rebels took from him.[7]

THE MARINE BRIGADE[8]

After this setback, five months elapsed before Doane realized his ambition to become an officer. On March 23, 1864, he transferred to and was commissioned a first lieutenant in the newly formed Mississippi Marine Brigade which played such an important part in the strategic operations on the Mississippi River.

After the capture of New Orleans in 1862 and Vicksburg July

[7] Doane Army Records, National Archives. Major General R. H. Sheridan, reporting to the Chief of Staff on February 3, 1866, says: "I was at times annoyed by guerrilla bands, the most formidable of which was under . . . Mosby. . . . I had constantly refused to operate against these bands, believing them to be substantially a benefit to me, as they prevented straggling and kept my trains well closed up, and discharged such other duties as would have required a provost guard of at least two regiments of cavalry." (Rodenbough, *From Everglade to Cañon,* 546)

[8] For the story of the Mississippi Marine Brigade and Doane's part in it, see W. D. Crandall and I. D. Newell, *History of the Ram Fleet and the Mississippi Marine Brigade.*

4, 1863, in a continued effort to sever the Confederacy in two, the Federals began moving reinforcements, provisions, and munitions down the muddy Mississippi. But all of it had to go through the heart of the Confederacy where thin, scattered forces lined both sides of the river. Concealed by its bends and banks, Confederate guns and guerrilla bands had little difficulty attacking, firing upon, and capturing the Union vessels. Federal gunboats patrolling the river were too few to cope with them.

Thus, the Marine Brigade, nicknamed "Ellet's Horse Marines," was organized to operate from river boats.[9] They would disembark, fight the guerrillas on land, and pursue them into the interior. Doane wrote, "I was in action ten times during the next six months including the battles of Chicot Lake and Port Gibson. I had the honor to command either the advance or rear guard in eight actions."

On May 7, 1864, Lieutenant Doane was in command of a detachment of marines who were ambushed and cut off near Yazoo City. Doane sent two men to learn the position of the enemy and the lay of the land. When they reported back, he ordered the marines to mount and dash through a fence gap. Fierce fighting and a hot pursuit followed as the enemy tried to head off the marines and keep them from reaching the main road. Through fields, over fences and ditches the marine cavalry galloped. Finally they came under the protection of the fleet guns. They had won the race. The only casualties were one man slightly wounded and one horse shot in the leg.

Another race, on the humorous side, occurred late the night of May 13 when the marines were carrying dispatches to Colonel John McArthur. Observing a big camp of soldiers, thinking they had located McArthur, cheered by the campfires and prospect of a rest and hot coffee, they trotted into its midst only to discover they were in the middle of the camp of

---

[9] One of the popular war songs of the day (the editor's grandmother used to sing it) was:

> I am Captain Jinks of the Horse Marines,
> I give my horse good corn and beans;
> Of course it's quite beyond my means,
> Though I'm Captain in the army.

Confederate General Wirt Adams. The Rebels were even more surprised than the marines. An immediate command, "Right about," moved the marines out at a gallop. They were chased back about forty miles, clear to Yazoo City, by Adams' cavalry.

The battle of Chicot Lake, early in June, 1864, was probably Doane's hottest action during the war.[10] It turned out to be a trap and a massacre for the Federals. Lieutenant Colonel George E. Currie, commanding the marine brigade, likened it to the Crimean War massacre described in Tennyson's "The Charge of the Light Brigade." Blundering Brigadier General Andrew Jackson Smith had ordered his men into an advance against the advice of Captain G. E. Fisher, who knew the country better.

The Rebels planned their strategy well. They deployed only a small part of their force in the front lines. Behind these lines lay an immense open field, and beyond that an impassable bayou stretching for several miles. Their main army was concealed and massed in the woods beyond the bayou. When the attack came the Rebels retreated their front-line forces according to plan, thus decoying the Federals to pursue them. The retreating Rebels crossed the bayou on a temporary bridge, then destroyed it. When the Federals reached the open field, they found themselves blocked by the bayou, with a murderous Rebel fire coming across the water from the shelter of the woods.

Lieutenant Colonel Currie describes the massacre:

> But the General thought he knew best, and . . . a line of infantry, a mile at least in length, was hurried to the stream, to receive volley after volley from the rebels on the opposite bank, sheltered by the woods as securely as though they were out of range of our shot and shell. Not a man flinched, though every man knew "someone had blundered." Our brave soldiers

[10] Chicot Lake, Arkansas, was an old oxbow dead-run of the Mississippi River. Lake Village (population, one hundred), the county seat of Chicot County, perched on its muddy banks. Crandall and Newell give the date of this engagement as June 5-6 (*Marine Brigade,* 413-418); Doane recalls it as June 15.

advanced as to certain death as though "cannons to
the right of them, cannons to the left of them
cannons in front, volleyed and thundered." How they
fell.[11]

In less than half an hour a hundred dead and wounded men
were lying in the field hospital, an old converted cotton gin
behind the lines.

On the left flank of the Federal side, the marines and Doane
fought creditably. For two days they held the enemy in check
and finally forded the bayou. Surprisingly, none of the marines
was killed and only one wounded. Twenty-four-year-old Doane
was developing as an ideal company officer. He trained and
commanded his men to fight with the utmost efficiency and, at
the same time, to protect themselves.

On the occasion of the Port Gibson battle of July 10-18,
1864, the Rebels withdrew in the face of 6,000 Federals who
took over the town. Two thousand marines, with Doane in
command of Company B, were left to occupy the village. [12]
However, this force proved too small, for the Rebels came back
and overwhelmed it. Withdrawing, Doane's outfit fought the
difficult rear-guard action.

As early as August 14, 1863, General Ulysses S. Grant recommended discontinuance of the Marine Brigade as a separate
organization, claiming it cost too much to maintain the brigade.
The marines, under General A. W. Ellet, had seven of the largest
and finest of the river boats for a force not exceeding 800 men.
Grant felt the boats could be used better for other army
transportation needs and the marines would be more effective if
taken off the boats and put on land altogether.

General Ellet was competent, though vaingloriously independent. He regarded himself as not subject to commands from the
other armed forces, though he made every effort to cooperate

[11] Ibid.
[12] Doane did not command a Negro company during the Civil War as Robert
Bowman stated in "Reconstruction of Yazoo County," *Publications of the
Mississippi Historical Society*, VII, 121.

with them. To further complicate matters, the Marine Brigade, though organized by the army, was assigned to navy command. Until October, 1863, General Grant could order the "horse marines" into action only through the time-consuming protocol of applying to acting Rear Admiral David D. Porter.

Finally General Grant had his way; orders came from Washington on August 3, 1864, discontinuing the brigade. The orders also sent the men and officers back to their former regiments, which obviously could not be done. How could First Lieutenant Doane, for example, be sent back to the regiment where he had been only a private? So the army put them all, officers and men, into a new regiment called the Marine Regiment, U.S. Volunteer Infantry, District of Vicksburg, which could be sent anywhere the action demanded. Doane was appointed first lieutenant of Company H of this regiment.

However, the enlisted men raised a big commotion over being transferred to the regular army and they hired a lawyer, James H. Purdy, a former army major, to take their case to the White House. President Lincoln was faced with the difficult decision of either discharging more than 1,000 soldiers in the midst of a critical war, or breaking government promises to these men. Fairly, he agreed that such promises should be sacredly fulfilled.

On December 5, 1864, the War Department dissolved the Marine Regiment and ordered the men discharged.[13] The end of the war was still four months away. The orders finally came through channels and reached Vicksburg in January. The officers stayed to muster out the men and pay them. Doane was honorably discharged at Vicksburg January 23, 1865; the roll shows his last pay to August 31, 1864. Although Doane was thereafter recommended for a colonelcy, the war came to a close and ended this opportunity.[14]

[13] Special Order 431, Secretary of War, December 5, 1864. All records and papers of the Mississippi Marine Brigade were delivered to the Adjutant General, District at Vicksburg, for transmission to Washington. It later developed these never reached their destination. The loss made the granting of pensions to the survivors difficult, and also obscured from the histories of the Civil War the accomplishments and glory of this brigade.

[14] Doane's statement, Army Records, National Archives.

RECONSTRUCTION IN THE SOUTH

After the war and a brief visit to Washington, Doane returned to Yazoo City, Mississippi, where he tried his hand at the mercantile business. On July 25, 1866, he married Amelia Link. On May 18, 1867, Doane became part of the military government in the state of Mississippi when he was appointed registrar for Yazoo County to register the new electorate. Seven months later, on December 6, Major General Edward O. G. Ord appointed twenty-seven-year-old Doane the mayor of Yazoo City to succeed Judge Daniel Jones, an old lawyer and competent mayor whom the federal law would not permit to continue merely because he had held that same office during the war. [15] On January 2, 1868, Doane was appointed justice of the peace, Beat No. 3, of Yazoo County.

One Confederate historian said that Doane was "among the first reconstruction civil officers of Yazoo County . . . an avant courier of the vandal horde which after him came down on us like a pack of wolves on the fold . . . he imposed and collected two dollars on every gun and pistol owned by a negro, and if this tax was not paid the weapon was confiscated. [16]

On May 18, 1868, Doane resigned as mayor of Yazoo City, and on the twentieth he handed in his resignation as justice of the peace, believing at this time that the military government was soon coming to an end. The new constitution for Mississippi had been drawn up and expectations were that it would be adopted and the state readmitted to representation in Congress. It was, however, defeated by Mississippi voters in a determined campaign.

Doane made up his mind to resume his army career. He got in

[15] 14 U.S. Statutes at Large 428; 15 U.S. Statutes at Large 14.

[16] Bowman, "Reconstruction of Yazoo County." Bowman is in error. The "vandal horde" to which he refers were the carpetbaggers who followed the military government. Historian H. M. Chittenden also incorrectly says Doane participated in the carpetbagger rule (*The Yellowstone National Park,* 1903 ed., 84); Doane had left Mississippi for the Indian frontier before these adventurers from the North began flocking to the South. Doane's commanding officer approved the gun regulation and told him to apply it to whites also, as the blacks were "imitative" of them. (Doane Army Records, National Archives)

touch with Senator John Conness of California, who wrote a letter on June 15, 1868, to Major General J. M. Schofield, Secretary of War, recommending Doane for a commission in the regular army. He was accepted.

With him on his new venture went Amelia, his wife of two years. We know little about her. She followed him to his stations in Kansas, Wyoming, and finally Fort Ellis in Montana Territory. They had no children.

CHAPTER 2

THE INDIAN FRONTIER: 1868 - 1870

EARLY EXPERIENCES

Doane's career as an Indian fighter started August 1, 1868[1] when he was appointed second lieutenant, Second U.S. Cavalry, and was sent to the boot camp of the day, Fort McPherson, Nebraska. He was soon transferred to Fort D. A. Russell (Cheyenne), Wyoming, then being established.[2] Less than a year earlier, November 13, 1867, the Union Pacific had reached this point. Soldiers were needed, not only to fight Indians but to deal with lawlessness among the whites, because with the rails came the end-of-the-track horde — boisterous, gambling, drinking, vice-indulgent, hardworking.

Doane's first assignments at Fort Russell were as quartermaster and as part-time commander of Troop H, Second Cavalry. His love of this great frontier country began here. He found these unmapped areas of the West a challenge to his craving for exploration and to his "sense" of geography. Concerning this period of his life, he later wrote: "In 1868 . . . in country I had never seen before and which was imperfectly

---

[1] Doane says July 5. Doane's Summary of Service, National Archives, written by him February 16, 1889, at the Presidio, San Francisco, California, with accompanying documents. (Hereafter cited as Doane Summary, National Archives. The Summary, while in chronological order, does not always conform to the month and day of other official records which the editors consider preferable.)

[2] Now known as Fort Warren, one of today's largest military installations, it was the big supply depot of the early frontier.

Fort McPherson, Nebraska, 1873. Officers Club, store, and post saloon. *Courtesy Nebraska State Historical Society.*

mapped, I never once failed in my course either in darkness or daylight though I had seen veteran officers who have served there for years entirely lost."[3]

Doane's first experience with Indian fighting came soon, when, as part of the rescue party, his company arrived to end one of the most dramatic Indian encounters of the West, the Beecher Island fight of September, 1868, in northeastern Colorado. Colonel George A. Forsyth and fifty citizen scouts had withstood a siege of nine days in sand foxholes dug on an island of Arikaree Fork while under constant attack by 900 Northern Cheyennes and Oglala Sioux. The results of this battle brought Doane again close to the reality of combat when he saw the Colonel, twice wounded, with one leg shattered by a bullet, and heard the men describe how they had dug a deep hole for water, had eaten their battle-killed horses, and conserved their ammunition.[4]

During these first six months in the territory, Doane was in charge of a supply camp on the South Platte River, spending much of that time scouting against the Indians. In answer to one winter call for help, he drove a pack train forty-seven miles in thirteen hours to supply a command which was out of rations.

EXPLORATION RESTLESSNESS

The approaching winter of late 1868 brought a lull in the Indian battles. But there was no lull in Doane's ambitions for exploration.

Here he was on the fringe of unmapped and unexplored regions — the Green and Colorado river canyons and the adjacent, waterless plateaus, for example. These had been discussed in his college classes and he had read vague references in

[3] Doane letter to Smithsonian Institution, September 1, 1874, Doane Summary, National Archives.

[4] For accounts of the Beecher Island affair, see General Nelson A. Miles, *Personal Recollections and Observations,* 145; General G. A. Forsyth, "A Frontier Fight," *Harper's New Monthly Magazine,* June, 1895, 42-62; M. J. Mattes, "Beecher Island Battlefield," *The Colorado Magazine* (Historical Society of Colorado), July, 1952, and references there cited.

the journals of western explorers who had never been able to penetrate the inhospitable terrain.

In 1540, Don Garcia Lopez de Cardenas had been brought to a halt on the impassable South Rim of the Grand Canyon. In 1868, 328 years later, little more was known about that part of the country. Only one crossing[5] of the river *El Vado de los Padres* had been found below today's Green River, Utah.

Forays of civilization were pushing the known and the passable further west. The Union Pacific, for instance, was moving track westward, with straining horses dragging up the earthen grade and sweating Irishmen pushing the rails ahead. At last the piling was going down for tandem bridges across the Green River in newly created Wyoming Territory; then the caps, the stringers, decking, and rails went on. On October 6, 1868, the first work train puffed slowly over the structure, testing its strength. Thus this great river of the West was crossed by rail.

Doane saw the possibilities. From Fort Russell, where he was stationed, he could now travel by rail to the Green River, embark in a boat, and float down to explore the rivers. He applied through military channels for permission and supplies to make this journey. But Doane was only a second lieutenant at a remote post in the west. He could hardly know that at the same time a geology professor at Illinois State Normal, John Wesley Powell, a former major in the army, was soliciting and obtaining financial help for the same trip from educational institutions in Illinois, and was arranging for rations from the United States government. In any event, the military took a dim view of the lieutenant's ambitions and refused his application. The honors went to Powell who started on the history-making trip May 14, 1869, from the rail crossing of the Green River. Doane took his disappointment as a soldier would.

---

[5] In Utah below Glen Canyon near the Arizona border.

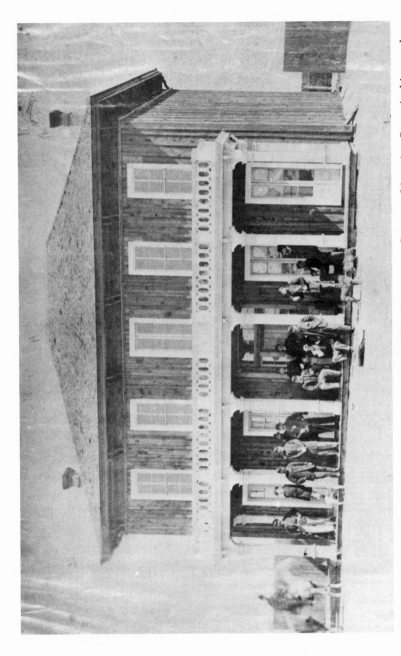

Fort D. A. Russell, Wyoming Territory, 1868. Commanding Officer's quarters. *Courtesy Wyoming State Archives and Historical Department.*

TO FORT ELLIS

On May 25, 1869, Second Cavalry Companies F (now Doane's company), G, H, and I moved out of Carter Station on the Union Pacific Railroad twelve miles west of Fort Bridger. Lieutenant Colonel Albert G. Brackett (in command of these troops until December) comments in his journals that "Mrs. Doane, Wife of Lieut. Doane, is the only lady accompanying the expedition."[6] The four companies marched via Taylor's Bridge (present-day Idaho Falls, Idaho) and Virginia City, Montana, 600 miles to Fort Ellis, arriving there on June 14, 1869. "These were the first soldiers regularly assigned to duty in Montana," according to Colonel Brackett.[7]

Beside Indian fighting, the main chores of the soldiers were the enlargement of their new post, exploration of the area, and the building of new roads.

Doane's first road assignment was with Captain E. W. Clift's expedition in August to explore a wagon route from Fort Ellis to the mouth of the Musselshell River on the Missouri River.[8]

An incident occurred on this expedition which resulted in Doane's having full command of Company F during its first year of warfare against the Indians in this territory. During the journey Captain Clift ordered each enlisted man to carry his own blanket on his saddle. But weary men rode wornout horses. Sympathetic Captain Oliver Ormsby G. Robinson, in command of Company F, allegedly allowed Company F blankets to drift back to a camp wagon, with Clift none the wiser. When the axle on the overloaded wagon collapsed, dumping the wagon into a ditch, Clift came galloping back — furious. Blankets were vanishing fast, but not fast enough.

[6] A. G. Brackett, "A Trip through the Rocky Mountains," Historical Society of Montana, *Contributions,* VIII, 330.

[7] U.S. Army Records show this post was established August 27, 1867, by Companies D and F, Thirteenth Infantry, reinforced September 2, 1867, by Company G, Thirteenth Infantry.

[8] Captain Clift's map is a good source, showing travel routes and settlements in 1869, old Indian trails north of Bozeman, road to Helena, Gallatin City, etc., location of Fort Ellis, Crow Agency, Bozeman Pass. The map can be found in Annual Report, Department of Dakota, 1870, Adjutant General's Office, No. 1869, National Archives; it is reproduced in this present volume as a foldout map.

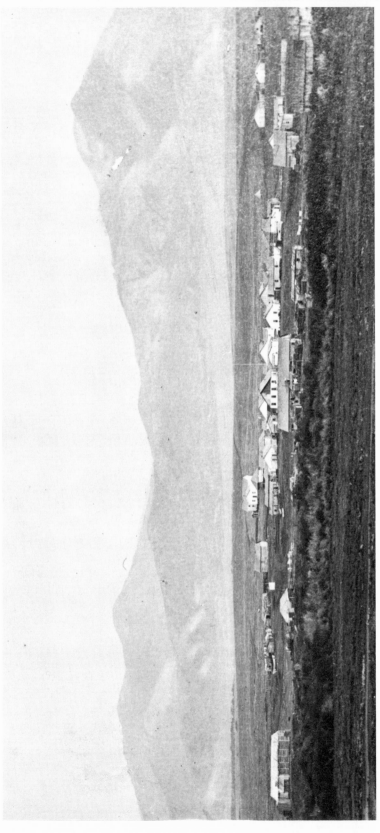

Fort Ellis, Montana Territory, July 1871. William Henry Jackson was a member of the 1871 Hayden Survey on its way to Yellowstone when he took this photograph. *Courtesy Yellowstone National Park.*

When questioned, Robinson squirmed, then said his top sergeant must have ordered it. Sergeant Alexander Anderson denied it. Robinson was arrested, court-martialed, and acquitted. But silent persecution and unpopularity followed because he had tried to shift the blame to the well-liked sergeant. In October Robinson was suspended for two months "for the good of the service." Doane wrote his superiors that Robinson was being unfairly treated. Finally the Captain could take the treatment no longer, went A.W.O.L., and in the end was written off the army rolls.

MASSACRE ON THE MARIAS

Doane's first experience in killing Indians came in the massacre on the Marias River. The planned winter attack had far-reaching effects in subjugating and winning peace from the Blackfoot confederation for the first time in its history. The maneuver also had far-reaching repercussions in an aroused public censure and a Congressional investigation of the massacre.

In 1889, when Doane was applying for the position of superintendent of Yellowstone National Park, he referred to this engagement: "[I was the] first and last man in Piegan camp January 23, 1870 . . . greatest slaughter of Indians ever made by U.S. troops."[9]

Under orders from the division and department commanders, Major Eugene M. Baker left Fort Ellis on January 6, 1870, with

[9] Other massacres of Indians (figures subject to variable accounts): (a) Colonel Patrick E. Connor against Shoshones and Bannocks on Bear River, Idaho, January 29, 1863: Indians killed, between 224 (Connor's count) and "nearly 400, two-thirds being women and children" (Mormon William Hull's count). (b) Major J.M. Chivington against Cheyennes and Arapahos at Sand Creek, Colorado, November 27, 1864: Indians killed 131, principally old men, women, and children. (c) General George A. Custer against Cheyennes on the Washita, Oklahoma, November 27, 1868: Indians killed, 103 warriors including Black Kettle; some women and children killed but mostly taken prisoners. (d) Colonel James W. Forsyth and Lieutenant Colonel Edwin V. Sumner against disarmed Sioux prisoners at Wounded Knee, South Dakota, December 29, 1890: Indians killed, eighty-four men, sixty-two women and children; other estimates, including General Miles, were about one hundred men and about one hundred women and children.

220 men and ten officers. The force marched thirteen days in the dead of winter, with temperatures dropping to 44° below zero, to attack a Piegan camp of Bear Chief and Big Horn on the Marias River (in present day north central Montana). At 8:00 A.M. on January 23, Doane, commanding Company F, led the attack in which 173 Indians were killed: ninety women, fifty children, and thirty-three men.

It seems worthwhile to give Doane's account of the affair, found in a little-known and obscure document — the only one he ever wrote of a battle engagement:[10]

Fort Ellis, M.T., March 21, 1874

On the 23rd of January, 1870, at daybreak, the expedition against the Piegan Indians struck one lodge of Indians on the Marias River. The Indians belonging to this lodge having been captured without any firing, F Company was sent forward by Major Baker along the trail of the Indians down the river. After following the trail at a gallop about four miles, two Indians were met on foot, with two squaws mounted on ponies. These were captured without resistance, and given in charge of Sergeant O'Kelly, who disarmed and secured them. The trail here ran parallel with the Marias River, which was hidden from view in a deep ravine of Bad Lands. First Sergeant Anderson was then sent out alone to the edge of the bluff to look along the river, lest we should pass some village without seeing it. While so engaged the company came in sight of a large drove of ponies herding on the edge of the bluffs, and presently the smoke from the Indian villages appeared just below. Sergeant Williams was detached with six men to cut out and drive away the herd, which he did very gallantly and judiciously, and at considerable risk, as it was within range of the

10 Rodenbough, *From Everglade to Cañon,* 552-553.

village, and, besides, the ground was full of ravines dangerous to ride over. In fact, the horse of one of the troopers fell into one of these narrow cuts, breaking three of his legs, and was killed in consequence.

At the same time Sergeant Moore was sent with several men to report to the First Sergeant, with instructions to charge down the bluffs *above* the villages, cross the stream and deploy on that side, while the company would come in below and between the Indians and the herds of ponies. This was executed to the letter; and as the company came down the bluffs on the trail, the First Sergeant was seen crossing the river above the village. He deployed his men properly and at a run, and in two minutes the Indians were completely surrounded. The other companies came up in a few minutes, and commenced firing, which was continued for an hour. During this time the First Sergeant kept his line effectively, having with him Sergeant Moore and about twelve (12) men. They were in great danger, as the dismounted companies were firing in their direction constantly, and they were obliged to maintain an exposed position in order to cut off the Indians who endeavored to break through their lines. Not an Indian got through though several were followed high up on the slope of the opposite Bad Lands, and killed with revolvers. The First Sergeant especially conducted himself with the utmost bravery and good judgment. He did everything that any officer could have done under the circumstances, and in a most creditable manner. While the firing was going on, Sergeant Wise, with a couple of men, drove off, under fire, several small herds of ponies which were on the other side of the river, doing it quickly and with discretion. Corporal Etheridge distinguished himself in killing Indians, taking great risks by standing in front of the lodges and firing into the doors. I saw him three times drop

Indians who had bows presented within a few feet of him, with the arrows drawn to an aim. He was a splendid shot, and killed several. Sergeant Howell displayed good judgment in destroying the lodges and in caring for the wounded squaws and children.

Sergeant O'Kelly was on guard that night, and is entitled to great credit for his energy and alertness, the camp being full of wounded, the sentinels firing at intervals all through the night, which was made hideous by the groans of the wounded, the howling of dogs, fire breaking out in the woods, and the stampeding of the pony herd in a tremendous windstorm.

G. C. DOANE, First Lieut. Second Cavalry.

The army took as prisoners 140 women and children and 315 horses, and destroyed forty-four lodges and all winter provisions and property. When Major Baker learned of a smallpox epidemic among the Indians, he quickly turned the women and children loose — but with no aid, food, or shelter. After the battle Doane was left in charge at the camp and ordered to destroy all property, count the dead and the prisoners, and collect the horses.[11]

The troopers returned to Fort Ellis on February 6, with one man killed and one with a broken leg. They had marched 612 miles in midwinter.

One of the charges by Montana citizens upon which this "punishment" of the Piegans was based was the claim "that Malcolm Clark [American Fur Company trader and former West Pointer] had been murdered by the Blackfeet on August 16, 1869; that one of his sons had been wounded, and his three daughters carried off into horrible captivity." Nathaniel P. Langford investigated these charges. He found that Clark had been killed by one of his Indian relatives as a result of an old

[11] *Report* 1870, Secretary of War, National Archives; 41 Congress, 2 Session, *House Exec. Doc. No. 185,* Library Congress Book 1418.

family argument. He found the son wounded but alive, and the daughters all at the Clark ranch, untouched. He helped them bury Clark.[12]

---

[12] The Langford manuscript on the Malcolm Clark affair, "A Frontier Tragedy," in his handwriting, is in Yellowstone Park Library, Catalog 7492, ACC 262. See also Helen P. Clarke (his daughter), "Sketch of Malcolm Clarke," Historical Society of Montana, *Contributions*, II, 255.

CHAPTER 3

EXPLORATION: 1870 - 1875

YELLOWSTONE

The most significant summer in Doane's life was 1870 — the year in which he commanded the military escort for the Washburn-Doane Expedition into what is now Yellowstone National Park. The expedition is discussed fully in Part II of this book. Doane's report, printed in full in Part II, has made his name a part of Yellowstone history.

In reviewing the circumstances which led to Doane's making this trip, we know he had been at Fort Ellis for over a year. His desire to explore the Green and Colorado Rivers had been frustrated two years earlier, but now at Fort Ellis he found himself stationed at a post whose gates opened onto another unmapped area — perhaps more intriguing than any other. Doane heard the early trappers' tales re-told. Gold seekers scouring the mountains brought back stories of a thermal wonderland, of steaming mountains, of multicolored lava pots, of burning rivers. In 1859-60 Captain William F. Raynolds had tried, and failed, to explore the area; he published his report in 1868. Doane must have read it — and thought to succeed where Raynolds had failed. In 1863 Walter deLacy, a Helena resident, had penetrated a portion of the Yellowstone area; he was a map maker and Doane was a map reader. Doane must have studied deLacy's noted 1865 map and felt the need for further refinements. And

Doane and other officers at Fort Ellis, early September 1871. L to R: Frank C. Grugan, 1st Lt., 2d Cavalry; Lewis Thompson, Capt., 2d Cavalry; George H. Wright, 2d Lt., 7th Infantry; *Doane,* 2d Lt., 2d Cavalry; Lewis C. Forsyth, Capt., Acting Quartermaster; A. B. Campbell, Asst. Surgeon; Dr. R. M. Whitefoot, Contract Physician; Sam T. Hamilton, 1st Lt., 2d Cavalry; Eugene M. Baker, Lt. Col., Commanding Officer, December 1, 1869 to October 15, 1872; Edward Ball, Capt., 2d Cavalry; Lovell H.

Jerome (rear), 2d Lt., 2d Cavalry; George L. Tyler, Capt., 2d Cavalry;
Edward J. McClernand, 2d Lt., 2d Cavalry; Charles B. Schofield, 2d Lt., 2d
Cavalry. The sash (crimson silk net) over Doane's right shoulder indicates
that he was Officer of the Day at the time the photograph was taken. In
1872 the sash was abolished for officers below the rank of brigadier
general. W. H. Jackson photo. *Courtesy Yellowstone National Park.*

the 1869 trek into the wonderland by the Folsom-Cook-Peterson trio must have strained Doane's patience.

This time Doane was determined not to repeat his mistakes of two years ago. Permission for an expedition required more than a simple request. Doane laid a groundwork not only with his post commander but also with his commander's superiors. He talked and corresponded about the matter with civilian acquaintances. Some civilians, such as Judge H. L. Hosmer and General H. D. Washburn, had influential military acquaintances. Among them all they managed to finagle a telegraphic order out of headquarters in St. Paul, and Doane was assigned to the expedition. Doane left for Yellowstone August 22 and returned to Fort Ellis September 24, 1870. He finished writing his Yellowstone report in January 1871.

The results of the Washburn-Doane Expedition were both national and favorable. Reports from the expedition convinced the famous government geologist, Ferdinand V. Hayden, to alter his survey plans for 1871 and go instead to Yellowstone. Thus began his several extensive surveys of the Yellowstone region. Also, General Sheridan directed Captains J. W. Barlow and D. P. Heap, of the Army Engineer Corps, "to make an exploration of the sources of the Yellowstone."

In the spring of 1871 Doane was sent to St. Paul on detached service. As soon as he returned to Fort Ellis he was sent into the Yellowstone area to join Hayden, whom he overtook at Upper Geyser Basin on August 6. The group left the Upper Geyser Basin and arrived at Yellowstone Lake August 9, camping on the south end of West Thumb.[1] Doane's knowledge greatly streamlined Hayden's work — except for one humorous misadventure. William H. Jackson, the photographer with the Hayden Expedition, tells the story on Doane:

As the Lieutenant had been around the [Yellowstone] lake, his familiarity with the country and its landmarks helped to make easier our course through

[1] Ferdinand V. Hayden, *U.S. Geological Survey of Wyoming and Montana* (Preliminary Report), 1872, 31-34.

Hayden Survey leaders in Yellowstone, summer 1871. L to R: A. Schönborn, topographer; James Stevenson, geologist; F. V. Hayden; Doane. W. H. Jackson photo. *Courtesy U.S. Geological Survey.*

Hayden Survey en route in Yellowstone, summer 1871

h man from right, with odometer cart, is Goodfellow. W. H. Jackson photo.

Hayden Survey party camped on Flat Mountain Arm of Yellowstone Lake, Summer 1871. W. H. Jackson photo. *Courtesy U.S.G.S.*

the dense forests interspersed with grassy glades, marshes, or lily covered lakes. But previous experience or sense of direction was not always to be relied upon when traveling through thick timber with many detours to escape entanglement in windfalls or thickets of dense pines. At one place, with the Lieutenant leading, we made our way up a gentle draw through the woods until we came out on a low divide and then began our descent on the other side. Continuing on our course, with no outlook and everything alike as two peas, after five or six miles our leaders were nonplussed by striking into a freshly made trail, so recent as to suggest another large party in our immediate neighborhood. As this was unthinkable, the conviction was forced upon us that we had doubled upon our own trail![2]

Of course it must be conceded that Doane was not lost for long, and, as Jackson said, one could easily get turned around in the heavy timber and rolling plateau where one cannot even see above the tree tops, but it still raises a smile to read in Doane's letter to the Smithsonian Institution three years later:

I always travel as an Indian does, without guide or compass, and do not know what it is to have the sensation of being lost.[3]

While south of Yellowstone Lake, Hayden, Doane, and two others took two side trips to the Continental Divide, which Hayden wanted traced on a map. Doane refers to this in his 1876 journal entry of November 30. The Continental Divide, incorrectly identified in his 1870 report, was corrected in the 1876 journal.

[2] William H. Jackson, *The Pioneer Photographer*, 119. The editor remembers Jackson talking about his first trip with Hayden, the last time we chatted together, at one of the annual dinners of the American Alpine Club in New York. This fine old gentlemen was then ninety-eight years old, yet completely alert and mentally active.

[3] Doane Summary, National Archives.

Doane interested Hayden in trying to locate the reputed but still elusive Two Ocean Pass and Bridger Lake. The pass was a natural phenomenon on the Continental Divide where a single stream divided, sending one fork flowing to the Atlantic Ocean, and the other flowing to the Pacific. The early trapper route into the Yellowstone area went through the pass. Trapper tales included how fish swam freely from one side of the Divide to the other.

The first trip of Hayden and Doane ruled out Two Ocean Pass as being in the area around Heart Lake. On their second side trip, from the South Arm of Yellowstone Lake, they went up the valley of the upper Yellowstone River to hunt for Bridger Lake. Hayden reported it did not exist. Doane insisted the lake they were then looking at was Bridger Lake.[4] From that point they followed the Continental Divide back to Yellowstone Lake, just missing the actual Two Ocean Pass area.[5]

From a camp on the east side of Yellowstone Lake, Hayden, Doane, and party made the first ascent of two peaks which Hayden named Mount Doane (elevation, 10,656 feet) and Mount Stevenson (10,362 feet) after James Stevenson, Hayden's right-hand man.[6] After this significant climb, the geological survey party headed back to Fort Ellis via Pelican Creek and Lamar River.

That autumn of 1871, Doane went down the Yellowstone River with the military escort provided for the Northern Pacific Railroad survey crew under Colonel J. A. Haydon.[7] This was

[4] Actually the lake does exist. Doane and Hayden had quite a discussion over this point. See Doane's Snake River journal, November 30 entry, Part III of this book.

[5] Although still somewhat north of the true Two Ocean Pass, they were very close to it; Doane's description in his 1876 journal is more accurate of Two Ocean Pass, but even then he apparently had not actually seen it and was describing some other location. See Part III this book, chapter 13, November 30 entry and note 8.

[6] Hayden named them on this occasion. See Part II this book, Chapter 11, September 7 entry and note 18; O. H. and L. Bonney, *Guide to Wyoming Mountains and Wilderness Areas,* 431.

[7] Not to be confused with Ferdinand Vandeveer Hayden, as one Montana historian has done. On the date Haydon was attacked by Indians in Baker's Battle, Hayden was in Upper Geyser Basin of Yellowstone with his survey parties (August 14, 1872).

Hayden Survey party camped near Steamboat Point on Yellowstone Lake, Summer 1871. W. H. Jackson photo. *Courtesy U.S.G.S.*

one of several assignments for the Fort Ellis soldiers to give full military protection to the surveyors, whose projects often antagonized the Indians into fierce retaliatory action.

Returning home to Fort Ellis, after the Northern Pacific assignment, Doane heard that his wife Amelia had suffered an accident while he was away. He learned more details from the Bozeman, Montana newspaper, *Avant Courier,* under the dateline October 26, 1871:

> Severe Accident — We regret to learn that Mrs. Doane, wife of Capt. [sic] Doane, of Fort Ellis, met with a severe accident on Tuesday of last week. Early in the evening Lieut. Scofield, accompanied by Mrs. Capt. Doane, started for a ride to Bozeman. The horses became frightened a short distance from the Fort, ran away, upset the carriage — turning it completely upside down — with Mrs. Doane underneath. Lieut. Scofield extricated her as soon as possible, but the unfortunate lady was suffering terribly, having, as it was afterwards proven, broken her leg in two places below the knee. She was carried to a cabin nearby, and meantime, a soldier passed the carriage and carried the news to the Fort that there had been a runaway. Colonel Baker immediately dispatched a squad of men to ascertain the particulars, and at a late hour in the night the lady was carried to the Fort on a stretcher.

On December 1, 1871, Doane received his well-earned promotion to first lieutenant and was assigned to Company G. That winter Doane was able to follow in the newspapers the history-making events then occurring in Washington, D.C. A bill to create Yellowstone National Park was introduced simultaneously in both Houses of Congress on December 18, 1871. In the *Helena Herald* of January 16, 1872, Doane read of the activities in Washington of his colleague from the Washburn-Doane Expedition:

The Hon. N. P. Langford, of Montana, the leader [sic] of the famous Yellowstone expedition of 1870 and several scientific and literary gentlemen are engaged in an effort to have the Yellowstone region declared a National Park.

The *Helena Herald* of January 31, 1872, under the heading "A National Park," carried an editorial stating that telegraphic dispatches that morning "announce that the bill introduced by Senator Pomeroy, providing for a national park on the headwaters of the Yellowstone," had passed the Senate.

Passage of the bill through the House a month later brought this editorial from the *Helena Herald* on February 28, 1872, under the heading, "Our National Park":

Our dispatches announce the passage in the House of the Senate bill setting apart the upper Yellowstone Valley for the purposes of a National Park. The importance to Montana of this congressional enactment can not be too highly estimated."

The bill was promptly signed by President Grant, becoming law March 1, 1872.

BAKER'S BATTLE

On July 14, 1872, Lieutenant Doane with Company G, under the command of Major Baker, started down the Yellowstone again with Colonel Haydon and his crew to continue the survey of the westward route for the extension of the Northern Pacific Railway. There were about 400 men in the military escort including infantry from Fort Shaw and cavalry from Fort Ellis. A month later, on August 14, the group was camped near the mouth of Pryor's Fork where Colonel Haydon had halted work the previous fall. Preparations were made to continue the survey. However, two days before, on August 12, 1,000 hostile

Sioux, ascending the river to attack the Crows, discovered the survey outfit. The Sioux attacked on the night of August 14,[8] when Major Baker happened to be dead drunk. No special security cautions had been taken.

First, some reconnoitering Sioux slipped in after dark, killed a watchdog, stole some saddles from the camp, and made off with six mules picketed near Major Baker's tent, all without being detected. Then, shortly after 2:00 A.M., the Indians attacked in force, expecting to capture the herd of horses. The horse pickets opened fire and drove the horses toward the corral. Lieutenant William Logan alertly threw his entire night guard of twenty-six men between the Indians and the herd. The Indians retreated with only fifteen horses.

Captain Charles C. Rawn, commanding four companies of Fort Shaw infantry, reported with them to Major Baker who scoffed at the idea of Indians around and ordered Rawn to keep his men in camp. Disgusted and angry, Rawn on his own responsibility deployed two of his companies next to a stream on the lower side of the camp.

By this time Captain Lewis Thompson, officer of the day, had investigated and reported to Baker. Half an hour after the beginning of the attack, Doane and his company, with the rest of the cavalry, were deployed by Captain Thompson on the line's left side. Defense of the camp had finally been set up.

The Indians, hidden in the willows on the lower side of camp, missed seeing Rawn's two companies take position there. They thought it open for them to attack and seize the horses. They began creeping forward at daylight.

Lieutenant W. J. Reed was waiting for them, and with parade ground precision ordered three volleys fired into their midst. Astonished, the Indians turned in disorderly flight, swarming

[8] August 14 is the correct date. One recent Montana history has three different dates for the same event and calls the Indians Cheyennes. Doane says 2,000 Sioux. Bradley and Barlow say the Indians were Sioux. Lieutenant James H. Bradley, *The March of the Montana Column*, 55 (hereafter cited as Bradley, *Montana Column*); J. W. Barlow, *Indian Interference with the Northern Pacific Railroad.* For the location of this and other Indian battlefields, see James Mooney's map, "Calendar History of the Kiowa Indians," *Bureau of American Ethnology Annual Reports*, 1895-96, XVII, Pt. 1, 141.

out of the timber.

Lieutenant James H. Bradley said, "The officers were . . . eager to follow. . . . Major Baker . . . ordered Rawn to get two of his companies ready, announcing his determination to take them and two companies of his 'busters' — as he was pleased to call the calvary — and pursue; but he soon forgot all about it or changed his mind."[9] Accounts agree in representing the Indians as greatly demoralized. Later they admitted forty killed (three left in the field) and probably a hundred wounded. An energetic commander with his wits about him would probably have gained a decisive victory.

Undoubtedly Doane agreed with Lieutenant Bradley's statement, "Baker's star as an Indian fighter shone out brilliantly on the Marias River in January 1870 . . . but suffered a great diminuation of luster on the Yellowstone August 1872."

The attack scared Colonel Haydon and diverted him from the project. Haydon turned toward the Musselshell on August 20 and disbanded his survey crew on September 25, blaming the failure to complete his survey on the military.

NAVIGATION OF THE YELLOWSTONE

While in garrison at Fort Ellis the winter of 1872-73, and as a result of his trips down the Yellowstone River, Doane wrote his report, *Navigation of the Yellowstone,* dated January 13, 1873.[10] The report had the effect of greatly stimulating agricultural interest in the fertile Gallatin Valley.

Doane stated that navigation of the Yellowstone was practicable and would be the most economical means of supplying the projected forts with lumber, forage, and food from the mountains and the Gallatin Valley. He detailed how transportation of supplies for the Baker escort to the Northern Pacific

[9] Bradley, *Montana Column,* 55.

[10] Doane Army Records, National Archives. A copy of this report was forwarded through Headquarters, Department of Dakota, to Division Headquarters, Chicago, which acknowledged receipt February 21, 1873.

survey in 1872 would have cost $1,012.50 by boat as against $34,856.00 by land.

THE JUDITH BASIN AND THE CROWS

Doane spent the summer and fall of 1873 at routine jobs of building barracks and quarters at Fort Ellis and scouting in the vicinity of the fort. In December, to his delight, another opportunity came for exploration: this time the Judith Basin, northeast of Fort Ellis. It started when he left the fort on December 16, 1873, with Special Agent F. D. Pease, to negotiate a new boundary and agency location with the Crow Indians.

Doane held a council with the Crows on December 22, going over the treaty of August 16, 1873, with them. He had little success in convincing the Indians they should move their agency farther east or be restricted to the new boundaries as the treaty stipulated. They refused to discuss these matters. They were only willing to discuss the annuity provisions of the treaty. However, Doane's straightforward diplomacy on this, his first contact with the Crows, made them peaceful neighbors to the Fort Ellis soldiery. His continuing intelligent dealing with the Crows through the following years brought their increasing friendship, an inestimable benefit in the Indian wars which followed. It was an outstanding and peaceful accomplishment equalled by few army officers of that day.

Continuing this trip, Doane traveled beyond the Crow Agency and explored the Judith Basin:[11] ancient buffalo grounds to the Crows, Nez Perces, Bannocks, Shoshones, Sioux, and other Indians. His report on the trip and exploration included maps, the location of the tribes, and appendices.[12]

[11] The Judith River today crosses U.S. Highway 87 about eighty-five miles east southeast of Great Falls, Montana. Stanford, Montana, is the county seat of Judith Basin County.

[12] Report to the Commissioner of Indian Affairs in the Department of the Interior on February 19, 1874. It contains the following appendices which are useful to historical research: (A) Description of the Crow reservation. (B) Report on the buffalo, their range, Indian hunting, wolfers. (C) Description of the country between the Yellowstone and Musselshell Rivers. (D) Description of Mauvais Terres or Bad-

Crow Indian Agency, Montana Territory. *Courtesy U.S. Signal Corps.*

THE CARROLL ROAD

In the spring of 1874, Doane, now in command of Company G and other troops, escorted a wagon train to the Missouri River above the Musselshell, where they established a fort and settlement called Carroll Landing. They did such work as was necessary to put the Fort Ellis-Carroll Road in condition for rough travel.[13] This road was of great importance in the Indian wars which were to follow. Upon completion of the job they returned to Fort Ellis May 29.

For the third time Doane went through Yellowstone Park in the summer of 1874. From his 1876 journal, October 18 entry, it is known that he traversed Tower Creek basin, Mount Washburn, and a peak at the north end of the Washburn Range.

AMBITIONS FOR AFRICAN EXPLORATION

No unexplored region in our times, neither the heights of the Himalayas, the Antarctic wastes, nor even the hidden side of the moon, has excited quite the same fascination as the mystery of the sources of the Nile. For two thousand years at least the problem was debated and remained unsolved. . . . By the mid-

lands of the Missouri in front (east) of the Judith Basin. (E) Meteorological observations at the Judith Basin and at Fort Ellis. He gives altitude of Fort Ellis as 4,711 feet, contemporary reports having been: Hayden, 4,789; U.S. Engineer officers, 4,750. The lowest temperature at Fort Ellis was -53° F. on January 24, 1872. The winter of his report, 1873-74, was the mildest then known in Montana Territory. (F) Report on Indian traders, whisky, and robe traffic. (G) Description of boundaries, corrections, tables of distances. For example, he gives the following mileages from Fort Ellis: Yellowstone Divide, nine miles; Yellowstone ford, twenty-seven; Crow Agency, thirty-four; Hunter Hot Springs, forty-seven. (H) Abstract of disbursements. "(I) Map of the district examined," as stated by Doane, but it is not with the manuscript, copy of which is at the Montana Historical Society, Helena.

[13] In less than a year twenty-five log houses were built at Carroll. Lieutenant James H. Bradley, "An Account of the Attempts to Build a Town at the Mouth of the Musselshell River," Historical Society of Montana, *Contributions,* II, 304-313; William Ludlow, *Report of a Reconnaissance from Carroll, Montana Territory, on the Upper Missouri, to the Yellowstone National Park, and Return, made in the Summer of 1875.*

dle of the nineteenth century . . . this matter had become . . . 'the greatest geographical secret after the discovery of America'.[14]

It was only natural that Doane's ambitions turned toward Central Africa, a blank space on the maps of the world.

In 1862 (four years earlier if we count when he first viewed and named Lake Victoria), John H. Speke discovered the source of the Nile at Ripon Ralls, Lake Victoria. But it would be almost fifteen years until the world accepted this fact. In the meantime, during the 1860's, the controversy of conflicting facts and theories about the Nile's true source would spawn many books eagerly read on both sides of the Atlantic. The public's imagination was captured by this dark mystery fully as much as today's generation focuses on space exploration.

And capturing the imagination most dramatically of all throughout America was the Stanley-Livingstone epic. Through the *New York Herald* accounts, the nation followed this epic avidly — and no one followed it more keenly than Doane.

In 1865, David Livingstone had returned to Africa, hopefully to settle once and for all the problems of the watersheds of Central Africa. Five years later the world still did not know for certain about the Nile, nor did they know what had happened to Livingstone. James Gordon Bennett of the *New York Herald* sent his crack foreign correspondent, Henry M. Stanley, to find Livingstone. He did, on November 10, 1871. But Livingstone's wanderings had settled nothing about the Nile. Stanley's report to the world in May of 1872, however, focused attention again on Central Africa. More headlines were made when Livingstone was laid to rest in Westminster Abbey on April 18, 1874. He had died in the heart of his beloved Africa on May 1, 1873. His faithful Africans had preserved his body and had carried it more than 1,000 miles to the coast.

But the Nile problem still remained. In far-off Montana Territory an army lieutenant had a solution. On September 1,

[14] Alan Moorehead, *The White Nile*, 1.

1874, in a fifteen-page letter to Joseph Henry, Secretary of the Smithsonian Institution, Doane set forth his plans for solving this 2,000-year-old riddle. [15]

On November 16, 1874, Professor Henry replied. Although Doane was certainly qualified, wrote Professor Henry, it was difficult enough to get a congressional appropriation for exploration in the United States, let alone trying to get one for Africa. He added:

> It is to be regretted that the proprietor of the New York Herald was not cognizant of your qualifications and desires since, in connection with the London Daily Telegraph, he has just sent out Stanley a second time to carry on African explorations.

In November 1874, Stanley left Zanzibar to answer definitively the watershed questions of Central Africa.

Dauntless, still hoping for government support, Doane obtained a leave from Fort Ellis, left for Washington, D.C. on December 30, 1874, and applied formally for assignment to a Nile project. Employing a technique he used years later much more extensively when he was applying for the superintendency of Yellowstone National Park, Doane began gathering letters of recommendation from influential persons in behalf of his proposal. For example, General of the Army W. T. Sherman wrote favorably about Doane to his brother, Senator John Sherman. Senator Sherman wrote to Secretary of War W. W. Belknap recommending Doane; Sherman was at the time chairman of the Senate Finance Committee. Belknap also received a letter supporting Doane from B. F. Potts, governor of Montana Territory.

Doane also worked on getting private financial backing. If Congress or the Smithsonian Institution failed to come through with any appropriations or if they were inadequate, Doane was planning for that contingency through an association with the American Geographical Society. Judge Charles P. Daly, the

[15] See Appendix to Part I this book for the complete text of this very revealing letter.

Society's president, promised to bring up Doane's request at the Society's annual meeting in February 1875 and to exert his influence with friends in New York and Philadelphia for additional funds.[16]

But all came to naught. Belknap studied Doane's application and pondered the political implications of sending an army man to explore a river in a far-off continent; the following note appears on the application:

> Feb. 1/75. The Secretary says he will make no such detail except Congress passes an act authorizing or directing him to detail an officer for such purpose.

In deep disappointment Doane returned to Fort Ellis. Four years later, while spending his "honeymoon leave" in Washington, D.C., he was evidently going through the Nile project file, still remembering his lost opportunity, for there appears in Doane's handwriting and signed by him, below the Secretary's note, the following:

> May 12, 1879. This is what defeated the project and gave Stanley the success I expected to achieve.

GUIDING THE SECRETARY OF WAR

Back at Fort Ellis in the spring of 1875, Doane supervised the building of warehouses and a new hospital, and the remodeling of the barracks, ending these chores when Secretary of War Belknap arrived at the fort on July 26, 1875.

The direct interest of the Secretary in Doane and in Yellowstone Park was an unexpected result of Doane's visit to Washington on the Nile project. The Secretary arranged for Doane to take him and a party of dignitaries, including officers and citizens, on a two-week pack trip through the Park from July 28

---

[16] Letter to Doane, February 15, 1875, from Carmichael (?); signature unclear. Doane Summary, National Archives.

ARRIVAL AT FORT ELLIS.

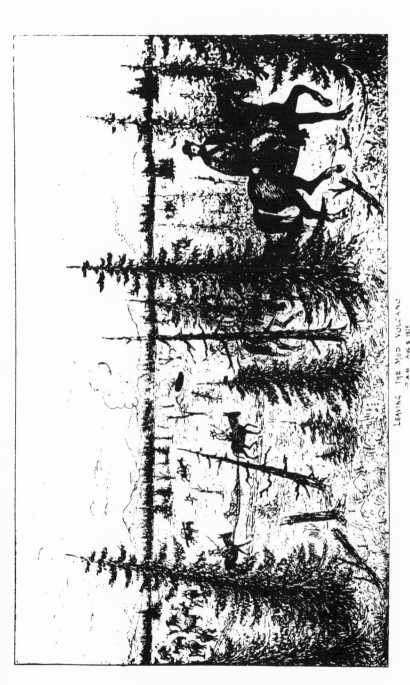

LEAVING THE MUD VOLCANO
7 AM AUG 8 1875

Drawings used to illustrate William E. Strong's book about the Belknap expedition, *A Trip to the Yellowstone National Park in July, August, and September 1875.*

to August 11, 1875. General William E. Strong wrote an interesting account of the expedition, noting that they visited all the points of interest covered by Doane's 1870 report.[17]

Their full itinerary of exploring, fishing, and hunting was disrupted by the abrupt illness of General R. B. Marcy, Inspector General of the Army, and the necessity of his immediate removal. He was too weak to ride a horse. Doane constructed a litter, carried by two mules, which allowed evacuation of the general, despite the extremely rough terrain and the doubts of the party members.[18]

Belknap returned to Washington to find troubles of his own. The following year, on March 7, 1876, he was to resign under political fire, accused of official corruption. Thus was lost for Doane the benefit of political influence he had gained that summer in the close association and friendship with the head of the War Department. Belknap's later trial and acquittal were little consolation.

It was fortunate for the United States that Doane had not been allowed to go to Africa. During the next three years his competent services were invaluable to the army in fighting the conflagrations of Indian war sweeping the plains.

[17] Strong, *Trip to the Yellowstone National Park*; *Annual Report,* Secretary of War, 1876. There were thirty-five members of this party including: General W. W. Belknap, Secretary of War; General Randolph B. Marcy, Inspector General, U.S. Army; General James W. Forsyth, General William E. Strong, Colonel George L. Gillespie, U.S. Corps of Engineers; Major N. B. Sweitzer, Assistant Surgeon Robert M. Whitefoot, U.S. Army; Frances Vinton Greene, Doane, and twenty-four enlisted men from Companies F, G, H, and L, Second Cavalry, Fort Ellis.

Yale University Library has in its Coe Collection two letters from Frances Vinton Green written to his parents, one from Virginia City, Montana August 25, 1875, and the other after he had returned to Washington September 4, 1875. They describe his trip with Doane through Yellowstone National Park and his return journey to Washington with brief stops in Virginia City, Denver, and St. Louis.

[18] At 6:30 A.M. on August 13, at the upper end of Yankee Jim Canyon, Doane met Captain William Ludlow going into Yellowstone Park. Doane traded his pack mules for Ludlow's six-mule team and wagon. It took three hours to exchange the loads. Doane drove the wagon to Fort Ellis. (Ludlow, *Reconnaissance of 1875,* 18, 30) See also Chapter 4, note 8.

CHAPTER 4

THE SIOUX WAR: 1876 - 1877

FORT PEASE

The short history of Fort Pease started in 1875 when forty traders from Bozeman tried to establish a settlement and trading post on the Yellowstone, seven miles below the mouth of the Big Horn River. They built the fort for protection: a few log huts connected by a palisade of logs enclosing a 200-foot square. Immediately the Sioux besieged the fort and kept the traders half starved and in a terrorized state, unable to hunt, trade, or profit.

Finally, Division Commander Lieutenant General Phil Sheridan had to send the four companies of cavalry from Fort Ellis, including Doane's company, to their aid. The soldiers left February 22, 1876, picked up fifty-four Crow warriors at the junction of the Stillwater, marched 208 miles in twelve days, arrived at Fort Pease on March 4, and rescued what was left of the garrison — eighteen white men and one Negro.

On March 17 Doane and more than 200 saddle-weary troopers rode back into the corrals at Fort Ellis after jogging through cold and mud and ice for 398 miles. They were hardly rested before being ordered back in the saddle to march the entire distance back again to Fort Pease, where they would wait for Custer on his last campaign.[1]

It was a long and turbulent summer that year of 1876, with Doane in the thick of the activity.[2]

The storm had long been gathering. The Indian Bureau, in direct violation of the U.S. treaty with the Sioux, had ordered all Indians back to their reservations by February 1, 1876. Time passed, the Indians ignored the order, the Indian Bureau called on the army – and the army acted.

The soldiers expected to collide with the hostile Sioux and Northern Cheyennes somewhere between the Little Missouri and Big Horn Rivers – determined to round them up, slaughter them, or drive them back to the reservations. The army posts of the West were stripped of every available officer and man who could be sent to the campaign.

The army planned that one column under Lieutenant Colonel George A. Custer (Fort Lincoln) would push the scattered Indians westward from North Dakota. Another under Brigadier General George Crook (Fort Fetterman) would sweep the tribes northward from Wyoming. The third column, under Colonel John Gibbon (Forts Shaw and Ellis), would move eastward from Montana, keeping the hostiles south of the Yellowstone River and closing the northern and western sectors of the nut-cracker on them.

At a crucial moment, Custer was called to Washington by the chairman of the War Department's Committee on Expenditure, Representative H. Clymer, who, aware of Custer's complaint against the exorbitant charges of the post traders, wanted him as a star witness against Secretary of War Belknap's involvment in the sale of post traderships. Custer's frank answers con-

[1] For the story of Fort Pease, see Doane Summary, National Archives; 44 Congress, 1 Session, *House Exec. Doc. No. 184,* 49-51; Clyde McLemore, "Fort Pease, The First Attempt at Settlement in Yellowstone Valley," *Montana Magazine of History,* II, No. 1, January 1953; Edgar I. Stewart, "Major Brisbin's Relief of Fort Pease," *Montana Magazine of Western History,* VI, July, 1956; H.H. Bancroft, *History of Washington, Idaho and Montana,* 710, 712; Bradley, *Montana Column,* 68; Topping, *Chronicles of the Yellowstone,* 167; Mary Allen Phinney, *Jirah Isham Allen,* 33-53.

[2] See Bradley, *Montana Column.* For a complete bibliography on the Custer massacre, see Colonel W. A. Graham, *The Custer Myth;* Edgar I. Stewart, *Custer's Luck.*

cerning Belknap and the President's brother Orvil Grant so infuriated President Grant that he replaced Custer with Brigadier General A. H. Terry to command the Dakota column. Custer was left only his own regiment, the Seventh Cavalry. The tangle delayed the Dakota column from starting until May 17, and threw off the timing of the whole campaign.

Doane left Fort Ellis April 1, 1876, in the Montana column of Colonel Gibbon, with Major James S. Brisbin as chief of cavalry and second in command. Crotchety Brisbin, suffering from rheumatism, was unable to mount a horse and rode in an ambulance. The column, bogged down by incessant rain, slogged its way eastward through Bozeman Pass and wallowed down to the Yellowstone River, making only thirty miles the first four days out of Fort Ellis. Even so, the Montana outfit was nearly six weeks ahead of the other columns, and accomplished no strategic purpose until Colonel Gibbon met General Terry at the Powder River June 9.

The Montana column arrived at the Crow Agency on the Yellowstone River April 9. Doane met with his old friends among the Mountain Crows, while Colonel Gibbon made talk with them. Twenty-five young Crows enlisted as scouts, which allied the Crow nation with the U.S. forces and removed it as a potential threat to the army.

Continuing down the Yellowstone River to Fort Pease below the mouth of the Big Horn, Doane spent twenty days there with the rest of the column, awaiting orders. Well advanced into the Sioux country, and without support from the other columns, the Montana outfit maintained an apprehensive and nervous vigilance there. On May 3, Cheyenne[3] raiders made off with all the horses of the Crow scouts. Next day, couriers returning to camp were attacked. The column finally moved out eastward on May 10.

[3] Bradley, *Montana Column,* 87, calls them Sioux.

SCOUTING THE SIOUX

On May 17 the scouts reported a 300-lodge Sioux village on the Tongue River. The Montana column immediately started across the Yellowstone River, the plan being to attack the Sioux village by daybreak next morning. But in four hours the cavalry managed to tug only forty water-logged horses across the river; four of the animals drowned. The infantry hadn't even started. Then darkness stalled the operation. Exasperated, amazed at the boldness of seventy-five Sioux who menaced the crossing, and dismayed by the ill omen of delay, Colonel Gibbon changed his mind, abandoned the effort, and ordered the cavalry to recross.

Thus Doane escaped what would later be the fate of Custer's men. He was with these 392 men who set out to attack the same village where Custer would later fail with 655. The next day Doane's orders sent him down to scout the mouth of the Tongue River where the Indian village had been seen.

On May 20, the Crow scouts reported to Colonel Gibbon that several hundred Sioux were sweeping toward the scouting party Doane was in. The Colonel sent his remaining cavalry and five companies of infantry to protect the scouting party. Fortunately, Doane's party had also discovered the Indians and had moved back to the concealment of the hills.

The Sioux continued to harass the column with fast raids. On May 23, Doane, with Company G, galloped out in hot pursuit of Indians whose rapid firing was heard echoing from the hills. Three miles away the soldiers found the bodies of two privates (A.W.O.L. from the camp) and two civilians, ambuscaded in a ravine and riddled with bullets. One of them, Private Stoker, from Company H, had been scalped.

THE COMMAND MOVES TO ATTACK

Meanwhile, the big Indian camp had been discovered moving toward the Rosebud. On June 8, per Gibbon's orders, Captain Walter Clifford's company, with Doane and Major Brisbin, floated down the river in patched-up boats (left by the former traders of Fort Pease) to the mouth of Powder River, intending to fortify there. At this point they met the chugging steamer *Far West* and General Terry, who had two companies of the Seventh Cavalry with him. Terry sent word for Gibbon to meet with him the next day while he and his staff steamed up the river on the *Far West,* accompanied by Captain Clifford's company, Doane, and Brisbin. They picked up Gibbon about eight miles from his camp.

The *Far West* reached the camp of the Montana column about noon, and General Terry invited all officers present to meet with him on board.

After a two-hour conference on June 9, these officers evolved a plan to send out the Seventh Cavalry under Custer to scout the country south of the Yellowstone River while the Montana column would return up the north bank, circle, and sweep the Indians south toward Custer. On June 10, the Montana column left. Doane was part of its command.

On June 17, Crook's Wyoming column was defeated and put out of action by the Indians on the upper Rosebud.

Doane, scouting up the Yellowstone ahead of the Montana column, returned on June 19 feeling "apprehensive." He had found no Sioux, but the Crow village they had previously left on the Big Horn "had disappeared."

On June 21, the last rendezvous of the columns was held at the mouth of the Rosebud. Another conference aboard the *Far West* between Generals Terry, Custer, and Gibbon, with Doane also attending, resulted in the decision that Custer would march south up Rosebud Creek in pursuit of the Indians whose mile-wide trail Major Marcus A. Reno had discovered on June 17. Gibbon's column (including Doane's outfit), with Terry along, would march west up the Yellowstone River, then south up the Big Horn River to the junction of the Big and Little Horn Rivers. The Indians were thought to be somewhere between.

Custer was offered, but declined, Brisbin's Second Cavalry, later explaining to his men that if the Seventh Cavalry couldn't handle the Indians another battalion wouldn't help much. Thus

Doane again escaped the fate of Custer's men.

At noon on June 22, in parade formation, amid the blare of trumpets, with Terry, Gibbon, and Brisbin reviewing, Custer left camp, marched two miles to the mouth of the Rosebud, then trooped fourteen miles more upstream. The Sioux were watching him now. Gibbon's infantry marched twenty-nine miles; his cavalry rode thirty-one miles.

Doane and civilian scout "Muggins" Taylor reconnoitered the north bank of the Yellowstone ahead of Gibbon's column. Mounted Sioux patrolled the south bank. They watched each other.

On June 23, Doane and Taylor saw thousands of buffalo. They killed and butchered enough for Gibbon's entire column, but that night only the cavalry feasted. The infantry ate beans and bacon, for the shortsighted quartermaster would not let the men stop to load the meat Doane had provided. That day Custer made thirty-three miles, Gibbon's column twenty-two. Everyone was hurrying. But Gibbon himself was quite sick and stayed on the boat; General Terry took over the command of his column.

On the twenty-fourth, Custer pushed his weary troopers all day and until two in the morning. They made a hard thirty-six miles – the Indian camp was still twenty-three miles away.

Doane spent most of a frustrating day watching the Montana column struggle to cross the Yellowstone River. The column made only six miles more that day up Tullock Creek, a tributary of the Big Horn.

MASSACRE

With a 5:00 A.M. start on June 25, Custer's tired troopers traveled nineteen miles more, and by noon were four miles from the Indian village, ready to charge.[4] Custer divided his men into three fighting units which by themselves would attempt the

[4] The numerous accounts vary slightly on time and distance. The editors have given what they believe to be the most reliable.

grand pincers movement mapped for the whole campaign — against the largest and most skilled military force ever assembled by Indians.

By midafternoon the outcome was determined. Custer and his 201 men were dead; Reno had been routed; Captain Fred Benteen had come back and joined Reno, as had Captain T.M. McDougall. All were now pinned down on the bluffs.

Meanwhile, on this same day, the Montana column was having its problems. While Custer's men were being butchered on the battlefield, while Reno's and Benteen's men were fighting for their lives on the bluffs, the Montana column was floundering hopelessly in the wild terrain south of the Yellowstone. Instead of heading up Tullock Creek, then over to the Little Big Horn, as suggested by Lieutenant Edward J. McClernand, the command, thinking Doane would best know this region, tossed the problem to him. Since this was east and south of the territory he was familiar with, Doane consulted with "Muggins" Taylor. Taylor and Doane advised the command to follow the ridge between Tullock Creek and the Big Horn River. Brisbin backed Doane and the route was changed.

Colonel Robert P. Hughes[5] says that had Gibbon's column followed Tullock Creek direct to the Indian village instead of making the march across to the Big Horn, it might have been possible for the column to arrive on the afternoon of the twenty-fifth in time to assist Custer. Colonel Hughes' statement misses the point that according to plan, the Montana column was not to join Custer until the twenty-sixth. Custer had outmarched the other column and precipitated the battle. Furthermore, Doane was following a basic rule of successful mountain warfare, to move along and control the ridges and sides of a valley before sending troops through the valley, even though they could move faster there.

Lieutenant James H. Bradley says that after learning of the change of route, his own scouting party cut across and found the soldiers "hopelessly involved in a labyrinth of bold hills and

5 Colonel Robert P. Hughes, "The Campaign against the Sioux in 1876," *Journal of the Military Service Institution,* XVII, No. 79, January 1896.

deep precipitous ravines entirely destitute of water."[6] Bradley's Crow Indians set the column on a slightly better route.

The Montana column reached the Big Horn about 3:00 P.M. after marching twenty-one miles. The infantry was exhausted. General Terry rested the men two hours, then moved them a couple of miles more, but they could go no farther that night. Yet Terry ordered Doane's company and the rest of the cavalry to keep going – a night march.

They thrashed aimlessly on in this unknown country enveloped in heavy rain, wind, and complete darkness. Finally, after several hours, they found themselves trapped in a dead end above vertical bluffs. Only then was a Crow scout called into the command consultations. He immediately led them out of the topographical horror. At midnight, after covering thirty-five terrible miles, they halted and unsaddled. In a few minutes the Montana column's cavalry dozed in a "slough of mud and disgust"; the infantry, twelve miles back, tossed in exhausted slumber.

Twenty-five miles away on the Little Big Horn, the bodies of Custer's dead lay stripped and naked. On the bluffs overlooking the hostile camp the men of Reno and Benteen hardly napped in the nightmarish blackness, exposed to constant enemy fire and impending attack.

On June 26, General Gibbon recovered from his sickness enough to rejoin his Montana column which had been under Terry's command since the twenty-third. Uneasiness pervaded the entire column. There had been no word from Custer. Fifteen miles away a heavy smoke rose to mark the battlefield.

Then three Crows came in, reporting the terrible story of the day before.[7] Terry immediately deployed his men in battle formation. Doane was in the cavalry on the right, the infantry, on the left. They moved out cautiously, expecting battle any minute.

The hostile village had decided to withdraw. That night a

---

[6] Bradley, *Montana Column*, 149.

[7] Graham, *The Custer Myth*, 19-24. The three Crows, Goes-Ahead, White-Man-Runs-Him, and Hairy-Moccasin, had ridden out with Custer, but had been sent back before he was surrounded and wiped out.

formidable Sioux rearguard watched Terry's command go into bivouac, only nine miles from Reno's position. Had Terry been an hour earlier or had he advanced farther, the Sioux would have attacked — with drastic results.

On June 27, Doane and the Terry-Gibbon command rode up to the Custer battlefield. Doane now gazed upon an impossible task for the army. Naked, tomahawked, and mutilated bodies lay bloody and dirty, covered with flies, swollen and discolored in the merciless Montana sun. Decent burial was impossible. There were only half a dozen shovels in the entire command. Doane saw troopers scatter a token of dust and sagebrush on the bodies, then slip away in horror.

The soldiers were allowed to rummage through the Indian campsite, souvenir-gathering from the dead. Doane picked up two or three beaded Indian moccasins.

Fifty-two of Reno's wounded were brought down to the valley and made as comfortable as possible. The next day eight bearers on foot were assigned to carry each wounded man. Over the rough ground this method of conveyance brought misery to wounded and bearer alike.

The command turned to Doane to solve the problem. He ordered a detail to construct litters such as he had built in 1875 to evacuate General Marcy from Yellowstone. Pairs of lodge poles twenty feet long, taken from the abandoned Indian camp, were lashed with two cross pieces on each pair. Dead horses were now skinned, the hides cut into strips, and the strips lattice-worked across the poles. On these frames buffalo robes and blankets were spread. One horse was hitched between the shafts of the poles in front, and another behind. One man led each horse.[8] The wounded rode comfortably to the steamer, *Far West*, which carried them down the Big Horn and Yellowstone Rivers to Fort Lincoln.

---

8 "The care and transportation of the wounded demanded attention. Hand litters were first made and their inefficiency demonstrated, when the fertile genius of Lieut. G. C. Doane, 2d Cavalry, evolved a mule litter, and upon these the wounded were carried very comfortably." T. F. Rodenbough and W. L. Haskin, *The Army of the United States*, 1896 ed., 186; Stewart, *Custer's Luck*, 477.

Type of litter devised by Doane to transport Reno's wounded to the steamer, *Far West*, after the Battle of the Little Big Horn. *Courtesy U.S. Signal Corps.*

Steamboat *Far West*, on which Doane met with other officers prior to the Custer fiasco. *Courtesy Montana Historical Society.*

AFTERMATH

At this stage, the Indians seemed to dissolve into the wild terrain south of the Yellowstone River. Actually they had divided into two main parties.

Doane spent the rest of the summer in the field, marching and scouting. The army licked its wounds, too beaten and bewildered to reorganize an offensive. On July 30, Doane was camped with the Second Cavalry at the mouth of the Rosebud when Colonel Nelson A. Miles arrived there by river steamer, bringing fresh troops of the Fifth Infantry — and renewed hope.[9]

Doane and Miles almost immediately developed a high respect for each other; they were friends the rest of Doane's life.

The combined command marched up the Rosebud to join forces with Crook. On August 10, Doane saw a cloud of dust rising beyond the distant hills. He heard the cry of "Sioux!" flash through the column. He heard orders shouted. A bugle sounded. The cavalry swung into a skirmish line; the infantry moved into position; the wagon train took shelter behind them.

Then a lone horseman galloped down the valley — Buffalo Bill Cody riding in advance of Crook's column. Soon Crook's outfit came up. Doane was now part of the largest U.S. Army force ever marshalled on the Montana frontier.[10]

There was more marching, deployment, and marching until the end of August when all the forces assembled at the mouth of the Powder River. There they disbanded and returned to their forts. Doane arrived back at Fort Ellis September 3. The country still belonged to the hostile Sioux.

In a letter which General Terry wrote to Division Commander Lieutenant General Phil Sheridan after that calamitous summer, he singled out Doane with a final paragraph:

---

[9] Virginia Johnson, *The Unregimented General, Nelson A. Miles,* 95.

[10] Miles, *Recollections,* 216. William Cody also described the scene in *Story of the Wild West,* 680. General A. H. Terry's payroll reports of 1876, National Archives, list Cody.

In this connection I desire to call the attention of the Lieutenant General Commanding the Division to the invaluable services rendered by Lieutenant Doane. I believe that I speak the sentiments of every officer and soldier who served under me in the field during the campaign of last summer, when I say that I feel the most hearty admiration for the zeal, skill and energy displayed by this accomplished gentleman and soldier.[11]

SNAKE RIVER EXPLORATION

One would underestimate Doane if he thought Doane had had enough of forced marches, hostile weather, and dangerous campaigning that rugged year of the Custer battle. During the summer maneuvers, Doane evidently was able to interest General Terry in one of his exploring projects, over Major Brisbin's head and without going through channels. On October 4, 1876, Terry issued orders, under authority of Division Commander Sheridan, which sent Doane on his winter exploration of the Snake River. Doane's journal and the story of this journey are included as Part III of this book. Suffice it to say here that the expedition was interrupted and never completed because Doane and his party were ordered back to Fort Ellis.

DOANE AND HIS CROW INDIAN SCOUTS

Two and one-half months after his return to Fort Ellis from the Snake River expedition, Doane was detached from Company G, Second Cavalry, on April 12, 1877, and placed in charge of Crow Indian scouts under the direct command of Colonel Nelson A. Miles.[12] Here "an officer in obedience of

[11] Doane Summary, National Archives.
[12] *Annual Report,* 1877, Secretary of War; 45 Congress, 2 Session, *House Exec. Doc. No. 1, Pt. 2,* Vol. 1794, Brisbin, 553. This annual report contains separate

Medicine, one of Doane's Crow Indian scouts, 1879. There were at least twenty Crows in Doane's detail. L. A. Huffman photo. *Courtesy Montana Historical Society.*

orders was secure from a fire in the rear,"[13] as Doane expressed it, still chafing over his recall midway in his 1876 Snake River exploration. Doane now had the freedom and initiative of his own command without having to channel every detail of his military life through company and battalion echelons. Not only that, but it gave the lieutenant a part in all the excitement and in all the adventure of living with the Indians. It was one of the most sought after assignments by a younger officer in the 1870's — to be with the Indian scouts.

Early in the summer of 1877 Doane lived with the Crow Indians in a village of 320 lodges at the mouth of the Big Horn River. Three thousand Indians camped there; 15,000 herded horses trampled the prairie grass, stirring great clouds of dust which mingled with the smoke of the tepee fires; 300,000 buffalo ranged the prairie to the north. Indian hunters dragged in a thousand carcasses each week to feed the tribe.[14]

Doane's Crow scouts were athletic young men, tall like himself, and brave. The prairie sun had burnished their bronze faces. Hard riding had trained them down to pure sinew and muscle. They reacted to every emergency without confusion or lost motion. The wilderness, and every sound and movement in it, was an open book to them. But the complications of civilization and its account books were beyond their experience. Two years later Doane was still trying to help them collect their first month's pay.

The Indian scouts were always in advance, ten, twenty, thirty miles ahead of the troopers, always watching. They would creep up to a high landmark, which they already knew, and with field glasses study the country ahead. If a raven flew up, a wolf or coyote ran out of a ravine, a band of antelope galloped off on a run, or a herd of buffalo stampeded they would know that

reports of Gibbon, Brisbin, Howard, Gilbert, Sturgis, and Miles on Nez Perce battles of 1877. (Hereafter this work will be cited as *Report* 1877, Secretary of War, with the name of the individual officer.)

[13] Doane's Snake River journal, Part III this book, Chapter 17, final sentence *Communiques* section. Three of Doane's companions on the 1876 expedition were sent with him in his new Crow Indian scout command — Sergeant Server and Privates Applegate and White.

[14] Scott, *Memories,* 49, 52; Doane Summary, National Archives.

White Swan, one of Doane's Crow Indian scouts. The names of seven others were known: Arapahoe, Big Nose, Big Otter, Found Things, Round Jean, Three Jesus, White Otter. *Courtesy Montana Historical Society.*

something had frightened them — perhaps an enemy — and would investigate further.

While camped at the Crow village, Doane paddled a canoe up the Big Horn River where he selected and staked out the site for the new military post to be called Fort Custer, at the mouth of the Little Big Horn fifteen miles down the river from the Custer battlefield.[15]

On June 28, Lieutenant Colonel Michael Sheridan picked up Doane and some of the Crow scouts who had been at the Custer battle, and together by horseback they revisited the battlefield of the year before. The sun-bleached bones of more than 200 men lay scattered on the ground. Only twelve officers were identifiable. Eleven, including Colonel Custer, were pineboxed, horsepacked, and boated back to Fort Lincoln.[16] Later, the remains of Colonel Custer were buried at West Point, New York; those of the other officers were buried in the Post Cemetary at Fort Leavenworth, Kansas. Captain Miles W. Keogh's remains were subsequently removed to Fort Hill Cemetery, Auburn, New York. Lieutenant John J. Crittenden was buried where he fell.[17] The unidentified remains of four officers and all enlisted men were consigned to the dust of the battlefield in anonymity.

[15] Thomas A. LeFarge, *Memoirs of a White Crow Indian,* 281.

[16] See Graham, *The Custer Myth,* 6-25, for actual stories of Curly and the other Crow scouts' participation. Sheridan reported that they had recovered all the bones. Less than a month later, on July 21, his brother Phil Sheridan visited the site and "reburied" seventeen skeletons; they were again "reburied" in April, 1879. The final "reburial," when a monument of granite was placed, was in July, 1881. There are 266 names on the monument: for 202 who died in the Custer massacre; the others with Reno or elsewhere.

[17] The vandalism of government "improvement," which in our day seems to recognize no bounds of restraint, removed his remains and headstone in 1932 to make way for a road.

G. C. Doane, 1878.

CHAPTER 5

THE NEZ PERCE WAR: 1877

ORIGINS OF THE CONFLICT

While Doane was participating in the clean-up of the Custer battlefield, hostilities had begun in the Nez Perce country of Idaho Territory that would bring him into that conflict.

The Nez Perces were justly aggrieved. For more than half a century they had lived the Christian ways of the white man on their Idaho reservation. Now, after complete peace and friendship, the U.S. Army under Brigadier General Oliver O. Howard had been ordered to hunt them down like animals and drive them off the old tribal lands.

As early as 1855, the Nez Perces had been forced to concede pieces of their territory. The big breakthrough for the white men came in 1860 when gold was discovered there. Appeasement availed the Indians nothing. The whites wanted all. They violated agreements, swarmed over the remaining reservation land, and even built the town of Lewiston on it.

As with other tribes, the United States could always bribe some individual Indians to sign any treaty. In 1866 they obtained one which would put the Nez Perces out of their most important valleys, the Wallowa, the Alpowai, and the Salmon River of western Idaho. Chiefs like Joseph, Looking Glass, Big Thunder, White Bird, and others refused to be bound by it.

The breaking point for the Indians came in June, 1877, with a series of retaliatory killings as the anger of the younger Indians of the tribe broke loose. General Howard moved against them June 13, 1877. The Indians fought back fiercely, and the Nez Perce war was on. Within a month three battles had been fought and the tally of dead was:

Battle of White Bird Canyon, June 17: Indians 0, Army 34; *Cottonwood Skirmish,* July 3: Indians 0, Army 11; *Clearwater,* July 11-12: Indians 4, Army 13.

In the parleys that followed, the army insisted on complete surrender but the Indians, remembering other times, did not trust the army and moved eastward across Idaho's Clearwater River. They argued among themselves for three days, then decided to head for the friendly Crows in Montana and enlist their aid. Chief Looking Glass argued that the Crows had always promised them safe passage to the buffalo hunting grounds, and more important "the Crows had promised that whenever the Nez Perces fought the whites the Crows would join them."[1] Looking Glass prevailed.

This was while Doane was in the Crow country.

On July 16 the Nez Perces collected what belongings they had managed to rescue from the last battle on the Clearwater, and broke camp. Families and warriors filed eastward over the 250-mile Lolo "trail" through the Bitterroot Mountains, bushwhacking through timber barricaded with deadfall, over boulders, across rockslides, chasms, and washed-out gullies.

General Howard battered his troops over the jagged "trail" after them, but dragged far behind. Soon he was wiring for help from Captain Charles C. Rawn (then superintending the construction of the embryonic Fort Missoula, Montana), Colonel John Gibbon (commanding the District of Montana at Fort Shaw, Montana), and Colonel Nelson A. Miles (commanding the District of the Yellowstone at Fort Keogh, Montana).

---

[1] Helen A. Howard and Dan L. McGrath, *War Chief Joseph,* 284.

TO JUDITH BASIN

On August 3 Doane with his Crow Indians, and in command over Lieutenant Charles C. De Rudio and E Company of the Seventh Cavalry, was ordered "to the Judith Basin to burn grass in order to drive the game farther westward."[2]

As Miles explained it afterwards in his December 27 victory report:

> From unofficial reports and newspaper accounts I judged the hostile Nez Perce Indians would, should they evade the troops in Montana, endeavor to reach the Judith Basin, and if pursued, would move north of the Missouri River. I ordered . . . Doane . . . to the Missouri, at and west of the Musselshell, with instructions to "intercept, capture or destroy the Nez Perces."[3]

Doane immediately requisitioned supplies and rations to be sent by water to Carroll, the trading post on the Missouri near the mouth of the Musselshell, and at the same time informed Miles that he would try to keep his force of Crows together, but that it was impossible "to state exactly what minor movements can be carried into effect."

Then Doane started back up the Yellowstone valley. With him went about sixty Crow scouts, De Rudio's E Company, and four of his own men — Sergeant Fred Server, Privates F. R. Applegate, and Oscar F. Long, all of Company G, and Private William White of Company F.

On his way he met a wagon train returning to Fort Keogh from Fort Custer escorted by the new West Point graduate, Second Lieutenant Hugh L. Scott.[4] Scott, quick to seize an opportunity for more excitement, talked a junior officer of E Company into switching assignments with him. Scott hurried to

---

[2] Fort Keogh Records, National Archives.
[3] *Report* 1877, Secretary of War, Miles, 540.
[4] Scott, *Memories,* 54.

Fort Keogh for Colonel Miles' approval while his orderly galloped twelve miles down the river to a camp on Sunday Creek to get regimental permission. Scott, by going with Doane, later told of Doane's part in the campaign.

Doane's force marched up Froze-to-Death Creek. One day they covered forty-five miles and joined again the big Crow camp which was now at the big bend of the Musselshell. The Crow village usually moved once a week, and now Doane moved with it. It gave him a chance to know what was going on, to keep the Crows on the soldier's side, and to participate in the Indian power politics of the plains. He could see the emissaries from other tribes come and go and learn the results of their parleys with the head chiefs of the Crows.

While Doane was at this Crow camp, a record-breaking storm occurred which the Indians referred to for years after as "the year of the big hailstorm." The terrific onslaught lasted only six minutes, but, in scout-interpreter J. I. Allen's words:

> There were many black eyes and bruised bodies, and destruction rampant everywhere. There seemed to have been a hotly contested battle, in which we suffered inglorious defeat. The cannonade of hail-stones killed over one thousand head of horses and ponies. When I saw the storm approaching I hurried inside my quarters. I found a lot of soldiers already there for shelter. Placing buffalo robes over our heads, we stood all together in the center of the lodge. . . . The monstrous hailstones began to cannon-ade the canvas covering of the lodge, tearing it from top to bottom. The gale took lodge poles, canvas and all, wrenched the buffalo robes out of our hands, hurled all with tremendous force to the ground, then swept along the valley for more than a mile. . . . The ground was covered with huge hailstones . . .; the hailstones did not merely tear the lodge canvas, they made holes more than a foot in circumference wherever they struck the tents. The Indians in camp

were paralyzed with fear and they charged the soldiers and scouts with bringing the storm. For some little time affairs assumed a serious aspect . . . [until] the interpreters . . . [explained] to them that we too had nearly all our horses and several mules killed. . . . Lieut. Doane issued the following orders: "fix up — repair lodges and get everything in trim again, we will not move camp for two days."[5]

Before leaving the big Crow camp for Judith Gap, Doane had the camp harangued, as "Colonel" Allen put it, for warriors to join him to fight the Nez Perces. The Crows only grunted, sign-talked, "The Nez Perce heart is Crow; the Crow heart is Nez Perce."[6] Understanding the Indian way, Doane left without them, hoping that after they thought it over they would change their minds. In the days that followed, the Indians kept drifting in to join Doane's outfit until they numbered about a hundred.[7] Doane's diplomacy was proving itself.

Doane and his command marched up Swimming Woman Creek, heading for the great natural gateway that was Judith Gap, the flat ten-mile-wide pass between the Little Belt and Big Snowy Mountains through which funnelled most of the travel in that area. Here the group camped to await the Nez Perce Indians.

Scott says, "[Doane] knew that country and the habits of the Indians so well that he could predict everything they did. Doane had told us where the Nez Perces were going to go a month and a half before they actually went."[8]

BATTLE OF BIG HOLE

The Nez Perces had reached the Big Hole Basin of Montana about August 7 and set up their tepees in a restful meadow on

---

[5] Phinney, *Jirah Isham Allen,* 83-84.

[6] Ibid., 95; Scott, *Memories,* 61. Allen received the nickname of "Colonel" at the Fort Pease fracas when he was in charge of the Big Horn gun.

[7] Scott says 200.

[8] Scott, *Memories,* 60.

the bank of the trout-filled Ruby Creek. Game was plentiful.

Before dawn August 9, Gibbon's 191 soldiers and citizen volunteers crept upon the sleeping camp. An early rising Indian trotting his horse out toward the pony herd collided with the creeping skirmishers. A shot was fired. Like the rush of a hurricane the soldiers swept into the sleep-dazed village, shooting to kill. Panicked, the Indians ran wildly, mostly for the willow thickets along the river where some of the soldiers were concealed. It was a scene of scattered and furious confusion — women screaming, warriors shouting orders, ponies stampeding, children yanked about and trampled, dogs barking, guns firing.

The soldiers killed seventy Indian women and children and nineteen warriors.

But, surprisingly, Chief Joseph succeeded in rallying his men. Some raced back to the slashed and smoldering tepees for their guns. Before it was over the Indians had turned the tables. Gibbon was wounded; his troops retreated under fire, then were surrounded and besieged. Thirty-four soldiers were killed, thirty-six wounded.

Howard with his pursuing troops finally caught up and rescued Gibbon August 11.

CONFLICTING ARMY COMMANDS

When Chief Joseph's people travoised over the tough and rugged Bitterroot Mountains, they crossed (or, perhaps better expressed, "crossed up") the lines of army command. Doane was soon caught in the middle of conflicting orders to him from separate commanders having no communication with each other.

In 1877 the army was organized with W. T. Sherman as general of the army, second only to the Secretary of War. His headquarters were nominally in Washington, D.C., although he was in the west most of that summer. The echelons of command, in descending order, were division, department, district, before breaking down into regiment, battalion, and company.

The Nez Perce war had started in the Pacific Division (Major General J. M. Schofield, San Francisco), Department of Columbia (under the command of Brigadier General O. O. Howard, Portland). Howard was ordered to pursue the Indians even though they passed out of his department. Now the war had swept into the Missouri Division (Lieutenant General P. H. Sheridan, Chicago), Department of Dakota (Brigadier General A. H. Terry, St. Paul), District of Montana (Colonel John Gibbon at Fort Shaw). The District of the Yellowstone (Department of Dakota) was headquartered, beginning July 27, 1876, at a camp on the Yellowstone River at the mouth of Tongue River (later known and hereafter referred to as Fort Keogh, near present Miles City, Montana), with Colonel Nelson A. Miles in command. Under him Colonel Samuel D. Sturgis was "in the field scouting," with twelve companies of the Seventh Cavalry.[9]

All these officers knew Doane's ability. As the Nez Perces moved toward Yellowstone, they wanted Doane at the spearhead of the army's effort. But their orders were not coordinated and worked at cross purposes. Doane, though only a lieutenant, was actually such a key man that the foul-up was disastrous to the army campaign and contributed in no small measure to Chief Joseph's successful retreat.

Sturgis complained afterwards:

> Some of the authorities in Montana . . . assumed to give him [Doane] orders counter to mine. . . . If he had remained where I had posted him and joined me as he had been directed, when he found the hostiles moving eastward, I not only would have had the benefit of his personal knowledge of the country (which was superior to that of any other individual in that country) but my force would have been so augmented as to justify my dividing it so as to occupy both the Stinking River and Clark's Fork passes at the

[9] Since these were field operations, the editors have designated the officers by their command rank. Brevet was an honorary rank, conferred by the Senate for "gallant action and meritorious services," with neither advanced command nor additional pay.

same time, and thus, in all human probability, the campaign would have been ended right there.[10]

Doane was first lieutenant, Company G, Second Cavalry, regularly under Major James S. Brisbin at Fort Ellis (District of Montana), but as special scout commander had been "detached" from Brisbin since April. He was now somewhat loosely on his own, but directly responsible to Colonel Miles (District of Yellowstone). Confusedly, orders were issued to him under his old regular command (District of Montana) as well as under the newly assigned command (District of Yellowstone).

While General Howard's Department of Columbia was fighting the Nez Perces, the Department of Dakota was still fully engaged in the Sioux war, although as those bands divided their forces, it was beginning to reach the stage of mop-up operations. Colonel Miles determined to prevent the juncture of any other Indians with Sitting Bull's band. Miles had been using Doane that summer towards this objective, keeping Doane with the Crows to maintain friendly relations there.

Miles had sent Doane to Judith Basin on August 3. On August 10, without knowing that on the same day Gibbon had been wounded, surrounded, and pinned down by the Nez Perces in the battle of the Big Hole, Miles ordered Colonel Sturgis from Fort Keogh with six companies of his regiment to Judith Basin "to the same end" he had previously ordered Doane, and with Doane ordered to report to Sturgis.

Sturgis sent forward an order for Doane to meet him at Judith Gap. Sturgis arrived on the Musselshell on August 19 and laid over a day, waiting for his supply train, but still within supporting distance of Doane.

At this time, even though troubled by poor communications, the minds of the military were beginning to run in the same channel.

On August 17, Colonel Gibbon, hospitalizing at Deer Lodge, and learning that Sturgis and Doane had gone to Judith Basin, sent two dispatches to Colonel Sturgis to move with all speed to

[10] *Report* 1877, Secretary of War, Sturgis, 508.

Fort Ellis, hoping to get him there in time to move up the Yellowstone River and head off the Indians before they crossed to the east side of that stream. The dispatches did not reach Sturgis until long afterwards (after Sturgis had fought the hostiles a running battle September 13 on Canyon Creek, in the vicinity of present-day Billings, Montana).

But Sturgis, on August 21, learning that the Nez Perces were still in the vicinity of Camas Prairie, decided to move back to the Yellowstone "aiming to reach that river near the mouth of the Stillwater . . . taking up a central position which might guard the various passes . . . all the way from the lower canon of the Yellowstone clear around to Clark's Fork a distance of 250 miles."

Sturgis sent orders to Doane to either join him, or to return to the special service Miles had assigned to him, namely, to Judith Basin with the Crows. "He did neither," Sturgis complained. Why?

Doane, one day in advance of Sturgis on August 21, probably intercepted Gibbon's order to return to Fort Ellis. Gibbon says he did.[11] Hugh L. Scott says:

> An Indian came in with a dispatch giving news of the Battle of the Big Hole. . . . Doane . . . saw that our supplies were too low to wait for the Indians to travel all that distance from the Big Hole, and so we went in to Fort Ellis to reshoe and refit.

On August 24, the Nez Perces and their outriders, moving eastward, attacked a Radersburg, Montana tourist party on the Firehole River in Yellowstone Park and two days later attacked another party, from Helena — A. J. Weikert and nine other men — on Otter Creek above Yellowstone Falls.[12]

[11] *Report* 1877, Secretary of War, Gibbon, 505.
[12] Stories of these Indian attacks became the classics of Yellowstone adventure. See Chittenden, *Yellowstone National Park,* 1964 ed., 100, 104; Howard and McGrath, *War Chief Joseph,* 234; Merrill D. Beal, *"I Will Fight No More Forever": Chief Joseph and the Nez Perce War,* 171; Andrew J. Weikert, "Journal of a Tour through Yellowstone National Park in August and September 1877," Historical

Doane, his Crow scouts, Lieutenant Scott, and de Rudio's company reached Fort Ellis August 26; and left the next day, August 27.

Sturgis says that having learned Doane had gone to Fort Ellis, he sent Doane "orders to take up a position in the lower canyon of the Yellowstone, keeping his Indian scouts well advanced toward the park, and in case the hostiles should move eastward, to join me rapidly; but in case they should come down the Yellowstone, to send me word to that effect and I would join him." [13] Gibbon by now was giving contrary orders. He says "Doane was ordered by telegraph to push up the Yellowstone to the bridge at the East Fork [today's Lamar River], cross that, and feel for the Indians up the right bank of the Yellowstone."

The Nez Perces were now camped on the Yellowstone River at Mud Geyser, below Yellowstone Lake. They had decided to move north down the Yellowstone River (past the present sites of Gardiner and Livingston, Montana) and join forces with the Crows. Chief Joseph sent an advance of nineteen warriors down the river.

Doane was already headed south up the river. But now his Crow allies began to slip away mysteriously in the night. The original one or two hundred dwindled to twenty faithful. "Colonel" Allen says:

> Lieut. Doane gave orders to me to keep to the rear, arrest deserters, and question them as to their reasons for deserting. I had not been long in the rear, before an Indian and his boy came along on the back track; I halted them and inquired where they were going. The Indian said, "I left my wife alone in camp, and I am afraid that something dreadful will happen to her . . . I had a dream last night about my wife, and I fear that all is wrong with her." I took the Indian and

Society of Montana, *Contributions,* IV, 185; Mrs. George F. Cowan, "Reminiscences of Pioneer Life," Ibid., 173.

[13] *Report* 1877, Secretary of War, Sturgis, 508.

his boy back to Lieut. Doane and told him the reason
that the Indian had given for wishing to desert; Lieut.
Doane replied, "Let them go." I went back to the
rear again and soon halted six more Indians. Some
had one excuse for deserting, some another, I let
them all go. I reported to Lieut. Doane in the evening, and he said, "We have enough anyway."[14]

As Doane pushed by the Devil's Slide on September 1,[15] he
observed smoke curling skyward farther up the canyon. Soon
the Crow scouts came dashing back. Nez Perces were as thick as
grass on the ground, they said, and were burning Henderson's
ranch.

The Crows threw off their saddles, painted their faces, put on
their war bonnets, and thus properly dressed for the occasion
by Indian standards, hurried back to the front again, riding
horseback. With Doane's permission Lieutenant Scott took Jack
Baronett[16] and ten men, and spurred after them, with the main
force to follow. Galloping through Mammoth Hot Springs they
found the still-warm body of Richard Dietrick sprawled dead
across the doorway of Jim McCartney's cabin. The retreating
Nez Perces had just shot him. Near Liberty Cap Jack Baronett
persuaded Scott to turn back before they were ambushed.

That night Doane's small force camped at Henderson's ranch
near an irrigation ditch which would provide both water and an
embankment for defending an attack. Doane ringed the camp

[14] Phinney, *Jirah Isham Allen,* 96; see Scott, *Memories,* 61.
[15] Gibbon gives this date as September 2. *Report* 1877, Secretary of War,
Gibbon, 506.
[16] The editors have adopted this spelling of the name. Jack E. Haynes said he
found this actual signature on old pay documents. The 1890 census has it Barronette.
W. E. Strong, who was careful with proper names and spent some time with Baronett,
spells it Baronette. T. C. Everts, whom Baronett rescued in 1870, spells it Baronet
(see Part II this book). There are other variations.
  The variety in Baronett's life itself far outdoes the variations in his name. Born in
Scotland in 1829, he had by the time he was twenty-three adventured from China to
Mexico to Australia. In light of Doane's later associations with him, it is interesting to
note that Baronett prospected for gold in Africa in 1853 and sailed the Arctic seas in
a whaler in 1854. See Chittenden, *Yellowstone National Park,* 1964 ed., 148.

with Cossack posts[17] to prevent any surprise attacks. There would be no raid here such as the one at Camas Meadows on August 20 when the Nez Perces raided General Howard's camp and ran off all his pack mules.

De Rudio had the post nearest the trail toward Mammoth. A commotion in the middle of the night aroused the entire camp. De Rudio came in, bringing a Negro. It was Ben Stone, the cook for the tourist party from Helena. Ben told his story. Doane listened; anything concerning the Nez Perce was now important military information—even if it had a slightly ludicrous touch.

As Ben told it (and as the editor heard the tale long years ago), when Ben approached camp the sentry called out, "Who comes there?" "Ben Stone," the Negro answered. "Come in, Ben Stone," and Ben came running as fast as he could.

Two of Doane's Crow scouts came up to shake hands. The trembling Ben panicked, declared one of these Indians was Chief Joseph himself.

Ben told Doane that when the Nez Perce attacked the tourist's camp, he could not believe it was Indians, but thought it was some of their own party playing a joke. He ran out shouting, "Stop this foolishness! You might kill someone! You can't scare us!" When he saw they were really hostile Indians he ran for his life. The dinner he was cooking never did get finished. The Indians fired several shots at him. He stumbled and fell in a creek, too breathless to move.

A soldier pointed to the ragged rip across the seat of his trousers. "Shot?" the soldier kidded. "Got that when I fell down," Ben confessed, "but I recollec' feeling somethin' crawlin' under me an' it were a piece o' lead."

Ben had reached Mammoth about the time the Nez Perces retreated through. He spurted up a gulch, shinnied up a tree and hid in the branches, his heart beating so loudly he said he thought the Indians could hear it. At night he came down, crawled out to peer over the hillside, then hid in some bushes.

---

[17] A group of three to six men maintaining watch and sentry. Thus the enemy cannot surprise the camp by throttling one sentry, for the rest of the post can always give an alarm.

THE HELENA (OR WEIKERT) PARTY . . . .

Some members of the Weikert tourist party from Helena, Montana, who were attacked by Nez Perce Indians in Yellowstone Park on August 26, 1877. L to R in center picture: Joe Robert, Andrew J. Weikert, Fred Pfiester. In ovals: upper left, Charles Kenck; lower left, Leonard Duncan; upper right, Prof. Richard Dietrich; lower right, Ben Stone. *Courtesy Montana Historical Society.*

"Five times, I started outa dem bushes, and five times I went back in again. A bear came into d' bushes, an' I didn't know what to do – be et by the bear or kilt by the Indians. But I decided fo' the bear – I had tried the Indians twice. I prayed Almighty God to take me outa dis trouble, an' He did. The bear stood up on his hind legs an' looked hard; den he ran away. An' here I is."

That night Ben prayed loud and long, thanking God for his goodness and deliverance. To the griping soldiers, he replied that he was going to thank Him as loud and as long as he liked whether the camp got any sleep or not. Finally the weary Doane ordered out a wearier guard to put silence on Ben.

The next morning Doane sent Lieutenant Scott with twenty men and some of the Crows over to scout the Yellowstone River near the mouth of the Lamar. Baronett Bridge was still intact. The patrol set fire to the grass as ordered and returned to camp. Sharp, black Nez Perce eyes watched them all day, and reported back to Chief Joseph the events of September 1 and 2.

Joseph afterwards admitted it had made a big change in their plans to go down the Yellowstone valley. They thought Doane's outfit was only the advance of a large army force. "With Howard's soldiers right behind us, we did not want to be caught between two forces of soldiers closing the ends of the Yellowstone canyon with high mountains on each side," Joseph said. So they crossed the Yellowstone River at Mud Geyser, went up Pelican Creek, across the mountains, and down Clark's Fork to its mouth on the Yellowstone (present day Billings). This took them away from Doane but put them within striking distance of Miles' forces and ultimately resulted in their defeat.

Doane had made a strategic and effective move. But a pompous colonel was now about to ruin the army plan.

On August 26, the day Doane returned to Fort Ellis, Howard was resting his wounded and battle-creased outfit at Henry's Lake, west of Yellowstone Park. He wired General Sherman (then at Fort Shaw) that he could not push his command much farther; he said he was ready to quit and march back to Fort Boise. Were not Sturgis and Miles nearby the hostiles?

Sherman wired him, "Miles is too far off . . . Sturgis is too slow. . . . If you are tired, give the command to some young energetic officer, and let him follow them."

Howard wired back on August 27, "You misunderstand me. I never flag. . . . We move in the morning. . . ."[18]

Doane intended to move forward that night of September 2 and meet the hostiles next day. Before he got away, a courier arrived from Lieutenant Colonel C. C. Gilbert ordering him to wait.

Gilbert's letter is of interest in this highly controversial matter since it has not heretofore been published. Datelined Fort Ellis, M.T., August 31, 1877, to Doane at "Barronette's Bridge, M.T." (where Gibbon's orders, not Sturgis', had sent Doane), it states:

> General Sherman and General Gibbon had a conference in my presence day before yesterday, the issue of which amounts to this, that I am to overtake you, assume the Command of you and your party, and then communicate with General Howard whose presence General Sherman much needs in the Department of the Columbia, and should Howard go at once I am to take the Command of his column. I expect to camp about 10 miles out from this Post this afternoon of Sept. 2d, that is to say the third day out.[19]

The next day after receiving this letter, Doane sent a message to Howard which provided the general with a clue as to what was afoot:

> The enclosed letter received by me last evening will need no explanation. I am here with one Co 7th Cavalry, about 30 citizens, and 42 Crow scouts. Camped at a burning ranch, fired by the Nez-Perces yesterday. Will await Col. Gilbert here but to-day am

[18] *Report* 1877, Secretary of War, Howard, 13.
[19] Doane Summary, National Archives.

sending you this to anticipate him. Please return a courier with the bearer of this (who may be able to find you to-night). I will look for an answer to-morrow night.

Gen. Sturgis on Aug. 29th was at Crow Agency. His command of 450[20] men, and Crow scouts besides, should be on Clarks Fork about Heart Mt. but I fear he is *not* there.[21]

Arriving at Doane's camp at Henderson Ranch on September 3, Gilbert proceeded to engineer a foul-up which ended with the generals calling each other names.

Heretofore Gilbert seemed to have been given an assignment that left him harmless to the army. He commanded Camp Baker (twenty miles northwest of White Sulphur Springs, Montana) which was little more than a sentry post at that time. On August 27, Gibbon had detailed him to Helena on an errand to open bids on a flour buying contract.[22] This was the same day Gibbon was dispatching valuable officers like Doane and Sturgis into battle positions.

But W. T. Sherman, general of the army, was in Helena at the same time Gilbert was there on the flour deal; also at this time Sherman was having the famous colloquy of telegrams with Howard. Whether to shame Howard, or knowing Gilbert no better, the general gave Gilbert a letter addressed to Howard, telling Howard in effect that he could turn his command over to Gilbert if Howard was too tired to fight.

To Gilbert it spelled the golden opportunity of his dull military career — a real command. Impetuously he rushed to reach Howard. Gibbon was caught in the quandary of supplementing Sherman's orders. He did this by instructing Gilbert to pick up Norwood's Company L (then in command of Lieutenant Schofield) at Fort Ellis and then Doane and his outfit on

[20] Actually about 360.
[21] Doane letter, AAG, Department of Columbia, September 1, 1877. National Archives.
[22] *Report* 1877, Secretary of War, Gilbert, 561.

the Yellowstone. Norwood's outfit was a good one. It had escorted General Sherman on his tour beginning July 18 from the mouth of the Big Horn through Yellowstone Park, arriving at Fort Ellis July 27; it had taken part "with great gallantry" in the Nez Perce fight at Camas Prairie on August 20.

Perhaps Gibbon thought Doane, Schofield, and their noncoms could keep Gilbert out of trouble. General Howard resentfully claimed it was an effort "to give Lieutenant Colonel Gilbert a command."

When Gilbert reached Doane he refused to let Doane go forward as Doane had planned and had been ordered. Gilbert said he "was only trying to reach Howard and did not want to be delayed by a fight and miss him. . . . Doane begged him with tears in his eyes to go forward the following day, but he refused." [23]

If Gilbert had followed Doane's urgings they would have met Howard at Baronett's Bridge September 4; [24] but Gilbert's fuzzy thinking pictured General Howard still at Henry's Lake where Sherman had wired Howard a week before.

Gilbert then turned the whole force of skilled officers, men, and Indian scouts twelve miles back down the Yellowstone, then westward over an old Bannock trail and up the West Gallatin and over to the Madison. There the backward march ended when they came across Howard's trail headed in the opposite direction, already eight days cold.

Gilbert had bunched his troops and pack trains at night in mountain pockets with half enough pasture and pushed and starved his animals until they could not carry a man. Doane could do nothing with him. The impetuous Gilbert kept up a gruelling, fruitless chase after Howard. Finally he took Jack Baronett and the best horses, still trying to catch Howard. Doane gathered what was left of the outfit, ambled back through the Park and down the Yellowstone, traveling slowly to recuperate the horses. He arrived back at Fort Ellis in October.

Gilbert's bedraggled group, reduced to about twenty officers

[23] Scott, *Memories,* 68.
[24] Gibbon's date.

and men, finally straggled back to Fort Ellis by way of Crow Agency.[25] Of all his horses, only twenty were thereafter serviceable to the army.[26]

Gilbert had wiped out two companies of U.S. Cavalry. He had destroyed Doane's effectiveness—at a time when it was most needed.[27] Chief Joseph's generalship could have done no more.

Joseph escaped again.

DOANE'S DIPLOMACY PAYS OFF

While Sturgis was looking for the Nez Perces on Clark's Fork, Nez Perce Chief Looking Glass rode ahead to the Crows seeking alliance and refuge. He had old friends among the leading men of the Crows. But the Crow's attitude had changed. Doane's influence with them had been effective. The River Crows were now allies of the army; the Mountain Crows were neutral; neither would offend their friends, the whites, by giving aid to the Nez Perces.

Joseph's only chance now was to flee to Canada and seek Sitting Bull and refuge there. The Crows stormed his rear guard for 150 miles before he reached the Musselshell. Joseph went through Judith Gap as Doane had predicted, even though it had involved the long detour around to the east.

Joseph would not be stopped until October 5, when he surrendered to Colonel Miles thirty miles short of the Canadian border.

Colonel Miles, in his victory report of December 27, 1877, summed up Doane's contribution to the Nez Perce campaign:

> [Doane] was very successful [in securing the services of the Crow warriors], and their services as allies with the force south of the Yellowstone, also in scouting

[25] *Report* 1877, Secretary of War, Gilbert, 561.
[26] *Report* 1877, Secretary of War, Brisbin, 553.
[27] Lieutenant De Rudio refitted at Fort Ellis, was ordered to Fort Benton, and later rendered some service in bringing in stray Nez Perces after Joseph's surrender.

the country along and north of the Yellowstone, west of this point, and in fighting and harassing the Nez Perces, were of very great value and obtained at a relatively small expenditure, in rations and ammunition, on the part of the government. Lieutenant Doane's services, first in organizing the Crows, and subsequently on the approach of the Nez Perces, with whom they had been in friendly relations, in retaining their loyalty to the government were highly important and valuable.[28]

Major James S. Brisbin, commander of Fort Ellis, says in the final two paragraphs of his annual report of October 26, 1877:

[Lieutenant Doane] did good service during the summer, frequently sending aid to General Miles, and one time preventing the Crows and Nez Perces from coming in contact, in which case, if they had, the Nez Perce would undoubtedly have obtained a fresh mount and escaped over the border, before Miles could have struck them.[29]

[28] *Report* 1877, Secretary of War, Miles, 499. Miles also wrote a letter of praise to Doane dated November 1, 1877, expressing "his entire approval of your action during the past summer campaign." Doane Summary, National Archives.
[29] *Report* 1877, Secretary of War, Brisbin, 553.

Fort Keogh, Montana Territory, 1877. Company of 5th Infantry in front of their barracks. *Courtesy U.S. Signal Corps.*

CHAPTER 6

FRONTIER DUTIES: 1877 - 1879

FORTS KEOGH AND CUSTER

Doane spent the winter of 1877-78 working again for Colonel Miles to ally the Crows against some of the remaining hostile bands of Sioux.[1] Also, he was traveling between Forts Keogh and Custer trying to collect back pay for the Crow Indians who had not yet received their money for the 1876 Sioux campaign. By now this pay was thoroughly buried in red tape. Doane had to hold the traveling paymaster in one spot long enough to send to Fort Ellis for the payrolls.

While Doane was at Fort Custer, reports came in on April 21 of an army wagon train hopelessly bogged down and out of food seventy-five miles to the south. It took Doane and his party three rugged days to travel the seventy-five miles of knee-deep slush, snow drifts, and swollen streams.

Doane gathered the party together and started for Fort Custer. There was only a trail. Doane says they marched by

> dodging snow drifts on slopes or taking them on a downhill pitch, crossing the ravines by forcing the loose stock through first and tramping down snow until it would bear the wagons. . . .

[1] Doane Army Records, National Archives.

[We] made one of the fords of Twin Creek and found swimming water; took boxes off wagons, used one of them for a boat, having covered it with tent flies and wagon sheets, ferried all property over in six loads, drove stock into water with lariats from opposite bank, and made them swim over. [Then we] floated the extra wagon bodies over with the boats and dragged the wagons across the bottom by an attachment of five chains, extra tongues, and ropes worked by a team on the opposite side. Afterwards floated the ambulance over in the same way, steadying them with the lariats to prevent their tipping over in the rushing current.[2]

Back at Fort Custer Doane learned that the new President of the United States, Rutherford B. Hayes, had appointed Phileteus W. Norris superintendent of Yellowstone National Park. Though no one could know it at the time, Norris would change things — he would build roads, would be able to take care of visitors, and would reside in the park, whereas the first superintendent, N. P. Langford, had seldom gone there. But it would also affect Doane, for Norris would begin to become knowledgeable about the region where Doane had previously held the limelight.

On May 1, Doane was back at Fort Custer still under the command of Colonel Miles and still trying to settle nine Crow accounts. He was holding the paymaster there while writing Fort Ellis again for the payrolls. By June the payrolls were settled and he was back at Fort Ellis.

Doane was interested to read in the Montana newspapers that Congress had passed the first appropriation bill in history for Yellowstone Park on June 13, 1878, for $10,000.

---

[2] Doane Summary, National Archives.

Fort Custer, M. T., c 1879. In the summer of 1877 Doane selected and staked out the site for these officers' quarters. L. A. Huffman photo. *Courtesy Jack Coffrin, Old West Gallery, Miles City, Montana.*

Fort Keogh, M. T., 1877. Officers' quarters. *Courtesy U.S. Signal Corps.*

THE BANNOCK UPRISING

Faced with utter destitution and starvation, one could scarcely blame the Bannock Indians for arming themselves in 1878, storming off their reservations, and battling to find food and sustenance. It is to the credit of the Fort Ellis officers that they sympathized with the Indians, tried to help them, and avoided battle and bloodshed by keeping the Indians policed and herded into small bands which were permitted to hunt without congregating into a large enough force to attack the army.

Doane was part of this effort. He was in command of Company L sent to Camp Mulkey near the Lemhi Agency in Idaho Territory that summer to serve under Captain Edward Ball.

Treaty parleys during the 1860's culminated in the signing of the Treaty of Fort Bridger with the Bannocks on July 3, 1868. Its all-important Article 2 provided that when the Bannocks desired a reservation a tract "which shall embrace reasonable portions of the 'Port Neuf' and 'Kansas Prairie' countries" would be selected. Six Bannock chiefs signed the treaty. The words "Kansas Prairie" was a clerical error — "Camas Prairie" had been intended by all concerned. Chief Taghee had always insisted that Camas Prairie be set aside for his Bannocks. The lowly camas tuber, harvested annually by them, was a vital part of the Bannock diet.

When Chief Buffalo Horn and his Bannocks saw cattle covering Camas Prairie in the spring of 1878, they reacted. The Bannocks had been protesting the invasion of the great plain by white men since 1871 when large herds of cattle and hogs were deliberately moved in. The hogs destroyed the root of the camas plant. When the Bannocks indignantly protested, citing the 1868 treaty, they were given to understand their land was "Kansas Prairie," not Camas Prairie. Obviously the white men were taking advantage of the clerical error to open Camas Prairie for settlement and the government was not going to interfere.[3]

[3] Fort Hall Records, National Archives.

Buffalo Horn and his warriors had had enough. They were not going to be pushed around any more. His band descended to Camas Prairie, shot and wounded three cowboys, and touched off the war. A vigorous campaign followed under General Howard.

Doane spent much of the summer in Idaho scouting the area of Horse Prairie, that country on the Beaverhead River north of Fort Hall, northeast of Camas Prairie, and west of Yellowstone Park.

By July the Bannock hostiles were breaking up into disorganized bands. Their leaders, Chief Egan and Buffalo Horn, had been killed. General Howard thought the Indians now "would endeavor to get to Lemhi and Fort Hall, or perhaps carry out their insane project of going to the buffalo country and thence to Sitting Bull."[4]

To keep the Lemhi Bannocks peaceful and apart, Brisbin authorized them to go on a hunt accompanied by soldiers of Doane's and Adams' companies. The other hostile Bannocks headed eastward across the Old Bannock Trail through Yellowstone Park until they ran into Colonel Miles near Heart Mountain on Clark's Fork in Wyoming Territory. There, the soldiers, aided by about seventy-five Crow scouts, surprised the twenty Bannock lodges on August 29, killing twenty-eight and capturing forty.[5] The remaining Indians were returned to the Fort Hall reservation that fall and hostilities ceased.[6] Doane was back at Fort Ellis in November.

Doane had performed well during the Bannock uprising, but it had been a frustrating experience for him — for a reason other than the Indians.

Doane still cherished ambitions to complete his Snake River exploration which had been halted by recall to Fort Ellis early

[4] Howard to McDowell, October 1878. 45 Congress, 3 session, *House Exec. Doc. No. 1,* Serial No. 1843, Part 2, 226.

[5] Miles reports eleven killed and thirty-five captured.

[6] See George F. Brimlow, *The Bannock Indian War of 1878,* 183; Brigham D. Madsen, *The Bannock of Idaho,* 224; Miles, *Recollections,* 294; Topping, *Chronicles of the Yellowstone,* 232-234; Members of the Potomac Corral of The Westerners, *Great Western Indian Fights,* 270; F. W. Hodge, *Handbook of American Indians,* I, 129.

in 1877. But while Doane harbored his hopes, Major Brisbin, at Fort Ellis, harbored his resentments. Brisbin was still rankled over the favoritism shown Doane by district and department commanders and over the fact that Doane had gone over his head for permission to make that 1876 Snake River Expedition. On June 2, 1878, Brisbin had written to his superiors, urging that the interrupted Snake River exploration be resumed and completed; he recommended that either Second Lieutenant E. J. McClernand or First Lieutenant J. U. Robinson lead the expedition. Brisbin then had Doane assigned to a less than major role in the Bannock campaign.

HONEYMOON

While Doane was at Horse Prairie, Idaho during the summer of 1878, he was not greatly surprised to learn that his wife, Amelia, was suing him for divorce at Virginia City, Montana, alleging desertion, abandonment, and extreme cruelty. They had no children. The divorce was granted September 23, 1878.[7] She resumed her maiden name of Amelia Link.

We can only surmise the reasons for the break-up that must have given the local gossips plenty of reason to talk. There was Amelia's accident in 1871 when she was out riding with Lieutenant Schofield. To be remembered also was the fact that in ten years of marriage Doane had hardly ever been home.

An army wife on the frontier in the 1870's led a lonely and difficult life, without conveniences, diversion, or companionship. Doane was away from the fort all of 1876 and 1877 except for a few days, and in 1878 it was the same story over again. The winter expedition of 1876-77, when he could have stayed home, may have been the final breaking point. But one never knows what really goes on in family troubles.

And the biggest scoop for the wagging tongues was yet to come!

[7] District Clerk Records, Virginia City, Montana; Doane Pension Records, Doane Army Records, National Archives.

From Horse Prairie, Idaho, on October 15, Doane applied directly to Washington for five months' leave, to take effect about December 15. It appears he was already making plans for a new marriage, but he was not taking the command at Fort Ellis into his confidence. In December, thirty-eight-year-old Doane would marry nineteen-year-old Mary Lee Hunter, of Hunter Hot Springs, Montana. Her father, Dr. Andrew Jackson Hunter, had been the government physician at Fort Ellis when Mary Lee was thirteen.

Major Brisbin fumed when he learned that Doane had gone over his head again. He wired Washington: "The leave . . . was obtained without knowledge or consent of his company or his post commander. He cannot be spared now and I request that his leave be suspended." Brisbin was "referred" to the "Department Commander," who had granted the leave.

The surprise wedding took place on December 16 in Helena, at the home of Captain T. P. Fuller with the Reverend Clark Wright performing the ceremony.[8] Governor and Mrs. Benjamin F. Potts of Montana Territory headed the list of guests. At the time, Mary Lee was attending St. Vincent's Academy in Helena while her family was living at isolated Hunter Hot Springs.

Doane and Mary Lee left from Helena by stage road via Virginia City to the railroad at Corinne, Utah.[9] "It was a four day trip to the railroad," Mrs. Doane recalled, "and a day was from 5 o'clock in the morning until 8 o'clock at night, and the last lap of the journey we rode all day and all night. It was quite a honeymoon."[10]

The newlyweds spent the winter in Washington, D.C. Doane was on full army pay.

[8] There is no public record of this marriage, although the Bozeman *Avant Courier* and the *Helena Daily Herald* published the news story. Some fifteen years later in New York City, following Doane's death, Reverend Wright made an affidavit that he had performed the marriage. This was enough to give Mary Lee her Army widow's pension.

[9] The Earl of Dunraven, in *Hunting in the Yellowstone,* described this stagecoach line on a trip he made in 1875.

[10] See Mrs. Doane's account in Merrill G. Burlingame, "The Andrew Jackson Hunter Family – Mary Hunter Doane," *Montana Magazine of History,* I, No. 1, January 1951, 5-13; Doane Pension Records, Doane Army Records, Doane Summary, National Archives.

Mary Lee Hunter Doane, Doane's second wife, 1880's. Mrs. Doane is wearing a navy blue dress she purchased in Philadelphia while she and her husband were on their wedding trip to "the states." Cobb's Doré Gallery (San Francisco) photo. *Courtesy Gallatin County (Montana) Pioneers Museum.*

CENTENNIAL TENT

But Doane was mixing love with opportunity. He had invented a new army tent and had already made some progress toward getting it adopted. Colonel John Gibbon, District of Montana, had endorsed it. Colonel Miles, District of Yellowstone, had ordered fifty of Doane's tents in 1877. [11] Doane had constructed one for Captain Bainbridge at Fort Hall in early 1877. [12] The tents had been tested by frontier use. Now Doane was in Washington where the tent had not been demonstrated but where the decisions were made. Imaginatively, he arranged for a demonstration with the brass of 1879. But he had no tent to demonstrate. It had not been part of his honeymoon luggage.

With the same dogged audaciousness which underlay all his projects, Doane pushed ahead. He asked for travel expense to the Philadelphia or Jeffersonville Quartermaster depot where labor and materials would be furnished to construct the tent "for presentation before the [Army Equipment] Board." The Army Equipment Board, the Adjutant General, and the Secretary of War approved his request. The Quartermaster General liked the tent idea but did not see why Doane had to supervise the work himself. About the trip he said curtly: "I think it a useless expenditure. Any tentmaker can make a tent from drawings without aid of any officer." [13] Doane went to Philadelphia anyway.

What was this tent? Why did Doane call it a "Centennial Tent?" Doane does not clarify the name. One can speculate that inasmuch as he presumably invented or perfected his design about 1876, he named it in honor of the 1776 army of American Independence. In any case, Doane was specific about the tent's design.

In his U.S. Patent Office application, filed March 29, 1879, Doane says:

[11] Letter from Doane to Army Equipment Board, February 20, 1879 (reproduced in this book). War Department Records, Adjutant General's Office, National Archives.

[12] See Part III, Chapter 17, *Communiques* section.

[13] Quartermaster General memo, February 21, 1879. War Department Records, Adjutant General's Office, National Archives.

I, Gustavus C. Doane, First Lieutenant, Second Cavalry, United States Army, have invented a new and Improved Army-Tent . . .

My invention relates to certain improvements in army-tents adapted to shelter a detachment of men . . .

The improvements consist, first, of means for equalizing and distributing the strain of the guy-ropes upon the tent, . . . without imparting any tearing or damaging strain to the canvas.

The improvements also consist in the peculiar construction and arrangement of a re-enforcement at the apex of the tent; the peculiar construction and arrangement of a set of reefing-cords for reefing up the side walls; in the means for attaching the re-enforcement straps to the guy-rope; in the peculiar arrangement and fastenings for the door in the side wall; in the means for forming a tight joint between the ground and the bottom of the side wall; and in the peculiar construction and arrangment of the cap at the top of the tent for covering the ventilation-opening. . .

In constructing this tent the best proportions to be observed are four feet six inches for the height of the wall, thirteen feet six inches slant height of roof, and eighteen feet six inches diameter of tent inside.[14]

In other words, Doane's tent provided a single pole, with sloping roof and vertical walls stretched into place by guy ropes, and with a ventilator in the peak. These basic principles have been used in U.S. Army tents since Doane demonstrated them. His tent differed from later army tents only in his being a circular one.

It is obvious that Doane had adapted his tent from the tepee of the Plains Indians, with modifications for army use. The Indian tepee required fifteen or more poles erected in cone

14 U.S. Patent No. 214996 granted May 6, 1879.

Washington D.C
February 20th 1879

To the Recorder
Board on Equipments
Washington DC
Sir

In presenting
the "Doane Centennial Tent" for your examination. I am unable to furnish a
Sample Tent for inspection. as I cannot
afford the expense. being on leave of absence
and from a distant Station. The Pattern of
the Tent having been favorably endorsed by the
District Commander of Montana (Colonel John Gibbon
7th Infantry) And Authority to manufacture fifty
Tents for the use of his Regiment having been
asked in 1877 by the District Commander of

the Yellowstone (Colonel Nelson A Miles 5th Infantry)
I have the honor to request- that I may be
ordered to Philadelphia - or to Jeffersonville
with authority to have constructed, from Common
or "A" tents on hand, under my direction. a
Centennial Tent - for the Inspection of the Board
Said Tent- to belong to the United States when
finished free of all liability- for Royalty: and
with further authority to Receipt- for said Tent
to the Officer responsible for the Property- at
the Q M Depot- where said Tent- may be
Manufactured - and to transport the same
to Washington for presentation before the Board
at- the expense of the Quartermasters Department

Very Respectfully
Your Obedient Servant -
G H Doane

Jt K 2 Cavalry
(On Leave of absence)

Address-
621- 13th St- N W
Washington DC

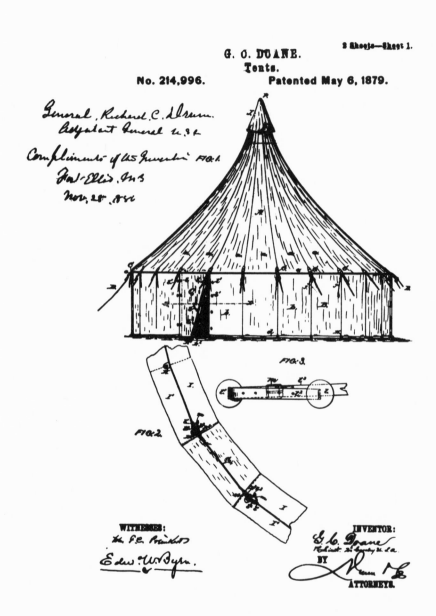

Drawings used by Doane to support his application for patent on his
centennial tent. *Courtesy National Archives.*

G. C. DOANE.
Tents.

No. 214,996. Patented May 6, 1879.

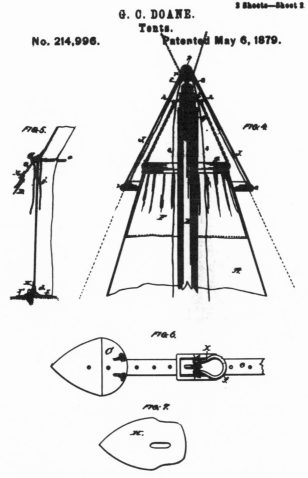

WITNESSES:

INVENTOR:
G. C. Doane

ATTORNEYS.

Centennial tents were still being used over a quarter of a century after
General Sherman turned down Doane's design, as this view of the Presidio

indicates, c 1906. Note two tents in left foreground; also, darker tents in left background are centennial models.

shape with two additional flap poles. For transportation, Indians lashed their poles to the sides of their horses, usually with a hide carrier secured across the butt ends in which they moved their household goods. The U. S. Army did not regard it as practical to travel in this manner or to carry so many poles. Doane himself had problems with obtaining and transporting tent poles on his 1876 Snake River Expedition when he used a tent more Indian- than centennial-like.

The centennial tent's single center pole design was a distinct advantage in respect to transportation, though it did preclude the building of an open fire inside the tent – a chief feature of the Indian tepee with its open center and its smoke flaps to veer the smoke away from prevailing winds. Doane's tent could, however, be used with a portable metal army camp stove.

Doane worked on his demonstration model in Philadelphia the spring of 1879; he got his leave extended an extra month and showed his tent to the officials. With endorsements and recommendations from the Montana field commanders on up almost to the top in Washington, the centennial tent seemed destined for army adoption. At last, however, General Sherman himself said No, and that was that. Except that centennial tents continued to be used, even dramatically.[15]

In June, Lieutenant and Mrs. Doane left Washington and returned west. Doane had been assigned to the new cavalry post of Fort Assiniboine, Montana, then in the process of construction. With packing boxes for furniture, Mary Lee began her frontier bridal housekeeping in a tent – presumably not a centennial tent. In October they moved into completed and spacious quarters.[16]

---

[15] See Chapter 7, *Greely's Expedition* section.
[16] Burlingame, "Hunter Family – Mary Hunter Doane."

Fort Assiniboine, M. T., 1879. L to R, in varying stages of completion: Guard house, adjutant's office, enlisted men's quarters. Photographer is standing near the site of the fort's 90-foot flag pole, looking north. Doane left from Fort Assiniboine for his 1880 Arctic exploration. *Courtesy U.S. Signal Corps.*

CHAPTER 7

ARCTIC EXPLORATION: 1880

HOWGATE AND GREELY

American participation in the era of Arctic exploration officially began on May 1, 1880, when an Act of Congress set in motion an expedition to the polar regions "for the purposes of scientific observations and exploration."

Doane was destined to command the first expedition, but strangely enough Arctic historians have heretofore failed to record this fact.

On November 18, 1877, Doane had volunteered for Arctic service. Captain Henry W. Howgate, Chief Disbursing Officer of the U.S. Army Signal Corps, at that time was promoting a colony-type expedition that would live in the Arctic a year or two and study it. Impressed with Doane's qualifications, Howgate promised him command of the expedition. However, Howgate also had in mind as expedition commander his protege, First Lieutenant A. W. Greely, who had lived in the Howgate home in Washington, D.C. for almost six years.

Greely, who was junior in rank to Doane, had undoubtedly become acquainted with Doane when Doane was assisting in the construction of telegraph lines in the West and Greely was the Signal Corps officer in charge; perhaps Greely had spoken favorably of Doane to Howgate.

Increasing interest in Arctic exploration resulted in an Arctic bill being introduced into Congress in 1878; it failed; no bill was introduced in 1879. On the passage of the 1880 bill, Doane was assigned to the expedition on May 5, 1880. He was the ranking officer.

This expedition went much deeper than desire for sheer adventure. It was part of the American contribution to the First International Polar Year (culminating in 1882-83) in which eleven nations would establish fifteen observatory stations in the polar regions. They would record a complete series of synchronized meteorological and magnetic observations, study the drifting water currents and the conditions and movements of the ice, and gather information about flora, fauna, and geology of the region, giving the world a better knowledge of the Arctic. The Americans were to maintain two of the stations, one at Point Barrow, Alaska, and another at Lady Franklin Bay, 81° 44' N, the farthest north of all the stations.

The project was the first time an international cooperative scientific research project was accomplished. It was conceived at the polar conference at Graz in 1875 and developed at Rome and Hamburg in 1879 and Bern in 1880.

This pioneer effort in the 1880's, of which Doane's expedition was the first step, provided the precedent for international cooperation which followed: the Second International Polar Year in 1932-33 and the International Geophysical Year in 1957-58. It also launched the race between nations to be the first to reach the North Pole. It was analogous to the race, in the 1960's, to put the first man on the moon.

On May 6, 1880, the Secretary of War wired the Army's Department of Dakota directing Doane to leave Montana with the eleven Second Cavalry men whom he had specially selected, including Sergeant D. L. Brainard and Privates Julius Frederick and Oscar Francis Long, who were to become heroes of Arctic survival on a later expedition.

Upon arrival in Washington, Doane learned that Greely had been placed in charge, with Doane as quartermaster and commissary officer. In that stage of the discussions, Doane waived his superior rank, with the private understanding that he would have charge of the advance exploration while Greely would remain at Lady Franklin Bay and be in command of the colony and station there. First Lieutenant William H. Lowe would serve under both.

S. S. GULNARE

However, in Washington where the expeditionary forces were gathering, a board of naval officers examined the *S.S. Gulnare,* the ship owned and donated for the expedition by Captain Howgate. The board condemned the *Gulnare,* an old 200-ton steamer built in Scotland, as unsuitable in hull and machinery for arctic service. No other suitable vessel was available. This ended government participation in the expedition; Greely withdrew as commander.

COMMANDER DOANE

Doane was caught in a dilemma: he could risk going in this faulty ship or perhaps lose the opportunity forever! He thought it over and finally agreed to command the expedition as a private citizen if the army would permit him. It did, granting him four month's leave. Lieutenant Lowe, with a twelve-month leave, agreed to accompany him.

The eleven enlisted men Doane had so carefully selected were sent back to Fort Ellis. In complimenting them, Doane characterized the skilled soldiers often found on the western frontier:

> In that small detachment of eleven men there were clerks, blacksmiths, colliers, sadlers, cooks, painters, sailors, carpenters, men who could make their own clothes, drive teams, pack, travel on foot or horseback, by sledges or on snowshoes, who would never get lost or bewildered, to whom the severities of a

winter in the northwest where the thermometer goes down to 50° below zero Fahrenheit were but a laughing stock. I felt as I saw them reluctantly go that the bone and sinew of the proposed expedition had departed and that they could not be replaced.[1]

The plan was for the *Gulnare* to land a scientific group in the Arctic, return to the United States to pick up supplies, and then next year plant another land party to replace that one.

On the date of sailing, the Supervisor Inspector of Steamboats for the District of Columbia inspected the *Gulnare* boilers and pronounced them in good condition and equal to new ones. The Attorney General of the United States decided the *Gulnare* could fly the American flag. Amidst great fanfare the *Gulnare* left from the Seventh Street wharves of Washington, D.C., on June 21, 1880. Doane joined the ship at St. Johns, Newfoundland, where it arrived some two weeks later, on July 7, with several boilers collapsed and the boat needing additional repairs. After much trouble with the crew, the boat, and the finances, the expedition finally left St. Johns July 30.

STORM

The *Gulnare* did prove unseaworthy.

On August 2, a terrific gale struck. The overloaded vessel strained and pitched, and the seams came apart. Huge seas incessantly broke over the ship fore and aft. The pumps clogged up with chips and shavings which had been left in the bilge during repairs at Alexandria, Virginia. They had to be cleaned every fifteen minutes. Next to the engine room the calking began to work loose and come out. Water spurted in with a hissing noise. The berths were drenched. Every time a wave struck, a barrel of water poured through an open crack in the stern which had showed daylight in calm weather. The drenched firemen and engineers worked in water up to their knees.

---

[1] Doane's *S. S. Gulnare* Report, O. H. Bonney Collection.

Freight got loose below and sacks of coal ground around the propeller shaft. Everything below, including the wood gratings of the fireroom floor, was afloat, slimy, and covered with coal. Bulwarks on the port side were stove in. The watersoaked material on deck became topheavy. A deckload of lumber was cut loose and floated away. Davits were ripped off and all the lifeboats were swept away. All control of the vessel was lost except holding her to the sea.

The end was near on August 4 with the vessel drifting towards the rocks and icebergs off Cape Farewell, the south tip of Greenland. Then the gale suddenly abated.

GREENLAND

Doane credited the two engineers who for two nights and a day did a masterful job of keeping the boat afloat. Held together by temporary repairs, the ship finally anchored safely on August 8 at Godhavn, on the Danish island of Disco, about midway up the west coast of Greenland, 70° 5' N latitude.

The innumerable delays, caused mainly by the unseaworthiness of the *Gulnare,* now made it too late in the season to go further north despite the fact, as Doane said, they had only reached the true starting point of a polar expedition.

While the crew made more repairs for the return trip, the land party did some exploring for a winter site. On August 20, Doane wrote the following letter to Theodor Smith, the Danish government official at Godhavn:

> Dr. Octave Pavy and Mr. Henry Clay are to remain this winter in either Ritenbank or Jakobshavn. Dr. Octave Pavy is the surgeon and naturalist and Mr. Henry Clay is secretary of the expedition.[2] Their object in remaining is the contemplation of my return next spring to make scientific and meteorological

[2] Both Clay and Pavy joined the Greely expedition the following year. However, they developed such enmities that Clay returned with Greely's ship *Proteus.*

observations, to make researches in botany, geology, climatology, etc., to study the glaciers and to accustom themselves to sledge travel and the hardships of Arctic life, all of which I consider important to the success of my future plans as specified above. I will leave them well provided with provisions, clothing etc., so that your government will not be put to any expenses on their account.[3]

On September 7, Doane and the crew began the seventeen-day return trip of 1,400 miles in the crippled *Gulnare,* reaching St. Johns on September 24. Doane and Lowe left the next day by the paquet steamer *Cortez* for Halifax, then traveled by sail to Washington. Thereafter Doane obtained a special order from Brigadier General H. Terry permitting him to "remain on temporary\duty at Fort Ellis until the opening of next spring when he will proceed to join his company." He finished the *Gulnare* report there March 16, 1881.[4]

DOANE'S DROLL SUMMARY

Doane's "preliminary remarks" in his report can be considered a classic discourse on the idiosyncrasies of explorers, into which Doane shows considerable insight.

Our Arctic Expedition of 1880 was a failure, not disastrous but complete. We only reached 70° 5' N latitude, the true starting point of a polar expedition, but little was accomplished and that little is not shown in this report.

The cruise of the *Gulnare* is the first acknowledged

---

[3] Doane's *S. S. Gulnare* Report, O. H. Bonney Collection.

[4] The editors found and own a rare copy of Doane's unpublished account of this little known event in the history of Arctic exploration. Doane's descriptions are graphic. F. Vilhjalmur Stefansson and his wife Evelyn, in correspondence with the editors, have expressed their opinion that Doane's document "has great historical value."

failure in Arctic annals. We did little, but left a great many things undone requiring some moral courage to refrain from doing. We did not change the names of all the localities visited as is customary, nor give them new latitudes and longitudes, to the bewilderment of the general reader. We do not dispute anyone's attained distance nor declare it impossible he should have been where he was. We did not hunt up nameless islands and promontories to tag them with the surnames of plethoric merchants and mildly enthusiastic females who had given us plugged tobacco and buttonhole bouquets. We did not erect any cenotaphs. A cenotaph is a monument erected to one who is buried elsewhere, or not buried at all. The Arctic style for such a structure is a pile of rocks, on the flattest of which is daubed in letters of tar the following stereotyped inscription: sacred to the memory of the heroic blank blank. Why a cenotaph should be erected where no one will see it and what use there is in erecting one at all are questions.

We raised no flags, converted no natives, killed none. We discovered no new evidences regarding the mosaic account of creation, nor the deluge, nor the unity of the races, nor the locations of ancient Troy, nor the garden of Eden. We found nothing in Greenland to put our nationality to the blush by comparison, nothing superior to the railroads and modern civilization. We did not see anything half as grand, half so sublime nor half so beautiful there than can be seen in the Yellowstone National Park and a dozen other localities at home. We did not even see what others have seen in the same regions; the primary geographical iceberg which in perspective towers above first class ships in the foreground and has a contemplative bear gazing seaward from its loftiest pinnacle oblivious to the herd of fat seals on the beach slope is not produced any more. Neither is the iceberg of the shop windows. The present ones are not so high by several hundred feet and instead of being in a freezing condition are rapidly thawing whenever afloat. Polar bears do not put their paws upon men's shoulders and smilingly permit their stomachs to be ripped open in the "Norwegian style" as formerly.

The rocks and bluffs of the Arctic regions are not all clouded with waterfall as pictured, nor is it dangerous to row a whaleboat lest it should run aground on a sleepy whale, be run through by the horn of a narwhal or captured by an angry herd of walrus.

Arctic scenery is grand but with little variety. The glacial phenomena alone in summertime are magnificent. In winter the auroras are added. At the pole during summer there is, of course, constant daylight yet nobody seems to have thought it worthwhile to call attention to the fact that solar observations only could be taken astronomically during that season. No one has proposed wintering at the pole. The proposition probably would not be carried into effect if ventured.

The object of this report is to endeavor to expose a few of the spacious plans, fallacies, reasonings, and ill-grounded conjectures which are called scientific, and to place the subject of circumpolar exploration on a basis of facts and reasonable probabilities. There is such a thing as science run mad and an enthusiasm which reaches lunacy. It is easy for our astronomers with the diameter of the earth's orbit as a baseline and nothing but ether as an intervening medium to stretch far out his distances to reach the blazing stars, but let that astronomer run against a ten foot wall and his terrestial progress is arrested. One cannot explore the earth's surface from an observatory, nor by mathematics nor by the power of logic; it must be done physically.

> The failure of the expedition as a government venture is officially charged to the *Gulnare.* Its failure as a private project will doubtless be conceded as due to the same cause. . .

Doane goes on to thank the many persons who had rendered assistance, including President Garfield, ex-President Hayes, and the members of the cabinet for many patient hearings and valuable time.

> Hoping that no more small appropriations may be made by the government to outfit Arctic expeditions to be followed by large ones for the purpose of rescuing the same, the following [report] is respectfully submitted.

> > [signed] G. C. Doane
> > 1st Lieut. 2nd Cavalry
> > U.S. Army

GREELY'S EXPEDITION

More attention should have been paid to Doane's timely admonition. The sequel to Doane's effort in the Arctic was that in 1881 the United States government again took over the project of reaching Lady Franklin Bay with an army expedition. Lieutenant Greely was assigned to command it.

Doane had decided against participation. The failure of the *Gulnare* and Captain Howgate's financial dealings in settling the obligations of the expedition may have had something to do with this decision.[5]

[5] A week after Greely's departure in the *Proteus,* General William Babcock Hazen, who had become Chief Signal Officer of the U.S. Army Signal Corps December 15, 1880, charged Howgate with the embezzlement of $200,000 in government funds. How much of this money had gone into the purchase of the *Gulnare* and the expenses of Doane's expedition is unknown. Soon after his arrest Howgate escaped and apparently was never apprehended, managing even to evade Alan Pinkerton and his men.

Greely's expedition reached Lady Franklin Bay, but the 1882 relief ship failed to reach Greely, and the 1883 relief ship sank. Only Greely and six men of an original twenty-five survived starvation and exposure before Commander Winfield Scott Schley rescued them on June 22, 1884.[6]

Among these survivors were Sergeant Brainard and Privates Frederick and Long – Doane's own choice of superb soldiers for an expedition. They strove unselfishly and without limit to provide for their comrades. Sergeant Brainard was one of Greely's party to reach the farthest point north (83° 24' N) of any exploration up to that time. He later attained the rank of brigadier general in the army.

Doane's photographer, George W. Rice, also returned north with Greely in 1881 as photographer. He was a constant inspiration in the struggle for survival. He died of exhaustion trying to recover a small cache of food from Baird Inlet.

Dr. Octave Pavy, whom Doane had left in Greenland, joined Greely at Godhavn in 1881, became surgeon of Greely's party, and was one of its personnel problems until his death June 6, 1884, sixteen days before the rescue.

Doane's quartermaster and subsistence planning was equally as sound as his selection of personnel. Greely erected quarters at Lady Franklin Bay using some of the lumber Doane had transported to Greenland for that very purpose. These quarters kept Greely and his men comfortable during the two winters they stayed there. At the turn of the century the same quarters gave Lieutenant Robert E. Peary winter shelter.

The last photograph taken at Greely's camp on Cape Sabine, when the survivors were rescued, shows a lone tent standing after the arctic blasts of the ordeal. It was Doane's centennial model, approved at the Arctic depot in Philadelphia in 1879.

The voyage of the *S. S. Gulnare* apparently ended Doane's ambitions for Arctic exploration. He did not make himself available for Greely's 1881 expedition, and on November 28,

---

[6] A. W. Greely, *Three Years of Arctic Service: An Account of the Lady Franklin Bay Expedition of 1881-84,* 2 vols.; A. L. Todd, *Abandoned: The Story of the Greely Arctic Expedition, 1881-1884.*

On June 22, 1884, about thirty minutes after Greely and the six other survivors were found, Ensign Charles H. Harlow photographed the battered centennial tent in which Greely and his companions had been living — and dying. *Courtesy National Archives.*

1881, he wrote from Fort Assiniboine to the Adjutant General in Washington the following:

> I state I am no longer a volunteer for duty with any so-called "Arctic Expeditions." Nor do I desire to be considered available for the same. This letter is written on account of my having so volunteered in 1877 to an officer on duty with the Signal Corps at the time; and my not knowing whether or not such letter may be on file in your office. In any case I am no longer under obligations. Nor am I a candidate for such duty.[7]

[7] Doane's Army Records, National Archives.

CHAPTER 8

THE FINAL DECADE: 1881 - 1892

SCOUTING AND RECRUITING

By 1881, Doane, then only forty-one years old, had led as long, as adventurous, and as arduous service in the army as any officer of that time. Now, with Mary Lee, he was beginning to think about an easier life.

In June 1881, he was sent to Fort Assiniboine to scout after molesting bands of Indians and half bloods. In November 1882, he was transferred to Fort Maginnis, Montana Territory, where he commanded Troop A, Second Cavalry, until September 1883.[1]

By 1883 the Indians had been herded onto the reservations and compelled to stay there. The buffalo, their only sustenance, were gone.[2] The red man would never again wage widescale war

[1] An interesting contemporary description of Fort Maginnis can be found in the letters of Frank Burke, a U.S. Signal Corps soldier who came to the fort on September 17, 1882. Burke's account is doubly relevant because of his interest in Arctic exploration. In 1881 he had been scheduled to accompany the Greely Expedition, but when the time came to join the party Burke was stationed at Crow's Nest in far western Montana and could not get east in time. See Charles T. Burke, ed., "Letters From the Wild West," *Montana The Magazine of Western History,* January 1969, 2. It is interesting to speculate about the discussions which must have taken place between Burke and Doane, two Fort Maginnis soldiers keenly concerned to get to the Arctic, each in his own way disappointed in the attempt, and both now reconciled to not going.

[2] That summer of 1883, the last of the northern herd, 50,000 to 80,000 head, crossed the Yellowstone at Fort Keogh and headed north. A cordon of hide hunters

on the plains. The biggest task of the frontier army was finished.

Doane applied for and was assigned to recruiting service. His applications almost apologized for seeking a "soft detail," as he called it, stating, "I have marched farther and oftener and have had more separate commands and detachments on frontier service and have had a greater number of days on actual duty than any officer in the regiment since the date of my joining the same."[3]

In his resplendent recruiting uniform, Doane could recount his experiences to dreamy-eyed youths and persuade them to enlist for the adventure of the frontier. Desertions from the dreary posts made it a constant task to keep the ranks filled.

From October 1883 until September 1884, Doane recruited from Jefferson Barracks, near St. Louis, in Milwaukee, and in Chicago.[4]

Urban life and its conveniences were pleasant: no long hours, hard marches, and warfare across rough country. He could spend every evening at home with Mary Lee. But the change would have future unforeseen results when Doane wanted to be superintendent of Yellowstone Park and found himself assigned to duties too far away.

In 1884, Doane was number five on the seniority list of first lieutenants. Captain William P. Clark, who had been on President Arthur's tour of Yellowstone Park in 1883, died. On September 22, President Chester Arthur signed Doane's promotion to captain of Clark's company (A, Second Cavalry).[5] Doane and his company were sent to the Presidio at San Francisco.

---

lined the Missouri River and slaughtered them. In November, Sitting Bull, his followers, and the white hunters accompanying them wiped out the final 10,000 buffalo near the Cannonball River in North Dakota, completing one of the most wasteful and disgraceful destructions of a natural resource ever committed by man. See Martin S. Garretson, *The American Bison.*

[3] Doane Army Records, National Archives.

[4] Doane Army Records, Doane Summary, National Archives.

[5] Doane accepted his commission and took the new oath at Jefferson Barracks, Missouri. He also sent in his oath of office from the Presidio at San Francisco, January 16, 1885, and again from Cochise's Stronghold in Arizona, May 10, 1886.

Jefferson Barracks, Missouri, c 1896. *Courtesy National Archives.*

THE APACHE CAMPAIGN

In September, 1885, unwelcome orders sent Doane from the Presidio to fight Geronimo's Apaches in Arizona. It was the last severe Indian outbreak in American history.

Mrs. Doane is quoted as saying that she had gone with the Captain from one bleak Montana army outpost to another, but now she was to be faced with the rigors of the hot Southwest. She followed her husband and lived in the small, arid towns adjacent to the army camps.[6]

The campaign centered in the vicinity of today's Chiricahua National Monument of Arizona. General George Crook, commanding the Department of Arizona, put Doane in command of the camp at Gila Canyon from January until March, 1886.[7]

On April 11, 1886, Brigadier General Miles, Doane's longtime friend, replaced General Crook. Miles found the troops of the Second Cavalry thoroughly disheartened and discouraged, strung out in tents along the tracks of the Southern Pacific at Bowie Station.[8]

He sent Doane to command the camp at Cochise's Stronghold, west of the Dragoon Mountains, with a heliograph station set up for communication. While Doane was there, Miles's troops pursued Geronimo across the Mexican border. Finally, on September 4, 1886, Geronimo surrendered.

Captain Doane and Mary Lee were on the platform at Bowie Station four days later when Geronimo and his men were taken aboard the train and sent to Fort Marion, Florida.

The oaths apparently were mislaid one after the other, necessitating this duplication, but years later they all turned up.

[6] Burlingame, "Hunter Family – Mary Hunter Doane."

Robert M. Utley reminds us in a recent article that an Arizona assignment was one of the most unwelcome which could come to an army man in the late nineteenth century. General George Crook complained, as Utley puts it, that the men considered Arizona a punishment to be endured, and had to be constantly prodded to prevent their lapsing into time-serving lethargy. Captain John G. Bourke called Arizona "that most woe-begone of military departments." See "Arizona Vanquished: Impressions and Reflections Concerning the Quality of Life on a Military Frontier," *The American West,* November 1969.

[7] See *Report* 1886, Secretary of War, for the report and map of Apache campaign.

[8] Miles, *Recollections,* 477.

Fort Bowie, Arizona Territory, September 1886. Fourth Cavalry band at flagstaff for retreat after Geronimo's surrender. *Courtesy U.S. Signal Corps.*

The Presidio, 1880's. Officers' quarters. *Courtesy California Historical Society.*

With the Apaches under control, Doane returned to the Presidio where he served until 1890.

DOANE SEEKS APPOINTMENT TO YELLOWSTONE PARK

Even as early as 1878 Major Brisbin had suggested to his superiors that the army ought to take charge of policing and preserving the Yellowstone National Park. Brisbin suggested a sergeant and four soldiers be stationed at the north entrance and a like number at the west entrance, with a soldier sent into the park with each party of visitors. He describes the beauty and the beast in the Park:

> Nowhere on earth are such wonders and game to be found and it will be a great shame if our authorities permit them to be destroyed.
> There are now in the park thousands of elk so tame a person can ride or walk about among them. . . . They are not slaughtered for their meat or skins but . . . simply for the pleasure of killing them. . . . There are many antelope, deer . . . grizzlies, cinnamon, brown and black bears, and flocks of 15 to 100 mountain sheep are met every day. . . .
> The action of the waters of the geysers and influence of the weather has induced an irregular cellular structure which gives a delicate and attractive appearance. . . . These formations are soft and can be cut with a saw or broken and carried away annually. Some of the most beautiful formations have already been entirely destroyed and will never be replaced during our lives or the lives of our children. This disposition to vandalism seems to possess everyone who enters the park and unless it is checked our wonderland will cease to be an object of interest.[9]

[9] Letter 347, June 5, 1878, to AAG, St. Paul. Fort Ellis Records, National Archives.

Colonel Ludlow had observed similar depradations a few years earlier. Reflecting upon the Yellowstone tourists, he wrote of the

> hopeless and unrestrained barbarity . . . of these sacrilegious invaders of nature's sanctuary. . . . To procure a specimen of perhaps a pound weight [of geyser sinter], a hundred pounds have been shattered and destroyed. . . . On our arrival in the basin we found several persons already encamped. . . . The visitors prowled about with shovel and ax, chopping and hacking and prying up great pieces of the most ornamental work they could find. . . .
> [On another day] we got back to camp just in time to prevent the fall of an uplifted ax, which a woman was just about to bring down on the summit of the Beehive [geyser]. . . . Our shouts reached her just in time, and subsequent remonstrance induced her at any rate to postpone the attack.[10]

Remonstrance was the limit of Ludlow's power; there were no sanctions he could employ. The General of the Army himself could have done no more. As a matter of fact, Phil Sheridan, in his visit to the Park in 1881, was appalled at the vandalism, but could only write:

> The craters of the geysers . . . were partly wedged up by good-sized trees pushed into them with buttend down, so that our large force of men could not pull them out, and visitors, men, women, and children, were mutilating the craters of the geysers in the most wanton and provoking manner.

Colonel James F. Gregory, Sheridan's aide-de-camp then, added his harsh and frustrated observation:

[10] Ludlow, *Reconnaissance of 1875.*

> If some means could be devised to prevent the van-
> dalism which seems to pervade the average American
> citizen, and restrain his propensities to . . . destroy
> every growing thing and to fill up with trees, sticks,
> etc., the wonderful craters. . . . We saw persons with
> hatchets who were hammering and cracking the beau-
> tiful tracery around the geysers . . . they did not take
> away what they broke off. They destroyed for the
> pleasure they had in their work.

Obviously the Park lacked proper legal protection. What little
it had was mired in apathy, error, confusion, and corruption. At
one point, the Wyoming Territory legislature intervened by
providing stringent measures for the protection of timber, game,
fish, and the natural phenomena of the Park. But many questioned whether a territory could exercise criminal jurisdiction
and judicial powers in a federal reservation. Furthermore, en-
forcement procedures soon turned out to be a kind of kangaroo
court affair in which the arresting officer, the justice of the
peace, and the Park administration split the fines.

The climax came when Congressman Payson of Illinois,
always a good friend of national parks, was unjustifiably arrested for failing to put out a campfire and was fined $50.00
and costs. This affair reached Congress in the Phillips Report of
February 1, 1886.[11] August 3, 1886, two days before adjourn-
ment, the Forty-ninth Congress passed a law detailing a company
of cavalry for the administration of the Park and omitting any
appropriation for the civilian superintendent and his assistants;
this ended civilian administration of the Park until October 16,
1916. Thus, from 1886 to 1916, army officers detailed to the
Park assignment acted as superintendents.

So, on August 6, 1886, L. Q. C. Lamar, Secretary of the Interior, faced with the reality of the situation, yet trying to retain
what control over future appropriations he could, retreated to the
face-saving provisions of an 1883 statute[12] which permitted him

---

[11] See 49 Congress, 1 Session, *Senate Exec. Doc. No. 51.*
[12] Act of March 3, 1883; 22 U.S. Statutes 627.

to request the troops himself. He asked that a captain, two lieu-tenants, and twenty cavalrymen be sent to Yellowstone, "also that the captain, as soon as designated, should report to the Inter-ior Department, by letter, for instructions."

The army went in on the double-quick to make secure their victory in the bureaucratic rivalry. The speed has amazed every frustrated observer of government in action. Immediate orders were issued. By August 17, Captain Moses Harris and Company M of the First Cavalry had marched the 230 miles from Fort Custer and were firmly entrenched in the new position; Camp Sheridan was laid out and bastioned — politically, at least.[13]

Doane learned too late that the civil administration of Yellowstone Park was being replaced by the army. He and his outfit had been too far away, across too many channels of army command, to be considered and dispatched through the tangles of red tape. Doane was deeply disappointed and discouraged. He had wanted the Yellowstone assignment as he had wanted nothing else during his army career.

Two and a half years went by — two and a half years of pleasant life at the Presidio at San Francisco, a welcome relief from the too-vivid days of misery in Arizona. Yet Doane still dreamed of Yellowstone Park — the enchanted land. He decided to apply for the assignment to replace Captain Harris. Harris and his outfit were due for a shift to garrison duty. Harris had even said the summer before that he was ready for a change; his two daughters, he thought, ought to be in school.

But again Doane seemed to be too late. He did not get his application off until March 9, 1889. As he should, he sent it through regular channels of command to reach the Secretary of War. He requested the Yellowstone detail for himself and his Troop A, Second Cavalry, pointing out that he had a better knowledge of Yellowstone Park, its geography and character-istics, than anyone else. He enclosed a complete summary of his army service. His battalion major, Thomas M. McGregor, and Lieutenant Colonel M. Graham, commandant at the Presidio,

[13] *Report* 1886, Secretary of the Interior, 49 Congress, 2 Session, *Exec. Doc. No. 1*, Pt. 5, Vol. I.

endorsed his application.

When the application reached Washington it hit a snag. Major General J. M. Schofield, commanding the army, inquired and found out from the quartermaster general that it would cost $6,957.80 to ship Doane and his men to Yellowstone.[14]

General Schofield sent Doane's application on to the Secretary of War commenting, "There is probably no better troop to relieve it, no officer better fitted for that special service, than Troop A 2nd Cavalry, and Captain G. C. Doane. The only objection known to me is in the cost of transportation. . . ."

Doane continued to work and muster support for his application. He obtained a recommendation signed by every member of both houses of the Montana legislature, and a petition signed by the mayor, council, and leading citizens of both Helena and Bozeman, with some thirty-eight names on it, including the principal officials of Gallatin County.[15] Governor Preston H. Leslie of Montana wrote a letter endorsing Doane and sent it with the other papers to Senator J. B. Beck. On April 1, Beck forwarded it to the Secretary of War.

W. W. Morrow, member of Congress from California, and T. H. Carter, delegate from Montana, signed a joint letter to the Secretary of War pleading Doane's cause. Doane wrote to General W. W. Belknap in Washington, and others.

General William E. Strong directed a letter to Secretary of the Interior, J. W. Noble, who referred it to the Secretary of War.

But before all of this reached him, the Secretary of War had, on March 30, declined to approve Doane's assignment, on account of the expense involved.

Almost desperate in his frustration, Doane wrote a letter to Washington on April 19. In it one can feel the impact of forlorn hopes, leaving scars that would not heal.

---

[14] Doane Summary, National Archives. Only $1,872.50 of this would have been required in cash. The balance of $5,085.30 was to be applied as a credit against the previous government financing of the Utah and Northern Division of the Union Pacific Railway.

[15] See Appendix to Part I for reproductions of two documents.

> If it were only a matter of expense, I can march from
> this post to the Park . . . on good roads mostly
> through an open country and in a distance of 950
> miles . . . at less expense than . . . remaining in gar-
> rison for the same length of time. . . . Troop A has
> not had any field duty since 1886. Such a march
> would be of great advantage in the way of instruction
> and could readily be made by the time the Park
> season begins on the 15th of June.

On May 8, 1889, Special Order No. 47 was issued from St.
Paul. It sent Captain F. A. Boutelle's troop from Fort Custer
and Captain Peter S. Bomus' troop from Fort Maginnis to
Yellowstone; Doane was not mentioned.

No one will ever quite know what happened. But when the
editors examined the official records in Washington there was a
clue — written in pen and ink in the margin of the printed
Special Order 47 of May 8, 1889:

> The orders of the Secretary of War referred to, were
> not issued from the AG Office but appear to have
> been given by the Secretary of War, while on his
> recent western tour of inspection.

It would seem that the Secretary of War was not even in
Washington when the stack of recommendations for Doane
came in and that he never saw them before his orders were
issued.

The Doanes spent a few more months at the Presidio. Then
the dreaded orders came: to go back to Fort Bowie — and the
dust and the heat! Transferred there, Doane refused to give up
his Yellowstone dream. At Fort Bowie on January 8, 1891, he
again wrote Washington asking for the Yellowstone assignment,
and again he enlisted the aid of his friends — General Strong,
Brigadier General John Gibbon, the Smithsonian Institution,
Interstate Commerce Commissioner W. G. Veazey, John L.
Hayden, Senator John H. Mitchell, W. W. Morrow in the House

of Representatives, Senator W. F. Saunders, and all his friends in the G.A.R.[16] and in the Society of California Pioneers,[17] and others.

Secretary of War Redfield Proctor wrote an identical letter to each of the persons who were supporting Doane:

> I beg to advise you that to comply would involve the transfer of this officer with his troop of cavalry from his present station at Fort Bowie, Arizona Territory, to the Park and it is consequently not deemed advisable to order him on this duty.

Instead, the Secretary sent the Sixth Regiment of Cavalry. He also sent Captain George S. Anderson from Fort Meyer, Virginia.

The situation had become one of irony and incredulity. In 1889, Doane had been too far from Yellowstone to justify his move. Now, in 1891, in Arizona, Doane was 1,000 miles from Yellowstone. Captain Anderson, in Virginia, was over 2,000 miles away.

END OF AN ERA AND A CAREER

In 1890, when the army ordered fifty-year old Doane back to Fort Bowie, Arizona, it was his first "field" duty since he had left Arizona in 1886 after the Apache campaign. The Doanes left San Francisco June 10, 1890. Arriving at Fort Bowie, he was almost immediately assigned to scouting patrols and was

[16] Doane was a member of George H. Thomas Post, G.A.R.

[17] The Society of California Pioneers was an organization of persons who had arrived in California before midnight December 31, 1849. Doane applied for membership May 6, 1889. His application for membership, his record of army service, the Memorial to him, and a letter from his widow, Mary Lee Doane, are still preserved in the Society's records in San Francisco. They were in a safe in a building completely destroyed by the earthquake and fire of 1906. The Society cautiously kept the safe closed for many months after the fire until it had thoroughly cooled. The records in the safe were thereby saved, whereas those in safes impetuously opened soon after the fire crumbled away to dust and ashes.

Camp San Carlos, A. T., c 1891. 1, enlisted men's quarters; 2, guard house; 3, officers' quarters; 4, officers' mess; 5, adjutant's office. San Carlos Indian Agency, where Doane was detailed, is in the background. Note two centennial model tents at the guard house. *Courtesy National Archives.*

stationed at Camp Crawford during July and August. On March 12, 1891, he was sent to the San Carlos Indian Agency and remained there until October 6, 1891, then returning to Fort Bowie.

The Arizona experience was too much of a change from the pleasant years in the Presidio at San Francisco. The powerful human frame, which had endured every hardship of nature and of border warfare, began to weaken. Strength of sinew and muscle no longer endured. His health began to fail. In December, 1891, he asked for disability retirement. But the army was in no position to take care of a faithful soldier.

Secretary of War Proctor had complained in his annual report of 1890, as did his predecessors, that the law did not adequately provide for the retirement of disabled army officers. While there were no restrictions on the total number of officers who could retire for age (sixty-four) or for years of service (forty), for other causes the retired list was limited to 400 officers (the "limited list").

In 1890, about half of the limited list was for Civil War disabilities, with openings occasioned only by death. Officers no longer fit for active duty had to stay in the army and seek easy assignments. It stymied the promotion of juniors. The Secretary suggested that at least the officers should be transferred from the limited list when they reached the age of sixty-four.[18]

When Doane's request for retirement came in, the limited list was full. He was fifty-one years old, with neither age nor years of service to get on the open list. The same law that all these years had kept him from being promoted to higher rank now prevented his retirement.

The limitations of the army system in Doane's time had permitted his promotion only when First Lieutenant James E. Batchelder had resigned in 1872 and Doane took his place as first lieutenant. Again, when Captain William P. Clark died in September, 1884, Doane was promoted to captain.[19] His own

[18] *Report* 1889-90, Secretary of War, Acts of 45 Congress, 2 Session, June 18, 1878; 20 U.S. Statutes 150; 22 U.S. Statutes 118; 22 U.S. Statutes 456.
[19] Doane became number 115 on the list of captains.

San Carlos Indian Agency, A. T., 1895. *Courtesy U.S. Signal Corps.*

G. C. Doane, 1890. *Courtesy Mrs. Wayne Herron.*

Fort Ellis as it looked to Doane when he visited there in 1892. Some of these officers' quarters had been built under his supervision and he had lived in one of them. Now the fort was abandoned. From a set of photographs given to Yellowstone National Park by Doane's widow. *Courtesy Yellowstone National Park.*

Mary Lee Doane, 1920's. Mrs. Doane was in her sixties when this photo was taken. *Courtesy Mrs. Wayne Herron.*

capability and seniority could not give him an increase in rank.

For Doane's failing health, his superiors did what they could — they gave him sick leave for six months. He returned to Bozeman, to the Gallatin Valley, and to the memories of the glory and adventure there in the 1870's.

The curtains were drawing on the great drama of exploration, conquest, and settlement of the West.

Fort Ellis, once the most important outpost in the Indian country, lay in weathered ruin, abandoned in August, 1886. Doane looked sadly at his old quarters. Cattle grazed the prairie and wandered through hingeless doorways; the buffalo were long gone. Freight and farm produce and troops now moved on steel rails. Chief Joseph had been freed and had gone to the Colville Reservation in Washington in 1885. Sitting Bull had been killed by police of his own race in December 1890. The last Sioux uprising had ended with the last massacre of Indians at Wounded Knee during the same month. General Sherman had died February 14, 1891, his task as the general of the Indian Wars completed.

Yellowstone Park: its wonders and wildlife had been preserved for all future generations — and every peak, stream, and contour in it had been mapped.

The curtain closed. There was no encore. Late in the spring of 1892, Doane seemed to successfully withstand a mild attack of pneumonia. Then, on the fifth day of May 1892, at the age of fifty-two years, a heart attack ended his life.

His funeral took place from the Doane residence at the corner of Main and Second Streets in Bozeman at 2:00 P.M., Sunday, May 8, 1892, attended by friends of the family, cavalry troopers, and members of the Gallatin Valley Pioneers, the Loyal Legion, and the Grand Army of the Republic.

The Stars and Stripes, under which he had served so ably, draped his coffin. A bugle sounded taps. A great and gallant soldier was laid to rest.

A month later his widow, Mary Lee Doane, sent a copy of his army service to the Society of California Pioneers, saying in her letter:

It is a great comfort to me to know that my Husband was loved and respected by all who knew him, and that I have friends at this time. . . . [T]he light of a happy home has gone out.

Mary Lee remained a widow. She lived in Bozeman for sixty years more, until her death on June 23, 1952.

APPENDIX TO PART I

by the editors

Fort Maginnis, M. T., 1883. Officers' quarters, duplex houses, in background; commanding officer's house third from left. Doane on horse in foreground. W. H. Culver photo. *Courtesy Montana Historical Society.*

APPENDIX A

POSTS WHERE DOANE WAS STATIONED

The following list summarizes, in chronological order, the posts where Doane was stationed or had some responsibility during his post-Civil War army career.

Fort McPherson. Nebraska. 1868 (August—). Few months of boot camp.

Fort Russell. Wyoming. 1868-1869. Indian skirmishes and scouting.

Fort Ellis. Montana. 1869 (June) – 1879 (June). Indian battles and scouting; road building. Yellowstone explorations. Snake River exploration. Fort Ellis was official headquarters for Doane during this decade, although he was sometimes elsewhere on detached service and other assignments.

St. Paul, Minnesota. 1871 (spring-summer). Detached service at Department of Dakota headquarters.

Fort Pease. Montana. 1876 (February, March). Rescue operation. (April, May). Waiting for Custer.

Fort Hall. Idaho. 1877 (January). End of Snake River Expedition.

Fort Keogh. Montana. 1877-1878. Crow Indian scout command under Colonel Nelson Miles. Chief Joseph chase.

Fort Custer. Montana. 1877 (June). Staked out this new fort. 1878 (April, May, etc.). Settling Crow scout payroll ac-

Spectators viewing Doane and the 2d Cavalry on dress drill at the Presidio on Washington's birthday, 1888. Alcatraz Island can be seen in right background; view is to the northeast across San Francisco Bay. Note also

the word "Examiner" in upper center of photo, presumably some sort of fence advertisement by the *San Francisco Examiner* newspaper. *Courtesy California Historical Society.*

counts.

Camp Mulkey. Idaho. 1878 (summer). Bannock uprising.

Fort Assiniboine. Montana. 1879 (June) — 1880 (May). Scouting. On leave for Artic exploration.

Fort Ellis. 1880 (September) — 1881 (June). Writing Arctic Expedition report for War Department.

Fort Assiniboine. 1881 (June) — 1882 (November). Scouting.

Fort Maginnis. Montana. 1882 (November) — 1883 (September). Scouting.

Jefferson Barracks. St. Louis, Missouri. 1883 (October—). Recruiting.

Milwaukee, Wisconsin. 1884. Recruiting.

Chicago, Illinois. 1884. Recruiting.

Presidio. San Francisco, California. 1884 (September) — 1885 (September).

Fort Bowie. Arizona. 1885 (September) — 1886 (October). Geronimo campaign.

Camp at Gila Canyon. 1886 (January-March).

Camp at Cochise's Stronghold. 1886 (April-August).

Fort Lowell. Arizona. 1886 (August-October).

Presidio. 1886 (October) — 1890 (June).

Fort Bowie. 1890 (June) — 1891 (December). Scouting.

Camp Crawford.[1] Arizona. 1890 (July-August).

Camp San Carlos. Arizona. 1891 (March-October). Duties at San Carlos Indian Agency.

---

[1] Camp Emmett Crawford was a temporary station in the Chiricahua Mountains southeast of Fort Bowie. It was probably set up for the purpose of heliograph communication by the army before the use of the electric telegraph. Established in 1886, there were apparently still some operations there to which Doane was assigned in July and August of 1890, as he had it so listed in the record of service which he kept. The camp was never carried as a separate installation in the reports of the Secretary of War, but it does appear on the army map of that period. The camp was named for Captain Emmett Crawford, the popular officer who lost his life in the pursuit of renegade Apaches.

APPENDIX B

DOANE'S SMITHSONIAN INSTITUTION LETTER

Doane's 1874 letter to the Smithsonian Institution (he calls it "Institute") is included here, in toto, because it is illuminating and reflects important aspects of Doane's personality. Doane appraises himself and expresses his ideas about exploration, still feeling the satisfaction of deserved praise for his scientific account of the Yellowstone exploration which Professor Henry had acknowledged in 1871.

Doane evidently had studied Livingstone's last words to Stanley in February 1872:

> [T]hen I shall strike south, and round the extremity of Lake Tanganyika. Then a south-east course will take me to Chikumbi's, on the Lualaba . . . on crossing the Lualaba, I shall go direct southwest to the copper mines of Katanga . . . eight days south of Katanga the natives declare the fountains [rivers] to be [Livingstone further details the route] . . . Then, coming down again, I can proceed north by the Lualaba to the fourth lake – which will, I think, explain the whole problem [of the source of the Nile. This journey will take] a year and a half.[1]

On his later expedition to determine this, after Livingstone's

[1] Henry D. Northrop, *Wonders of the Tropics or Explorations and Adventures of Henry M. Stanley,* 336.

death, Stanley left Zanzibar on November 17, 1874, and ended his trip August 11, 1877, with only 115 of his original 356 having survived warfare and pestilence. Sixty of these were suffering from dysentery, scurvy, and dropsy. Stanley found the Lualaba to be the source of the Congo, not of the Nile. He had followed it to the Atlantic coast and opened a waterway into the heart of Africa.

In typesetting Doane's letter from his handwritten copy, we have retained his spelling, punctuation, capitalization, and underlining.

.   .   .

To
       Professor Joseph Henry,
              Secretary of the Smithsonian Institute,
                     Washington, D.C.
                            Sir:
     I beg leave to address you in relation to something which has been to me a subject of Study for several years, but has more especially been a matter of thought since my Expedition and Report upon the Yellowstone Basin in 1870.

     I now desire to make an Expedition to the Headwaters of the Nile, with the paramount object of following its longest channel to the sea.

     The interest that you must feel in that Country which has engaged the attention of the Scientific world since Modern Science has deserved a name, is my warrant for writing you; but I nevertheless do so under circumstances of great embarassment. First, that from the nature of the Proposition made, I must necessarily assume the possession of certain qualifications, and discuss the same. And Secondly, from an apprehension that I may not be able without undue elaboration to convey distinct ideas in relation to the contingencies of an enterprise involving Many Chances which can only be calculated when in the immediate presence of events.

To give you an idea of my training for this work I beg leave to rehearse the following.

I was born in Northern Illinois in 1840. The Family moved to St. Louis in 1844. Crossed the Plains to Oregon in an ox-wagon in 1846. Went by sea to California in 1849, where I grew to manhood and graduated at the Pacific University in 1861. Went to Boston via Panama & New York in December 1862. Served in the Eastern Army until April 1864. In the Western Army on the Miss River until January 1865. Lived in the South until May 1868. Commissioned July 5th 1868, and have served on the frontier ever since. I have been in all the States except four, all the Territories, except New Mexico, Arizona and Alaska. Have been accustomed from earliest youth to all the hardships, and some of the dangers of frontier life. Have always found my principal enjoyments in exploration, boating and hunting, and have always made Geography a practical study.

It is a well established fact that some men have a special qualification, which enables them to travel without difficulty not only in known, but also in unknown districts. As the Mountain Men express it, "to go by the signs of the Country". This faculty of finding passable trails, water, wood, grass, and at the same time keeping the true course under all circumstances, without Guide, Map or Compass, is by those who cannot do these things often pronounced instinctive. I do not regard it as such in any sense.

To elaborate the Mental Analysis by which these things are accomplished would be lengthy; perhaps tedious. Suffice it to say that this faculty depends upon a knowledge of the laws by which the modelling of the earth's surface is governed, combined with a correct judgement as to effects produced which observation alone can give. The laws of formation are wonderfully simple depending as they all do on the fact that water always runs down-hill. In addition to this, an understanding of the conditions under which Forests are to be found, and a correct eye for distances, enable a Man of judgement and self reliance, to travel wherever he may wish, not by a process of searching out, nor stumbling upon, but by correct courses, the best trails, and with an absolute certainty of reaching his destination. "Keeping the direction", is done by a mental working of Latitudes and Departures from the true line of direction. This enables one to go at all points of the Compass; winding through Forests, and turning impassable Mountains or Canons, in a manner which will utterly bewilder an inexperienced voyageur, and yet return to his true course and resume it without failure. The immeasurable advantage of this mode of travel over that of following a Compass, is at once seen in a broken Country, or in a desert when departures must be made for water, either case involving the abandonment of selection as to route, and troublesome measurements which cause great delay.

This faculty of travel I possess when I first joined the Regiment in 1868 during Expeditions in the Department of the Platte, and on the frontier of Kansas, in a Country I had never seen before, and which was imperfectly mapped. I never once failed in my course either in darkness or daylight; though I have seen veteran officers who have served there for years, entirely lost. I have repeatedly traversed the dense forests of the National Park in the darkest of nights, to reach camps at locations where I had never been, and which I did not know, with the same unerring certainty. So far, all the Mountaineers I have ever travelled with, have "given up" that I could go where they could not, in an unknown region. I always travel as an Indian does, without guide or Compass, and do not know what it is to have the sensation of being lost. If furnished the Latitude and Longitude of two points, I should not doubt for an instant my ability to go from one to the other, and to do so by as practicable a road as could generally be found, and without material delay arising from any lack of knowledge of the Country.

Now this knowledge of the "Rules of Travel", if I may so call them, can be learned on one Continent as well as another, as Water, which carves the features of all the Continents, works by an universal law. Let the Traveller be posted as to the general deductions of Geography, which every true student should know, and by mere application of principles to climatic conditions, the conformation of any Country becomes a plainly written page, which a well informed Man needs no guide to interpret for his benefit. For Example

Clothe the region of our Great Lakes with the conditions of a Tropical Climate, and you have a picture of the System of the Nile, as far as the application of natural laws is concerned. The differences of configuration depend upon the Mountain ranges and watersheds. These are detected by the eye and explain themselves.

From these general ideas I deduce the conclusion, that to be qualified to explore one Country, is to be qualified to explore any other. And from what has been said heretofore, it is evident that measures, which to the uninformed would seem the visions of desperate rashness, to the well posted Man of resources in travel would often be the results of almost Mathematical Calculation. The Man who knows what he is aiming at, and has the nerve to execute is invincible.

The Career of Livingstone affords many instances bearing upon this subject. His first journeys were entered upon without any intelligent plans of operation. It was only after 15 years of wanderings that he began to get a true idea of the drainage system of Africa. But Sir Roderick Murchison [President, Royal Geographical Society], from very scanty data, had worked out from Analogy that system as far as the Congo and Zambesi Rivers are concerned, and announced the result, in advance of Livingstone's dispatches, to the same effect. It was only during the last years of his life that the Great Traveller appears to have realized the importance of studying the watersheds, rather than the water channels. When at Lake Dilolo on the head of the Zambesi, he failed to learn from personal observation whether that Lake also runs a stream into the Congo; a discovery which, if it be, as surmised, would define the eastern watershed bounding both those rivers throughout their whole length (not in a particular, but in a general sense). On several occasions he expresses a fear lest he may be following sources of the Congo rather than the Nile, yet he never once speaks of adopting the infallible method of getting upon the summit of a watershed and following it, to establish the divide between two Rivers. When on the Eastern sources of the Zambesi he seems to have overlooked the fact that sources of great rivers, running in opposite directions from the same watershed are always near each other, and often interlace. It was only at the last, that he seems to have reached that self reliance in his own judgement, which enabled him to travel by the Trend of the Country itself, the only safe system. Then he was on the "right track", and the results, up to the time of his death proved so. If the Fountains of Ptolemy and Herodotus have an existence, (and if they have not, there are others) they are to be found by climbing the divide between Lake Bangweolo, and the Zambesi, and following the watershed until the margin of each basin is defined in their common boundary, the Divide. These ideas are based upon Livingstone's facts as given by himself. Had Livingstone recieved a training for Exploration previously by a few years spent in travel through the wild districts of North America, in a healthy climate, and in a temperate zone, where rapid progress may be made, and vast districts traversed in a year, he would have been spared many disappointments and much grievous labor. He would doubtless then have solved his Nile problem while in the vigor of Manhood; instead of dying in the wilderness, broken down, and without success. The farcical attempts to relieve Livingstone, made at various times, by the English, though their failures be covered up in a verbiage of new discoveries and so on, are simply laughable, so ridiculous were the preparations, in view of the end to be accomplished.

The expedition of Stanley, its object being to hunt a man, and not to explore a Country, was a success, both as to means, and results, but Stanley lacks calibre. He does well what he is sent to do, but does not rise to the Conception of Great Achievments. Imagine a man in the full vigor of Life, seated on the shore of Lake Tanganyika and listening to Livingstone's stories of the great Lacustrine river Lualaba! How could he have turned back as he did! He should have embarked upon the broad current of that unknown River, and followed it to Egypt or – destruction.

My plan of operations would be, to travel by water through districts known and to explore the watersheds on the borders of districts unknown. The first Method, at the outset would dispense with the Armies of Porters and Guides which have been such a curse to English Travellers. It would lessen expenses, save time, enable the transportation of larger supplies, and the preservations of larger collections, to be returned, by the same channel, on reaching the limit of navigation. It is besides a more healthy way of journeying, as water is a powerful absorbent of Malaria. Moreover it would evade many of the toils expected from travelling by land. By exploring thoroughly the watersheds I should be enabled to trust myself on the current of any stream running toward the Nile basin, with a certainty not to be derived from any other source.

For an outfit, I would propose the following. A very small Steam Launch with a supply of Cordage, Extras for the Engine, Canvass and repairing materials, including ship Carpenters' Tools, a liberal supply of Arms, Ammunition and Camp Equipage. A few Instruments and Mechanics. All the above articles, could be supplied to an officer by the Department. Myself and a Junior Officer to be detached for the duty, which would give full pay during absence, and expenses of travel to Zanzibar. The above matters arranged, $10,000 Ten Thousand dollars would suffice for supplies and hire, for a two years' trip as the pay of the two officers would amount to over $6,000 Six Thousand Dollars more, during the same period and this would also be applied to the work.

I would hire but two white men, a Photographer and an Engineer, and would qualify myself to dispense with both if necessary. Would have the Launch bolted so that it could be taken to pieces and rebuilt readily, and the little Engine, so that its heaviest section could be carried by two men.

I should then propose to go up the Zambesi to the Victoria Falls 940 miles, make the Portage, rebuild the Launch, select the largest of the Northeast branches of the Upper River and follow it to shoal water. Then make a thorough survey of the Nile divide, select one of the streams running Northeastward to the head of which I would transport the Engine and supplies, rebuild the Launch, and embark on reaching the first Lake or a large stream. I would whipsaw Lumber and build a Barge of capacity enough to carry a bullet-proof armor of hard-wood and make it secure against "Boarders". This would be towed by the Launch. These preparations having been completed I should feel myself Master of the Situation; free to negotiate, fight, or run, as the exigency might require. And I firmly believe that no human force in Africa could then prevent me from reaching either Gondokoro or the Sea.

In the Course of the Exploration I should assume Livingstone's facts, unless disproved by observation, but would in all cases be guided by my own judgement of the Country traversed, making all things subservient to the finding and following of the Nile Channel. In case Falls were encountered the labor of rebuilding would have to be borne, but mere Rapids would have to be worse than the Dalles of the Columbia to stop the Expedition on its way. On the water, and going with the current, one can take desperate chances. I do not believe in the much talked of dangers of African Travel, but am prepared to assume the worst, and risk all.

It would be a special pleasure to make this Expedition under the Auspices of the National Institute if it may be so arranged. If successful, the expenditure of one tenth the cost of the Annual Explorations by Professor Hayden and others would solve a great probelm in Science, and open the water Channels of the heart of a Mighty Continent to the current of Civilization.

To get the necessary Authority and supplies are the first considerations. From your position at the Capital, and from your relations in Science, you will be able to correctly advise me as to the "modus operandi" in the premises, for I do not know how to commence working for an outfit, or Authority to go.

Having never had a leave of absence I can doubtless get to

Washington this winter, where I have a Friend or two in Authority. I am prepared to do anything in the way of honorable effort to succeed in this project, and as it is no "soft detail" that I require should not hesitate to ask for it.

Please do me the favor to advise, and criticize also if you deem it best. You are at liberty to refer this letter at discretion.

Hoping that the above ideas may meet with your favorable consideration

I have the honor to remain
Very Respectfully
Your Obedient Servant
G C Doane
1st Lt. 2d Cavalry

Fort Ellis, Montana Ty
September 1st 1874.

APPENDIX C

LETTERS SUPPORTING DOANE'S PARK APPLICATION

The following three pages consist of a facsimile of the petition sent to the U.S. Secretary of the Interior on March 6, 1889. It is signed by the members of the Sixteenth Legislative Assembly of the Territory of Montana, both the House and the Council; and by the mayor and aldermen of Helena, Montana. The fourth page is a cover letter by Montana Congressman Thomas H. Carter giving his own support to the petition. The petition itself calls attention to Doane's special qualifications for the superintendency of the "the world's greatest pleasure ground, the Yellowstone National Park" and urges his appointment to this post.

The next four pages present a letter to Congressman Carter requesting him "to use all possible effort to secure his [Doane's] immediate detail with his Company — that this season may see him in charge" at Yellowstone. The letter is signed by members of the City Council of Bozeman — mayor, marshal, etc. — and by over two dozen other Montana citizens.

These documents are interesting not only in demonstrating the strong support Doane had in Montana but also in presenting a kind of who's-who-in-Montana roster of signatures from the late 1880's.

TO THE HONORABLE

The Secretary of the Interior:

Sir:

We, the undersigned, members of the Sixteenth Legislative Assembly of the Territory of Montana, feeling a special interest in the world's greatest pleasure ground, the Yellowstone National Park, would respectfully petition you to request the Honorable the Secretary of War to detail Capt. G. C. Doane, 2 Cavalry U. S. A. as Superintendent thereof. Capt. Doane was one of the earliest explorers of the Park, and his official report, made more than eighteen years ago, was one of the first published documents to call the attention of the curious and scientific to this greatest display of nature's handiwork. Since his first explorations he has made repeated visits to the Park, each of which has enabled him to contribute something new and of value to the country and to the scientific world, with reference to the vastness, the resources, and the curiosities of this most wonderful region. The thorough knowledge of every part and portion of the Park thus acquired, his military education and record, and his scientific and literary tastes qualify him in a peculiar degree for this responsible position. We feel sure that in preferring a request for his detail as above suggested, you would be most effectually promoting the public interest in that regard.

We are, with great respect,

Your very obedient servants,

Charles K. Cole
President of the Council

Lee Mantle
Speaker of the House

Wm H. Roberts   Member of the "House"
W. _____   "   "   "
Gail T. Morris   "   "   "
C. P. Blakley   "   "   "
Clinton _H_ Brooks   "   "   "
_____ O Joslyn   "   "   "
A. W. Pickman   "   "   "
Jno Davis   "   "   "
John R Comfort   "   "   "
W. C. Gillette   "   "   "
_____ Johnson   "   "   "
_____ Courtney
Loring B Ree   "   "   "
_____   "   "   "
_____
_____
Jno D Ward
_____ Harker
_____ Hand
H. A. Hunt
_____
              Members of the "Council"

Wm M Thompson. Deer Lodge Co.   Lawrence A Brown
W. A. _____ _____   C. W. Hoffman
H. M. Buckford Missoula Co.   William Thompson
Jerry _____ Chateau Cascade   Geo. M. Hatch
Will Kennedy. Jefferson Co.
C. R. Middleton, _____

         I hereby certify that the foregoing are
the individual signatures of the members
of the Council of the 16th Legislative
Assembly of Montana

                         Jas R Eardley
                           Ass't Clerk of
                              Council

I hereby certify that the
foregoing are the individual
signatures of the members of
the House of the 16th
Legislative Assembly of Montana

Benjamin White
Chief Clerk

Thomas O. Fuller   Mayor of Helena Mont
A. O. Simmons   Alderman 7th Ward
Jacob Loeb   "Alderman 4th Ward
J. S. Keeley   "   3 Ward
Wm Harrison   "   5 Ward
John North   "   2nd "
C. J. Donnelly   "   1st "
Marcus Lissner   "   1 Ward
G. A. Kinner   "   7 "
Henry Klein   ½ Ward
R. S. Henry   "   6" Ward
Moses Morris   4" Ward
Hugh Kirkendall   3 Ward
J. B. Colewell   8th Ward

I hereby certify that the above and foregoing are
presumably known to be the signatures of the Mayor
and Aldermen of the City of Helena, Montana

Alex. C. Botkin
City Clerk

Washington D.C. 29th 1889

I heartily concur in the foregoing
statement and petition. In my opinion
the appointment of Captain Drain
would prove very satisfactory to all
citizens of Montana.

T. H. Carter M.C.
Montana

To The Secretary of War

Bozeman. Montana.

March 9th. 1889.

To Hon. Thos. H. Carter —

Delegate from Montana —

Sir:

We respectfully represent
that we are citizens of
Montana. —

That, as such, and as
citizens of the United States,
we are interested in the
proper management of the
"National Yellowstone Park."

That, the Park should
be under control of a person
fitted by education, character
and scientific attainment
for such a position. — As such
a person would, naturally,
bring to it practical effort,
securing its proper development
and the best results from Expenditure of the public appropriations. —

That, such a person
Exists in Captain G. C. Doane,
2d. U.S. Cavalry — the first to
appreciate and publish to

to the world the wonders of
the Park.—

That, under him, we
feel assured such work
would be done that the
main features of it would
recive the attention yet
needed.— the many centres
of interest yet unvisitable
would rapidly become
known to the public; and
by reason of the intelligent
investigation he would,
we know, explend, the history,
Causes and capabilities of
the region would recive the record
they have never yet had.—

Therefor, we respect-
fully ask you to use all
possible efforts to secure
his immediate detail,
with his Company.— that,
this season may see him
in charge.

We remaining, Very
Respectfully, Your Obedient
Servants.—

J. V. Bogert,
Mayor of Bozeman, M.T.

G. W. Hghsmith
& W. Mackenzie
J. Libby
E. F. Ovenhouse

A. D. Clark City Marshal

City Council of Bozeman. M.T.

James M. Robertson Sheriff of
    Gallatin Co M.T.
Jos. S. Radford
    Asst. Cashier Gallatin Valley Nat Bk
E. B. Martin
H. U. Kase
A. Peter Koch ; Cm. Bzg. Nat Bk
H E Martin
Jno. J. Mendenhall

Geo W. Monroe Register U.S. Land Office
Wm. L. Ines Recvr.   "   "
R H Crawford
J. L. Staats Attorney at Law
Jas. W. Freeman, County Clerk & Recorder
J. A. Garrett — Clerk Dist Court

Sanford Ruffner
John Chrisman

F. L. Briscoe
V. B. Place
A. W. James & Son

Matt. W. Alderson Bus. Mgr. Avant Courier
M. W. Penwell
F. M. Higgins · M. D.

Wm. B. Bowen

A. R. Cutting
H. P. McNaughton
Brennan Bros. & Co.
R. M. Whitefoot M. D.
R. C. Burns
C. Hohenschuh
Jas. F. Keown
A. D. McPherson   Probate Judge

PART II

THE YELLOWSTONE EXPLORATION OF 1870

INTRODUCTION TO PART II

by the editors

CHAPTER 1

KNOWLEDGE OF YELLOWSTONE PRIOR TO 1870

We realize today that the Washburn-Doane Expedition was not the first to observe Yellowstone wonders. Yet it was Doane's journal and to some extent the writings of other members of the party which brought to the world the first scientific knowledge of the unusual Yellowstone phenomena. And indeed these writings and other publicity generated by expedition members led directly to the establishment of Yellowstone National Park.

Prior to 1870, the weird world of the Yellowstone was the source of wild rumors and fantastic legends. Listeners put little credence in the stories of the early trappers, embellished, stretched, and co-mingled as they were with other tall tales of the campfire or the saloon.

There were also a few written accounts: news clippings, journals, manuscripts; but in 1870 these were scattered or largely unknown. And to the extent known, they were suspect. Even the truth seemed too preposterous to be believable. Yellowstone was truly *terra incognita.*

INDIANS

While the Indians had a greater faith in the work of the Creator than the white man with his Towers of Babel, the whites regarded Indian belief as mere superstition, and all the more so when the talk was about Yellowstone. Even Doane believed the Indians were too superstitious of the thermal wonders of the region to visit there. He so stated in his journal entry of September 15, 1870. Yet old Indian trails crossed the area for intertribal visitation, and as routes to warpath and buffalo grounds. Some are still in use today, such as the old trail through Two Ocean Pass to Bridger Lake and north along the east side of Yellowstone Lake. Aborigines from the Mississippi Valley had traveled the great distance and visited the region. Their pottery was found by early park superintendent P. W. Norris.[1]

At some time·in the past an Indian warrior stood on the edge of one of the hot pools near Old Faithful and tossed an arrowhead into the bubbly depths. The evidence to prove that even the Indians were susceptible to mankind's temptation of throwing objects into the hot springs was turned up when Ranger George D. Marler found the arrowhead while cleaning the pool of tourist-introduced debris.[2]

Captain John Mullan, reporting to the War Department, February 14, 1863, tells that he learned of the existence of the Yellowstone hot springs and geysers from the Indians.[3]

The Piegan Indians were familiar with the region, and told young Jesuit Father Francis Xavier Kuppens about the wonders of the Yellowstone. They eventually led him to the Falls, the Lake, and geysers while he was on a buffalo hunt with them in 1865.[4]

But the Yellowstone Park region was not suitable for permanent habitation. In winter, heavy snows and penetrating cold on the high plateaus were too severe for man or game, causing both to migrate out of the region, as they do today. In summer,

[1] W. H. Holmes, "Aboriginal Pottery of the Eastern United States," *Bureau of American Ethnology,* Vol. XX, 201. See also P. W. Norris, *Annual Report of the Superintendent,* for years 1878-1881.
[2] Now called Arrowhead Spring. George D. Marler, "Firehole Geyser Basin 1959," *Yellowstone Geyser Observations and References,* Vol. III, 9.
[3] N. P. Langford, *The Discovery of Yellowstone Park, 1870,* 1923 ed., 17.
[4] Francis X. Kuppens, "The Origin of the Yellowstone National Park," *The Woodstock Letters,* Vol. XXVI, No. 3, 400-403.

and, in fact, during all seasons, the Indian's bounty of life, the great herds of bison, ranged principally outside the Park region. Yellowstone was a travel corridor, a sort of no-man's-land among the Indian tribes.

On their first day in the present Park area, the Washburn-Doane party encountered Indians traveling the same route they were following.

EARLY TRAPPERS

Prior to Doane's journal, the white man's written accounts and references to the Yellowstone wonders began with William Clark's journal entry that the Yellowstone River had "a considerable fall" somewhere in the mountains. He then crossed out this statement and wrote "No" after it; even Clark did not believe what he heard about the Yellowstone. On July 15, 1806, his party reached its closest point to the Yellowstone region, going through Bozeman Pass about sixty miles north of the Gardiner entrance to Yellowstone Park.

Clark's map of 1814 was based on information given him by the fur trappers. He showed "John Colter's 1807 route," which has caused 150 years of argument about where Colter traveled in the Yellowstone vicinity. Clark's manuscript map (now at Yale University), from which the 1814 map was prepared, shows Colter passing "Hot springs brimstone" at a point south of the Gallatin River, which the editors interpret to be Mammoth Hot Springs. Then Colter crossed the Yellowstone River at what the editors interpret to be the old Indian crossing below Tower Falls. Colter then followed the old Indian trail eastward to Clark's Fork.[5]

Early park superintendent Norris, hunting guide Frederick Bottler, and others were continually discovering evidence of the presence of white men — old blazes,[6] axed tree stumps, a

[5] O. H. and L. Bonney, *Guide to the Wyoming Mountains and Wilderness Areas,* 2d ed., 25.
[6] H. M. Chittenden, *The Yellowstone National Park,* 1912 ed., 35. In 1933 O. H. Bonney found a blaze, HB, with the arrow pointing south toward the west shore of

decaying corral, caches of steel traps,[7] and even an earth-roofed log fort: four logs high with portholes.[8]

Somewhat like today's visitor in Yellowstone National Park were the curiosity-filled fur trappers of the early 1800's, who went out of their way to see for themselves just how the Yellowstone phenomena fitted into the wild rumors and camp-fire exaggerations of that day. Some left written accounts of their visits; most, by word of mouth, added to the incredibility of the rumors.

Baptiste Ducharne visited the Grand Canyon, the Falls, Yellowstone Lake, and some of the geyser regions in 1824 and 1826. Living in Montana in 1882, at the age of 102 years, he was able to describe the visits.[9] Daniel T. Potts wrote a letter dated July 8, 1827, to his brother Robert in Philadelphia, describing Yellowstone Lake and the West Thumb paint pots. His brother published the account.[10] Joe Meek visited the region (probably Norris Geyser Basin) in 1829 and compared the frosty morning's view to "the City of Pittsburg." His travels, written by Mrs. Victor, were published in 1870.[11]

Warren A. Ferris made a special trip to the Upper Geyser Basin to satisfy his curiosity and camped there May 18-20, 1834. He had heard of the geysers from "more than twenty men." He said they were discovered in 1833 by a party led by Manuel Alvarez. Ferris wrote several articles in the 1840's and later. His map, which turned up among family papers a hundred years later, would have answered many cartography problems of the day.[12]

Shoshone Lake. It was on a knoll east of and overlooking the junction of trails from Lone Star Geyser, Bechler River, and Shoshone Lake (about two miles NNW of the northwest corner of Shoshone Lake). See also Part II, Chapter 12, note 16.

[7] Chittenden, *Yellowstone National Park,* 36.

[8] Norris, *Annual Report,* 1880, 29, 36; Cornelius Hedges, "Journal," Historical Society of Montana, *Contributions,* V, 377.

[9] E. S. Topping, *Chronicles of the Yellowstone;* Chittenden, *Yellowstone National Park,* 1964 ed., 39; Helen F. Sanders, *History of Montana,* 657.

[10] *Philadelphia Gazette,* September 27, 1827; *Niles Weekly Register,* October 6, 1827.

[11] Frances Fuller Victor, *River of the West,* 75.

[12] Warren A. Ferris, *Life in the Rocky Mountains 1830-35.*

In 1832 Captain Benjamin L. E. Bonneville came to Wyoming and built Fort Bonneville, the first fur fort in the area. During the following years, he made maps, carefully observed and noted plant and animal life, and made friends with the Indians. Decades later, when the Historical Society of Montana sought to restore historical information about the West which had been destroyed in the Helena fire of January 9, 1874, they wrote to Bonneville. He replied, "You ask me if I know of the thermal springs and geysers. Not personally, but my men knew about them and called their location the 'Firehole.' "[13]

JIM BRIDGER

In 1866 Jim Bridger told N. P. Langford "of the existence of hot spouting springs in the vicinity of the source of the Yellowstone and Madison rivers, and said that he had seen a column of water as large as his body spout as high as the flagpole in Virginia City, which was about sixty feet high."[14] Langford believed Bridger because he felt Bridger's imagination was not sufficiently fertile to invent the story.

Osborne Russell, with Jim Bridger's trapper brigade, traveled through the Yellowstone region in 1835, including what is known today as the Lamar River valley and "Gardner's Hole," now called Swan Lake Flat. In 1836 the men, followed a few days later by Bridger, went through the Park area by way of Pacific Creek, Two Ocean Pass, Atlantic Creek, and the east shore of Yellowstone Lake; then over to the Lamar River, across the ford below Tower Creek, over to the Gardner River and Gardner's Hole, and down the Yellowstone River. In 1837, they followed a similar route to the outlet of Yellowstone Lake. In 1839 Russell visited the Shoshone Lake Geyser Basin, describing the "Hour Spring" (probably Union Geyser). He also visited the Firehole Basin which he described. He wrote a complete account of his early trips to the Yellowstone region, but it

---

13 "Captain Bonneville's Letter," Historical Society of Montana, *Contributions,* I, 109.
14 Langford, *Discovery,* 17.

was not published until 1914.[15]

We now know that Jim Bridger was in the Yellowstone region again in 1846, traveling from Fort Bridger up the Green River, over Two Ocean Pass, then around Yellowstone Lake to its west arm. He and a small party including James Gemmell left the main camp there and spent a week sightseeing in the Upper and Lower Geyser Basins, came back and, skirting the west side of the Lake, visited the Falls and Mammoth Hot Springs "to enjoy the baths and to recuperate our animals," as Gemmell told the story many years later (1895).[16]

Bridger himself left no writing. He never learned to write his own name. Even the carving "James Bridger—1844" on Names Hill near LaBarge, Wyoming, must have been another's work. But Lieutenant J. W. Gunnison in 1852 had written Bridger's sharply focused description of the wonder of Yellowstone.[17]

In 1860, Bridger, as guide to the Corps of Topographical Engineers under Captain William F. Raynolds, tried to get that party into the Yellowstone area from the southeast. The party crossed Union Pass, descending the Gros Ventre River into Jackson's Hole, intending to recross the divide from there back into the Yellowstone region. They missed the first opportunity for an officially authenticated report of Yellowstone because, amazingly, Bridger, the great guide of the West, for once in his life lost his way. The party floundered around for six days coming down the Gros Ventre River, probing up ravines and valleys trying to find the way north through Jackson's Hole. Then, instead of heading up Pacific Creek and over Two Ocean Pass, it wasted another week getting across the Snake River. Finally Bridger led the party across Teton Pass into Pierre's Hole (Teton Basin) where Bridger recognized enough landmarks to escape from his secret dilemma. The party never did get into the Yellowstone area; the excuse was "heavy June snows." Captain Raynolds had to be content with "listening to marvellous tales of burning plains, immense lakes, and boiling springs

[15] Osborne Russell, *Journal of a Trapper, 1834-1843.*

[16] William F. Wheeler, "The Late James Gemmell," Historical Society of Montana, *Contributions,* II, 331.

[17] Lt. J. W. Gunnison, *The Mormons, or, Latter-Day Saints,* 151.

without being able to verify these wonders" which had been told to him by Robert Meldrum and Jim Bridger. Raynold's map showed an empty space penetrated by the Yellowstone River, passing a Sulphur Mountain, Falls of the Yellowstone, and Elephant's Back Mountain.[18]

PROSPECTORS

Gold seekers scouring the mountains in the early 1860's crossed portions of the Yellowstone area, carrying back with them rumors of the thermal wonderland. One of the largest prospecting parties was organized in August and September, 1863, by Walter W. deLacy, ex-civil engineer who, with forty gold prospecting buddies (with dropouts along the way, the forty dwindled to fourteen), went up the Snake River through Jackson's Hole, passing east of Shoshone Lake and through the Firehold Basin, panning for gold in all streams along their route. DeLacy's map was his great contribution. It was better than previous maps but was not entirely accurate. Carl I. Wheat speaks of the "cartographic impact" of deLacy's 1865 map, and his 1870 map "as one of the great maps of Western cartography."[19]

Other parties and individuals passed through this region during the Montana mining craze, with accounts appearing now and then in local newspapers, and these in turn were sometimes picked up by news correspondents and the stories sent out over Western Union wires. By 1869, those who read them began to be aware that there was a strange volcanic region in the Far West, and wondered what it really was. The day was fast approaching to quash rumors and establish fact by studied exploration.[20]

[18] Not published until 1868, *Senate Exec. Doc. No. 77.* Some of this is reprinted in F. V. Hayden, *Sixth Annual Report of the U.S. Geological and Geographical Survey of the Territories,* 20 *et seq.*

[19] Carl I. Wheat, *Mapping the Transmississippi West,* V, Part 2, 270. Walter W. deLacy, "A Trip Up the South Snake River," Historical Society of Montana, *Contributions,* I, 113; H. H. Bancroft, *History of Washington, Idaho and Montana,* 632 (includes map). See Hayden's criticism of the map in *Sixth Annual Report,* 244.

[20] Chittenden, *Yellowstone National Park,* 1964 ed., 64.

Very truly Yours
D. E. Folsom

C. W. Cook

Nathaniel P. Langford tried talking up the organization of an expedition to the upper Yellowstone in 1867 and again in 1868, but he did not get beyond the talking stage.[21] Frankly, no one wanted to venture into the hostile Indian country.

FOLSOM, COOK, AND PETERSON

Early in the summer of 1869 the newspapers throughout the territory announced that a party of citizens from Helena, Virginia City, and Bozeman, with an escort of soldiers from Fort Ellis, "would leave Bozeman about the fifth of September, for the Yellowstone country, with the intention of making a thorough examination of all the wonders with which that region was said to abound."

Again, an Indian scare broke out and troops were shifted from Fort Ellis and could not be sent. Enrolled members "began to discover that pressing business arrangements elsewhere would prevent their going." The party dwindled down to three – David E. Folsom, C. W. Cook, and William Peterson, who decided to go anyway since they were all prepared.

Folsom, Cook, and Peterson left Fort Ellis on September 18, 1869, traveled through the Yellowstone region and arrived at Madison junction fifteen days later on October 3. They were back home at Diamond City, forty miles east of Helena, on October 11.

From Fort Ellis, Folsom, Cook, and Peterson took about the same route to the area of Tower Falls which the Washburn-Doane Expedition followed a year later.[22] From the mouth of Tower Creek they went up Lamar River for a day and cut back westerly to the Falls of the Yellowstone. They described the Upper Falls and gave its height as 115 feet, and the Lower Falls

21 Langford, *Discovery,* 19.
22 Their published journal did not mention Tower Falls itself or its height, but did describe basalt "from 30 to 40 feet thick standing in hexagonal columns" and other rock strata which identified the locality. In *Haynes Bulletin,* December 1922, and January, February, and May 1923, Charles W. Cook, in reconstructing the story of the expedition, verified their visit to the Falls.

"narrowing in till it is no more than 70 feet wide . . . makes a final fearful leap of 350 feet."

On September 23 Folsom, Cook, and Peterson continued up the Yellowstone River, fording across to the left bank 6.5 miles above the Falls. Later that day, "some twelve miles from the Falls," they visited Mud Volcano, Dragon Mouth Spring, and Sulphur Caldron.

Then "we ascended to the head of the lake [along the north shore] and remained in its vicinity for several days." On September 25 they "concluded to follow up the west shore to the head of the lake and then turned to the northwest." The original account then mentions the geyser basin at Thumb. They spent only three days by pack and saddle horse traveling the length of the Firehole geyser basins, and apparently saw only one geyser eruption.

To give the reader an idea of the interesting but limited information the Folsom-Cook-Peterson account contained, the editors quote a portion in full: from their Yellowstone Lake stop past Shoshone Lake and through the Firehole geyser basins.

Imagine you are reading about country which you either had heard unbelievable tales about or had never heard of before; avoid mentally filling in details or adding to the picture from your own knowledge of Yellowstone Park, for that is the way you would have had to do it in 1870.

> September 29th, we took up our march for home. Our plan was to cross the range in a northwesterly direction, find the Madison River, and follow it down to civilization. Twelve miles brought us to a small triangular-shaped lake, about eight miles long, deeply set among the hills. We kept on in a northwesterly direction, as near as the rugged nature of the country would permit; and on the third day (October 1st) came to a small irregularly shaped valley, some six miles across in the widest place, from every part of which great clouds of steam arose. From descriptions

which we had had of this valley, from persons who had previously visited it, we recognized it as the place known as "Burnt Hole," or "Death Valley." The Madison River flows through it, and from the general contour of the country we knew that it headed in the lake which we passed two days ago, only twelve miles from the Yellowstone. We descended into the valley, and found that the springs had the same general characteristics as those I have already described, although some of them were much larger and discharged a vast amount of water. One of them, at a little distance, attracted our attention by the immense amount of steam it threw off; and upon approaching it we found it to be an intermittent geyser in active operation. The hole through which the water was discharged was ten feet in diameter, and was situated in the centre of a large circular shallow basin, into which the water fell. There was a stiff breeze blowing at the time, and by going to the windward side and carefully picking our way over convenient stones, we were enabled to reach the edge of the hole. At that moment the escaping steam was causing the water to boil up in a fountain five or six feet high. It stopped in an instant, and commenced steeling down – twenty, thirty, forty feet – until we concluded that the bottom had fallen out; but the next instant, without any warning, it came rushing up and shot into the air at least eighty feet, causing us to stampede for higher ground. It continued to spout at intervals of a few minutes, for some time; but finally subsided, and was quiet during the remainder of the time we stayed in the vicinity. We followed up the Madison five miles, and there found the most gigantic hot springs we had seen. They were situated along the river bank, and discharged so much hot water that the river was blood warm a quarter of a mile below. One of the springs was two hundred and fifty feet in diameter, and had every indication of spouting powerfully at times. The waters from the hot springs in this valley, if united, would form a large stream; and they increase the size of the river nearly one-half. Although we experienced no bad effects from passing through the "Valley of Death," yet we were not disposed to dispute the propriety of giving it that name. It seemed to be shunned by all animated nature. There were no fish in the river, no birds in the trees, no animals — not even a track — anywhere to be seen; although in one spring we saw the entire skeleton of a buffalo that had probably fallen in accidentally and been boiled down to soup.[23]

The trip was written up for publication, but the article was rejected by eastern periodicals, with avowals to the effect that they did not publish such fiction. *The Western Monthly,* of Chicago, finally used a 5,000 word version (after editorial deletions) in their July 1870 issue.[24] Thus Folsom and Cook produced what was probably the first authentic report of an expedition which set out for the specific purpose of exploring the Yellowstone region. But the Folsom-Cook-Peterson Expedition made little if any contribution to the scientific knowledge of the area. Its main importance was the local interest which it stirred up in Montana and the informal information which the trio brought back. Out of this context it was easier to put together the Washburn party.

In 1870, then, it still remained for the Washburn–Doane Expedition to bring the world authentic and scientific knowledge of Yellowstone.

---

[23] C. W. Cook, "The Valley of the Upper Yellowstone," *The Western Monthly,* Vol. IV, No. 19 (July 1870), 66-67.

[24] See Appendix to Part II this book for a bibliographical note on *The Western Monthly* July 1870 issue and the Folsom-Cook accounts of their trip.

CHAPTER 2

FORT ELLIS 1870

Fort Ellis had been unable to supply a troop escort in 1869 for a Yellowstone exploration. Was 1870 a better year?

As it was, the military situation at Fort Ellis was not favorable for any of its officers to be absent on exploration and Doane narrowly missed being able to go on the 1870 expedition at all. It required maneuvering behind the scenes to bring it about. If Major Eugene M. Baker, Doane's commanding officer, had not felt the pressure of higher authority and seen the political advisability of sending a competent military escort, he would not have done so. Major Baker was already on the spot publicly in Washington on account of the massacre of the Piegans on the Marias the preceding January.

In August, 1870, Fort Ellis was the hottest spot on the turbulent, embattled, and dangerous Indian frontier. This was no time for Lieutenant Doane, one of its ablest officers, to engage in his long-cherished ambition of exploration.

The fort that summer was understaffed and undermanned, with only eight officers and 132 enlisted men present, about half its usual force.

A large number of Crow Indians had broken loose from the nearby agency that summer and had scattered into the mountains. How many, what hostile plans they had, or where they were now, no one knew for sure. About 250 lodges of them had wintered at the agency south of the Yellowstone River a few miles from Bozeman Pass. Since their flight, settlers in the Gallatin and Yellowstone valleys went to bed each night armed and waiting, fearful of being raided before dawn. The military had to protect Fort Ellis as well as the settlers.

The fort was almost centered at the territorial overlap of the most powerful tribes—Snakes and Bannocks to the southwest, Flatheads, Nez Perces, and Pend D'Oreilles to the northwest, Blackfeet to the north, Sioux to the east and northeast, and the entire Crow tribe and the fighting Cheyennes practically at the fort's postern gates on the east. The post itself and every route to it was vulnerable, and surrounded by Indian tribes. Shrieking war cries of the Indians swept down through the heavily traveled Flathead Pass, thirty miles north, through Bridger Pass, seven miles northeast, and Bozeman Pass, five miles east.

In July, two of the cavalry companies under command of Captain Lewis Thompson had left Fort Ellis to deal with Indian troubles near Fort Shaw. White intruders were after gold on Indian lands. The Indians were retaliating with raids and murder of frontier settlers.[1]

On August 10, First Lieutenant James E. Batchelder and Second Lieutenant George H. Wright had departed with nine enlisted men. They were to build a road to Camp Baker, Montana Territory, which would set up a roadblock on the Smith River corridor through which hostile Blackfeet were raiding the Montana settlers.

Two officers were absent on leave.

Captain O. O. G. Robinson, who should have been commanding Doane's Company F, had long gone A.W.O.L. Second

---

[1] Army General Order No. 72, June 4, 1870, received at Fort Ellis July 5, directed that intruders on Indian lands should be kept off by military force, if necessary. If one be technical, Fort Ellis itself was an intrusion. By the Laramie Treaty of September 17, 1851, the Indians and the treaty commissioners defined the territory where Fort Ellis was located and south to the Yellowstone River as belonging to the Blackfoot tribe. Although this treaty was never ratified by the U.S. Senate, it is the best authority for the carefully defined territorial boundaries of the various tribes at that time. The Blackfoot reservation was later reduced by Executive Order of July 5, 1873, which took the Gallatin Valley out of the reservation. *Bureau of American Ethnology*, Vol 18, 786.

Lieutenant Doane had been in sole command for nearly a year. If he went on the Yellowstone exploration, Company F would be without any commissioned officer.

Under the circumstances, it is surprising that Doane had more luck in obtaining this assignment to one of his exploring ambitions than he did on other occasions. One factor was added to the picture, however. Doane was a little more alert this time, anticipating refusal.

Previously, by chance, Chief Justice of the Territory H. L. Hosmer had learned that Doane was keenly interested in Yellowstone exploration. He so informed General Washburn who promptly wrote to Doane. Doane quickly replied from Fort Ellis on August 12:

> Your kind favor of the 9th ult. came yesterday, and I reply at the first opportunity for transmittal. Judge Hosmer was correct in regards my *earnest desire* to go on the trip proposed, but mistaken in relation to my *free agency* in the premises. To obtain permission for an escort will require an order from General Hancock, authorizing Colonel Baker to make the detail.
>
> If Hauser and yourself will telegraph at once on rec't to General Hancock at Saint Paul, Minn., stating the object of the expedition, etc., and requesting that an order be sent to Comdg. Officer at Fort Ellis, M.T., it will doubtless be favorably considered. Colonel Baker has promised me the detail if authority be furnished. I will reimburse you the expenses of the messages which should be *paid both ways* to insure prompt attention.
>
> I will be able to furnish Tents and Camp equipage better than you can get it in Helena — and can furnish them without trouble to your whole party. Hoping we may make the trip in company I have the honor to remain,

Your Obdt Servt

G. C. DOANE

Please let me know what steps you take in the matter as soon as convenient.[2]

Washburn and Hauser immediately sent a joint telegram to
Major General Hancock as Doane suggested. This proved to be
the effective move that set up Doane as the officer in charge of
the military escort.

On August 14, 1870, Major Baker received the telegram from
General Hancock, Headquarters, District of Montana, St. Paul,
ordering the military escort.

[2] Samuel T. Hauser Papers.

CHAPTER 3

THE 1870 PARTY

NINE CIVILIANS

On August 1, 1870, twenty civilians were enthusiastically enrolled in the Yellowstone exploration party. Then rumors of the warlike maneuvers of the Crows reached their ears. Courage declined. The majority found sudden emergencies arising in their businesses. Even James Stuart, fearless frontiersman that he was, could not get the federal judge to excuse him from jury duty.[1]

A new roster was made up. Remaining were the following eight men:

General Henry Dana Washburn (1832-1871) was the chosen leader of the nine civilian expeditionary members. Well experienced in military command, he had served in the Civil War including the Vicksburg campaign and Sherman's March to the Sea, and had been breveted brigadier general. He was discharged and breveted major general on July 26, 1865. He then served two terms in the U.S. Congress, from Indiana, declining re-election at the end of his term March 3, 1869. On April 17, 1869, President Grant appointed him surveyor general of Montana, for which he qualified May 18.

After the party's return he left Helena by stage on December

[1] Langford, *Discovery*, 31.

3, 1870, to visit his people in Indiana; he died there January 26, 1871.

Samuel T. Hauser (1833-1914), then thirty-seven years old, was president of the First National Bank of Helena. He was a natural-born promoter and had worked hard to organize the expedition. Originally a civil engineer, he had prospected and promoted mining ventures in Montana, and had promoted banks in Virginia City, Missoula, and Butte.

He became territorial governor in 1885.

Nathaniel Pitt Langford (1832-1911), another dedicated man with political influence, worked tirelessly to get this expedition going. Born in New York, he had collected Montana's taxes when the territory was created in 1862 (as "Collector of Internal Revenue"). President Andrew Johnson had tried to appoint him governor of Montana in 1868 but the Senate refused to confirm any of Johnson's appointments and Langford was unable to take office. As one of Montana's original vigilantes, Langford wrote an account of early day desperadoes and frontier justice called *Vigilante Days.* He was thirty-eight years old at the time of the Yellowstone expedition.

He would become first superintendent (1872-1877) of Yellowstone National Park, serving without compensation (but only visiting the park a few times). However, he was also national bank examiner in Montana (1872-1885) during the same period, so the tax payers cannot be said to have neglected entirely to pay him. On July 29, 1872, together with James Stevenson, he made the first ascent of the Grand Teton in Wyoming.

Cornelius Hedges (1831-1907), then thirty-nine years of age, had come to Montana to pan gold, stayed to practice law. He had been on the vigilante committee that wiped out the Plummer gang and helped bring law and order to Montana. He had the legal foresight and was the first member of the party to propose the idea of a Yellowstone National Park.

He became U.S. District Attorney for Montana in 1871 and 1872, and was probate judge for five years. He was Grand Secretary of the Masonic Lodge in Montana from 1874 to his death.

Besides an active political life, he became an editorial staff
writer on the *Helena Herald*.

Truman C. Everts (1816-1901) at fifty-four years was the
oldest member of the party. He was then Montana's current
assessor of Internal Revenue. The search of more than a month
for him when he became lost in the Yellowstone wilderness
would create national publicity for the expedition.

Walter Trumbull (1846-1891), the son of U.S. Senator
Lyman Trumbull, of Illinois, was Everts' aide as assistant
assessor of Internal Revenue. Also a newspaper correspondent,
Trumbull's articles concerning the loss of Everts would focus
national attention on the Yellowstone region. Later, as clerk of
the U.S. Senate Committee on Judiciary in Washington in 1872,
Trumbull assisted with the Yellowstone National Park bill.

Benjamin Stickney, Jr. (1842-1912) was a prominent Helena
storekeeper and pioneer, accustomed to making wholesale pur-
chases at wholesale prices. He contributed to the expedition by
assembling the required thirty days' provisions and by collecting
the cost from each party member.

Warren C. Gillette (1832-1912), then thirty-eight years old,
had been a pioneer merchant in Bannock, Virginia City, and
then Helena. He was one of the best mountain men in the
group.

Also politically active, he later became a member of the Con-
stitutional Convention of Montana in 1889.

Only **Jacob Smith** (1838-?), last to enlist with the group,
seemed to be lacking influence. He listed himself as "hide
dealer." Langford said that after all the other men had signed
up for the expedition, Smith wanted to go, too. "Jake
was . . . unfitted to be a member," Langford wrote in his diary,
". . . where vigilance and alertness were essential to safety
. . . he seemed to think that his goodnatured nonsense would
always be a passport to favor."[2] He turned out as Langford
expected. On the night of September 13, with Indians in the
locality and a real threat to the party, Jake refused to take his
turn on guard duty and General Washburn, silently suffering

[2] Ibid., 32.

Henry D Washburn
1869

Nathaniel P. Langford

Cornelius Hedges.

Benj. Stickney

W. E. Gillette.

G. C. Doane, September 1871.

with undisclosed tuberculosis, took Jake's place.

This, then, was the small party of civilians who were determined to explore the Yellowstone wilderness despite the dangerous Indian frontier.

WALTER DELACY

An interesting question is why Walter deLacy did not join the Washburn party. In some sense he was the most "natural" expedition member in Helena.

In 1863 he had explored the Snake River and had discovered Shoshone Lake; he was also an experienced map maker. His knowledge was recognized, for example, by the first legislature of the new Territory, which, in the winter of 1864-65, commissioned deLacy to make a map of Montana, to be used in laying out counties. This was the 1865 map which Carl Wheat has called "one of the more famous Western maps," made by Montana's "great cartographic pioneer[;] . . . he had wrought a memorable map of a new Territory, and had he never done anything else, he would have given us sufficient reason to honor his memory."[3]

From 1867-1871, deLacy was employed in the office of the surveyor general of Montana; thus he was working with Washburn while the expedition was being planned.

Perhaps deLacy simply could not get time off from his work to accompany Washburn. The members of the party financed the expedition themselves and deLacy may not have had enough money for his share. He might even have been one of the twenty who had originally signed up and then backed out when the Indian scare occurred.

In any event, in his earlier exploration deLacy had traveled through a different part of the country − up the Snake River, past Shoshone Lake, and into the *Lower* Geyser Basin. Any knowledge he had of that country would have been of little benefit to the party going in from Fort Ellis and up the Yellow-

---

[3] Carl I. Wheat, *Mapping the Transmississippi West*, Vol. V, Part I, 149, 148, 153.

stone River.

An account of deLacy's own 1863 expedition was not published until 1876,[4] although he had written a letter about it earlier, which reported that "at the head of the South Snake, and also on the South fork of the Madison, there are hundreds of hot springs, many of which are 'geysers'."[5] DeLacy did not attempt to capitalize on what he had seen, except as a map maker. It must be remembered that in 1863, when he made this trip, Montana as a territory did not yet exist. There were no settlements except boom mining camps. There was no telegraph and no *Helena Daily Herald,* in fact no newspapers at all, to seek a report from deLacy and spread it across the nation — a nation then divided and wracked with Civil War. There was no audience to hear lectures and no one to use deLacy for railroad financing propaganda.

DeLacy's direct contribution to the Washburn-Doane Expedition was to compile the information furnished by the Folsom-Cook Expedition and put it on a map which was used by Langford on the 1870 trip.

FORT ELLIS AND MAJOR BAKER

The Washburn group was now ready. On Tuesday, August 16, 1870, the *Helena Herald* announced their departure: "At 9 o'clock tomorrow morning the roll will be called on Main Street, at the foot of Broadway, and the expedition will take up its march to the front." The general feeling of the party was summed up by Hedges: "I think a more confirmed set of skeptics never went out into a wilderness than those who compose our party."[6]

The faster traveling members of the Washburn party arrived in Bozeman the following Friday night at 7:00 P.M. Two days

---

[4] W. W. deLacy, "A Trip Up the South Snake River in 1863," Historical Society of Montana, *Contributions,* I, 113.

[5] R. W. Raymond, "Mining Resources of the States and Territories West of the Rocky Mountains," 1869, *House Exec. Doc. No. 54,* 40 Congress, 3 session, 142.

[6] Chittenden, *Yellowstone National Park,* 1912 ed., 73.

later they camped on the East Gallatin River about one half mile from Fort Ellis, where Lieutenant Doane had put up a tent for them.

On Sunday, General Washburn rode over to the fort and was shown into Major Baker's office. The August sun was reaching through the window of the log headquarters building casting a dusty beam across the cluttered pine desk of the major. An empty whisky bottle lay in the corner of the room. On the desk was the hand-scrawled and almost crumpled telegram from General Hancock concerning the expedition. It was a week old.

Washburn and Baker greeted each other cordially as old soldiers would. Both had served ably in the Civil War. Washburn had enlisted as a private, then risen to brevet brigadier general, and finally brevet major general. Baker had served in the army since July 1, 1859, had been captain in the First Cavalry through most of the War, and had been breveted colonel in December, 1868. This was the first year for both in Montana. Washburn had been appointed surveyor general of the territory in 1869. Baker had arrived at Fort Ellis in December of 1869. Baker knew Washburn's political influence.

Major Baker opened the conversation. He complained that nearly all of his force was in the field fighting Indians, that he had no men to spare, and that it was dangerous to leave Fort Ellis in such an understaffed position.

Washburn waited until the major had finished. Then he pointed out the justification of the assignment on the grounds that the military knew nothing about the territory south of Fort Ellis and that it ought to be reconnoitered by an experienced army officer.

With a gesture towards the desk, Major Baker stated that in view of the orders from General Hancock, he would send five men and a lieutenant.

The major called his adjutant, Lieutenant James G. MacAdams, and told him to draw the order detailing Doane, one sergeant, and four privates from Doane's company.[7]

MacAdams asked the major who would command Company

---

[7] Langford, *Discovery,* 61; Special Order No. 100, August 21, 1870.

F while Doane was gone.

"Fill in your own name," Baker ordered the adjutant.[8]

This settled the matter as far as Baker and Washburn were concerned. Washburn rode back to his camp half a mile away content that with Doane leading the military escort, the success of the expedition was assured.

In the meantime, Doane busied himself with final preparations for this venture into the land of the legendary where the earth was on fire and spouted waters higher than a flagpole.

[8] Post Returns, Fort Ellis, National Archives.

CHAPTER 4

WRITINGS OF THE 1870 PARTY

Six members of the Washburn-Doane Expedition wrote some sort of account of the exploration. In order to round out the story of the 1870 expedition and to show different viewpoints and attitudes, the editors have added to Doane's daily entries excerpts from the journals and writings of other members of the party.

DOANE'S CONTRIBUTION

Doane's contribution was his factual report, the first scholarly paper of its kind about the Yellowstone region. Doane's journal of 25,000 words is a scientific development of his observations. Doane had an excellent education on everything that was scientific knowledge in the year 1870 and his mind continued to study and explore. With fact-of-the-matter directness he dispels any doubt that the unbelievable wonders of the Yellowstone did exist. Humor and human foibles are almost absent from Doane's manuscript; these he presumably left for his colleagues to record.

Doane himself once said that a journal of exploration should be

> a faithful delineation. Such a report one likes to travel by — truthful, plain, and unembellished; a

simple narrative of facts observed. It gives evidence of a correct eye and a sound judgment; of capacity for the work undertaken.[1]

His Yellowstone journal follows this faithfully.[2] In Doane's later journals – of his 1876 Snake River Expedition and his 1880 Arctic Expedition – Doane moves away from a strict adherence to his own admonition and does embellish the simple factual narrative with expressions of more personal feelings and with a delightful wit, even flecked with touches of sardonic humor. But he never loses his "correct eye" and his "sound judgment."

In the case of Yellowstone-1870, unembellished facts observed were precisely what was needed. We today, realizing the uniqueness and the immensity of the awe-inspiring phenomena which confronted Doane and knowing that he fell in love with Yellowstone for the rest of his life, can only marvel even more at the restraint in his writings which prevented emotion from clouding the factual and scientific clarity so necessary for the first genuine information and understanding of the region – a region previously so misunderstood and surrounded with terrible and sublime tales.

---

[1] T. F. Rodenbough, *From Everglade to Cañon with the Second Dragoons, 1836-1875,* 406.

[2] In Doane's day, as always, observers differed about the proper balance between "objective" and "subjective" perspectives. Thomas Moran, for example, a contemporary of Doane's and a soon-to-be-initiated devotee of Yellowstone, would have found fault with Doane's sparse subjectivity. Moran was the painter and illustrator who accompanied the 1871 Hayden Expedition to Yellowstone. He went two years later to the Grand Canyon in Arizona with Major John Wesley Powell. In commenting on Powell's *Scribner's* articles, Moran praised the descriptions as "strong and vigorous," but expressed to Powell his major reservation:

> You do not once (if I recollect right) give your sensations even in the most dangerous passages, nor even hint at the terrible and sublime feelings that are stirred within one. . . . It seems to me that the expression of these impressions and thoughts tend to realize the descriptions to the reader & are almost as necessary as the descriptions themselves."

(Thurman Wilkins, *Thomas Moran: Artist of the Mountains,* 89)

LANGFORD'S STORY

Nathaniel Pitt Langford was observant too, but he was also a story teller and campfire raconteur; he saw the human touches as much as he did the physical objects and marvels. He wrote about them all. Note his story of Jake Smith and the card game on August 27 and the naming of Tower Falls on August 28. His stories were often lengthier and more popularly written than Doane's accounts. His articles in *Scribner's Monthly* (a total of about 17,000 words in the May and June issues of 1871) had vastly wider distribution than Doane's journal. However, Langford's own complete journal was not published until thirty-five years later, under the title *The Discovery of Yellowstone Park, 1870*. It was about 38,000 words in length.

TRUMBULL'S WRITING

Walter Trumbull, more accustomed to newspaper writing than the others, added a touch of human interest and subtle humor to his writing. His picture sketches made during the journey often had this same touch. Trumbull's humor appears as he describes the comedy of fears and failures of the grizzly bear hunt on September 8, and the saga of the luckless pack horse on September 9. His description of the Firehole geysers is readable, concise, journalistic reporting. His writing is to be found in the *Overland Monthly* of May and June, 1871, a total of 10,000 words.

HEDGES' JOURNAL

Cornelius Hedges' journal is a brief daily jotting of notes of what he saw, what he did, and how he felt (even down to details such as "sat in the rain under tree, moodily meditating"). His descriptions are kept to a minimum but are precise where needed. An example of a complete daily entry is given for

August 22. Hedges' journal of about 8,750 words was published in the Historical Society of Montana, *Contributions,* V, 1904, 370.

WASHBURN'S NOTES

General Henry Dana Washburn's scantier notes of about 3,000 words were published in the *Helena Daily Herald* on September 27 and 28, soon after the party returned to Helena in 1870. As surveyor general of Montana Territory, Washburn no doubt would have included a full discussion of the Yellowstone expedition in his annual report for the fiscal year ending June 30, 1871, but he died of tuberculosis on January 26, 1871, only four months after the end of the expedition. The 1871 annual report made by his successor, John E. Blaine, contained no reference whatsoever to the Washburn-Doane Expedition of 1870.

Washburn had the viewpoint of a surveyor. His mind mapped out the lay of the land, and he gathered data which would enable him to make graphic description and to prepare a reliable map.

Washburn's *Helena Daily Herald* articles dwell mainly on the Yellowstone canyon and its Upper and Lower falls, the Crater Hill area, the loss of Everts, and how the party classified and named some of the geysers (see excerpt under September 19). His notes were republished in *Mining Statistics West of the Rocky Mountains,* March 21, 1871 (*House Executive Document No. 10,* 42 Congress, 1 session).

The whereabouts of Washburn's personal diary is unknown. The latest mention of it is found in a news story which appeared in *The Tacoma* (Washington) *Ledger,* July 9, 1911, where the general's widow, Serena Washburn, was quoted as saying, "However, the general had with him a diary he had kept regularly, and the notes in this gave all but the memory pictures and details which would have made his story, by word of mouth, so valuable."

EVERTS' EPIC ACCOUNT

Truman Everts wrote a 12,300-word epic of his wanderings and sufferings in "Thirty-seven Days of Peril," *Scribner's Monthly,* November 1871, which is a story in itself, almost as incredible as it is painfully instructive and entertaining. Simply told, he gives his thoughts, reactions, and emotions, even his hallucinary discussions with old friends. Excerpts used include his getting lost on September 9, his rescue on October 16, and his summary of the expedition. Everts' account was also published in Historical Society of Montana, *Contributions,* V, 1904, 395.

JAKE SMITH'S COMMENT

It is of record that Jake Smith kept no diary. According to Langford on September 21, "Jake Smith to-day asked me if I expected that the readers of my diary would believe what I had written. He said that he had kept no diary for the reason that our discoveries had been of such novel character, that if he were to write an account of them he would not be believed by those who read his record, and that he would be set down as a liar. He said that he did not mind being called a liar by those who had known him well for many years, but he would not allow strangers that privilege."[3]

---

[3] Langford, *Discovery,* 181.

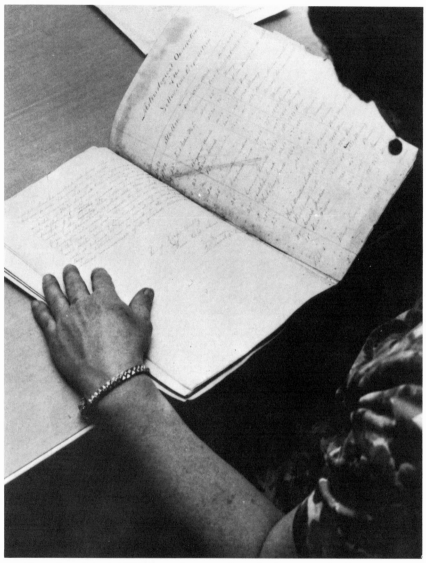

Doane's original 1870 journal, opened to final page and Meteorological Observations chart, being inspected by Miss Minnie Paugh, Special Collections Librarian at Montana State University, Bozeman.

CHAPTER 5

THE STORY OF DOANE'S ORIGINAL 1870 JOURNAL

The editors follow Doane's original manuscript copy of the journal – the first time it has been used in any publication.

In September, 1967, they located this manuscript copy of the journal at Montana State University, Bozeman, Montana, where it had just reached the light in a currently conducted classification of the University's archive collections. The manuscript copy had been donated to the University by Doane's widow, Mary Lee Hunter Doane.

Handwritten in an era before such manuscripts were typewritten, the script is in excellent penmanship, easily read. Carefully written on the ruled pages of an old buckram-bound, ledger-like book, about 8 by 12 inches, it is evident that it had been given to a professional or skilled scrivener to make this copy. It is not Doane's handwriting, although in Doane's own hand there are corrections; and in the case of the meteorological observations, he had filled in most of the figures himself.

In the post records of Fort Ellis there is a Special Order No. 3 by Colonel Baker dated January 3, 1871, detailing Private Charles Moore[1] of Company F to "daily duty as clerk to report to Second Lieut. Doane for purpose of making out papers, etc. connected with the Yellowstone Expedition." Special Order No. 18 of January 23, 1871, relieved Moore as clerk to Doane.

[1] This is the same Private Moore who had accompanied Doane on the expedition.

of which observations were to be taken at different
points on the route.

First day   We left Fort Ellis on the morning of the 22d taking
the road to the Yellowstone river in an easterly direction
. Bar. 25.25. Ther 92° noon Elevation **4911 ft.**

This road follows the general course of the
East Gallatin, over a hilly country of limestone
formation, with scattering pine timber on the
northern slopes. The ravines and small valleys
are grown up with Quaking Aspen, and Willow.
The strata of rock are nearly perpendicular,
composed of cliff limestones, interspersed with shale
and slate, having nearly a vertical dip to the
westward, and greatly broken up by volcanic

were caught in abundance and we fared sumptuously
with the single exception that the river water tasted
strongly of chemicals, and that all other available water
tasted still worse than the river. Those of the party who
sported silver watches now discovered that they were
no longer silver, but a greasy pinch back yellow, discolored by the gases in the atmosphere of the springs.
Arms were also affected; the polished surfaces becoming
spotted with black. Distance twelve miles —
Bar 22.75 Ther 60° Elevation 7487 feet
September 2th we remained in camp on the river, and visited
springs in the neighborhood. Along the banks of the stream
there are a dozen cauldrons of greyish clay mud, varying
from 6 to 40 feet in diameter, and from three to ten feet in
depth, each with its vent of sulphur vapor, and shiny

Portions of two pages from Doane's 1870 journal. Meteorological observation insertions can be seen in Doane's handwriting. *Courtesy Montana
State University Library.*

Doane was still suffering from the effects of his infected thumb.

While Doane dated his report December 15, 1875 [sic], it probably was not dispatched to Headquarters in St. Paul until late in January. General W. S. Hancock, Department of Dakota, acknowledged its receipt and wrote Doane on February 9, 1871, of "his warm commendation," stating that "it does you great credit as an officer of intelligence and fidelity in the performance of duty." On February 8, 1871, Hancock sent the report to the Adjutant General of the Army, recommending publication. W. T. Sherman, General of the Army, submitted it on February 16, 1871, to the Secretary of War with recommendations that the report be printed.

W. W. Belknap, Secretary of War, concurred and on February 24, 1871, sent it to the Committee on Territories of the United States Senate where, on March 3, 1871, it was ordered printed. It appeared as *Senate Executive Document No. 51*, 41 Congress, 3 session.[2]

Comparing the manuscript to its Senate publication of 1871, the editors find the manuscript superior. The Senate printing had practically no paragraphing, whereas Doane had carefully paragraphed his manuscript; Doane's original paragraphing is used here. The Senate edition had also introduced punctuation changes which changed the sense in some cases, and editorial word changes which were poorly selected or inaccurate. For example, where the editing had changed Doane's "Madison Lake" to read "Henry's Lake," it destroyed the meaning and value of his observations.

---

[2] Doane himself had also sent a copy of his journal to the Smithsonian Institution. They wrote him a letter on May 2, 1871:

> We are happy to announce that this paper was received and its account of the geological and physical character of the remarkable section of which it treats is very interesting. We were about having it printed when an ascertainment [was made] that a . . . copy . . . had been ordered published by Congress.

Note on Format

The editors have provided chapter titles and subheadings for each chapter, in both cases using present-day nomenclature and spelling. In the text itself, spellings have been left as Doane had them – e.g., Gardiners river, Fire Hole, cañon, Butler for Bottler, etc. Also, the paragraphing of the Doane text follows his original manuscript; this was not done in the Senate printing of Doane's journal.

Both Doane's original manuscript and its Senate printing introduced each new day's entry with the notation "fourth day," "twelfth day," etc. and often followed it with the date – e.g., "Morning of the 25th," "September 2d," etc. The editors have standardized and supplemented these notations to read, e.g., **Thursday, August 25, fourth day.**

The summary paragraphs introducing each chapter (6-16) are by the editors.

The text of the Doane manuscript is set with a maximum line width.

The Doane journal text is supplemented throughout with excerpts from writings by other members of the Washburn-Doane Expedition. These are set in italics with the name of the author in brackets at the beginning of each quotation.

The editors' comments, interspersed throughout Chapters 6-16, are set with a shorter line width, as per this paragraph.

For explanation of the chapter-opening map sections, see Appendix to Part II, C, "The Maps," especially pages 400n3 and 403.

DOANE'S JOURNAL

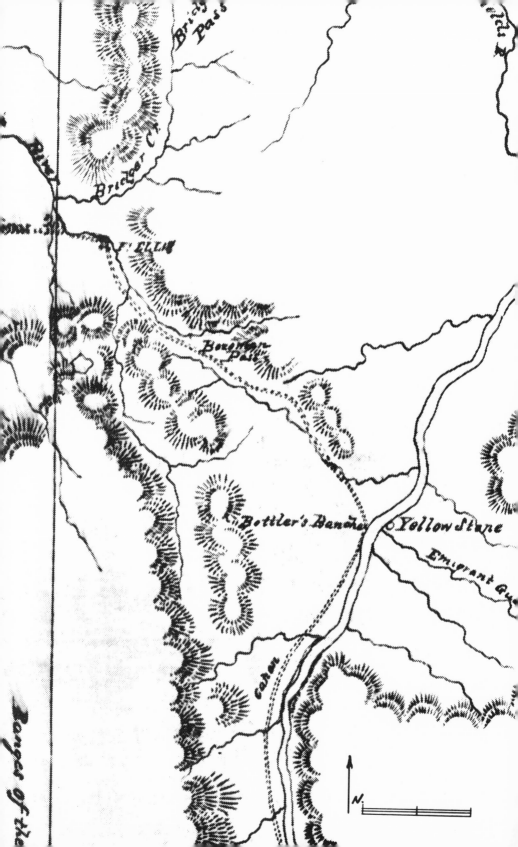

CHAPTER 6

FORT ELLIS TO BOTTLER'S RANCH

Doane begins by quoting Major Baker's order of August 21. Personnel listed. The party follows the Gallatin River east (present U.S. Highway 10) from Fort Ellis, then cuts off southeast along Trail Creek to the Yellowstone River, and follows this south to Bottler's Ranch (U.S. 89), which they reach on their second day out, August 23.

ORDERS AND PERSONNEL

Fort Ellis, Montana Territory,
December 15, 1870.

Sir: The subjoined special order was received from your office by me on the 21st of August, 1870:

(Special Order No. 100 – Extract.)

Headquarters Fort Ellis, Montana Territory,
August 21, 1870.

. . .

II. In accordance with instructions from Headquarters District of Montana, Lieutenant G. C. Doane, Second Cavalry, will proceed with one sergeant and four privates of Company F, Second Cavalry, to escort the surveyor general of Montana to the falls and lakes of the Yellowstone, and return.[1] They will be supplied with thirty days' rations, and one hundred rounds of ammunition per man. The acting assistant quartermaster will furnish them with the necessary transportation.

By order of Major Baker.

J. G. MacAdams,

First Lieutenant Second Cavalry, Acting Post Adjutant.

In obedience to the above order, I joined the party of General H. D. Washburn, en route for the Yellowstone, and then encamped near Fort Ellis, Montana Territory, with a detachment of Company F, Second Cavalry, consisting of Sergeant William Baker, Privates Charles Moore [a bugler], John Williamson, William Leipler, and George W. McConnell. The detachment was supplied with two extra saddle horses, and five pack mules for the transportation of supplies. A large pavillion tent was carried for the accommodation of the whole party, in case of stormy weather being encountered; also forty days' rations and an abundant supply of ammunition.

The party of civilians from Helena consisted of General H. D. Washburn, Surveyor General of Montana, Hon. N. P. Langford, Hon. T. C. Everts, Judge C. Hedges, of Helena, Samuel T. Hauser, Warren C. Gillette, Benjamin C. Stickney, Jr., Walter Trumbull, and Jacob Smith, all of Helena, together with two packers and two cooks.[2]

They were furnished with a saddle horse apiece, and nine

---

[1] Chittenden noted: "There is a significant absence in this order of any reference to geysers or hot springs; and the discreet post commander evidently did not intend to commit himself to a recognition of their existence on the strength of such knowledge as was then available." (*Yellowstone National Park*, 1912 ed., 73)

[2] Langford names them, "Mr. ——— Reynolds and Elwyn Bean, western slope packers, and two African boys as cooks." This was not Charlie Reynolds who died in Reno's command at the battle of the Little Big Horn on June 25, 1876. Langford gives the name of one of the cooks as "Newt", who had "a large black dog of seeming little intelligence, to which we have given the name of 'Booby.' " (*Discovery*, 59)

pack animals for the whole outfit; they were provided with one aneroid barometer, one thermometer, and several pocket compasses, by means of which observations were to be taken at different points on the route.

GALLATIN VALLEY

Monday, August 22, first day. We left Fort Ellis on the morning of the 22d, taking the road to the Yellowstone river in an easterly direction. Barometer, 25.25; thermometer, 92° noon; elevation, 4,911[3] feet.

This road follows the general course of the East Gallatin, over a hilly country of limestone formation, with scattering pine timber on the northern slopes. The ravines and small valleys are grown up with quaking aspens and willows.

The strata of rock are nearly perpendicular, composed of cliff limestones, interspersed with shales and slate, having nearly a vertical dip to the westward, and greatly broken up by volcanic agencies underneath. Six miles from Fort Ellis we crossed the Yellowstone divide, a ridge of considerable height forming the apex of two water sheds; one sloping to the Gallatin, the other to the Yellowstone.[4] At the point of crossing the ridge is depressed several hundred feet below its usual altitude allowing a tolerable wagon road over the pass.

The summit affords a fine view of the beautiful Gallatin Valley, with its cordon of snow capped peaks, its finely timbered water courses, and its long grassy declivities, dotted with the habitations of pioneers and blooming with the fruits of industry now ready for harvest. Barometer, 24.10; thermometer, 70°; elevation, 6,140 feet.

[3] The figure only is in Doane's handwriting. It was inserted in a blank space which was left in the handwritten manuscript by the scrivener. Most altitude figures are similarly inserted by Doane.

[4] Marked as Bozeman Pass on Doane and Washburn maps. For a further description of this route by Doane, see his October 11 entry in his Snake River Journal, 1876, Part III of this book. Present-day U.S. Highway 10 goes through Bozeman Pass (elevation 5,712 feet) about eleven miles east of Bozeman, Montana, a little north of the early-day route.

At the head of the East Gallatin ravine, a fine seam of coal has been struck in the bed of the stream where it can be worked to advantage, beneath the carboniferous limestone found in such localities. We traveled thence through a natural pass between high ridges, and down a gentle declivity about three miles, striking the valley of Trail Creek, leading to the Yellowstone, and camping on this creek at a point distant about fifteen miles from Fort Ellis.[5] This stream is shut in by high hills, wooded at the summits, and with grassy slopes. Occasionally, masses of lava are seen projecting from the highest points.

The valley formation is composed of the débris washed down from the hills, together with traces of original drift.

Trail Creek at the place of our encampment is a small sized trout stream of great clearness and purity; the general direction of the stream is southeast. Barometer, 24.30; morning, thermometer, 54°; elevation, 5,803 feet.

INDIANS AND GUARD DUTY

The party made camp at 4:00 P.M., having traveled the fifteen miles from Fort Ellis since 11:00 that morning. An ominous foreboding of Indian attack and massacre hung over the civilian members of the party as it did over every departure from the settlements in those days. Practically every one of them had gone through the experience of having friends and acquaintances killed by the Indians. Langford wrote in his diary on this, the first day out:

[Langford] . . . *plans for guard duty . . . Hedges is to be my comrade-in-arms . . . We two are to stand guard the first half of this first night — that is, until 1 o'clock to-morrow morning;*

5 To follow this old route today, drive east 8.5 miles from Bozeman, Montana, on U.S. Highway 10, turn south on the Trail Creek cutoff, a gravelled road between U.S. 10 and 89. P.W. Norris called it Trail Creek Pass in his *Annual Report of the Superintendent* for 1877 and 1881.

then Washburn and Hauser take our places. Fresh Indian signs indicate the redskins are lurking near us, and justify the apprehensions experienced in the letter which Hauser and I received from James Stuart, that we will be attacked by the Crow Indians. I am not entirely free from anxiety. Our safety will depend upon our vigilance. We are all well armed with long range repeating rifles and needle guns, though there are but few of our party who are expert at off-hand shooting with a revolver.[6]

James Stuart was an old frontiersman with a Shoshone wife who had been rescued and ransomed by him from hostile Indians who had killed her first mate and had captured her. Her apprehensions probably added to those of Stuart himself.

Langford and Hauser had written Stuart in early August, urging him to join the expedition, even expecting him to captain the civilian group. Stuart had written the following reply:

Deer Lodge City, M.T., Aug 9th, 1870
Dear Sam & Langford:—
Stickney wrote me that the Yellow Stone party had dwindled down to eight persons. That is not enough to stand guard, and I won't go into that country without having a guard every night. From present news it is probable that the Crows will be scattered on all the head waters of the Yellow Stone, and if that is the case, they would not want any better fun than to clean up a party of eight (that does not stand guard) and say that the Sioux did it as they said when they went through us on the Big Horn. It will not be safe to go into that country with less than fifteen men,

[6] Langford, *Discovery,* 64.

and not very safe with that number. I would like it better if it was fight from the start; we would then kill every Crow that we saw and take the chances of their rubbing us out. As it is, we will have to let them alone until they will get the best of us by stealing our horses or killing some of us; then we will be so crippled that we can't do them any damage.

At the commencement of this letter I said I would not go unless the party stood guard. I will take that back, for I am just d----d fool enough to go anywhere that anybody else is willing to go, — only I want it understood that very likely some of us will lose our hair. I will be on hand Sunday evening unless I hear that the trip is postponed.

Fraternally Yours,
JAS. STUART.

Since writing the above, I have received a telegram saying, "twelve of us going certain." Glad to hear it, — the more the better. Will bring two Pack horses and one Pack Saddle.[7]

It is interesting to note that nowhere in his journals does Doane express any apprehension over the Indians, although he writes of caution on August 24. Of course he was a soldier writing an official report which would go through channels, and an officer does not speak of fear even if he feels it. Then, too, Doane had been through battles of the Civil War, had led the destruction of the Piegan band on the Marias only a few months before, and probably felt ready to deal with the Indians, usually Crows he had seen hanging

[7] Ibid., 26.

around the post at Fort Ellis. But it must be remembered that in treating with the Indians he was always a competent professional soldier, unlike many of the impassioned and panicky frontier riflemen. On this first day it was already apparent that Doane would be the most serious and scientific member of the party with his observations.

Langford often noted the lighter side as well as the serious. He tells of some of the horseplay that first night.

[Langford] *In the course of our discussion Jake Smith expressed his doubt whether any member of our party except Hauser (who is an expert pistol shot) is sufficiently skilled in the use of the revolver to hit an Indian at even a close range, and he offered to put the matter to a test by setting up his hat at a distance of twenty yards for the boys to shoot at with their revolvers, without a rest, at twenty-five cents a shot. While several members of our party were blazing away with indifferent success, with the result that Jake was adding to his exchequer without damage to his hat, I could not resist the inclination to quietly drop out of sight behind a clump of bushes where from my place of concealment I sent from my breechloading Ballard repeating rifle four bullets in rapid succession, through the hat, badly riddling it. Jake inquired, 'Whose revolver is it that makes that loud report?' He did not discover the true state of the case, but removed the target with the ready acknowledgment that there were members of our party whose aim with a revolver was more accurate than he had thought. I think that I will make confession to him in a few days. I now wish that I had brought with me an extra hat. My own is not large enough for Jake's head. Notwithstanding the serious problems which we must deal with in making this journey, it is well to have a little amusement while we may.* [8]

---

[8] Ibid., 65.

The journal by Hedges carries only routine details that first day.

[Hedges] *Monday 22. Had a fine bed and sleep, merry company. Didn't wake till morning. All staid together last night for first time. Dog woke me up barking at horses. Smith is disgusted at prospect of standing guard. Were to start at eight. My horse gives me no end of trouble about running away. Didn't get off till eleven. Followed up fork of East Gallatin and struck across a gentle divide on to Trail Creek. Camped about four – made 20 miles, – ahead of packs all the time – little showers – cool – scenery fine – snow in sight across the Yellowstone. W. traded horses before starting. Caught the first trout. Trumbull opened bank and lost. S. put up his hat to shoot at for 25 cents a shot. L. and I stood guard first part of night. I got pretty cold but slept well.* [9]

Early in his article Trumbull names the other members of the party plus

[Trumbull] *two packers and two unbleached American citizens of African descent. Each member of the party was mounted on horse back and there were twelve pack animals . . . At Fort Ellis we were joined by Lieutenant Doane of the Second Cavalry, with a squad of soldiers, well mounted, and armed with needle carbines and revolvers. We citizens carried an assorted armory, consisting of Henry, Ballard, and Spencer rifles, revolvers, and bowie knives. We intended to hunt for all sorts of large game, Indians only excepted. No one desired to find any of them . . . The party camped on Trail Creek. At this place a night watch was established; which was maintained throughout the entire trip in order to keep the Indians from breaking the Eighth Commandment.*

The following day we reached the Yellowstone and camped at Botteller's which is the frontier "rancho" as you ascend that river. During the day the party traveled in detachments. Three

9 Hedges, "Journal," 373.

hunters kept several miles ahead; next, were two skirmishers in front of the main body; and a half-mile farther back, came the main body itself, together with the pack-train. As the skirmishers neared the river they discovered three Crows; not sitting on a tree, but riding in their direction. With keen military sagacity, they . . . rallied on the main body with astonishing rapidity.[10]

[Washburn] *Stood guard. Quite cold . . . Crows (Indians) near.*[11]

Tuesday, August 23, second day. On the 23d we followed the valley of Trail Creek twelve miles, to within sight of the valley of the Yellowstone. Approaching the river, the country became more and more volcanic in appearance, with large masses of trachyte lava cropping out from the high ridges on the right and left. Many of these masses showed a perpendicular front of several hundred feet, with projections resembling towers, castles, and other objects of interest. Several miles away on the right, in the highest range bordering the valley, is Pyramid Mountain, a snow-capped peak, and farther[12] to the southward a long range, also covered with snow. On the left of the valley the foot hills were clothed with beautiful verdure, and the higher summits of the ranges grown up with pine timber. Crossing a low ridge in the afternoon we came in full sight of the Yellowstone valley and stream. The view from this point was extremely grand covering a vista of some thirty miles along the river of the valley of which is here several miles wide, and shut in by volcanic mountains of immense height on the opposite side; these peaks are of a dark lava with ragged summits that stand out in bold relief against the sky. Heavy masses of snow fill the upper ravines in the summertime, feeders of hundreds of

10 Trumbull, "Yellowstone Expedition," 431.
11 Langford, *Discovery*, 64n.
12 Sometimes Doane used the word "farther;" at other times he used "further." The Senate document has just as inconsistently changed it to the opposite spelling many times. Here Doane used "farther" and the Senate document switched it to "further."

springs, which trickle through dense masses of forest on the mountain sides. The valley descends from the foothills in gentle declivities, covered with luxuriant grass, and the channels of numerous streams come down from the ranges above on either side. Descending to the valley we followed up the stream, camping at "Butler Ranch," eight miles above.[13] A few antelope were seen during the day, but no other game. Distance traveled twenty miles. In the afternoon we met several Indians belonging to the Crow agency, thirty miles below.[14]

In the evening a severe rain storm set in lasting with intervals throughout the night, and on the following morning the mountains were covered with newly fallen snow. We remained in camp at Butler's[15] until 12 o'clock on the 24th.

[Langford] *At 8 a.m. to-day we broke camp. Some delay occurred in packing our horses, Lieutenant Doane and the escort went ahead, and we did not see them again until we reached the night camp*

. . . we saw our first Indians as we descended into the valley of the Yellowstone. They came down from the east side of the valley, over the foot hills, to the edge of the plateau overlooking the bottom lands of the river, and there conspicuously displayed themselves for a time to engage our attention. As we passed by them up the valley they moved down to where their ponies were hobbled. Two of our party, Hauser and Stickney, had dropped behind and passed towards the north to get a shot at an antelope; and when they came up they reported that, while we were observing the Indians on the plateau across the river, there were one hundred or more of them watching us

---

[13] Alternate U.S. Highway 89 (built 1960-1) in part follows up the west side of the Yellowstone River just as the old route did.

[14] The old Crow Agency was on the south bank of the Yellowstone River about four miles east of the mouth of Shields River, about ten miles east of Livingston, Montana. The buildings were rude, mostly adobe. It was later abandoned, moved to the junction of Little Rosebud Creek and Rosebud Creek (not Rosebud River which is farther east). See William Ludlow, *Report of a Reconnaissance from Carroll, Montana Territory, on the Upper Missouri, to the Yellowstone National Park, and Return, made in the Summer of 1875*, 57.

[15] The correct spelling is Bottler although various writers, including Doane, have erroneously used other spellings.

*from behind a high butte as our pack-train passed up the valley.
As soon as they observed Hauser and Stickney coming up nearly
behind them, they wheeled their horses and disappeared down
the other side of the butte. This early admonition of our exposure to hostile attack, and liability to be robbed of everything, and compelled on foot and without provisions to retrace
our steps, has been the subject of discussion in our camp to-
night, and has renewed in our party the determination to abate
nothing of our vigilance, and keep in a condition of constant
preparation.*

*With our long-range rifles and plenty of ammunition, we can
stand off 200 or 300 of them, with their less efficient weapons,
if we don't let them sneak up upon us in the night. If we
encounter more than that number, then what? The odds will be
against us that they will "rub us out," as Jim Stuart says.*

*We learn from Mr. Boteler that there are some twenty-five
lodges of Crow Indians up the valley.* [16]

[Hedges, August 23] *Everts taken sick and laid up, eating
corn and berries . . . [I] Had milk and butter for supper. Spent
all the evening in drying clothes . . . Took horn of whiskey and
went to bed and soon was warm as toast.* [17]

[Langford, August 24] *Mr. Everts was not well enough to
accompany us, and it was arranged that he should remain at
Boteler's ranch, and that we would move about twelve miles up
the river and there await his arrival.* [18]

[Langford, August 25] *Mr. Everts came into camp just at
night, nearly recovered, but very tired from his long and tedious
ride over a rugged road, making two days travel in one.* [19]

[16] Langford, *Discovery,* 68.
[17] Hedges, "Journal," 373.
[18] Langford, *Discovery,* 70.
[19] Ibid., 72.

Bottler's ranch, 1871. L to R: unidentified young man, two Bottler brothers, A. C. Peale, Negley. W. H. Jackson photo. *Courtesy Yellowstone National Park.*

MISSION AT BOTTLER'S RANCH
by the editors

Doane was aware that the Crows were watching him as he pushed his small escort ahead of the main Washburn Expedition southward up the Yellowstone River. He and his five men passed the Indians lurking across the river that afternoon. His small force would have been easy prey for the braves of the Crow nation, but Doane boldly trotted his pack train right by them, seemingly without military precaution. He calculated this would lead the older warriors to suspect Doane's group to be only the advance of a larger army force. The Indians would not beat the war drums until they were sure, and by that time he would be far away.

He was hurrying to Bottler's ranch. He did not want an audience when he talked to Frederick Bottler[20] about two missing guns from Fort Ellis.

The story as Doane had heard it was that while Doane and the other officers were away earlier that summer, Bottler had gone over to the fort to play cards with the soldiers. The men had put up two army needle guns and some ammunition in a faro game and Bottler had won them.

Doane knew Bottler by reputation — that he was one of the most determined, resourceful, and courageous characters who had settled beyond the frontier. In 1870 he was the only rancher anywhere on the mighty upper Yellowstone. He was self sufficient. His .place was an oasis in the wilderness for good eating, comfort, and hospitality for every party on its way through this wild, unsettled region.

Doane was thinking how he would confront Bottler about the guns. He was also thinking of the

[20] Frederick Bottler (1843-1914) had come west in 1865 to the Alder Gulch placers at Virginia City and had later gone to the Gallatin River valley near Bozeman, Montana before he moved to the upper Yellowstone River.

ever present danger to Bottler from the Indians. If anything happened to Bottler, the military also would soon be involved.

Arriving at the ranch, he sent his men to unload the packs and tend the camp chores while he went to talk to Bottler.

Neither Doane's journal nor those of the others tell the story of Doane's encounter with Frederick Bottler. It came from Floyd Bottler, son of the frontiersman, ninety years after it happened. Floyd himself was then an old man.[21]

"Dad got word that Doane was coming," Floyd Bottler tells. "Dad had the guns on the wall over the bed an' he says, 'I made up my mind I'd fight before I gave up my guns. Them was good guns and I needed them and I was going to keep them. My other gun was lost in the Gardner River when I nearly drowned in June.'[22]

"So, by golly, Lieutenant Doane came over. Dad asked him in. Dad sat on the bed, and Doane sat in that chair over there, across from the bed.[23]

"Dad said Lieutenant Doane would look at the guns, and then look at him, then look at the guns, then look at him. For a long time neither said anything.

"Then Doane spoke. 'Bottler,' he says, 'I come

[21] Tape recording in O. H. Bonney Collection. Floyd Bottler did not fix the date but since it was Doane's first meeting with Bottler, circumstances would place it on this occasion. Most of the Fort Ellis commanding officers were absent on Indian fighting early in 1870. Floyd Bottler had heard his father tell the story many times.

[22] In June 1870 P. W. Norris and Frederick Bottler had started out to explore the area of present-day Yellowstone Park. Deep snows thwarted their efforts to cross the Madison Range to the geysers there. When descending to the Yellowstone valley below Mammoth Hot Springs, Bottler was swept away crossing the Gardner River, losing his rifle, ammunition, most of his clothing, and nearly his life. That ended their expedition — leaving the honors to Doane and the Washburn party. (Norris, *The Calumet of the Coteau*, 237)

[23] At the time of the tape recording, Floyd pointed to the actual straight back chair in his living room in which Doane had sat. It was one of a set made by his father out of birch wood in 1869. Another one of these chairs is now at Norris Geyser Basin.

over to take them guns from you. They're government property, but,' he says, 'a man living in this country needs those guns. Now you keep them but,' he says, 'when you come around Fort Ellis you keep them guns scabbared and well out of sight or I'll have to take them away from you.' "

Their eyes met again and held for a long moment. Then both men rose and their hands met in a strong clasp. They turned and walked out into the ranch yard. [24]

[24] The site of Bottler's ranch is four miles south of Emigrant Post Office, 33.7 miles south of Livingston, 27.3 miles north of Gardiner, and 33 miles north of Mammoth Hot Springs. It is on the west side of the river and highway. In 1969 there was a white house and a big barn on the location where Frederick Bottler had his home for many years. The old 1870 buildings were about half a mile from here. No remnants of these remain, for a French settler cut up all the old logs for firewood. In 1893 Bottler had a fine modern house, 6,000 head of sheep, and 960 acres of land here.

Doane describes Bottler's ranch further in his journal entry of October 12, 1876, Part III of this book.

The Earl of Dunraven visited the ranch in 1874 and mentioned it with fond memories in his book: "We lay at Bottlers for three days full up to our eyes of hominy, milk, and other products of the dairy and the farm ... what a refreshing wash we had and how we did enjoy our supply of fresh eggs, chicken, cream, butter, and cheese, and plenty of Japan tea." (*Hunting in the Yellowstone*, 300)

Bottler's Ranche • Yellow Stone

Emigrant Gulch

Cabin

Manning's Cr.

CHAPTER 7

BOTTLER'S RANCH TO THE GARDNER RIVER

Yellowstone trout fishing described. Instead of crossing the Yellowstone River, as U.S. Highway 89 now does, the Washburn-Doane party continues south along the west bank, passing through Yankee Jim Canyon, described by Doane. They camp, on August 25, at the junction of the Gardner and Yellowstone Rivers, near what is now Gardiner, Montana.

Wednesday, August 24, third day. Throughout the forenoon it rained occasional showers, but before 12 o'clock the clouds rolled away in heavy masses along the mountain sides, the sun came out, and the atmosphere was clear again. From this point a beautiful view is obtained. The mining camp of Emigrant Gulch, is nearly opposite on a small stream coming down from the mountains on the other side of the river. A few settlements have been made in this immediate vicinity and small herds of cattle range at will over the broad extent of the valley. Our camp was situated at the base of the foot hills, near a small grove from which flowed several large springs of clear water, capable of irrigating the whole bottom in front. The soil here is very fertile and lies favorably for irrigation. Timber is convenient, water everywhere abundant, and the climate for this region remarkably mild. Residents informed me that snow seldom fell in the valley; stock of every kind subsist through the winter without being fed or sheltered. Excepting the Judith basin I have seen no district in the western territories so eligible for settlement as the upper valley of the Yellowstone. Several of the party were very successful during the morning in fishing for trout, of which we afterward had an abundant and continued supply. The Yellowstone here is from fifty to one hundred yards wide, and at the lowest stage, four feet deep on the riffles, running over a bed of drift boulders and gravel, with a very rapid current. The flow of water is fully equal to that of the Missouri at Fort Benton, owing to the rapidity of the current, though the channel is much more narrow.

TROUT FISHING IN THE YELLOWSTONE RIVER

The Yellowstone trout are peculiar, being the largest variety of the genus caught in waters flowing east. Their numbers are perfectly fabulous, but their appetites extremely dainty. One may fish with the finest tackle of eastern sportsmen, when the water appears to be alive with them, all day long, without a bite. Grasshoppers are their peculiar weakness, and using them for bait, the most awkward angler can fill a champagne basket in an hour or two. They do not bite with the spiteful greediness of eastern brook trout, but amount to much more in the way of subsistence when caught. Their flesh is of a bright yellow color on the inside of the body and of a flavor unsurpassed. The barometer stood here 24.20 [25.10]; thermometer, 58° [40°]; elevation, 4,837 feet.[1]

We moved in the afternoon at 2:30 p.m. following the course of the valley, crossing several small streams and numerous dry gulches on the way. After traveling about six miles, we crossed by a difficult pathway a spur of the mountain coming down with a bluff bank on the edge of the stream,[2] beyond which the

[1] The first figures are those which appeared in the manuscript; the figures in brackets were in the Senate printing. This format will be hereafter followed when the figures differ.

A chart, "Meteorological Observations of the Yellowstone Expedition," appeared in the Senate printing of Doane's journal. This chart is reproduced in the Appendix to Part II of this book. Comparison of figures may also be made using this chart.

[2] At this point Alternate U.S. Highway 89 crosses the Yellowstone River. Still visible from the bridge is the old southward trail crossing the mountain spur, as

valley opened out to a bottom of large extent, and great beauty, back of which the foot hills rose up in successive plateaus to the summit range. On the opposite side the steep lava mountains came in close to the stream, their lofty fronts covered with stunted timber, and their summits of naked granite piercing the sky.[3] Several small streams ran in from the right, their banks bordered with wild cherry and cottonwood; the branches of the former broken down in many places by grizzly bears in gathering the fruit. A large portion of the bottom land is subject to overflow by the mountain streams, and bears a crop of grass, in many places waist high. The river is skirted with shrubbery and cedars, the latter having short, thick trunks, too short for ordinary lumber, but yielding most beautiful material for small cabinet work, and of a nature susceptible of an exquisite polish. We followed up this valley [about six miles][4] and camped on the bank of the stream upon a high plateau of drift boulders, and at the opening of an immense cañon, the lower cañon of the Yellowstone.[5] Our mess table was here supplied with antelope, hare, ducks, and grouse killed during the day, together with fish caught *ad libitum* in the afternoon.

Guards were established here during the night, as there were signs of a party of Indians on the trail ahead of us, all the members of the party taking their tours of this duty, using, in addition, the various precautions of lariats, hobbles, &c., not to be neglected while traveling through this country. The night was very clear, and somewhat chilly, a strong wind setting in down the cañon towards morning.

From observations taken at this point it appears that the maximum variation between high and low water mark in the Yellowstone is less than eight feet. Distance 12 miles.

---

described by Doane here, and again in his journal entry for October 16, 1876, Part III of this book.

[3] Emigrant Peak.

[4] Words in brackets in Senate printing but not in Doane manuscript.

[5] This is known today as Yankee Jim Canyon. For fuller story see Part III of this book, Chapter 6, *Wagon Wreck in Yankee Jim Canyon* section and note 19.

This is the only known photograph of the 1870 Yellowstone expedition. Two unidentified members of the party are

YANKEE JIM CANYON

Thursday, August 25, fourth day. Morning of the 25th, barometer 25.00 [25.10]; thermometer, 40°; elevation, 4,837 ft.

Threading our way for a distance of one mile among the enormous granite boulders, we came to the foot of the canon, through which the trail was very narrow, admitting but one animal at a time, and passing over a high spur of the mountain overlooking the river, which at this point is forced in tremendous rapids, surging through a narrow gorge, and over immense boulders in the bed of the stream. The lava walls rise hundreds of feet above this trail, which passes in many places under projecting boulders, holding tenure of their places by a very slight gravitation, and threatening continually a resumption of their journey to the river bed below. Huge masses of trachyte lava, heaped together in every conceivable form obstruct the narrow way, affording refuge in their interstices to numbers of rattlesnakes, which made hostile demonstrations on being disturbed, and remained masters of the situation after we had passed. After scrambling over rocks for a distance of two miles, we came to where the valley opens again slightly, and the trail, leaving the river, passes to the summit of a ridge on the right, where we found at an elevation 1,000 feet above the river a small but beautiful lake. On descending presently from the mountain we again entered the river valley, which was here from one and a half to two miles wide.

The rock formation after passing the narrow gorge was of limestone strata, with superincumbent sandstones and shales; small deposits of gypsum appeared, and over all, drift boulders were scattered, even on the summits of the higher hills; behind these, granite peaks rose up, worn at their bases by drift currents. The soil here lost its fertility, the level lands being covered with a heavy growth of sage brush, and the few streams of water impregnated with alkali. The general trend of the river is to the southeast. About noon we passed a very singular formation on the right,[6] the strata of limestone turned up edge-wise, formed a hill several hundred feet in height, on the face of which the softer portions of the strata having been washed away, caused the more solid limestones to stand out from the hillside in two immense walls, the crests of which were covered with stunted pine trees. Near these a dark stratum of coal was visible, also a red stratum reported to be cinnabar, which we did not, however examine.[7] From this point to the mouth of Gardiners River, a distance of twelve miles, the valley was full of original drift. The boulders were of Quincy granite, and wherever found were worn off smooth as if by the action of water. The ground rose rapidly as we proceeded, passing from a dead level alkali plain to a succession of plateaus covered slightly with a sterile soil through which the limestones cropped out constantly.

In many places, deep ravines were worn down in the strata by the waters from the melting snow, numerous springs were seen, far up on the mountain sides, but their waters sank among the arid foot hills without reaching the river.

This desert region enclosed by mountains clothed with verdure, and on the banks of a large stream, is one of the anomalies common in the West, where the presence of lime-stone or sandstone in horizontal strata, especially, almost always means want of water, and consequent desolation.

We camped at the mouth of Gardiners river,[8] a large stream

[6] Langford noted passing a singular formation which they named Devil's Slide. (*Discovery,* 14)

[7] Both Cinnabar Mountain and the former pioneer hamlet of Cinnabar take their name from the bright red, mercuric sulphide ore which was thought to be in the nearby Devil's Slide, but proven later to be only colored stone.

[8] Should be spelled Gardner River, according to modern U.S. Geological Survey rules. However, to be historically accurate, one could follow usage of the early trappers and settlers who, as with similar geographical designations (e.g., Jackson's Hole), called it Gardner's River, *with* the apostrophe.

Gardner River flows into the Yellowstone River just south of the North Entrance to Yellowstone Park. Yellowstone is the oldest name in the Park, but Gardner is the next oldest, dating back to 1832 when free trader Johnson Gardner trapped at Fort Union for the American Fur Company. The name of the town of Gardiner, Montana, is a corruption of Gardner. There are rumors but no records anywhere of a Jim Gardiner. A. L. Haines, Yellowstone Park historian, thinks this name developed from Jim "on the Gardner" McCartney, who was compelled to move outside the Park

coming in through a deep and gloomy cañon from the south. This was our first poor camping place, grass being very scarce, and the slopes of the range covered entirely with sage brush. From this camp was seen the smoke of fires on the mountains in front, while Indian signs became more numerous and distinct.

Many prospect holes of miners were passed during the day, and several abandoned camps of the previous year.

The river at this point shrinks to half its usual size lost among the boulders of the drift; immense masses of which choke up the stream in many places, forming alternate pools and rapids, which afforded great delight to the fishermen of our party. Some of the huge masses of granite in the bed of the stream are hollowed out by the action of the water into many singular forms.

We here found numerous specimens of petrified wood, but no traces of fossils, except in the solid limestone of the higher ledges. Two or three miles above, and on the opposite side of the Yellowstone from this point, is the mouth of Bear Gulch, an almost inaccessible mining district not being worked at present but said to yield well during the season of operations. Distance 18 miles.

> Langford's diary is relevant here to illustrate the differences in the interests and attitudes of the two men — Langford and Doane. Above, Doane concentrates on the natural phenomena, while Langford takes time out to make a few human interest observations, such as, on August 23:

[Langford] *Jake Smith has sent the first demoralizing shot into the camp by announcing that he doesn't think there is any necessity for standing guard. Jake is the only one of our party*

boundaries after the boundary survey was made.

When at this point (now Gardiner), the 1870 expedition was within five miles of Mammoth Hot Springs, but by keeping close to the Yellowstone they missed this wonder which was discovered by Hayden the following year. Dr. Ferdinand V. Hayden (1829-1887) led U.S. Geological Survey expeditions through the Park in 1871, 1872, and 1878.

*who shows some sign of baldness, and he probably thinks that
his own scalp is not worth the taking by the Indians.*

*Did we act wisely in permitting him to join our party at the
last moment before leaving Helena? One careless man, no less
than one who is easily discouraged by difficulties, will frequently demoralize an entire company. I think we have now
taken all possible precautions for our safety, but our numbers
are few; and for me to say that I am not in hourly dread of the
Indians when they appear in large force, would be a braggart
boast. . .*[9]

*August 25. — . . . Jake Smith stood guard last night, or ought
to have done so, and but for the fact that Gillette was also on
guard, I should not have had an undisturbed sleep. We know
that the Indians are near us, and sleep is more refreshing to me
when I feel assured that I will not be joined in my slumbers by
those who are assigned for watchful guard duty.*"[10]

Langford also gives us a clue to the general campfire
conversations and pasttimes:

[Langford] *As I write, General Washburn, Hedges and Hauser
are engaged in an animated discussion of the differences between France and Germany, and the probabilities of the outcome of the war. The three gentlemen are not agreed in deter-
mining where the responsibility for the trouble lies, and I fear
that I will have to check their profanity. However, neither
Washburn nor Hedges swears. . .*[11]

[9] Langford, *Discovery*, 69.
[10] Ibid., 72.
[11] Ibid., 71.
This was the period of the Emperor Louis Napoleon III of France, Bismarck of
Prussia, and the Franco-Prussian War of 1870-71. The French had moved out August
1, and the hardest battles of the war were fought before the Washburn-Doane party
left Fort Ellis on August 22. The central act in the tragedy of the French began on
August 19 with the investment of the French army under Marshal Bazaine at Metz.
There were other discussions among the members of the Washburn-Doane Expedition about the war; for example, Hedges says on September 22, "Had quite a
confab with General about comparative fighting qualities of French and English,"
and on September 25 Hedges says that he went over to Bannack George's "cabin and
got later paper and learned for first time that Napoleon was a prisoner and republic

Langford's feeling about Jake Smith, expressed in his diary, was shared by other party members. This sketch is one Trumbull made during the expedition.

This woodcut, modeled on Trumbull's drawing, was done by a New York artist and used to illustrate Langford's second *Scribner's* article, June 1871; the illustration was captioned "Jake Smith guarding the camp from hostile Indian attack. 'Requiescat in pace.' "

[And three evenings later] *as we have been writing, there has been a lively game of cards played near my left side, which Hedges, who has just closed his diary, says is a game of poker. I doubt if Deacon Hedges is sufficiently posted in the game to know to a certainty that poker is the game which is being played; but, putting what Hedges tells me with what I see and hear, I find that these infatuated players have put a valuation of five (5) cents per bean, on beans that did not cost more than $1 a quart in Helena, and Jake Smith exhibits a marvelous lack of veneration for his kinswoman, by referring to each bean, as he places it before him upon the table, as his "aunt," or, more flippantly, his "auntie." Walter Trumbull has been styled the "Banker," and he says that at the commencement of the game he sold forty of these beans to each of the players, himself included (200 in all), at five (5) cents each, and that he has already redeemed the entire 200 at that rate; and now Jake Smith has a half-pint cup nearly full of beans, and is demanding of Trumbull that he redeem them also; that is, pay five (5) cents per bean for the contents of the cup. Trumbull objects. Jake persists. Reflecting upon their disagreement I recall that about an hour ago Jake, with an apologetic "Excuse me!" disturbed me while I was writing and untied the bean sack on which I am now sitting, and took from it a double handful of beans.*

It seems to me that a game of cards which admits of such latitude as this, with a practically unlimited draft upon outside resources, is hardly fair to all parties, and especially to "The Banker."[12]

[Hedges] *Caught three fish — very tired — took some whiskey and felt better . . . The last of my box of cigars went to-night. I went to bed early to be ready for second watch. We*

proclaimed in France."

Langford says on September 27: "About noon I met a horseman who had left Virginia City this morning . . . He paused long enough to let me scan a newspaper which he had, from which I learned of the capitulation of the French at Sedan." (*Discovery*, 182) Sedan capitulated and Napoleon III was taken prisoner September 2, 1870.

[12] Langford, *Discovery*, 76.

had nice bed on river sand, the dashing waters and winds in cedar tops made music, the stars shone brilliant, temperature moderate. It would be hard to fix a better bed for a tired man. Got mad at my horse to-day and struck him with fish pole.[13]

[13] Hedges, "Journal," 374.

CHAPTER 8

GARDINER TO TOWER FALLS

After fording the Gardner River the party enters the area later known as Yellowstone National Park and follows the great Bannock Trail along the northern heights of Mount Everts, midway between the Yellowstone River (north) and the Grand Loop Road (south of Mount Everts). The Trail crosses Blacktail Deer Plateau slightly farther to the north than the Grand Loop Road now does. Camp is made near Tower Falls. August 27 and 28 are spent exploring the area.

THE TRAIL ACROSS MOUNT EVERTS

Friday, August 26, fifth day. Morning — Barometer, 24.80; thermometer, 49°; elevation, 5,215 feet. Noon — Barometer, 23.10; thermometer, 72°; elevation, 7,331 feet. We left camp at 11 o'clock a.m., and crossed Gardiners river which at this point is a mountain torrent about twenty yards wide and three feet in depth. We kept the Yellowstone to our left, and finding the cañon impassable, passed over several high spurs coming down from the mountains, over which the way was much obstructed by falling timber; and reached, at an elevation of 7,331 feet, an immense rolling plateau extending as far as the eye could reach.[1] This elevated scope of country is about thirty miles in

[1] The route followed traverses the back of Mount Everts. It is now part of the horse trail system of the Park, was part of the Great Indian Trail, its once deeply worn lodge-pole ruts still evident in places. A readily accessible spot to see these ruts is found by crossing the Gardner River on a footbridge 1.15 miles south of Gardiner's stone arch, four miles north of Mammoth Hot Springs. At the top of the hill above

extent, with a general declivity to the northward. Its surface is an undulated prairie dotted with groves of pine and aspen. Numerous lakes are scattered throughout its whole extent, and great numbers of springs, which flow down the slopes and are lost in the volume of the Yellowstone.

THE BLACK CANYON OF THE YELLOWSTONE

The river breaks through this plateau in a winding and impassable cañon of trachyte lava over 2,000 feet in depth; the middle cañon of the Yellowstone, rolling over volcanic boulders in some places, and in others forming still pools of seemingly fathomless depth.[2]

At one point it dashes here and there, lashed to a white foam upon its rocky bed, at another it subsides into a crystal mirror, wherever a deep basin occurs in the channel. Numerous small cascades are seen tumbling from the rocky walls at different points, and the river appears from the lofty summits a mere ribbon of foam in the immeasurable distance below.

This huge abyss through the walls of flinty lava, has not been worn away by the waters, for no trace of fluvial agency is left upon the rocks; it is a cleft in the strata brought about by volcanic action, plainly shown by that irregular structure which gives such a ragged appearance to all such igneous formations.

Standing on the brink of the chasm, the heavy roaring of the imprisoned river comes to the ear only in a sort of hollow hungry growl, scarcely audible from the depths, and strongly suggestive of demons in torment below. Lofty pines on the bank of the stream "dwindle to shrubs in dizziness of distance." Everything beneath has a weird and deceptive appearance. The water does not look like water, but like oil. Numerous fish-hawks are seen busily plying their vocation, sailing high above

the footbridge, one hundred feet north of the Park register box, the old line of travel is seen. The original Bannock Trail was partly erased here by the heavy use of the wagons to Cooke City, but obsidian chippings are still found.

[2] The middle canyon is now known as Black Canyon. It was the "Third Canyon" of Hayden Surveys. It can be seen only by foot travel.

the waters and yet a thousand feet below the spectator.

In the clefts of the rocks down, hundreds of feet down, bald eagles have their eyries, from which we can see them swooping still farther into the depths to rob the ospreys of their hard-earned trout.

It is grand, gloomy, and terrible; a solitude peopled with fantastic ideas, an empire of shadows and of turmoil.

MOUNT EVERTS PLATEAU

The great plateau had been recently burned off to drive away the game, and the woods were still on fire in every direction. In the morning I had ridden forward on the trail, hoping to find a passage through the canon and after having endeavored to descend its precipitous banks in several places without success, I had climbed to the summit of the plateau, and followed the trail of two hunters who had camped with us on the previous night and were gone in advance after game. Mr. Everts and Private Williamson accompanied me; the latter killed an antelope on the trail immediately after reaching the summit, which we left as an indication to the party following. Our course led along the great plateau about three miles to the right of the cañon, toward which the ground fell off with a slight declivity.

Passing over the high rolling prairie for several miles, we struck at length a heavy Indian trail leading up the river, and finding a small colt abandoned on the range, we knew they were but a short distance ahead of us. The plateau formation is of lava in horizontal layers as it cooled in a surface flow; these are upheaved in places by a subterraneous action into wave like undulations, and occasionally granite shafts protrude through the strata, forming land marks at once permanent, and generally of picturesque form. They resemble dark icebergs stranded in an ocean of green rising high above the tops of the trees in wooded districts or standing out grim, and solid, on the grassy expanse of the prairie land.

On the lower verge of this plateau we bade farewell to drift, its altitude being far above the line of operations of the ice period. I noticed that the grass in many places was here too green to burn, though already parched in the lower valleys we had already traversed, and that many flowers were just in bloom.

It was still early summer in this elevated region, far above the perpetual snow line of the mountains on the Gallatin.

TOWER JUNCTION

In the afternoon the trail led us through a deep cañon to the south, which opened out on a small valley at the confluence of the East Fork of the Yellowstone.[3]

The main stream here turns to the southwest, the branch coming in through a deep rocky valley, in a course due east. The opening formed at the junction of the two streams is probably three miles in diameter, and of nearly circular shape. The mountains on the opposite side, and towards the head of the East Fork, are composed wholly of lava, heaped up in every imaginable form. In the center of the valley rises a table mountain, perpendicular on its sides, and capped with a horizontal stratum of trap rock about fifty feet in depth. Standing isolated in the surrounding level valley, and between the channels of the two streams, it has a very singular and remarkable appearance.[4]

The channel of the Yellowstone where it enters this valley cuts to the depth of three hundred feet through a bed of gypsum, overlaid by a stratum of trap, the columns of which show great perfection of chrystalization.

The valley itself abounds in springs, small lakes, and marshes. The slopes and ravines to the right and beyond the Yellowstone are heavily timbered with pine, affording a strong contrast to the bare rocks on the opposite side of East Fork.

Descending from the plateau through a steep ravine into the

[3] Now called Lamar River, named for Secretary of the Interior L. Q. C. Lamar.
[4] Junction Butte.

valley, and skirting for a distance of two miles a swampy flat, we came to the first warm spring found on the route. This spring is on the right of the trail and of small size, temperature milk warm, and is highly impregnated with sulphur.

Passing thence, the trail leads over a spur of the mountain coming in from the right, and through a deep ravine, crossing Warm Spring Creek,[5] where we camped for the night in company with the two hunters afore mentioned. The remainder of the party did not arrive until the next day. We passed a mile before going into camp near a small lake, the "wickey ups" of fifteen lodges of Crows, the Indians whose trails we had been following across the plateau. Distance traveled 18 miles.

> From this and other comments by Doane, obviously the party was not always together, and this sometimes accounts for a different perspective. Langford gives his version of the trip across Mount Everts on August 26:

[Langford] *In the morning Lieutenant Doane and one of his men, together with Mr. Everts, had started out ahead of the party to search out the best trail. At 3 o'clock p.m. we arrived at Antelope creek, only six miles from our morning camp, where we concluded to halt. On the trail which we were following there were no tracks except those of unshod ponies; and, as our horses were all shod, it was evident that Lieutenant Doane and the advance party had descended the mountain by some other trail than that which we were following. Neither were there any marks of dragging lodge poles. There are seemingly two trails across the mountain, — a circuitous one by as easy a grade as can be found, over which the Indians send their families with their heavily laden pack horses; and a more direct, though more difficult, route which the war parties use in making their rapid rides. This last is the one we have taken, and the advance party has doubtless taken the other.*

Our camp to-night is on Antelope creek, about five miles

5 Tower Creek.

from the Yellowstone river. After our arrival in camp, in company with Stickney and Gillette, I made a scout of eight or ten miles through the country east of our trail, and between it and the river, in search of some sign of Lieutenant Doane, but we found no trace of him. Parting from Stickney and Gillette, I followed down the stream through a narrow gorge by a game trail, hoping if I could reach the Yellowstone, to find a good trail along its banks up to the foot of the Grand cañon; but I found the route impracticable for the passage of our pack train. After supper Mr. Hauser and I went out in search of our other party, and found the tracks of their horses, which we followed about four miles to the brow of a mountain overlooking the country for miles in advance of us. Here we remained an hour, firing our guns as a signal, and carefully scanning the whole country with our field glasses. We could discern the trail for many miles on its tortuous course, but could see no sign of a camp, or of horses feeding, and we returned to our camp.

Saturday, August 27. – Lieutenant Doane and those who were with him did not return to camp last night ... We left camp about 9 o'clock, the pack train following about 11 o'clock, and soon struck the trail of Lieutenant Doane, which proved to be the route traveled by the Indians. The marks of their lodge poles were plainly visible.[6]

[Trumbull] *In the evening we camped on a clear mountain stream, not more than ten miles from our previous camp ... Two of the party, who went ahead, missed the camp, and were out overnight, although every endeavor was made to find them. They, however, got along well, by building a shelter of pine boughs, in front of which they made a large fire.*

By the brook-side we found a number of prospect-holes, and some blazed trees, showing that enterprising miners had preceded us. A gentleman got a pan of dirt from one of the holes, and succeeded in panning out two nuggets, evidently from different gulches, their combined value being about $8.[7]

6 Langford, *Discovery*, 73.
7 Trumbull, "Yellowstone Expedition," 433.

CAMP ON TOWER CREEK NEAR THE FALLS

Saturday, August 27, sixth day. Barometer, 23.70; thermometer, morning, 46°; elevation, 6,546 feet. We remained in camp at Hot Spring Creek[8] awaiting the arrival of the rest of the party. In the morning I rode down to the confluence of the two rivers, and found the East Fork to be a smaller stream than Gardiners river. This valley showed evidence of diminished volcanic action, calcareous mounds being frequently seen, which had originated in the action of hot springs, the waters of which had now ceased to flow.

The valley was full of drift, and numerous prospect holes indicated the enterprise of the miners in penetrating these unknown regions so far.

At the mouth of Hot Spring Creek we found a system of sulphurous and mineral springs, distributed for a distance of two miles in the bottom of the deep cañon through which the river runs. These springs were invariably small, several of them having the temperature at the boiling point; many of them were highly sulphurous, having in fact more sulphur than they could carry in solution, and depositing it in yellowish beds along their courses.

Several of them were impregnated with iron, alum, and other substances. The sulphurous fumes could be detected at the distance of half a mile.

The gypsum walls of the canon were very remarkable, the excess of sulphur in the combination over the proportion of limestone giving a brilliant yellow color to the rocks in many places. The formation was usually very friable, falling with a natural slope to the edge of the stream, but occasionally masses of a more solid nature projected from the wall in curious shapes of towers, minarets, &c., while above, and over all the solid ledge of trap, with its dark and well defined columns made a rich and beautiful border enclosing the pictured rocks below.

Standing on the margin of the stream a few hundred yards further down, is Column Rock, a huge pile of alternate layers of

[8] Tower Creek.

basalt, and amygdaloid cement, several hundred feet in height, surmounted by a pinnacle of trap the columns of which are exactly perpendicular and of a perfect outline.[9]

The great curiosity of the locality however is the Tower Fall, of Hot Spring Creek, where that stream is precipitated in one unbroken body from an amygdaloid ledge a sheer descent of 115 feet, into a deep gorge, joining the Yellowstone a few hundred yards below.[10]

At the crest of the Fall, the stream has cut its way through the amygdaloid ledge, leaving tall spires of rock, from fifty to hundred feet in height, and worn in every conceivable shape. These are very friable, crumbling under slight pressure; several of them stand like sentinels on the very brink of the fall.[11] A view from the summit of one of these spires is exceedingly beautiful; the clear, icy stream plunges from a brink a hundred feet beneath, to the bottom of the chasm over two hundred feet below, and thence rushes through the narrow gorge, tumbling over boulders and tree trunks fallen in the channel. The sides of the chasm are worn away into caverns lined with variously tinted mosses, nourished by clouds of spray which rise from the cataract, while above, and to the left, a spur from the great plateau rises over all, with a perpendicular front of four hundred feet. The falls are accessible either at the brink, or foot, and fine views can be obtained from either side of the cañon. In appearance they strongly resemble those of the Minnehaha, but are several times as high, and run at least eight times the volume of water.[12] In the basin we found a large petrified log imbedded in the débris. Nothing can be more

[9] Now called The Needle, this 260-foot spire of volcanic breccia is seen below the highway 0.8 mile north of Tower Falls, near the west wall of the canyon.

[10] Hauser triangulated the height of Tower Falls as 110 feet; Stickney ventured to the verge of the fall, and, with a stone attached to a strong cord, measured its height as 105 feet. A Yellowstone Park pamphlet gives it as 132 feet.

[11] Langford describes one of these grotesque towers as The Devil's Hoof, a fifty foot rock with a supposed similarity to the proverbial foot of his Satanic majesty. This eroded pinnacle may be seen through the timber on the east side of Tower Creek, just north of Tower Creek crossing, 0.5 mile north of Tower Falls parking area. One is impressed by the honors given the devil for the Yellowstone Park region.

[12] Minnehaha Falls in today's Minnehaha Park of Minneapolis, Minnesota, are sixty feet high, and are world famous through Longfellow's "Hiawatha."

Tower Falls. A Thomas Moran woodcut done before he had been to
Yellowstone; used to illustrate Langford's first *Scribner's* article, May
1871.

Tower Falls, 1871. W. H. Jackson photo. *Courtesy U.S.G.S.*

Tower Falls. A Thomas Moran watercolor, 1872. *Courtesy Thomas Gilcrease Institute, Tulsa, Oklahoma.*

chastely beautiful than this lovely cascade, hidden away in the dim light of overshadowing rocks and woods, its very voice hushed to a low murmur unheard at the distance of a few hundred yards. Thousands might pass by within a half mile and not dream of its existence, but once seen, it passes to the list of most pleasant memories. In the afternoon the remainder of the party arrived, having lost the trail on the previous day.

Here again one may contrast Doane's concentration on a description of Tower Falls in the preceding paragraphs with Langford's portrayal of the more human element:

[Langford] *It is proper at this point to interpolate an account of the circumstances under which the name "Tower" was bestowed upon the creek and fall.*

At the outset of our journey we had agreed that we would not give to any object of interest which we might discover the name of any of our party nor of our friends. This rule was to be religiously observed. While in camp on Sunday, August 28th, on the bank of this creek, it was suggested that we select a name for the creek and fall. Walter Trumbull suggested "Minaret Creek" and "Minaret Fall." Mr. Hauser suggested "Tower Creek" and "Tower Fall." After some discussion a vote was taken, and by a small majority the name "Minaret" was decided upon. During the following evening Mr. Hauser stated with great seriousness that we had violated the agreement made relative to naming objects for our friends. He said that the well known Southern family — the Rhetts — lived in St. Louis, and that they had a most charming and accomplished daughter named "Minnie." He said that this daughter was a sweetheart of Trumbull, who had proposed the name — her name — "Minnie Rhett" — and that we had unwittingly given to the fall and creek the name of this sweetheart of Mr. Trumbull. Mr. Trumbull indignantly denied the truth of Hauser's statement, and Hauser as determinedly insisted that it was the truth, and the vote was therefore reconsidered, and by a substantial majority it was decided to substitute the name "Tower" for "Minaret." Later, and when it was too late to recall or reverse the action of our party, it was surmised that Hauser himself had a sweetheart in St. Louis, a Miss Tower. Some of our party, Walter Trumbull especially, always insisted that such was the case. The weight of testimony was so evenly balanced that I shall hesitate long before I believe either side of this part of the story. [13]

[Trumbull] *It was decided to be in bad taste to name prominent objects after members of the expedition.* [14]

Trumbull then goes on to tell the same story as Langford about the naming of Tower Falls. It is of interest to note, however, that the party did name Mount Washburn, Mount Langford, Mount Doane, and Mount Everts after members of the party.

Sunday, August 28, was almost a day of leisure at Tower Falls which they called "Camp Comfort." For breakfast Hedges tells that they had:

[Hedges] *fish and venison, brown bread, biscuit, and butter, tea and coffee. Large party of us went down to explore and measure the falls . . . Returned to camp and found nearly all playing cards, read the Republican and then, as there was no prospect of moving camp I returned on our trail to Prospect Point, about one thousand feet above the river . . . here I sit on the brink writing these lines.* [He then describes the view.] *Read Harper in the evening most of the company playing cards.* "[15]

Langford says that Washburn rode out during the day to make a reconnaissance and returned at 3 o'clock; he had been to the top of Mount Washburn and had seen Yellowstone Lake.

[13] Langford, *Discovery*, 79n.
[14] Trumbull, "Yellowstone Expedition," 433.
[15] Hedges, "Journal", 277.

Langford also mentions that "Booby," the dog, was painfully suffering from sore feet and that they were trying to devise some sort of moccasins for him. Over a week later Langford reports some progress: Booby is

[Langford] *taking more kindly, day by day, to the buckskin moccasins which "Newt" made and tied on his feet a few days ago. When he was first shod with them he rebelled and tore them off with his teeth, but I think he has discovered that they lessen his sufferings.* [16]

THE BANNOCK TRAIL

Sunday, August 28, seventh day. We remained in camp, visiting the different localities of interest in the neighborhood. The Indians we had been following crossed the river a short distance above the mouth of Hot Spring Creek on what is known as the Bannock Trail, leading from the headwaters of the Snake river, around by the way of the headwaters of the Madison and Gallatin rivers and through this district to the great buffalo range between here and the Missouri. [17] The two hunters previously spoken of followed this trail across the range to the head of Rose Bud Creek. They found on the headwaters of the East Fork, the skeletons of two hunters murdered by the Indians two years ago. [18] They also report the existence of

[16] Langford, *Discovery*, 80, 134.

[17] Langford locates the trail of the Indians ". . . off to the left, to the brink of the Yellowstone, which it follows up about three-fourths of a mile, and then crosses to the east side." (*Discovery*, 81)

[18] One of these skeletons was Jack Crandall. The stream where he was murdered is known as Crandall Creek to this day. E. S. Topping says Jim Gourley and Bill Cameron were the two hunters (mentioned by Doane) who found them. He says Finley was the other murdered prospector. (*Chronicles of the Yellowstone,* 76) P. W. Norris says his name was Adams. (*Annual Report* for 1880)

Three other members of Crandall's party escaped. Losing their horses and camp outfit they made a long, nightmarish retreat to the old Crow Agency; they brought back the first knowledge of the Clark's Fork mining region. Topping gives the names of the three as Arch Graham, Bob Anderson, and Jim Lee; Norris correctly says that Adam Miller was one of them. The story had gained considerable alteration and

numerous hot springs, geysers, jets of steam issuing from the rocks, and other curiosities at different points about the sources of that stream. They report the country beyond the range at a distance of seventy miles, to fall off to a rolling prairie, black with buffalo as far as the eye can reach. They found strong indications of gold on the head of Rosebud, but were deterred from prospecting by fear of the Sioux.

DOANE'S THUMB SERIOUSLY INFECTED

Since leaving Fort Ellis, I had suffered considerably with a pain in the thumb of my right hand, which was now increased to such an extent as to amount to absolute torture. I had it lanced here three times to the bone, with a very dull pocket knife, in the hope of relief, which however did not come. It proved a felon of the most malignant class, and was destined to subject me to infernal agonies. I passed the night walking in front of the camp-fire, with a wet bandage around my arm to keep down the pain.[19]

---

embellishment by the time it was published in the *Park County News* (Livingston, Montana), November 23, 1923.

[19] Langford reported on August 28: "It ought to be opened, but he is unwilling to submit to a thorough operation." (*Discovery*, 81) Hedges wrote on August 27: "Lieut. had a felon on his thumb cut by Langford;" on August 28: "Langford opened felon for Lieut;" and on August 31: "Lieut. D. in pain all night. Langford and Washburn up all night with him." ("Journal," 377)

Great Plat...

Hot Spring Cr

Hot Springs

Mt Washburn

Gr Cañon

...nell Cr

Hot Spring

...hill
Great Falls mile

...t...ell Cr

Ot... Cr

Ala... Cr

Tient Pass

N

Grater Hills
& Springs

Mud Volca...
& Springs

CHAPTER 9

TOWER FALLS TO YELLOWSTONE CANYON

The party follows the high ridges, almost along today's modern highway from Tower Falls to the summit of Mount Washburn. Doane
describes the view from Mount Washburn. On the evening of the
twenty-ninth, Doane, Washburn, and Hedges go down Sulphur Creek,
visit Washburn Springs, and have their first view of the Grand Canyon
of the Yellowstone. On August 30 the party descends Cascade Creek,
camps above the Falls of the Yellowstone. Next day the group explores
the Falls.

Monday, August 29, eighth day. We broke camp about 8
o'clock and for a distance of six miles climbed the divide separating Warm Spring Creek from the Yellowstone, skirting along
the cañon of the former stream. The ground for that distance
rises very rapidly and is much broken by creek beds running
parallel with the river.[1]

Following the highest ridges we presently came to a point
from whence could be overlooked the grand cañon, cleaving the
slopes, and breaking through the lofty mountain ranges, directly
in front. Its perpendicular sides wherever visible of the yellow
sulphuric tint above described, and its crest on either side of the
river, mantled with heavy timber, extending beyond in an unbroken forest as far as the eye could reach.

---

[1] Although the pack train went along the east flank of Mount Washburn, several
members of the party took a side trip to its summit.

This, the upper cañon of the Yellowstone, is about twenty miles in length, extending to the foot of the great falls, is impassable throughout its whole extent, and only accessible to the water's edge at a few points and by dint of severe labor.

Through the mountain gap formed by the cañon, and on the interior slopes some twenty miles distant[2] an object now appeared, which drew a simultaneous expression of wonder from every one in the party.

A column of steam, rising from the dense woods to the height of several hundred feet, became distinctly visible. We had all heard fabulous stories of this region and were somewhat skeptical as to appearances. At first it was pronounced a fire in the woods, but presently someone noticed that the vapor rose in regular puffs, and as if expelled with a great force. Then conviction was forced upon us. It was indeed a great column of steam, puffing away on the lofty mountain side, escaping with a roaring sound, audible at a long distance even through the heavy forest.

A hearty cheer rang out at this discovery and we pressed onward with renewed enthusiasm.

Following the ridge leading to the peak nearest the cañon, and the highest of the range, we were soon at its base; then making a detour to the right[,][3] crossing several ugly ravines, and through a gap in the ridge we passed over the "Elephants Back"[4] and entered the great basin of the Yellowstone lake.

Observations were taken from the summit of the peak, which we named Mount Washburn.[5] Noon, barometer, 20.80; ther-

---

[2] The distance is evidently a misprint, as pointed out by Chittenden (*Yellowstone National Park,* 1964 ed., 70), because Doane later writes that the party heard the roaring sound of the steam, impossible if the distance were twenty miles.

[3] Bracketed punctuation, wherever indicated, was in the Senate document but not in Doane's original manuscript, and is needed.

[4] Elephant's Back is now called Washburn Range. This is not to be confused with the present-day Elephant Back Mountain just west of Lake Junction, and which was named by Hayden in 1871. The name appears on Raynold's map, 1860.

[5] In the early years of the Park one traveler reported that the summit of this much visited mountain had a profusion of old card holders, peach and sardine cans, crammed with names of all visitors, from cabinet officers on down. Earliest date was that of the Washburn-Doane party of 1870.

Langford reported an elevation of 9,800 feet with his aneroid barometer. Latest

Atop Mount Washburn with the Hayden Survey, 1871. Unidentified
packer with Jackson's photographic outfit on mule. W. H. Jackson photo.
Courtesy U.S.G.S.

mometer, 50°; elevation, 9,966 feet.

THE VIEW FROM MOUNT WASHBURN

The view from the summit is beyond all adequate description. Looking northward from the base of the mountain, the great plateau stretches away to the front and left with its innumerable groves and sparkling waters, a variegated landscape of surpassing beauty, bounded on its extreme verge by the cañons of the Yellowstone. The pure atmosphere of this lofty region causes every outline of tree, rock, or lakelet to be visible with wonderful distinctness, and objects twenty miles away appear as if very near at hand.

Still further to the left, the snowy ranges on the headwaters of Gardiners river stretch away to the westward,[6] joining those on the head of the Gallatin, and forming, with the Elephants back a continuous chain, bending constantly to the south; the rim of the Yellowstone Basin.

On the verge of the horizon appear like mole hills in the distance, and far below, the white summits above the Gallatin Valley. These never thaw during the summer months though several thousand feet lower than where we now stand upon the bare granite, and with no snow visible, near, save in the depths of shaded ravines.[7]

Beyond the plateau to the right front, is the deep valley of the East Fork, bearing away eastward, and still beyond ragged volcanic peaks, heaped in inextricable confusion, as far as the limit of vision extends.[8]

On the east, close beneath our feet yawns the immense gulf of the Grand Cañon, cutting away the bases of two mountains in forcing a passage through the range. Its yellow walls divide the landscape nearly in a straight line to the junction of Warm Spring Creek below. The ragged edges of the chasm are from

topographic map elevation is 10,243 feet.

[6] The Gallatin Range.

[7] What Doane is trying to say is that there is no snow on the summit of Mount Washburn at this time of year except in the shaded ravines.

[8] The Absaroka Range.

two hundred to five hundred yards apart, its depth so profound that the river bed is no where visible. No sound reaches the ear from the bottom of the abyss; the sun's rays are reflected on the further wall and then lost in the darkness below. The mind struggles and then falls back upon itself despairing in the effort to grasp by a single thought the idea of its immensity. Beyond, a gentle declivity, sloping from the summit of the broken range extends to the limit of vision, a wilderness of unbroken pine forest.

Turning southward a new and strange scene bursts upon the view. Filling the whole field of vision, and with its boundaries in the verge of the horizon, lies the great volcanic basin of the Yellowstone; nearly circular in form, from fifty to seventy-five miles in diameter, and with a general depression of about two thousand feet below the summits of the great ranges which forms its outer rim. Mount Washburn lies in the point of the circumference northeast from the center of the basin. Far away in the southwest the three great Tetons[9] on Snake River fill another space in the circle, and connecting these two points are crescent ranges, one westward and south[10] past the Gardiner's River and Gallatin, bounding the lower Madison and thence to the Jefferson, and by the Snake river range to the Tetons. [11]

[9] Langford says, "Some member of our party has asked what is the meaning of the word 'Teton' given to these mountains. Lieutenant Doane says it is a French word signifying 'Woman's Breast,' and that it was given to these mountains by the early French explorers, because of their peculiar shape. I think that the man who gave them this name must have seen them from a great distance; for as we approach them, the graceful curvilinear lines which obtained for them this delicate appellation appear angular and ragged. From our present point of view the name seems a misnomer." (*Discovery*, 113)

Such misnaming has often been a puzzle even down to our own present day until the editors researched the matter. Alexander Ross seems to be the first to have used the name *Trois Tetons,* applying it to the cratered buttes known in modern times as the Twin Buttes and Big Southern Butte in Idaho near Craters of the Moon National Monument. Their shape more resembles the female breast. Some time after 1824 the name became transposed, probably by Peter Skeen Ogden in 1825, to what we know today as the Teton peaks, since both geographical features were in the region of the "Upper Snake River" and the peaks were more prominent. (Bonney, *Guide to Wyoming Mountains,* 217)

It is interesting to note here the knowledge Doane had acquired.

[10] Madison Plateau.

[11] Not today's Snake River Range which is south of the Teton Range and Teton

Another eastward and south, a continuous range by the head of Rosebud, enclosing the source of the Snake, and joining the Tetons beyond.

Between the south and west points this vast circle is broken through in many places for the passage of the rivers; but a single glance at the interior slopes of the ranges, shows that a former complete connection existed, and that the great basin has been formerly one vast crater of a now extinct volcano.

The nature of the rocks, the steepness and outline of the interior walls, together with other peculiarities to be mentioned hereafter, render this conclusion a certainty.

The lowest point in this great amphitheater lay directly in front of us and about eight miles distant. A grassy valley, branching between low ridges running from the river toward the center of the basin.[12] A small stream rose in this valley breaking through the ridges to the west in a deep cañon, and falling into the channel of the Yellowstone, which here bears in a northeast course, flowing in view as far as the confluence of the small stream, thence plunged into the grand canon and hidden from sight. No falls can be seen, but their location is readily detected by the sudden disappearance of the river. Beyond this open valley, the basin appears to be filled with a succession of low converging ridges heavily timbered, and all of about an equal altitude.

To the south appears a broad sheet of water the Yellowstone lake. Across the grand cañon, on the slope of the great mountain wall, is the steam jet seen this morning, and in the next ravine beyond it are six more of inferior volume. Still further south are others to the number of perhaps twenty, and to the southwest more of them scattered over the vast expanse of the basin, rising from behind the wooded hills in every direction. The view in this respect strongly resembles that from the Alleghanies where they overlook iron and coal districts, with all their furnaces in active operation, save that one looks in vain

Pass. Doane is referring to the north end of the Teton Range: Teton Peaks 1 to 44. (See Bonney, *Field Book The Teton Range,* 77)

[12] Cascade Creek.

here for the thrifty towns, country villas, steamboats, and rail-road depots. The surface formation of Mount Washburn on the northern or outside slope is a spongy lava. The body of the peak is of feldspathic granite. Its southward, or inward slope, is very precipitous with evidence of once having been much more so; at present however having a talus of material broken away by the elements.

Scattered over the outside slopes we found beautiful speci-mens of sardonyx, identical with those found on the Sierra Nevada.[13]

Descending the mountain side a couple of miles, we camped on the head of a small stream flowing [from the] west into the grand cañon. Distance traveled, 12 miles. Bar[ometer,] 23.00; ther[mometer,] 50°; elevation, 7,270 feet.

Coming into camp in advance, passing through a grove of pine on the margin of a little creek, I was met face to face on the path by two magnificent buck elk, one of which I wounded, but lost in the woods. Shortly afterward Mr. Smith started up a small bear which also got away. The ground was everywhere tracked by the passage of herds of elk and mountain sheep. Bear signs were everywhere visible.

WASHBURN HOT SPRINGS

In the evening, accompanied by Mr. Washburn and Mr. Hedges, I followed down the channel of the creek to the brink of the grand cañon.[14] Passing for a mile down an open glade with a heavy coating of rank green grass, and dotted with clumps of pine, we came to a bed of whitish substance extending for a hundred yards on each side of the creek, and through which its channel ran. Having no chemical tests we were at a loss to classify this deposit; some thought it volcanic ashes.

This formation abounds in the vicinity, in deep beds under-

[13] Sardonyx is a kind of onyx having deep orange-red, translucent layers of quartz-like material.
[14] Now known as Sulphur Creek.

lying the ridges of the valley and overlaid by masses of lava almost entirely composed of obsidian.[15]

A mile below this point small hot springs of sulphur, sulphate of copper, alum, and mud, were found in great numbers, and soon we came to an opening in the woods at the foot of a bluff where there appeared a system of boiling hot springs of muddy water, with clouds of vapor escaping therefrom.[16] The large ones were five in number, of which the first measured 25 X 30 feet, hot, with slight ebullition in the centre; water slate color, and not flowing. The second four feet in diameter boiling violently, and flowing water dark brown, muddy, but without deposit. The third, 20 X 25 feet measurement, brown muddy water, boiling up three feet in the center, with an occasional violent rush of vapor to the height of one hundred feet.

This spring flows periodically; it lies close under a projecting bank of sulphurated calcarious formation, and in one corner of the spring rises a sort of honey comb deposit, of beautifully variegated colorings, and composed of sublimated sulphur on a bed of metallic luster resembling silver. This deposit is several feet in height, and would weigh many tons. The vapor is forced through the interstices of this honeycomb with a loud hissing

[15] A. C. Peale, geologist with the Hayden party in 1872, states: "The top of the cañon above the falls is made up of obsidian, which is porphyritic, containing crystals of sanidine . . . It passes into a perlite-like rock of a light-bluish color, in some places is white." (Hayden, *Sixth Annual Report,* 131)

Arnold Hague, great geologic authority on Yellowstone Park, says: "A Tourist visiting all the prominent geyser basins, hot springs, Yellowstone Lake, and the Grand Canyon and Falls of the Yellowstone, is not likely to come upon any other rock than rhyolite, excepting, of course, deposits from the hot springs, unless he ascends Mount Washburn . . . These 2,000 square miles offer as grand a field for the study of structural forms, development of crystallization, and mode of occurrence of acidic lavas as can be found anywhere in the world . . . Obsidian, pumice, pitchstone, ash, breccia, and an endless development of transition forms alternate with the more compact lithoidal lavas which make up the great mass of the rhyolite . . . In mineral composition these rocks are simple enough . . . Chemical analyses . . . present comparatively slight differences in ultimate composition . . . Difficulty [is] met with by the scientific traveler in recognizing the uniformity and simplicity of chemical composition of the rhyolite magma over the entire plateau, owing to its great diversity in superficial habit." (*Geological History of the Yellowstone National Park,* 7-9)

[16] Now called Washburn Hot Springs. From the Canyon-Tower road, 4 miles north of Tower Junction, the Grand Canyon of the Yellowstone can be seen through a huge gash in the wooded terrain. These springs are east of the road, on the southern base of Mount Washburn.

sound.

Above this spring thirty feet, on the bank, is a fourth, similar, and measuring 7 × 8 feet, and beyond another of black, paint like consistency which deposits a crater from the ejected material. [17]

Around these larger are dozens of smaller springs, vapor jets, and mud spouts. The ground in the vicinity is in layers, like pie crust, which break through or settle when trodden upon giving one a sensation of extreme uncertainty, as a rush of hot sulphur vapor invariably rises from the fracture. It was with extreme difficulty, and some little risk, that we obtained specimens of the deposits.

Langford, in contrast to Doane's factual description, dramatizes the area as though it were a bit of hell:

[Langford] *Toiling on our course down this creek to the river we came suddenly upon a basin of boiling sulphur springs, exhibiting signs of activity and points of difference so wonderful as to fully absorb our curiosity. The largest of these, about twenty feet in diameter, is boiling like a cauldron, throwing water and fearful volumes of sulphurous vapor higher than our heads. Its color is a disagreeable greenish yellow. The central spring of the group, of dark leaden hue, is in the most violent agitation, its convulsive spasms frequently projecting large masses of water to the height of seven or eight feet. The spring lying to the east of this, more diabolical in appearance, filled with a hot brownish substance of the consistency of mucilage, is in constant noisy ebullition, emitting fumes of villainous odor. Its surface is covered with bubbles, which are constantly rising and bursting, and emitting sulphurous gases from various parts of its surface. Its appearance has suggested the name, which Hedges has given, of "Hell-Broth springs," for, as we gazed upon the infernal mixture and inhaled the pungent sickening vapors, we were impressed with the idea that this was a most perfect realization of Shakespeare's image in Macbeth. It needed but*

[17] Inkpot Spring.

the presence of Hecate and her weird band to realize that horrible creation of poetic fancy, and I fancied the "black and midnight hags" concocting a charm around this horrible cauldron. We ventured near enough to this spring to dip the end of a pine pole into it, which, upon removal, was covered an eighth of an inch thick with lead-colored sulphury slime.

There are five large springs and half a dozen smaller ones in this basin . . . Around them all is an incrustation formed from the bases of the spring deposits, arsenic, alum, sulphur, etc. . . . and it was with the greatest difficulty that I obtained specimens of the incrustation. This I finally accomplished by lying at full length upon that portion of the incrustation which yielded the least, but which was not sufficiently strong to bear my weight while I stood upright, and at imminent risk of sinking in the infernal mixture, I rolled over and over to the edge of the opening; and, with the crust slowly bending and sinking beneath me, hurriedly secured the coveted prize of black sulphur, and rolled back to a place of safety. [18]

THE BRINK OF THE CANYON

Continuing on our way three miles further, we came to a dense growth of small timber on the brink of the grand canon, and were stopped by its sheer wall, which fell off fifteen hundred feet to a bench grown up with pines, through which ran an apparently narrow chasm, so deep that the waters could not be seen, nor heard.

It was a second edition of the bottomless pit. The small stream had hollowed out a channel through the lower bench several hundred feet in depth additional, but even looking down through this fissure did not enable us to see the Yellowstone.

After resting on the brink and gazing long with wonder into the fearful gulf below, we returned to camp having had a walk of ten miles, profoundly impressed with the laborious nature of our undertaking and more than satisfied with the opening up of the campaign.

[18] Langford, *Discovery,* 83.

After visiting the Hot Springs, Hedges says:

[Hedges] *It was after sundown when we got back to camp. Was all sweat through. On guard with Langford. We had huge fires. Jake Smith set fire to a pine that came near burning us all out. Roasted some venison by fire and enjoyed it hugely. Easiest night I have had on guard.*"[19]

CAMP ON CASCADE CREEK NEAR CANYON VILLAGE

Tuesday, August 30, ninth day. We moved at 9 a.m., in a southerly direction, with a detour to the right to avoid a marshy ravine, and in three miles struck the head of the low valley seen from Mount Washburn yesterday; following its windings for several miles we came to the lowest point, where the stream above referred to enters the cañon, and here camped. Distance traveled eight miles. This valley is from one half to three miles wide with branches in every direction among the wooded ridges, is clothed with a heavy mantle of excellent grass, abounds in springs of pure water, and was formerly the bottom of a lake.

The profile of the creek bank showed the following[:] bed of the stream dark lava, surface flow[;] above, obsidian and granite pebbles, six feet, then quartzose sandstone two feet, limestone one foot, and volcanic ashes one to four feet, thus showing several estuary deposits above the volcanic rocks.

In company with others of the party I rode down the creek, following the brink of its cañon which gradually deepens to three hundred feet, as far as its junction with the Yellowstone. As we approached the Grand Cañon a dull roaring sound warned us that the falls were near at hand.

I had been suffering greatly during the forenoon being obliged to gallop from one spring to another to keep wet the wrappings of my hand; following this cañon kept me away from water so long that the pain became utterly unsupportable. I abandoned my horse, and have no distinct recollection of how I

---
[19] Hedges, "Journal," 380.

got to the water's edge, but presently found myself with my arm up to the elbow in the Yellowstone a few yards below the foot of a graceful cascade. In a few minutes the pain becoming allayed, I proceeded to explore the locality. I had descended the cañon at a point where the creek joined the river, precipitated into a gorge just above its juncture in a lovely cascade of three falls, in the aggregate one hundred feet in height. This was named Crystal Cascade, and the stream Cascade Creek.[20] In the bed of the gorge were to be found an infinite variety of volcanic specimens, quartz, feldspar, mica, granites, lavas, basalts, composite crystals, in fact everything from asbestos to obsidian, was represented by fragments in the bed of this stream; there were also clay stone specimens, of which we afterwards learned the origin.

At the foot of the gorge, and on the margin of the Yellowstone, stood a high promontory of concretionary lava literally filled with volcanic butternuts; many of these were loose, and could be taken out of the rock with the hand; broken open, they were invariably hollow, and lined with minute quartz crystals of various tints. This formation is rare, but occurs frequently in the Great Basin.

From the outer point of this promontory can be seen the foot of the Upper Fall of the Yellowstone, and I climbed to the summit to obtain a view.[21]

UPPER YELLOWSTONE FALLS

After ascending about 600 feet a plateau is reached overlooking the cataract, which is inaccessible at its brink without the use of ropes. The river comes down for half a mile above, over a series of lava ledges, each terminating in a fall of from ten to fifteen feet. Of these there are five. Then with a tremendous

---

[20] Hedges suggested these names.

[21] 2.52 miles south of Canyon Village at the west end of Chittenden Memorial Bridge, take the Canyon Rim scenic route. From it will be seen the Yellowstone River rapids, Upper Falls of the Yellowstone, and Crystal Falls (North Rim Trail leads to the latter), all described here by Doane.

Upper Fall Yellowstone.
115 ft.

Moore.

Upper Falls of the Yellowstone, sketched by Pvt. Moore during the 1870
expedition.

Upper Falls of the Yellowstone. Moran woodcut modeled on Moore's sketch; used to illustrate Langford's first *Scribner's* article, May 1871.

Upper Falls of the Yellowstone. Moran watercolor, 1872. *Courtesy Thomas Gilcrease Institute, Tulsa, Oklahoma.*

current, and confined in a rocky channel narrowed to a space of eighty feet, it is hurled from the brink of a perpendicular wall, a sheer descent of a hundred and fifteen feet.[22] So rapid is the current that the great mass of foam shoots out clear of the rock and falls far out in its basin, striking upon a covered ledge at an angle which causes a portion of the water to be projected like a broad fan, into the air, with a hissing sound, to the distance of sixty feet, and afterwards dissolving into clouds of spray. The depth of water on the brink is about four feet, and the concussion of the fall is tremendous. A lava promontory overhangs the basin on either side, giving fine opportunities for observation. After watching the rushing waters for an hour, other members of the party arrived, with whom I returned to camp. Bar[ometer,] 22.60; ther[mometer,] 40° [46°]; elevation, 7,697 feet.

[Langford] *Lieutenant Doane* [tonight] *has crawled out of his blankets, and is just outside the tent with his hand and forearm immersed in water nearly as cold as ice. I am afraid that lock-jaw will set in if he does not consent to have the felon lanced.* [23]

Wednesday, August 31, tenth day. The day was spent without moving camp examining the falls and cañon. Returning in the morning to the Upper Fall, we measured its height given above and followed down the cañon. The brink of the lower fall is visible from the ledges of the upper; distance between the falls, a little over half a mile. The cañon between the falls is lava, alternating with the sulphur formation, is 450 feet deep, and about 200 yards across. The stream flows over lava, granite, and boulders.

LOWER YELLOWSTONE FALLS

The lower fall at its brink is ninety feet across, and without rapids above, though the current is very swift. It is precipitated

22 Official height is 109 feet.
23 Langford, *Discovery,* 87.

Lower Falls of the Yellowstone, sketched by Pvt. Moore during the 1870 expedition.

Lower Falls of the Yellowstone. Moran woodcut used to illustrate Langford's first *Scribner's* article, May 1871.

clear of the rock a perpendicular descent of three hundred and fifty feet,[24] the cañon at its foot being eight hundred feet in depth.

A promontory of the wall rises one hundred and twenty feet above the brink and overhanging the basin, from which the view is inconceivably grand. The heavy body of water dissolving into a sheet of foam, pours into an immense circular caldron overhung by the gigantic walls. From the depths of the abyss comes up a humming sound very different from the wild roaring of the upper cataract.

From a projecting promontory a mile below, the finest view is obtained.[25]

Both of these cataracts deserve to be ranked among the great waterfalls of the continent. No adequate standard of comparison between such objects, either in beauty or grandeur, can well be obtained. Every great cascade has a language and an idea peculiarly its own, embodied, as it were, in the flow of its waters. Thus the impression on the mind conveyed by Niagara may be summed up as "overwhelming power;" of the Yosemite as "Altitude;" of the Shoshone Fall, in the midst of a desert, as "going to waste." So the Upper Falls of the Yellowstone may be said to embody the idea of "Momentum," and the Lower Fall of "Gravitation." In scenic beauty the upper cataract far excels the lower; it has life, animation, while the lower one simply follows its channel; both however are eclipsed as it were by the singular wonders of the mighty cañon below. This deepens rapidly; the stream flowing over rapids continually. The ground on the brink rises also, to the foot of Mount Washburn, the falls being at a low point in the basin. Therefore the canon walls increase in altitude, in following down the stream.

GRAND CANYON OF THE YELLOWSTONE

Several of the party descended into the chasm a short distance below the fall, but could not reach its foot. A mile below,

[24] Official height is 308 feet.
[25] Inspiration Point.

Grand Canyon of the Yellowstone, from the brink of the Lower Falls, 1871. W. H. Jackson photo. *Courtesy U.S.G.S.*

The Great Cañon and Lower Falls of the Yellowstone. Woodcut illustration for F. V. Hayden's *Scribner's* article, February 1872.

Grand Canyon of the Yellowstone. Moran oil, 1893. *Courtesy Thomas Gilcrease Institute, Tulsa, Oklahoma.*

several steam jets play across, a few feet above the water.[26] The walls of the cañon are of gypsum, in some places having an incrustation of lime, white as snow, from which the reflected rays of the sun produce a dazzling effect, rendering it painful to look into the gulf. In others the rock is crystalline and almost wholly sulphur, of a dark yellow color, with streaks of red, green, and black, caused by the percolations of hot mineral waters, of which thousands of springs are seen, in many instances, flowing from spouts high up on the wall, on either side. The combinations of metallic lusters in the coloring of the walls is truly wonderful, surpassing doubtless anything of the kind on the face of the globe. The ground slopes to the cañon on the opposite or east side, and from it to the low valley on the west.

Three miles below the fall the chasm is ten hundred and fifty feet deep. In some places, masses of the rock have crumbled and slid down in a talus of loose material at the foot; in others, promontories stand out in all manner of fantastic forms, affording vistas of wonder utterly beyond the power of description. On the caps of these dizzy heights, mountain sheep and elk rest during the night.

I followed down the stream to where it breaks through the range, on horseback, threading my way through the forest on game trails with little difficulty. Selecting the channel of a small creek, and leaving the horses I followed it down on foot, wading in the bed of the stream which fell off at an angle of about thirty degrees between walls of the gypsum.[27] Private McConnell accompanied me.

On entering the ravine we came at once to hot springs of sulphur, sulphate of copper, alum, steam jets, &c., in endless variety, some of them of very peculiar form. One of them in particular of sulphur had built up a tall spire from the slope of the wall standing out like an enormous horn with hot water trickling down its sides.

The creek ran on a bed of solid rock, in many places smooth and slippery, in others obstructed by masses of débris fallen

[26] Seen from Artist's Point.
[27] Sulphur Creek (south of Mount Washburn).

from the overhanging cliffs of the sulphurated limestone above.

After descending for three miles in the channel we came to a sort of bench or terrace, the same one seen previously in following down the creek from our first camp in the basin. Here we found a large flock of mountain sheep, very tame, and greatly astonished no doubt at our sudden appearance. McConnell killed one, and wounded another, whereupon the rest disappeared, clambering up the steep walls with a celerity truly astonishing.

We were now fifteen hundred feet below the brink. From here the creek channel was more precipitous and for a mile we climbed downward over masses of rock and fallen trees splashing in warm water ducking under cascades, and skirting close against sideling places to keep from falling into boiling caldrons in the channel.

After four hours of hard labor since leaving the horses, we finally reached the bottom of the gulf, and the margin of the Yellowstone, famished with thirst, wet and exhausted.

The river water here is quite warm, and of a villainously alum and sulphurous taste. Its margin is lined with all kinds of chemical springs, some depositing craters of calcareous rock, others muddy, black, blue, slaty, or reddish water. The internal heat renders the atmosphere oppressive, though a strong breeze draws through the cañon. A trying sound comes constantly to the ear, mingled with the rush of the current. The place abounds with sickening and purgatorial smells.

We had come down the ravine at least four miles and looking upward the fearful wall appeared to reach the sky. It was about 3 o'clock p.m., and stars could be distinctly seen; so much of the sunlight was cut off from entering the chasm.[28] Tall pines on the extreme verge appeared the height of two or three feet.

The cañon, as before said, was in two benches, with a plateau on either side about half way down. This plateau, about a hundred yards in width, looked from below like a mere shelf against the wall; the total depth was not less than twenty-five hundred

[28] Although the editor has explored many great canyons, he has never noticed this phenomenon.

feet and more probably three thousand. There are perhaps other cañons longer and deeper than this one, but surely none so combining grandeur and immensity with peculiarity of formation and profusion of volcanic or chemical phenomena.[29]

Returning to the summit, we were five hours reaching our horses, by which time darkness had set in, and were without a trail in the dense forest, having fallen timber to evade and treacherous marshes to cross on our way to camp. I knew the general direction, however, and took a straight course, using great caution in threading the marshes, wherein our horses sunk up to their bodies nevertheless. Fortune favored us and we arrived in camp at 11 o'clock at night, wet and chilled to the bone. To me it was terribly fatiguing after the excitement had passed away, as I was becoming very weak from continued loss of rest or sleep.

---

[29] Langford writes, "As it is impossible to explore the entire cañon, we are unable to tell whether the course of the river through it is broken by other and larger cataracts than the two we have seen, or whether its continuous descent alone has produced the enormous depth to which it has attained. Rumors of falls a thousand feet in height have often reached us before we made this visit." (*Discovery*, 88)

CHAPTER 10

YELLOWSTONE CANYON TO LAKE JUNCTION

From Canyon Village their route parallels Grand Loop Road south along the Yellowstone River through Hayden Valley. The party inspects Crater Hills (west), then, 4 miles to the south, the Dragon's Mouth Spring and other nearby thermal features. The group fords the river and parallels the Grand Loop Road but follows the east bank to Lake Junction. The party then camps for a day on Yellowstone Lake two miles east of Fishing Bridge near East Entrance Road.

Thursday, September 1, eleventh day. We moved out at 10 A.M., heading the Cascade ravine through open timber and following the summit of one of the low ridges to the river, striking a game trail along its bank at a point two miles above the upper fall.

The stream here changes its character altogether, running in the center of an open glade, bank full, with grassy margins, a slow current, and spread out to a width of from two hundred to four hundred feet. The bottom is pebbly, or quicksand, the water of crystal clearness, and cold again.

The little valley is marshy, for which reason we traveled on the slopes of the ridges, crossing at intervals, open glades between them. Through one of these flows Alum Creek a small stream coming in from the west, its bed dyed of an inky blackness by the deposit from its strongly impregnated waters.[1]

---

[1] Alum Creek, named at this time by the party, is 5.1 miles south of Canyon Junction. The early trappers created some yarns about it. Jim Bridger tells that one

HAYDEN VALLEY

Six miles above the falls we entered a wide valley[2] of calcareous formation, open and branching among timbered ridges on either side of the river, which runs through its centre in a northeast[3] course, an old lake bed,[4] as are all the grassy sections of the basin.

On the north side of the river appeared the great steam jets before alluded to, in ravines opening into this valley. A good sized stream, known as Hellroaring River, emptied in near by from the north.[5] From the southwest a shallow stream came in also, and in front near the centre of the valley were several large white hills to which we directed our course.

Elk were feeding in small bands on the other side of the valley, and large flocks of water fowl were frequently seen sporting in the river channel.

THE CRATER HILLS

The white hills or the "Seven hills" as we afterward named them, proved well worth a visit;[6] here is a group of large

day he forded the creek and rode out several miles and back. He noticed the return journey was only a small fraction of the distance going, and that his horse's feet had shrunk to mere points which sank into the solid ground, so that the animal could scarcely hobble along. Seeking the cause, he found it to be in the astringent quality of the alum-saturated water which shrank distance itself. (Chittenden, *Yellowstone National Park,* 1903 ed., 49)

"The headwaters of this stream are so strong with alum that one swallow is sufficient to draw one's face into such shape that it is almost impossible to get it straightened out again for one hour or so." (Andrew J. Weikert, "Journal of a Tour through Yellowstone, 1877," August 26, Historical Society of Montana, *Contributions,* III)

[2] North end of what is now called Hayden Valley after Dr. Ferdinand Vandeveer Hayden, the U.S. government geologist.

[3] Northwest.

[4] Doane observed well. Hayden Valley was once an arm of a vast, prehistoric lake of which Yellowstone Lake is a remnant. Today the valley is a favorite with grizzlies, elk, and waterfowl.

[5] Probably Sour Creek and tributaries. Present-day Hellroaring Creek is northwest of Tower Junction.

[6] Now called Crater Hills. From a point 10.5 miles north of Lake Junction, 5.3 miles south of Grand Canyon, they may be seen about 1.5 miles south and west of the highway.

mounds varying from 200 to 500 feet in height, each of which has been deposited by the action of a single spring, and at their basis a system of nature's chemical works on the grandest scale. I climbed to the summit of the two loftiest of these hills; their formations are identical, all being composed of calcareous matter, solid within, but shelly on the exterior, and when decomposed, of a snowy whiteness. The slopes were covered with shales, slid down from above. On the summits were the ruins of craters of great size, and former solidity, now choked up with débris.

From hydrostatic pressure all the springs had burst out below at the foot of the slopes, but through innumerable small vents, all over the surface of the hills, hot sulphur vapor escaped, subliming around the vents in splendid crystals of large size. The rocks were everywhere warm, and in some places hot to the touch; wherever the horses feet broke through the crust, hot vapor escaped. Everywhere the rocks gave forth a hollow sound beneath our tread, and in many places the intense heat caused them to bulge out in a scaly formation which broke through on the slightest pressure of the foot, whereupon scalding vapor poured out in such volumes as to cause a hasty retreat.

THE SULPHUR SPRINGS

The greatest spring[7] in appearance lies at the foot of the highest hill[8] and is intensely sulphurous, great clouds of vapor constantly escaping. It measures 15 × 20 feet on the inside; the water boils up constantly from three to seven feet in height the whole surface rising and falling occasionally with a flux, and reflux of four feet additional, overflowing its basin, and receding every few minutes. The basin is built up with a solid rim, or lining of pure chrystaline sulphur four feet in width, all around the edge, probably amounting to forty tons in weight. The water is clear, but of a whitish cast, and above the boiling

[7] Sulphur Spring.
[8] Now called Sulphur Mountain (7,800 feet). According to Langford, the party named this largest hill Crater Hill. (*Discovery*, 101)

point, steam being evolved from its surface. The basin cannot be approached nearer than twenty feet distant on account of the scalding vapors. A small channel leads down the slope, and for several hundred feet its bed is incrusted with a sulphur deposit, showing that the spring occasionally flows a considerable quantity of water. This deposit is from three to ten inches deep.

Farther along the base of the same hill is a sulphurous cavern twenty feet in visible depth, and eight feet in diameter, out of which issued jets of vapor with a sound like the puffing of a high pressure steamboat. These jets pulsate regularly, and the vapor is intensely hot.

Scattered along the bases of the next hills near by were great numbers of small sulphur springs of the same character and deposits of the larger one, any one of which would be counted a great curiosity in any district but this. About one hundred yards below is a spring of slate-colored water 70 × 30 feet, an immense caldron boiling constantly.

THE MUD POTS[9]

Still further on is a basin of perhaps four acres containing from twenty to thirty mud springs, varying from two to twenty feet in diameter and of depths below the surface, from three to eight feet. The mud ejected is of different degrees of consistency, but generally about the thickness of common mortar, and mostly of an iron brown color. It boils slowly like mush, with bubbles of gas escaping, and is spouted to various heights, from two to forty feet, falling with dull splashes around the edges of the craters which are being built up continually, and continually caving in, to be worked over and ejected as before. Some of the springs throw up yellow mud, others white, and a

9 All the mud-contained eruptive features in this locality change constantly. In the past sometimes they have undermined or engulfed the road, necessitating its rerouting. Whether the engineers decide road or natural features more precious to save from destruction in the future remains to be seen. Today, a scenic side road about 10.7 miles south of Canyon Junction leads to Mud Volcano, Dragon's Mouth Spring, and to a mud geyser which erupts every few seconds to a height of twelve feet.

few pink. The different springs of all classes had no apparent connection with each other, though often but a few feet apart, the mud being of different colors, the basins having different levels, and the pulsations being independent, one being frequently in violent ebulition, while another near by was quiescent. A Plasterer would go into ecstasies over this mortar, which is worked to such a degree of fineness that it can be dried in large lumps, either in the sun, or in a fire, without a sign of cracking, and when once dry is a soft finely grained stone, resembling clay slate when dark, or meerschaum when white. Mortar might well be good after being constantly worked for perhaps ten thousand years.[10]

In a ravine near by was a large flowing spring of alum water, and several of sulphate of copper. Springs of this latter class are always clear and deep with beautiful basins, raised slightly at the rim, and lined with incrustations of brilliant colors.

Scattered over the whole area of one fourth of a mile in diameter in addition to the above, were hundreds of small spouts of vapor, water, and mud.

In a basin by itself was a black mud spring, 20 × 40 feet throwing mortar a distance of seventy feet. This substance was so strongly impregnated with sulphuric acid, as to burn the tongue like fire, in its intense sourness.

All the mud springs are double, and most of the water springs also, each one having in addition to its crater, and generally in the margin thereof, or near it, a honey comb vent in the ground, or rock, through which sulphur vapor escapes with a frying sound; doubtless a vent for the internal fires below. This rule applies in all localities in the basin.

The amount of pure chrystaline sulphur deposited in this locality is very great; probably one hundred tons could be gathered, in sight, on the surface. The continuous supply will one day be turned to account in the manufacture of acids on a large scale.[11]

[10] Chittenden noted that this "mortar" has actually been used with good results in "calsomining" walls. (*Yellowstone National Park*, 1903 ed., 216)

[11] Note that the idea of preserving the region as a national park, free from

There being no water fit to drink in the vicinity we moved on up the valley about five miles through grassy hills and level bottoms passing several isolated caldrons of grey mud on the way, and camped in a group of them on the river bank at the head of the valley. Here trout were caught in abundance and we fared sumptuously with the single exception that the river water tasted strongly of chemicals, and that all other available water tasted still worse than the river. Those of the party who sported silver watches now discovered that they were no longer silver, but a greasy pinch back yellow, discolored by the gasses in the atmosphere of the spring. Arms were also affected; the polished surfaces becoming spotted with black. Distance, twelve miles. Bar[ometer,] 22.75; ther[mometer,] 60°; elevation, 7,487 feet.

Friday, September 2, twelfth day. We remained in camp on the river, and visited springs in the neighborhood. Along the bank of the stream there are a dozen caldrons of greyish clay mud, varying from 6 to 40 feet in diameter, and from three to ten feet in depth, each with its vent of sulphur vapor, and slimy crater from three to five feet in height.[12] Just above camp the bed of the river is full of hot water spouts, with bubbles of gas escaping.

DRAGON'S MOUTH SPRING

In a ravine over the ridge, hot vapors pour out in every direction, and here is a remarkable group. A small stream of green water flows down the ravine having its source in a rocky cave in the bank, with an aperture of 6 by 8 feet – a perfect grotto, lined with brilliant metallic tints of green, red, and black, and from which steam escapes in regular pulsations to a distance of forty feet, forcing out the water in waves which break over an outside horizontal rim about once in ten seconds.[13] A few

commercialism, had not yet formed in the minds of the party. See September 19 entry.

[12] Sulphur Caldron.

[13] Later named Dragons Mouth Spring for its darting tongue of boiling water and steam. It has continued its activity to the present time.

yards farther down are several boiling springs of yellow muddy water, the largest of which is 80 feet in diameter, and near it a great honey comb sulphur vent a hundred feet in diameter, through which the vapor rushes with a loud hissing sound.

MUD GEYSER

One hundred yards from the bank of the river, and below these springs is a geyser of dark muddy water; its basin is two hundred feet across on the outer rim, and about six feet deep, with a channel cut through one side for the passage of flood water from the hills. The area is floored with a strata of mud rock deposited from the water, forming a circular plateau in the middle of which is an oblong crater 45 × 75 feet with an irregular vapor vent, and system of steam jets adjoining, covering the whole space to the outer rim on the right. This was a periodic geyser having eruptions every six hours and in the following manner:

The crater being full of boiling water, and the vapor vent active, suddenly columns of steam shoot up through the water to the height of three hundred feet. The ground trembles, the vapor hisses through the vent with increased force, the water of the crater is violently agitated, being thrown up in vast columns, to the height of thirty and forty feet, splashing out as far as the rim of the basin with great force. This continues for half an hour, the water increasing in quantity in the crater all the while. Then the steam ceases suddenly to escape, the water settles and commences to lower in the crater, continuing to fall to the depth of thirty-five feet, leaving bare the incrusted and funnel shaped walls which converge at that depth to the diameter of seven feet. The water here stands for a time[,] the steam jets cease to hiss[,] the vapor vent to give forth its fumes and all is quiet. After the lapse of an hour the water stoutly rises again, the vents become active and at the end of the regular period the whole performance is repeated as before.[14]

[14] Now designated as Mud Geyser. It has shown little activity since the 1870's. See Allen and Day, *Hot Springs of Yellowstone National Park,* 418; and Peale in Hayden, *Twelfth Annual Report,* 95.

MUD VOLCANO OF 1870

A few hundred yards from here is an object of the greatest interest. On the slope of a small and steep wooded ravine is the crater of a mud volcano, thirty feet in diameter at the rim, which is elevated a few feet above the surface on the lower side and bounded by the slope of the hill on the upper, converging as it deepens to the diameter of fifteen feet at the lowest visible point, about forty feet down. Heavy volumes of steam escape from this opening, ascending to the height of three hundred feet. From far down in the earth came a jarring sound in regular beats of five seconds with a concussion that shook the ground at two hundred yards distant. After each concussion, came a splash of mud as if thrown to a great height; sometimes it could be seen from the edge of the crater but none was entirely ejected while we were there. Occasionally an explosion was heard like the bursting of heavy guns behind an embankment and causing the earth to tremble for a mile around. These explosions were accompanied by a vast increase of the volumes of steam poured forth from the crater.

This volcano has not been long in operation, as young pines crushed flat to the earth under the rim of mud, were still alive at the tops. The amount of matter ejected was not great considering the power of the volcano.

The distances to which this mud has been thrown are truly astonishing. Directly above the crater rises a steep bank a hundred feet in height, on the apex of which the tallest tree near is one hundred and ten feet high, the topmost branches of this tree were loaded with mud, two hundred feet above, and fifty feet laterally away from the crater. The ground and fallen trees near by were splashed at a horizontal distance of two hundred feet. The trees below were either broken down or their branches festooned with dry mud which appeared in the tops of trees growing on the side hill from the same level with the crater, fifty feet in height, and at a distance of one hundred and eighty feet from the volcano.

The mud to produce such effects must have been thrown to a

perpendicular elevation of at least three hundred feet. As the diameter of the vent is small in comparison to its depth, it would admit of an initial propulsion varying little from a vertical line. It was with difficulty we could believe the evidence of our senses, and only after the most careful measurement could we realize the immensity of this wonderful phenomenon.

> This "mud volcano" does not appear to be the same feature which is designated as such today. Langford says that to reach it from Mud Geyser,

[Langford] *ascending a small hillock . . . it is about midway up a gentle pine-covered slope . . . Hedges, having ventured too near the rim on that side [leeward], . . . was thrown violently down the exterior side of the crater by the force of the volume of steam emitted during one of those fearful convulsions.* [Hedges did not mention the incident.]

> Like Doane, Langford too could hardly believe his senses on this occasion. Langford called this "the greatest marvel we have yet met with."

[Langford] *General Washburn and I again visited the mud vulcano* [sic] *to-day* [September 3]. *I especially desired to see it again for the one especial purpose, among others of a general nature, of assuring myself that the notes made in my diary a few days ago are not exaggerated. No! they are not! The sensations inspired in me to-day, on again witnessing its convulsions . . . were those of mingled dread and wonder. At war with all former experience it was so novel, so unnaturally natural, that I feel while now writing and thinking of it, as if my own senses might have deceived me with a mere figment of the imagination.* [15]

[15] Langford, *Discovery,* 103.
    Langford also on this same day details some other interesting occurrences, including his own near death:
      Saturday, September 3. – This morning General Washburn and I left
      camp immediately after breakfast and returned four miles on our track

Langford could not understand why F. V. Hayden had very little to say about this remarkable curiosity when the eminent geographer saw it the following year. Then Langford returned here in 1872,

[Langford] *and the omission by Hayden was explained as soon as I saw the volcano in its changed condition. The loud detonations which resembled the discharges of a gunboat mortar were no longer heard, and the upper part of the crater and cone had in a great measure disappeared, leaving a shapeless and unsightly hole much larger than the former crater.* [16]

Hayden later reported (in 1878) a geyser here with eruptions eighteen to forty feet high, lasting 4½ to thirty minutes at one to 4½ hour intervals. To illustrate further the changes at this location, in 1948 seasonal Park Ranger Lowell Biddulph discovered a new activity nearby. Now known as Black Dragon Caldron, it started as a three or four foot ground opening in the middle of a timbered area. It was

of September 1st to Crater Hill and the mud springs, for the purpose of making farther examinations . . . In the basin where we had found so many mud springs we to-day found a hot boiling spring containing a substance of deep yellow color, the precise nature of which we could not readily ascertain. We accordingly brought away some of it in a bottle (as is our usual custom in such cases of uncertainty), and we will have an analysis of it made on our return home. . .

A half mile south of these springs we found an alum spring yielding but little water and surrounded with beautiful alum crystals . . . it was unsafe to stand near the edge of the spring. This, however, I did not at first perceive; and, as I was unconcernedly passing by the spring, my weight made the border suddenly slough off beneath my feet. General Washburn noticed the sudden cracking of the incrustation before I did, and I was aroused to a sense of my peril by his shout of alarm, and had sufficient presence of mind to fall suddenly backwards at full length upon the sound crust, whence, with my feet and legs extended over the spring, I rolled to a place of safety. But for General Washburn's shout of alarm, in another instant I would have been precipitated into this boiling pool of alum. . .

Everything around us − air, earth, water − is impregnated with sulphur. We feel it in every drop of water we drink, and in every breath of air we inhale. Our silver watches have turned to the color of poor brass, tarnished. (*Discovery,* 102)

[16] Ibid., 108.

throwing mud out on the trees, which dried in about two weeks. Shifting 200 feet eastward, it gradually formed a larger pool with steep banks. In a dry year this caldron tends to diminish activity in August, but today it is still filled with black mud (from iron sulphide), bubbling actively from the action of carbon dioxide gas, hydrogen sulphide, and hydrogen.[17]

In the morning I had forded the river intending to go down on the other side and examine the steam jets on the Hellroaring River, but the day being warm I was overcome with pain and weakness and obliged to return without seeing them, to my great disappointment.

DOANE'S INFECTION IS WORSE

[Langford] *Lieutenant Doane's felon has caused him great suffering to-day, and I have appealed to him to allow me to lance it. I have for many years carried a lancet in my pocketbook, but I find that I have inadvertently left it at home. So all this day, while on horseback, I have been preparing for the surgical operation by sharpening my penknife on the leathern pommel of my saddle as I rode along. I have in my seamless sack a few simple medicines, including a vial of chloroform. Lieutenant Doane has almost agreed to let me open the felon, provided I put him to sleep with the chloroform; but I feel that I am too much of a novice in the business to administer it. However, I have told him that I would do so if he demanded it.*[18]

Saturday, September 3, thirteenth day. We forded the river opposite camp and followed up the stream on the east side passing several of the grey mud caldrons in the first two miles of our course on the river bank. A cañon of small depth here

[17] Biddulph to Bonney, personal interview, September 4, 1966.
[18] Langford, *Discovery,* 101.

commences impassable in many places and without difficulty, we bore off to the left on the summit of the wooded ridges. In six miles we struck the river again at a point where it falls over a sloping ridge of lava in roaring rapids in a distance of half a mile.

The trail is easily passable to the crossing of a creek seven miles from camp and coming down through a marshy valley from the range on the left.[19] Fording this we were caught in an impassable labyrinth of fallen timber and obliged to retrace our steps. Recrossing the creek, we followed down its valley over marshy ground for two miles, when a broad sheet of water suddenly appeared in front. Crossing the creek once again at a miry ford, skirting an estuary three miles further along the margin of a heavy forest on the left, we then passed over a sand levee, grown up with sage brush, and found ourselves on the open beach of the great Yellowstone Lake. Camped in a grove on the lake shore.[20]

At the head of the creek is a large basin covered with an incrustation of sulphur, and behind the first ridge a number of steam jets were seen rising into the air; these we did not visit.[21] Distance, 12 miles. Bar[ometer], Lake shore, 22.60; ther[mometer,] 58°; elevation, 7,714 3/5 feet.

[19] Pelican Creek.
[20] Almost on the site of today's Indian Pond (Squaw Lake) Campground.
[21] Sulphur Hills area.

Mud Volcano
& Springs

Rapids

Yellow Stone Lake

N.

CHAPTER 11

ALONG THE EAST SIDE OF YELLOWSTONE LAKE

Doane describes Yellowstone Lake. The party leaves camp on September 5, traveling the east shore of Yellowstone Lake, following the present location of the East Entrance highway to Lake Butte, about 10 miles beyond Lake Junction. The men continue south through Brimstone Basin, camping at the confluence of Beaverdam and Rocky Creeks on September 6. On September 7, Doane and Langford climb a high mountain peak (Colter Peak) and describe its view. There Langford sketches the first accurate outline map of Yellowstone Lake. Meanwhile the main party moves camp 4 miles west to the south end of Southeast Arm.

YELLOWSTONE LAKE

Sunday, September 4, fourteenth day. We did not move camp.[1] The lake lies close to the east range in the rim of the great basin, and presents an appearance at once beautiful and imposing. Its eastern shore extends southward from camp in a line broken by various inlets to the distance of twenty-six miles.

[1] Langford says, "Walter Trumbull suggested that a proper deference to Jake Smith's religious sentiments ought to be a sufficient reason for not travelling on Sunday, whereupon Jake immediately exclaimed, 'If we're going to remain in camp, let's have a game of draw.' " (*Discovery,* 110)

Hedges said that Washburn went to look at the trail on the east side of the lake. Obviously Washburn was working hard, going out a day in advance of the rest of the party to reconnoiter, as he had on the previous Sunday and other occasions. ("Journal," 384)

Yellowstone Lake. Moran woodcut illustration for Hayden's *Scribner's* article, February 1872.

Its general form is triangular, with apices in the south, south-west, and north points, the latter being below our camp three miles and at the mouth of the creek crossed yesterday. The Yellowstone leaves the lake a mile beyond this angle and from the west side, starting with a slow current in a channel one fourth of a mile wide and deep enough to swim a horse. The shore on the east side for five miles is a broad and level beach of sand, and the lake is shallow for some distance out from the edge. This sand is composed almost entirely of obsidian and those minute crystals known as California diamonds. Near camp on the edge of the lake is a small boiling spring having numerous spouts far out in the water.[2] At the mouth of the creek are large swampy districts flooded and the resort of myriads of water fowl.

The sand of the beach forms a ridge on the shore cast up by the waters like those seen on Lake Michigan near Chicago.

Farther down the south shore spurs of the range come down into the basin with bluff fronts. On the south side these promontories project far into the lake in great numbers, dividing it into bays and channels. On the west side is a low bluff of the timbered ridges with a sand beach in front along the margins of the waters.

The greatest width of open water in any direction is about eighteen miles. Several islands are seen, one of which is opposite the channel of the river and five miles from the east shore.[3] Another is ten miles further south, and two miles from the shore[,] a mountain isle with a bold bluff all around to the water's edge. These islands doubtless have never been trodden by human footsteps, and still belong to the regions of the un-explored. We built a raft for the purpose of attempting to visit them, but the strong waves of the lake dashed it to pieces in an hour.

Numerous steam jets pour out from the bluffs on the shore at different points. The waters of the lake reflect a deep blue

[2] Beach Springs.
[3] Now called Stevenson Island. Doane visited it in 1876. See Part III this book, October 26 entry.

color, are clear as crystal and doubtless of great depth near the center. The extreme elevation of this great body of water, 7,714 3/5 feet, is difficult to realize;[4] place Mount Washington, the pride of New England with its base at the sea level at the bottom of the lake and the clear waters of the latter would roll 2,214 feet above its summit. With the single exception of Lake Titicaca, Peru, it is the highest great body of water on the globe.[5] No shells of any description are found on the lake shore, nor is there any evidence of the waters ever having stood at a much higher level than the present; twenty-five feet will cover the whole range of the water marks; its annual rise and fall is about two feet.

THE TROUT OF YELLOWSTONE LAKE

Its waters abound with trout to such an extent that the fish at this season are in poor condition for want of food. No other fish are seen, no minnows, and no small trout. There are also no clams, crabs, nor turtles — nothing but full grown trout. These could be caught in mule loads by wading out a few feet in the open waters at any point with a grasshopper bait. Two men could catch them faster than half a dozen could clean and get them ready for the frying pan. Caught in the open lake their flesh was yellow; but in bays where the water was strongly impregnated with chemicals it was blood red. Many of them were full of long white worms, woven across the interior of the body and through to the skin on either side. These did not appear to materially affect the condition of the fish which were apparently as active as the others.[6]

[4] The calculations of altitude with only a barometer are remarkably accurate. The U.S. Geological Surveys of 1955 and 1960 give the elevation of Yellowstone Lake as 7,733, a difference of only nineteen feet.

[5] Lake Titicaca is 12,507; Lake Tahoe, California-Nevada, is 6,275. Ferdinand C. Lane says the highest lake in the world is probably somewhere in the Himalayan or Karakoram ranges. He says Lake Pomopso, north of Bhutan, some 20 miles long, is at least 16,000 feet high where it lies at the base of 24,700 foot peak Kalhakangri. Lake Askal Chin in the same region has an elevation of 16,600 feet. (*The World's Greatest Lakes,* 223)

[6] See August 24 entry for trout description. For further reference to the worm-infested trout, see Hayden, *Fifth Annual Report* for 1871, 97-98.

POCKETKNIFE SURGERY

I had on the previous evening been nine days and nights without sleep or rest and was becoming very much reduced. My hand was enormously swelled and even ice water ceased to relieve the pain. I could scarcely walk at all, from excessive weakness. The most powerful opiates had ceased to have any effect — consultation was held, which resulted in having the thumb split open and Mr. Langford performed the operation in a masterly manner, dividing thumb bone and all; an explosion ensued followed by immediate relief. I slept through the night, all day and the next night and felt much better. To Mr. Langford, General Washburn, Mr. Stickney, and the others of the party, I owe a lasting debt for their uniform kindness, and attention in the hour of need.

[Langford] *Last evening Lieutenant Doane's sufferings were so intense that General Washburn and I insisted that he submit to an operation, and have the felon opened, and he consented provided I would administer chloroform. Preparations were accordingly made after supper. A box containing army cartridges was improvised as an operating table, and I engaged Mr. Bean, one of our packers, and Mr. Hedges as assistant surgeons. Hedges was to take his position at Doane's elbow, and was to watch my motion as I thrust in the knife blade, and hold the elbow and fore-arm firmly to prevent any involuntary drawing back of the arm by Lieutenant Doane, at the critical moment. When Doane was told that we were ready, he asked, "Where is the chloroform?" I replied that I had never administered it, and that after thinking the matter over I was afraid to assume the responsibility of giving it. He swallowed his disappointment, and turned his thumb over on the cartridge box, with the nail down. Hedges and Bean were on hand to steady the arm, and before one could say "Jack Robinson," I had inserted the point of my penknife, thrusting it down to the bone, and had ripped it out to the end of the thumb. Doane gave one shriek as the released corruption flew out in all directions upon surgeon and assistants, and then with a broad smile on his face he exclaimed, "That was elegant!" We then applied a poultice of bread and water, which we renewed a half hour later, and Doane at about eight o'clock last night dropped off into a seemingly peaceful sleep, which has been continuous up to the time of this writing, two o'clock p.m.*[7]

September 5. – Lieutenant Doane continued to sleep all last night, making a thirty-six hours nap, and after dressing his thumb and taking an observation to determine our elevation, which we found to be 7714 feet above the ocean, we broke camp at nine o'clock.[8]

Monday, September 5, fifteenth day. We moved at 9 a.m. south along the eastern shore passing at intervals the extinct craters of several springs crumbling away from the action of the waves. In two miles we came to a low promontory whence several steam jets arose with a loud roaring sound.[9] Beyond is a small bay bounded by a deposit of yellow clay full of concretions in curious forms of saucers, stockings, pencils, and the like. The bottom of this bay is lined with a whitish sediment which discolors the water along the shore. Hot sulphur springs and lukewarm ponds were abundant.

After traveling six miles we were obliged to leave the beach and follow the pine ridges in many places through fallen timber with some difficulty. We passed several large alkaline soda springs and numerous swampy hollows between the ridges, camping in a beautiful little valley near the shore of the lake. Distance 15 miles. [Barometer, 22.50; thermometer, 44°; ele-

---

7 Langford, *Discovery,* 111.

8 Ibid., 114.

9 Steamboat Springs on Steamboat Point. Osborne Russell reports that Bridger's party of sixty trappers camped here August 19, 1836. Russell and several others camped here again August 3, 1837. (*Journal of a Trapper, 1834-1843,* 1955 ed., 44, 62)

A Bridger story is that whenever he fished Yellowstone Lake he went to the boiling springs along the west shore. He let his bait down through the hot upper layers of water (whose specific gravity is less than that of the cool lake waters underneath). Having hooked his trout in the cool, habitable zone, Bridger yanked him into the boiling water, cooking him on the way out!

vation, 7,714 3/5 feet.] [10]

This point affords a fine view of the lake. A strong wind from the west had been blowing all day, and the waves rolled in, to the height of four feet. The beach here is of volcanic gravel mixed with calcareous shales, among which we found many beautiful specimens of colored rock crystals and petrifactions.

THE CLIMATE OF YELLOWSTONE LAKE

The climate and vegetable growths of the Great Basin are strikingly different from those of the surrounding country. The summer, though short, is quite warm, notwithstanding the elevation of the district.

Rains are frequent in the spring months and the atmosphere is comparatively moist. All the grasses grow rank and are not of the seeded varieties common to the country, being green and luxuriant, when the lower valleys are parched by the sun.

Ferns, Whorttle berries, thimbleberries, and other products of a damp climate abound, all being of diminutive growth. It is a miniature Oregon in vegetable productions, the pines being about the height of those on the East Virginia shore, and other growths lessened in proportion. Musquitoes and gnats are said to be numerous in the early summer, but we saw none at all. The snows of winter are very heavy, but the cold is not severe for such an altitude. Doubtless the internal heat and immense amount of hot vapor evolved exert a powerful agency in moderating the rigor of the climate.

The basin would not be a desirable place for winter residence. The only two men I have been able to find who ever wintered there both came out affected with goitres in the spring. It is a disease very common among the Mountain Crows many of the old squaws having enormous growths of the tumors filling the whole space from the chin to the breast. [11]

[10] Bracketed words were written, then crossed out by Doane, in his manuscript.
[11] Again, note Doane's sharp observations. One of the unanswered problems of modern medical science is the greater incidence of goitre in certain mountain regions, as for example, in the state of Colorado. It is possibly due to a lack of iodine and other minerals in the pure water of mountain streams.

[Langford] *To-night a conference of the party was held, to decide whether we would continue our journey around the lake, or retrace our steps and pass along the north side of the lake over to the Madison. By a vote of six to three we have decided to go around the lake. Mr. Hauser voted in favor of returning by way of the north side. My vote was cast for going around the lake.*

> If they had gone around the north shore they would have missed "Old Faithful" and all the spectacular features of the Firehole River.

Tuesday, September 6, sixteenth day. We broke camp at 10.30, bearing eastward over the ridges for an hour, then turning south into an open valley through which runs quite a stream of yellow sulphur water heading in the mountain range close by. [12]

On the slope of this range covering an area of three square miles is a formation known as a Brimstone Basin. [13] The whole lower range of the slope for that space is covered with masses of either blue clay or yellow calcareous deposit perforated by millions of minute orifices through which sulphur vapor escapes, subliming in masses around the vents.

These brimstone basins are numerous, and many of them miles in extent. They are generally found on the lower slopes of mountains, or at the foot of bluffs, but frequently occur in level districts. The latter class are always wet and generally impassable, the crust of the earth being very thin with a whitish mass of soft hot mud beneath the most dangerous marsh imaginable. Several of our horses were scalded by breaking through in passing over such places.

From this valley our route was greatly obstructed by fallen timber obliging us to follow the lake shore whenever practicable, and this was often miry, being a bed of soft clay

[12] Columbine Creek.

[13] East of the north end of Southeast Arm. Langford and Doane explored this mountain side. Langford noted the area was similar to "Crater hill" but says the volcanic action in this vicinity was decreasing.

covered with coarse lava pebbles growing larger in size as we advanced. In the afternoon we reached the lower end of the lake at its southeast angle. Here a large stream comes in through a swampy valley grown up with willows and about four miles in width.[14]

The whole valley is filled with pools of water, a resort for great numbers of water fowl, but the soil bears up the weight of a horse though muddy on its surface.

The ground was trodden by thousands of elk and sheep. Bear tracks and beaver trails were also numerous and occasionally was seen the footstep of a California lion.[15] The lake shore was barricaded with stranded pine trees in huge rafts of drift-wood; we endeavored to cross the valley on the beach; but after struggling through the tangled willows for two hours, found the creek channel to be a wide and deep slough impassable for man or beast. Retracing our steps we rode along the mountain side up the valley a couple of miles and camped on its border at the confluence of a small stream.[16] Distance, ten miles.

During the night we were several times disturbed by the dismal screaming of California lions, and in the morning found their huge tracks close around the camp.

LANGFORD MAPS YELLOWSTONE LAKE[17]

Wednesday, September 7, seventeenth day. In company with Mr. Langford, I climbed to the summit of a neighboring peak the highest of the east range.[18] We were four hours reaching the highest point climbing for over a mile over shelly feldspathic

[14] Upper Yellowstone River. The region here today is still unspoiled – about as Doane describes it.

[15] More commonly known today as the mountain lion. Doane, it will be remembered, as a child grew up in California and hence probably used this name. This animal *Felis Concolor* is known by many names: cougar, puma, panther, painter, red tiger, American lion, catamount. Its former habitat was from Canada to Patagonia.

[16] Beaverdam Creek.

[17] Langford's sketch (reproduced in this present volume) was the first authentic map of Yellowstone Lake.

[18] See editors' note on Mount Langford and Mount Doane at end of this chapter.

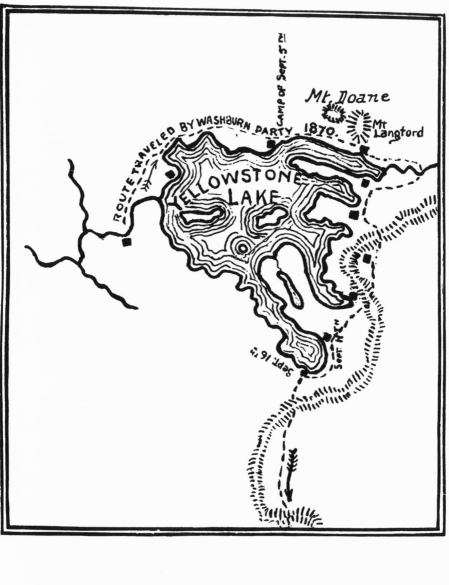

Yellowstone Lake as sketched by Langford from atop Mount Langford on September 7, 1870, and completed September 10 and 13. Note camp sites marked.

granite[19] after leaving our horses at the limit of pines. Summit at noon, bar[ometer,] 20.35; ther[mometer,] 65°; elevation, 10,327 feet.

The view from this peak commanded completely the lake enabling us to sketch a map of its inlets and bearings with considerable accuracy. On the southwestern portion of the lake rose a high mountain[20] of a yellow rock, forming a divide or water shed in the centre of the great basin beyond which the waters flowed south and west.

The stream we failed in crossing on the previous day rises in the southeast range running east several miles and joining another stream from the southwest at Bridger's lake,[21] a sheet of water about two miles in diameter at the foot of a rocky peak about twenty-five miles to the south from whence, the stream flows due north in a straight valley to the Yellowstone Lake.

This valley has a uniform width of about three miles, is level and swampy through its whole extent with numerous lakelets of considerable size scattered at intervals over its surface. South of Bridger's lake and beyond the snake river divide were seen two vast columns of vapor thirty miles away which rose at least five hundred feet above the tops of the hills. These were twenty times as large as any we had previously seen but lay a long

[19] Doane described the summit of the peak they climbed as feldspathic granite. Actually, the summits of both Colter Peak and the next prominent peak to the north (labeled Mount Doane on Washburn's map) are of dacite, a gray volcanic rock resembling granite, being of different composition than the other peaks of the Absaroka Range to the north, which are largely of volcanic breccia. Mounts Langford and Doane, as named on the U.S. Geological Survey maps, are mere cone-like rubble piles of breccia.

[20] Mount Sheridan.

[21] For Bridger Lake, see Part III this book, November 30 entry. It would be interesting to know from what source Doane had learned about Bridger Lake in 1870. Langford says, "Doane says that he thinks he has seen on an old map the name 'Bridger' given to some body of water near the Yellowstone." (*Discovery,* 118) The Doane map of 1870 shows Bridger's Lake in its approximate location, but much too large. The name had not appeared on deLacy's 1865 map, Raynold's map, or Mullan's map, and the editor has been unable to locate an earlier map than Doane's and Washburn's which showed it. Bancroft has a deLacy map which the footnote would indicate was published in 1870 or before; it shows Bridger Lake, the nonexistent "Madison Lake," and lacks the detailed outline of Yellowstone Lake as sketched by Langford. (*History of Washington, Idaho, and Montana,* 1890 ed., 633)

distance out of our course and were not visited.[22]

Looking east one mountain succeeds another with pre-cipitous ravines, volcanic, rugged, and in many places im-passable, as if all the fusible portions of the mountains had melted and run away leaving a vast cinder behind.[23] There were no ranges of peaks, it was a great level plain of summits with the softer portions melted out, the elevations all coming up to the same level and capped with horizontal beds of surface lava. This formation extended to the limit of vision. The deep and narrow valleys were grassed and timbered, had sparkling streams and furnished basins for numbers of small lakes; in fact there are lakes here everywhere[,] on the summits of mountains and on their terraced slopes[,] in valleys and in ravines, of all sizes, shapes, and qualities of water.

Descending the mountain we followed the trail of the party, crossing the stream a mile above our camp where it is a hundred feet wide and three feet deep with a moderate current. Thence we followed to the right through a beautiful open forest across the grassy valley, passing two little gems of lakes at the foot of high ridges on the west side. Presently the trail turned up the slope of the mountain where night overtook us. After traveling some distance I discovered we were following a band of elk, having missed the trail in the darkness. We then struck out for the lake shore on which our course was regained but presently lost again after more elk; we then built a fire and examined the ground carefully for tracks, found the right direction and at 10 o'clock at night arrived in camp on the lake shore to the relief of our companions, who supposed us lost in the mountains. Our camp to-night is due south from the head of the Yellowstone,

[22] There is no explanation for these columns of vapor. They might have been peculiar clouds. The old hot springs at the northern end of Jackson Lake would be about thirty miles southwest. Today these springs are covered by the dammed waters of Jackson Lake.

[23] He is describing the volcanic Absaroka Range, so named by the U.S. Geological Survey in 1885. Langford (*Discovery,* 119) called it the Wind River Range which today is officially *only* south of Togwotee Pass. The Hayden Survey (1871-72) called it The Yellowstone Range. Captain W. A. Jones (1873) called it the Sierra Shoshone. See Hayden, *Preliminary Report of the U.S. Geological Survey of Montana,* 1; Jones, *Reconnaissance in Northwestern Wyoming and Yellowstone Park,* 1873, 21.

on the other side of the lake. Long wooded promontories here extend out into the basin inclosing bays several miles in length. These are so numerous as to render it impossible to give a correct profile of the shore without actual measurement, the perspective in such distances rendering appearances very deceiving. Distance, nine miles.

NOTE ON THE SEPTEMBER 7 CAMP
by the editors

Langford locates this camp ". . . on the westerly side of the most southeasterly bay of the lake . . ."[24]

Yellowstone Park Ranger Lee L. Coleman (now retired) believes that in 1931 he located exactly this campsite.[25] He found there three spent Spencer cartridges. Guns were fired at intervals at this campsite to direct the exploring Langford and Doane to it.

Mr. Coleman says, "The Trail Creek camp as it is now known is the best and most logical place to camp on this portion of the lake shore. It is well sheltered, a nice little fresh water creek comes down off the mountain, and horse feed is available not too far away."

At this camp both Washburn and Hauser expressed their satisfaction with the sketch of the lake shore Langford made that day from the top of the mountain; Doane suggested to Washburn that because Langford was the first to reach the summit of the mountain, the peak should be named for him.

Back in Helena after the expedition, Washburn compiled a map of the Yellowstone region, incorporating Doane's suggestion. At this time Langford suggested that Doane's name be given to the adjoining peak to the north.

[24] Langford, *Discovery,* 126.
[25] Coleman to Bonney, September 1964, O. H. Bonney Collection.

NOTE ON MOUNT LANGFORD AND MOUNT DOANE
by the editors

[Langford] *Soon after the return of our party to Helena General Washburn ... told me that in recognition of the assistance I had rendered him in making a fair outline of Yellowstone lake ... he had named for me the mountain on top of which I stood when I made the sketch of the south shore of the lake. I called his attention to the fact that Lieutenant Doane had been my comrade in making the ascent and suggested that Doane's name be given to the adjoining peak to the north. He approved of this suggestion, and the map* [reproduced in this present volume], *with these mountains so named, was transmitted to the Interior Department.* [26]

The Mount Langford and the Mount Doane of 1870 are not the same as the peaks designated today by those names.

The editors are indebted to Aubrey L. Haines, historian of Yellowstone National Park, for being the first to correctly locate the peak climbed by Doane and Langford. The peak they climbed, correctly located on the Doane and the Washburn maps (labeled Mount Langford on Washburn's map), is shown on the present U.S. Geological Survey topographic maps as Colter Peak (10,683 feet). Doane and Langford gave an altitude of 10,327. Doane also refers to this peak as Mount Langford in his report.

Mount Langford, as shown on today's U.S. Geological Survey maps, is not the peak climbed by Langford and Doane. It was so designated by the Hayden Surveys of 1871-72.

According to Langford's diary, Hayden on his 1871 map transferred the name of Mount Langford to a peak far to the northeast. Later the name was

[26] Langford, *Discovery,* 126.

transferred back to the southeast corner of Yellow-stone Park, but still on the wrong peak, despite Lang-ford's efforts to get it straightened out.

Mount Doane, as shown on today's U.S. Geological Survey maps, is not "the adjoining peak to the north" of the original Mount Langford. The peak originally called Mount Doane by agreement between Washburn and Langford is now known as Mount Schurz. The present Mount Doane was named by Hayden in 1871.[27] It would appear that Doane did not know about Washburn and Langford naming a peak for him in 1870: Doane was with Hayden in 1871 when Hayden named a different peak Mount Doane, and it seems likely that had Doane known about the Wash-burn map he would have called the duplication of names to Hayden's attention.

The matter is not made simpler by pointing out that in fact there are now two mountains in Wyoming named for Doane. In addition to Mount Doane in Yellowstone Park, which commemorates his 1870 expedition, there is a Doane Peak in the Teton Range, named by the Grand Teton National Park officials in 1938 to commemorate Doane's 1876 Snake River trip.[28]

[27] See Part I this book, Chapter 3, note 6.
[28] See Part III this book, Chapter 12, November 23 entry and note 8.

CHAPTER 12

SOUTH OF YELLOWSTONE LAKE

The party continues west along the south end of Yellowstone Lake, crossing south of the Promontory, Chicken Ridge, and Flat Mountain, where Mr. Everts is lost on September 9. On September 11 the party reaches West Thumb and stays until the fifteenth, searching for Mr. Everts. On September 14 the snow is 20 inches deep, and is falling constantly.

CROSSING THE PROMONTORY

Thursday, September 8, eighteenth day. We traveled across a high promontory running into the lake[,] winding among steep ravines and through fallen timber lying in heaps with full grown living forest above it.[1] This timber must have been deadened by fire, the trunks being bare of limbs and much decayed, but in such masses as to be impassable in many places causing us to make wide detours to find a trail.

The standing forest is very dense; the pack animals ran between trees, often wedging themselves in so tightly as to require some trouble in extricating them. Several of the packs burst causing numerous delays. Our faces were scratched, clothes torn, and limbs bruised squeezing through between saplings.

[Langford] *On one of these occasions when we were in a vast net of down timber and brush . . . and when our tempers had*

---

[1] Now known as the Promontory.

been sorely tried and we were in the most unsocial of humors, speaking only in half angry expletives, I recalled that beautiful line in Byron's "Childe Harold":

> There is a pleasure in the pathless woods,
> [There is a rapture on the lonely shore,]

which I recited with all the "ore rotundo" I could command, which . . . produced an instantaneous response of uproarious laughter, which . . . had the effect . . . to create a pleasure in the pathless wilderness we were traveling.[2]

After a hard day's work traveling at all points of the compass for a distance of at least fifteen miles we struck a stream leading north through a deep ravine, and followed it down.[3] Presently the ranges opened out skirting a pretty little bottom in which we camped. Distance direct, 7 miles.

HEDGES AND EVERTS CLIMB A HIGH POINT

[Hedges] *General Washburn and myself, after pitching camp and disposing of supper (on the 7th) took a ramble to spy out a route for our next day's drive. At about a mile from camp, in nearly a due-east course, we came upon a game trail, passed an old Indian tepee at least a year old, skirted a little lake about 50 feet above the main lake, snugly tucked up about the foot of a high, bold, bluffy point partly open and partly covered with standing and fallen timber. At that time we only ascended a short distance . . . We were anxious to know what could be seen from the top of that mountain, and Mr. Everts proposed to me that I should go with him as soon as breakfast was over in the morning, September 8. Accordingly we went . . . The point reached the night before was soon passed, and we stood upon*

[2] Langford, *Discovery*, 130.
[3] Probably Grouse Creek. According to Langford, they camped about a mile from the lake. (Ibid., 127)

what appeared as the top seen from the base, but we found it but one step to a much bolder point, whose base was concealed from our view below. Not knowing the persistency of the man, I asked him if we had better go to the top, and his quick response was, "By all means." The sides of this mountain were in places so nearly perpendicular that we made slow and labored progress. Sometimes losing our foothold, we would slide back several feet . . . Thrice we halted on what seemed from below to be the summit, and still we found the top beyond us, which we reached by a final desperate attempt . . . Here we stood on a broad, level, rocky rim to a high plateau, pine covered as it receded, which commands a most magnificent view of the whole lake . . . In admiration of the pluck and perseverance of my companion, I told him that point should be named Mount Everts . . . During the half hour that we remained on this mountain, probably 1,200 feet above the lake's surface, we traced almost its entire outline, as well the part that we proposed to traverse as that over which we had already come . . . This was only the day before he got separated from us, and so strong was my faith that he knew our course and would appear at some point in our advance that I scarcely entertained a fear till we finally reached the farthest point where we left the lake.

In descending the mountains Mr. Everts took a shorter line to camp . . . I found Mr. Everts in camp when I reached it . . . The company, of course, assented to my proposed name for the mountain we had visited.[4]

Messrs. Hedges and Stickney wandered off from the party in the morning but struck the shore of the lake and followed it, meeting us shortly after going into camp. In the evening a grizzly bear with cubs was roused by some of the party, but as

[4] *Helena Daily Herald,* October 8, 1870. This article by Hedges was written to commemorate Everts' disappearance the month before, on September 8. Also see Hedges, "Journal," 385.

This peak (9,235 feet), now unnamed, is the first high point directly south of the Southeast Arm. It is the most northerly point of Two Ocean Plateau. For some reason General Washburn gave the name Mount Everts to the heights east of Mammoth Hot Springs, five or so miles west of the spot where Everts was found. In this manner the first suggested designation of Mount Everts has been forgotten.

they had not lost any bears she got away with her interesting family undisturbed. These animals are very numerous in the basin, the green grasses, berries, and pine nuts affording them abundant supplies of food, but our party kept up such a rackett of yelling and firing as to drive off all game for miles ahead of us.

The numbers of springs of water on the slopes of these ridges is surprising, large districts on the hill sides being swampy and impassable. The water from the granite rocks is always good, from all others bad.

The small lakes are perfectly alive with otter, which may be seen playing upon their surfaces at night fall by hundreds. Beaver, mink, and muskrat are also abundant.

Trumbull, as a participant in the bear hunt, gives a good account of the actual facts:

[Trumbull] *Six of the party decorated themselves as walking armories, and at once started in pursuit. Each individual was sandwiched between two revolvers and a knife, was supported around the middle by a belt of cartridges, and carried in his hand a needle carbine. Each one was particularly anxious to be the first to catch the bear, and an exciting foot-race ensued until the party got within 300 yards of the place where the bear was supposed to be concealed. The foremost man then suddenly got out of breath, and, in fact, they all got out of breath. It was an epidemic. A halt was made, and the brute loudly dared to come out and show itself, while a spirited discussion took place as to what was best to do with the cubs . . . It was decided to advance more cautiously to avoid frightening the animal, and every tree which there was any chance of climbing was watched with religious care, in order to intercept her should she attempt to take refuge in its branches. An hour was passed in vain search for the sneaking beast, which had evidently taken to flight. Then this formidable war party returned to camp, having a big disgust at the cowardly conduct of the bear, but, as the darkie said, "not having it bad." Just before getting in sight of camp, the six invincibles discharged their firearms simultaneously, in order to show those remaining behind just how they would have slaughtered the bear, but more particularly just how they did not. This was called the "Bear Camp"....*

Jake Smith, with his usual lack of scriptural accuracy, remarked, "I always considered Daniel a great fool to go into a den of bears."[5]

FROM SOUTH ARM TO FLAT MOUNTAIN ARM

Friday, September 9, nineteenth day. We moved in a westerly course over the summit of a high promontory,[6] thence descending into a narrow open valley and crossing a small stream rising in the promontory between two arms of the lake and flowing south.[7]

This creek rising as it were in the very midst of the Yellowstone lake, is the source proper of Snake River[;] five miles below it empties into a stream flowing from a heart shaped lake five miles in diameter.[8] This stream is about seventy feet wide, three feet in depth and is the main fork of Snake river. This explains the origin of the old story of the "two water" lake or spring, to the effect that the two streams, the Yellowstone emptying into the Gulf and the Snake river, into the Pacific had

[5] Langford, *Discovery,* 129.

[6] Chicken Ridge and Continental Divide, west of South Arm.

[7] Surprise Creek. It flows into Heart River and actually is one of the sources of the Snake River. One must stretch it some to have it rise "in the very midst of Yellowstone Lake."

[8] Heart Lake. "Named prior to 1870 for an old hunter by the name of Hart Hunney who in early times plied his trade in this vicinity. He was possibly one of Bonneville's men, for he seems to have known the General well.... The spelling, *Heart,* dates from the expeditions of 1871. The notion that the name arose from the shape of the lake seems to have originated with Captain Barlow [Barlow-Heap Expedition, 1871]. (Chittenden, *Yellowstone National Park,* 1964 ed., 174) See Part I this book, Chapter 3, *Yellowstone* section.

Notwithstanding Doane's 1870 "heart-shaped lake" reference, Barlow's contribution, and the fact of its present-day name, many persons (including Chittenden in 1895) have suggested that Lewis Lake, to the west, actually appears more heart-shaped.

Oddly, Doane's 1870 map reverses Heart Lake; i.e., the peninsula indents it from the south shore rather than (correctly) from the north.

a common source. The proximity is truly unparalleled, the
waters of one stream actually running from between the waters
of the other.[9] Passing thence westward we became entangled in
fallen timbers of the worst description on steep hillsides and
among impassable ravines but finally emerged into an open flat
on the promontory and camped at the fountain head of the
Snake river. Distance, five miles. [Barometer, 22.65; thermometer, 45°; elevation, ------.]

On going into camp it was discovered that a pack horse was
missing. This animal a small cayuse had been uniformly un-
fortunate, miring down in marshes, tumbling over log heaps and
rolling endwise down steep banks; he was found a couple of
miles back firmly wedged between two trees.

[Trumbull] *The lost pack-horse was an extraordinary animal
— a beautiful, golden stallion of vast proportions, some thought
as much as thirteen hands high. Some people would have called
him of buckskin color, but he was of that intensely brilliant hue
which buckskin assumes when wet and in the shade. He was one
of the animals which, in fording the Yellowstone, managed to
flounder into deep water and saturate his pack; and whenever
we waded through a slough, he was sure to be the horse that got
stalled. In such cases he invariably waited until the packers,
with their patience severely tried, went back and lifted him out
by main force. On this particular occasion, he had proven himself the acrobat of the pack-train by turning a number of somer-
saults backward, down the hill, pack and all; and when found,
was astride a log lengthwise, his feet just touching on either
side, but either unable to extricate himself, or too proud and
patient to make an effort to do so. He consequently very
resignedly contemplated his position and surroundings. He was
too proud and spirited to betray any emotion, though his situation was undoubtedly distasteful to his feelings. In war, he
might have been a lion; in peace, he was certainly a lamb. He*

[9] Doane mislocated Two Ocean Pass, which is some twenty miles to the southeast. Osborne Russell describes it accurately in *Journal of a Trapper, 1834-1843*.
(1955 ed., 43)

The "Yellowstone Wonder." Woodcut illustration for Langford's second *Scribner's* article, June 1871.

was just the kind of a horse that, in a race, would have driven every thing else before him . . . He was dubbed the "Yellowstone Wonder." [10]

EVERTS IS LOST

Mr. Everts did not come in with the rest of the party and men sent back on the trail found no traces of him. We fired signal guns and kept watch fires during the night, but without success. Supposing that he had passed to the right or left we moved on the next day leaving men behind on the trail.

[Everts] *We had a toilsome day. It was quite late in the afternoon. As separations like this had frequently occurred, it gave me no alarm, and I rode on, fully confident of soon rejoining the company, or of finding their camp. I came up with the pack-horse, which Mr. Langford afterwards recovered, and tried to drive him along, but failing to do so, and my eyesight being defective, I spurred forward, intending to return with assistance from the party. This incident tended to accelerate my speed. I rode on in the direction which I supposed had been taken, until darkness overtook me in the dense forest."* [11]

Because no one knew at that time the seriousness of Everts' disappearance, a bit of tomfoolery was certainly not out of order:

[Langford] *Last night there occurred an incident which I would gladly blot from these pages, but a faithful record of all the events of camp life in connection with this expedition demands that I omit nothing of interest, nor set down "aught in malice" . . .*

Hedges, being tempted of one of the Devils which doubtless roam around this sulphurous region . . . asked me if I was

[10] Trumbull, "Yellowstone Expedition," 490.
[11] Everts, "Thirty-seven Days of Peril," 2.

hungry. I replied that such had been my normal condition ever since our larder had perceptively declined.

Langford then tells how he and Hedges, while on guard duty, ate the two prized partridges which the cook had specially set aside for tomorrow's breakfast. In the morning's discussion over the missing birds, the guilty pair kept their silence and let the blame fall upon Booby, at which time the poor dog was pelted with stones and sticks.

[Langford] *Suddenly the camp was electrified by Gillette asking, "Who was on guard last night?" "That's it," said one. "That's where the birds went," said another. This denouement was too much for Hedges and myself, and amid uproarious laughter we made confession, and "Booby" was relieved from his disgrace and called back into the camp, and patted on the head as a "good dog," and he has now more friends in camp than ever before.*

Such practical jokes surely relieved inevitable tensions brought on by such close and continued contact both with one another and with a formidable environment. One gets some idea of this tension in reading Langford's closing diary entry just the day before his horseplay story:

[Langford] *I growled at Hauser and scolded him a little in camp tonight because of some exasperating action of his. I here record the fact without going into details. I think that I must try to be more patient. But I am feeling somewhat the fatigue of our journey. However, there is something to be said on the other hand, and that is that there is no one of the party better able to bear its labors and anxieties than I, and therefore I should be the last man to lose my patience.*

I know of nothing that can try one's patience more than a trip of any considerable length by wagon train or pack train through an uninhabited region, and the most amiable of our race cannot pass this ordeal entirely unscathed. Persons who are not blessed with uncommon equanimity never get through such a journey without frequent explosions of temper, and seldom without violence. Even education, gentle training and the sharpest of mental discipline do not always so effectually subdue the passions that they may not be aroused into unwonted fury during a long journey through a country filled with obstructions. Philosophy has never found a fitter subject for its exercise than that afforded by the journey we are now making, which obliges the members of our party to strive to relieve each other's burdens. [12]

CAMP ON FLAT MOUNTAIN ARM

Saturday, September 10, twentieth day. We broke camp at 10 a.m., taking a westerly course through fallen timber and over steep ridges[,] striking a long slender arm [13] of the lake in the afternoon[;] camped on this inlet, distance five miles. Parties then went back on the trail and laterlly, hunting Mr. Everts. Messrs. Hauser and Langford ascended a high peak near camp and fired the woods in hope of giving him a point of direction. [14] We also fired signal guns during the night.

According to Everts' account, he got up early on the tenth, confidently retracing the trail.

[Everts] *While surveying the ground my horse took fright, and I turned around in time to see him disappearing at full speed among the trees. That was the last I ever saw of him. It was yet quite dark. My blankets, gun, pistols, fishing tackle, matches — everything, except the clothing on my person, a couple of knives, and a small opera glass — were attached to the saddle.* [15]

---

12 Langford, *Discovery,* 132.
13 Flat Mountain Arm.
14 Flat Mountain (9,204 feet).
15 Everts, "Thirty-seven Days of Peril," 2.

> In his excitement Everts then lost his spectacles, a
> tragedy because of his nearsightedness. Later he lost
> his two knives and one shoe. His field glasses became
> his most valuable article, a lens enabling him to start a
> fire.

In the evening large numbers of fish were caught, Private
Williamson catching fifty-two large trout, all that two men
could carry, in less than an hour. The night passed away and the
missing man did not come. In the early morning we were
serenaded by a couple of lions, their melancholy voices echoing
through the heavy forest with a peculiar, wild and mournful
sound. We had blazed trees at all our camps throughout the
whole trip, leaving on each a record with dates, route and distances marked on these hewn sections.[16] Here we also hung up
in sight a few rations, hoping Mr. Everts might strike our trail
and follow after we had gone.

Sunday, September 11, twenty-first day. I started in advance,
with Messrs. Hauser and Langford, rounding the arm of the lake
at the head of which a narrow valley with a small stream comes
in; thence striking due west up a steep ridge we reached on its
summit a plateau of open woods, with grassy spaces between
and a perfect network of small lakes, their surfaces covered with
the broad leaves of the tiger lilly.[17] These extended for miles
on either side as the promontory is very extensive running far
out into the waters of the great lake.

[Hedges] *The most graphic map of the lake that I could*

16 A clue as to why none of these blazes has been located was suggested by Lee
Coleman, Yellowstone Park ranger (now retired), "Harry Trischman, an old time
ranger in Yellowstone, told me the Army Superintendent ordered the removal and
obliteration of all the old names and dates throughout the park. I have seen many
trees with large, overgrown blazes that have the face cut off by later axe work,
showing a deliberate effort to remove whatever appeared on the blaze. Chances are,
many historic items were lost by this 'cleanup' order."

17 Doane probably meant the yellow pond lily (*Nuphar polysepalum*), the common waterlily of high mountain lakes, blooming in midsummer. The waxy yellow
flowers are up to five inches across. The large, nutritious seeds were gathered by the
Indians.

*present my readers would be the human hand with fingers ex-
tended and spread apart as much as possible. The main portion
of the lake is the northern, which would represent the flat of
the hand. There is a large southwest bay, nearly cut off, that
would represent the thumb, while there are about the same
number of narrow southern inlets as there are fingers on the
hand.''*[18]

AT WEST THUMB (east side)

After an easy ride in a direct line of seven miles, we reached
the extreme westerly and longest arm of the lake, a lovely bay
of water six miles across and with steam jets rising at its
southern extremity in great numbers.[19]

Opposite the head of this arm is the great yellow mountain
seen from Mount Langford several days ago.[20] This is the central point from which radiate double barriers separating the
waters of the Yellowstone from the Snake, and the latter from
the Madison, Snake river flowing on the east side of the mountain southerly, and the Fire Hole branch of the Madison, rising
in a small lake to the west of the range, the main branch coming
from Madison lake south of this.[21] This mountain may be said

[18] Later, when it was realized that Delusion Lake (the index finger) was not an
inlet, the simile to the human hand was dropped except for "West Thumb." Professor
R. W. Raymond made an amusing observation:

> The gentleman who first discovered this resemblance must have thought
> the size and form of fingers quite insignificant, provided the number
> was complete. The hand in question is afflicted with elephantiasis in the
> thumb, dropsy in the little finger, hornet bites on the third finger, and
> the last stages of starvation in the other two. (L. P. Brockett, *Our
> Western Empire*, 1243)

[19] West Thumb.

[20] Mount Sheridan. Langford refers to this as "Brown Mountain." See Bonney,
Guide to Wyoming Mountains, 429.

[21] The Senate document incorrectly reads Henry's Lake. Henry's Lake is not the
source of the Madison (see Chapter 14, note 10). Doane's 1870 map shows a lake east
of the Continental Divide which he designates Madison Lake and shows it on the
Firehole drainage. There is no such lake on the Firehole drainage. But see discussion
under "The Maps," in Appendix to Part II. Doane was actually referring to Shoshone
Lake which is on the Snake River drainage. Doane's sentence illustrates the inaccurate knowledge of the geography of the region in 1870. It was confused because

to be the focus of volcanic action in the basin, the greatest phenomena being observed within a radius of thirty miles from its summit. From its yellow sulphurated appearance it can be readily distinguished, and is the central and most important landmark in the great basin. We camped on the arm of the great lake, three miles north of its extremity and on the east side. Here we remained in camp during the 12th, 13th, 14th, and 15th, searching constantly for Mr. Everts. During the night a heavy snow storm set in which continued at intervals throughout the next day.

THE SEARCH FOR EVERTS

Monday, September 12, twenty-second day. Today parties went out in couples on the search. Messrs. Smith and Trumbull followed the lake shore around the head of the promontory to within sight of our previous camp. They returned in the evening and reported having seen human footsteps in the sands of the beach. Mr. Smith was positive he saw several Indians on foot who retreated into the woods on being approached. They were probably white men, as a man was met in the neighborhood a few days afterwards, who stated that he belonged to a small party in the vicinity.

> Everts' account indicates that on September 11, the day before, he had tried to cut across the South Arm-Flat Mountain Arm promontory and had come upon Heart Lake.

of the intertwined drainage of the rolling Madison Plateau, all at the same elevation. (See Chapter 13, notes 2 and 4; Part III, Chapter 10, October 29 entry).

Hayden states that what is known as Shoshone Lake was referred to as Madison Lake prior to that time. (*Sixth Annual Report,* 244; explorations for 1872)

The Park visitor today may observe the divide of waters between the Snake River (south) from the Yellowstone (east) at the point where Grand Loop Road crosses the Continental Divide, 12.6 miles east of Old Faithful and 4.3 miles west of West Thumb.

Along this same highway at Craig Pass, 6.8 miles east of Old Faithful, 10.2 miles west of West Thumb, Isa Lake flows both west into the Firehole drainage which ultimately empties into the Atlantic Ocean, and south into the Snake River drainage, which empties into the Pacific Ocean.

In the middle of this promontory is one lake of considerable size and at a high elevation above that of the Yellowstone. [22]

Messrs. Washburn and Langford took a southerly direction toward the base of the yellow mountain for a distance of eleven miles. They saw from the divide the lake from which Snake river issues, also a small lake at an elevation of eight hundred feet above it. [23] Beyond this divide they became entangled in an immense swampy brimstone basin, miles in extent, abounding in sulphur springs, small geysers and stream jets. [24] The ground was covered with turf or calcareous deposits in a thin scale overlying hot white mud. Mr. Langford's horse broke through several times coming back plastered with the white substance and badly scalded. They were unable to penetrate to the lake on account of the instability of the footing.

> Everts said he started for a group of hot springs on the third day, September 12. These were the Heart Lake Geyser Basin at the foot of Mount Sheridan. This was the same day that Langford and Washburn searched the area. In writing about it, Everts described:

> [Everts] *The lake* [presumably Heart Lake] *is fed by innumerable small streams from the mountains, and the countless hot springs surrounding it. A large river flows from it, through a cañon a thousand feet in height, in a southeasterly direction, to a distant range of mountains, which I conjectured to be Snake River; and with the belief that I had discovered the source of the great southern tributary of the Columbia, I gave it the name of Bessie Lake, after the "Sole daughter of my house and heart."* [25]

---

[22] Delusion Lake (7,822 feet), eighty-nine feet higher than Yellowstone Lake.
[23] Heart Lake and Witch Creek Lake above.
[24] Heart Lake Geyser Basin, reached today only by trail. From highway 14.2 miles north of South Entrance, 7.5 miles south of West Thumb, take trail east six miles.
[25] Everts, "Thirty-seven Days of Peril," 4.

For seven days Everts hovered here, a delay which put him completely out of reach of his colleagues. It stormed furiously. He was reluctant to leave the hot springs which warmed him, and the supply of elk thistle roots which he boiled and ate. On the third night of the storm, during his sleep, he broke through the crusted border of a hot pool and scalded his hip.

WEST THUMB GEYSER BASIN

Tuesday, September 13, twenty-third day. The snowy weather continued with intervals of hail and rain; large fires were kept up and the search continued. I rode around the head of the lake to the steam jets visible from camp. This was the largest system we had yet seen.

Located at the extreme point of the most westerly arm of the lake, and on a gentle slope reaching along the shore for a mile, and extending back into the woods for the same distance, this system embraced every variety of hot water and mud springs seen thus far on the route with many others heretofore unseen.

Four hundred yards from the lake shore is a basin of mud having a bright pink color. This is a system of itself being seventy feet in diameter and projecting thick mud through small craters of a conical shape around the edge of the basin while the center is one seething mass.[26] The deposit speedily hardens into a firm laminated clay stone of beautiful texture, though the brilliant pink color fades to a chalky white.

Near and around this basin are a dozen springs from six to twenty-five feet across, boiling muddy water of paint like consistency, in colors varying from a pure white to a dark yellow; then come several flowing springs, from ten to fifty feet in diameter of clear hot water, the basins and channels of which are lined with deposits of red, green, yellow, and black, giving them an appearance of gorgeous splendor; these deposits were too friable to preserve, crumbling at the touch. The bright

[26] Thumb Paint Pots.

colors were on the surface of the rock only, not extending to its interior.

Below these were several large craters of bluish water impregnated with sulphate of copper; these boiled to the height of two feet in the centre and flowed large streams of water. Their rims were raised a few inches in a delicate rocky margin of a fringe like appearance deposited from the water. Beyond these are two lakes of purple water, hot but not boiling these give deposits of great delicacy of coloring.[27]

Nearby are two more Bluestone springs the largest we have yet seen; one, 30 x 40 feet and of temperature 173° flows a stream into the other one, about seventy feet distant, and six feet lower. This latter spring is 40 x 75 feet[,] temperature 183°, a stream of a hundred inches of water flows from it. The craters of these springs are of calcareous stalagmite, and lined with a silvery white deposit which illuminates by reflection the interior to an immense depth. Both craters have perpendicular but irregular walls and the distance to which objects are visible down in their deep abysses is truly wonderful. No figure of imagination[,] no description of enchantment can equal in imagery the vista of these great basins. West of these is a group of clear hot water which surpass them all for singularity, though not in beauty. These are basins of different sizes and unknown depths in which float what appear to be raw bullock hides, as they look in a tanner's vat, waving sluggishly about with every undulation of the water the resemblance is complete.

On examination the leathery substance proves to be a fragile texture something like the vegetable scum in stagnant pools, ("and yet it is not vegetable") with brilliant colors of red, yellow, green, and black, on the shaded side. It is easily torn and could not be preserved unless indeed by pressure like rose leaves. It has the thickness and flabbiness of rawhide, and is quite heavy when wet. Digging down into the basin I found that this singular substance filled the whole depth, layer upon layer being deposited; and stranger than all the lower strata were

[27] Abyss Pool, Black Pool, and several other beautiful hot springs.

solidified, turning to pure finely grained sheets of alabaster specimens of which I brought in.

On the margin of the lake is a double row of calcareous springs at the boiling point, here 185° which do not flow except at intervals. These build up craters of solid limestone from five to twenty feet in height[;] many of these stand in the waters of the lake and several are partially broken away by the erosive action of its waves. There are two flowing ones with low craters, from twenty to thirty feet in diameter, which run as much as fifty inches of boiling water each. Of these, the walls of the crater are visible to a great depth, inclining at a sharp angle under the bed of the lake, and separated from it by thin barriers of shelving rock.[28]

All along the shore for a mile runs a terrace of calcareous stalagmite in a deposit of from twenty to fifty feet in depth the edges of which are worn to a bluff bank by the action of the waters. This stratum has been deposited by the mingled streams of mineral waters of every sort which flow from the springs above and flood its whole surface.

The rock is stained with variegated colors which speedily fade, but specimens obtained from the lower beds and bleached in the lake are the purest of alabaster. Scattered over the surface of this terrace are masses of calcareous tufa which when dried will float in water.

Not less than a thousand inches of hot water flow into the lake at this point, and, numberless jets can be seen boiling up far out in its basin.

In this enumeration I have described but a few of the largest springs; there are hundreds of them including vapor vents, mud spouts, and still caldrons.

They are scattered through the woods in such numbers as to require the utmost care to prevent stumbling into them at every turn. Occasionally this anomaly is seen of two springs at different levels both boiling violently[;] one pours a large and constant stream into the other yet the former does not diminish,

[28] Fishing Cone.

nor does the latter fill up and overflow. Most of the springs however seem to be independent of each other and to come from immense depths, having different levels at the surface, different temperatures and pulsations; seldom are found the waters and deposits of any two exactly alike. It is impossible to adequately describe and utterly impossible to realize from any description more than a faint idea of the beauties and wonders of this group.

FOREST FIRE ON FLAT MOUNTAIN

The fire kindled on the summit of the mountain [three days ago] has by this time spread to a vast conflagration before the devouring flames of which tall pine trees shrivel up and are consumed like grass. The whole summit of the mountain sends up a vast column of smoke which reaches to the sky, "a pillar of cloud by day and of fire at night."

I returned to camp in the evening profoundly impressed with the greatness of the phenomena we were witnessing from day to day, and of their probable future importance to science, in unraveling mysteries hitherto unsolveable.

Messrs. Hauser and Gillette, returned in the evening unsuccessful in their search; the snow, hail, and rain by turns continued and lions were again heard during the night.

> Hauser and Gillette became more or less lost trying to reach camp, but the "dog 'Booby' took the lead when they were at fault, and brought them into camp all right." [29]

Wednesday, September 14, twenty-fourth day. We remained close in camp, the weather continued stormy. The snow was now twenty inches deep and fell almost constantly. Our pavilion tent served us admirably[;] without it we should have suffered great inconveniences for lack of shelter.

The water fowl of the lake deserve a passing notice. These

[29] Langford, *Discovery*, 151.

include swans, pelicans, gulls, Canada geese, brants, and many varieties of ducks and dippers. There are also herons and sand hill cranes. Of pelicans, immense numbers sail in fleets along the lake, in company with the majestic swan. The gulls are of the same variety as those found in San Francisco Harbor. [30] I think the pelicans are identical with those found in the great lakes on the northern border but am not sure as we did not get a specimen.

There are several low flat islands in the lake which are always white with them at the close of the day.

Of birds and animals of the forest, I have seen of each several not down in the books, comprising of birds a sort of large mockingbird, two varieties, belonging, I think, to the genus corvus. Two kinds of woodpeckers, two or three species of grouse, also a guidebird, [31] resembling a blackbird, but larger. I saw but one of these. The day I went to the bottom of the grand canon it hopped and flew along from rock to rock ahead of us during the whole trip down, waited perched upon a rock while we were resting, and led us clear to the summit again in the same manner making innumerable sounds and gestures constantly to attract attention. Others of the party remarked birds of the same kind and acting in the same manner. The common birds of the basin are Eagles, hawks, ravens, ospreys, prairie chickens, and grouse. Of animals I saw several species of squirrels and weasels which do not appear in the books. We saw no snakes of any kind in the basin.

[Langford] *Lieutenant Doane to-day requested me to loan him this diary from which to write up his records, as the condition of his thumb has interfered with his use of a pen or pencil. I have accordingly loaned it to him, and Private Moore has been busy the greater part of the day copying portions of it.* [32]

[30] Today, Park gulls, banded for identification, are found spending their winters along the California coast.
[31] A colloquial term not in use today. Roger Tory Peterson told the editor that he had never heard of the term.
[32] Langford, *Discovery,* 152.

Thursday, September 15, twenty-fifth day. The snowstorm abated[,] clouds hung overhead in heavy masses, an oppressive dampness pervaded the atmosphere, the snow melted away rapidly under the influence of a warm wind from the west.

The only traces of Indians we had seen were some shelters of logs rotten and tumbling down from age together with a few poles standing in former summer camps. There were no fresh trails whatever. Appearances indicated that the basin had been almost entirely abandoned by the sons of the forest.

A few lodges of Sheep Eaters, a branch remnant of the Snake tribe, wretched beasts who run from the sight of a white man, or from any other tribe of Indians are said to inhabit the fastnesses of the mountains around the lakes, poorly armed and dismounted, obtaining a precarious subsistence and in a defenseless condition. We saw however no recent traces of them.

The larger tribes never enter the basin, restrained by superstitious ideas in connection with the thermal springs.

A party of three can travel with perfect safety as far as Indians are concerned in any part of this district, by keeping close watch upon their horses at night as the lions would make short work with them if an opportunity was afforded, horse flesh being their favorite diet.

Friday, September 16, twenty-sixth day. We moved around the arm of the lake[33] to the hot springs previously described, camping near them; distance, five miles. [Barometer, 22.70; thermometer, 44°; elevation, 7,714 3/5 feet.] [34]

The shore line is bordered by a levee of obsidian lava pebbles and calcareous fragments, cutting off and enclosing ponds of water behind it from which the surplus waters flow out through crevices in the dike. These ponds are the accumulated waters of thousands of springs breaking from the ground all along the line of the beach. The lake bottom is everywhere free from caverns and gradually sloping to deep water. The ruins of old spring

[33] West Thumb.
[34] Words in brackets crossed out in Doane manuscript.

craters appear at intervals along the shore.

In the afternoon the snow had diminished to a general depth of six inches and exposed locations were bare. We spent the evening in collecting specimens from the different springs and laying in a supply of fish for future use.

Crater Wells & Springs

Geyser Region

Fire Hole Basin

Crater

Geyser

Lieut. Doane 1870

Madison River

MADISON L.

ROCKY

Hot Springs

MOUNTAINS

Prismatic Basin

Hot Springs

N.

Snake R.

CHAPTER 13

WEST THUMB TO OLD FAITHFUL

Leaving West Thumb on September 17, in a northwesterly direction, the party travels south of the present-day west-bound Loop Road to Old Faithful. They see Shoshone Lake and reach the Firehole River, following it to the Old Faithful geyser area where they spend two days. Upper Geyser Basin is described at length.

Saturday, September 17, twenty-seventh day. In the morning we noticed a great commotion among the hot springs — many heretofore quiescent were now active and flowing. Others which previously boiled gently, sent up clouds of steam and threw water to the height of three and four feet. Evidently they have their periods of increased action like those we saw on the Yellowstone below.

FINAL SEARCH PARTY FOR EVERTS

Before leaving camp a council was held which resulted in our leaving Mr. Gillette, with Privates Williamson and Moore, to make a final effort in the search for Mr. Everts. They were provided with one pack mule and ten days' rations. They were to go back to Bozeman by our former route or at discretion make a search and follow on our trail.

Langford reported the party depressed at the thought of abandoning the search for Everts. Hauser, encouraging Gillette, said helpfully, "I think that I should be willing to take the risk of spending ten days more in this wilderness, if I thought that by so doing I could find a father-in-law." Uproarious laughter showed they all knew Gillette had been extending many social courtesies to Miss Bessie Everts.

About this time, Everts was at Heart Lake. The sun came out. It then occurred to Everts that he could make a fire with his opera glass. With renewed hope he decided to move on but could not decide which way. He started south to the Snake River and Idaho, but became confused in the rugged topography. His goal – a notch in the mountain barrier – came no closer. He gave that up.

Then he decided to go west into the Madison Valley, the short route to civilization, and stumbled off in that direction until a precipice obstructed his route. He could find no way around. He lit a fire. It got out of hand, flashed into a full scale forest fire and he fled to escape the conflagration.

Finally dropping from exhaustion, he experienced an hallucination – an old preacher friend standing nearby insisting that Everts retrace his steps. Trudging the long route around Yellowstone Lake and down Yellowstone River seemed hopeless, but Everts followed the ghostly advice. On and on he stumbled by day, resting by night, wondering if he would ever come out alive. He nibbled now and then on a few thistle roots which he carried in his pockets.

A GLIMPSE OF SHOSHONE LAKE

Starting at 9 o'clock in a northwesterly course[1] we traveled

[1] Langford noted: Today's tourist, "looking south from Shoshone Point [mid-

up a gradual declivity through open timber four miles to the summit of the divide, then descending for about the same distance we crossed a deep open valley containing a headwater tributary of the Fire Hole branch of the Madison.[2] The course then lay over the summit of a very steep ridge a thousand feet in altitude, the face of which was covered with masses of fallen timber through which we found a passage of the utmost difficulty. Passing the summit[3] a glimpse was obtained of a good sized lake[,] the source of the Fire Hole.[4] Skirting then a ridge to the northward over a country very much broken we soon began to descend and finally reach the bottom of an open ravine abounding with springs of good water where we camped.[5] Distance, twelve miles. Bar, 22.70 [22.65]; ther, 40° [50°]; elevation, 7,535 feet.

FIREHOLE RIVER

Sunday, September 18, twenty-eighth day. We broke camp at 9 o'clock traveling along the slopes of the ridges, skirting the ravines through falling timber and passing in many places over swampy terraces for a distance of three miles, when we suddenly came upon a mountain torrent forty feet wide and running through a gorge of trachyte lava two hundred feet in depth; this was the Fire Hole river heading in a lake a few miles to the south.[6] Following down the course of this stream we

point on the Old Faithful-West Thumb road] may catch a glimpse of a portion of the prostrate forest through and over which we struggled." (*Discovery,* 162*n*)

[2] Doane is wrong here. They are in the valley of DeLacy Creek which flows into Shoshone Lake on the Snake River drainage. Hauser and Langford felt they were on Snake River headwaters, not Firehole waters, and they were right.

[3] Again the Continental Divide.

[4] Shoshone Lake. See discussion of error under "The Maps," in Appendix to Part II; also Hayden, *Sixth Annual Report,* 244. The Continental Divide separates the Shoshone Lake drainage from hat of the Firehole River at a point only four miles west of the lake.

[5] Spring Creek.

[6] The Firehole was the name given to this region by the early trappers.

Topping says: "Kit Carson, Jim Bridger, Lou Anderson, Soos, and about twenty others on a prospecting trip . . . saw the geysers of the lower basin and named the river that drains them the Fire Hole." (*Chronicles of the Yellowstone,* 16)

presently passed two fine roaring cascades, where the water tumbled over rocks to the depths of twenty and fifty feet successively.[7] These pretty little falls if located on an eastern stream would be celebrated in history and song; here amid objects so grand as to strain conception and stagger belief, they were passed without a halt.

Shortly after, the cañon widened a little and on descending to a level with the stream, we found ourselves once more in the dominions of the Fire King.

Scattered along both banks of the infant river were boiling springs depositing calcareous craters. These varied from two to twelve feet across, and were all in active eruption, the cones deposited varying from three to forty feet in height and sometimes covering a space of one fourth of an acre. A feature of these craters is that they gradually seal themselves up and stop the flow of their waters by depositing around the interior edges a deep fringe of rocks the points of which finally meet across the openings of the craters forming a sort of sieve which finally closes entirely, forcing the waters to break out in some other place. Numbers of these self-extinguished craters are seen scattered along both banks of the stream, having now become cones of solid rock. Most of the waters are clear, and the deposits are usually calcareous, but we found a few springs of water resembling ink, from which the deposit was a black hard rock composed largely of silica and extremely flinty, shattering the blades of our hatchets and giving forth showers of sparks when struck by them.

The valley here descended rapidly and we soon saw in front dense columns of steam rising above the hills. After traveling two miles among these springs of various kinds and through several bogs on the slopes, we came suddenly upon an open

The Firehole must not be confused with the Burnt Hole and the latter's name origin, as some writers do. According to Russell, the Burnt Hole was on the Madison River about forty miles northwest of present Madison Junction, putting it in the broad valley about ten miles west of present Hebgen Dam. (*Journal of a Trapper, 1834-43*, 1921 ed., 101) Ferris gives it a similar location (*Life in the Rocky Mountains, 1830-35*, 85), as does Hayden. (*Sixth Annual Report*, 24)

[7] Kepler Cascades, 1.6 miles south of Old Faithful.

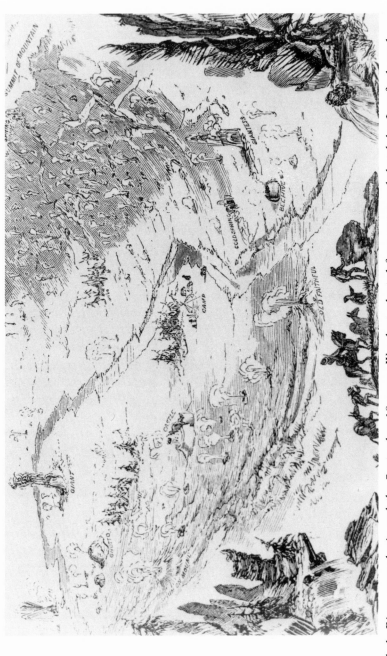

Firehole River geyser basin and the September 18 camp. Woodcut adapted from notes and sketch by Langford; used with his second *Scribner's* article, June 1871.

rolling valley of irregular shape about two miles in width and three in length.

This valley is known in the wretched nomenclature of this region as the Fire Hole, and contains phenomena of thermal springs unparalleled upon the surface of the globe.[8] Crossing the river we moved down to a central point of the valley and camped in a little grove of pine timber near the margin of a small marshy lake around which were to be seen numerous fresh signs of buffalo driven out by the noise of our hasty intrusion.[9] Distance, six miles. Bar, 23.80 [22.70]; ther, 43° [40°]; elevation, 6,626 feet.

The valley is of triangular shape with an obtuse angle on the south side of the river which runs parallel with its longer side and about three hundred yards from the foot of the range.

At the apex of the obtuse angle a stream fifty feet wide comes in from the south joining the main river in the midst of the valley below its central point. The mountain ridges on all sides are fifteen hundred feet in height, composed of dark lava in solid ledges, are heavily wooded and very steep. Small groves of timber also cover the highest points of the valley, which is a succession of ridges, and of rounded knolls capped by springs, the intervening depressions being rendered marshy by the overflow of their waters. The whole surface of the basin to an unknown depth is a calcareous bed deposited from the springs.

OLD FAITHFUL

Near the head of the valley immediately after crossing to the south side of the river we came to one of the geysers which was at the time throwing water with a loud hissing sound to the height of one hundred and twenty-five feet: in a few minutes the eruption ceased and we were enabled to approached the

[8] Upper Geyser Basin.

[9] Langford's picture indicates they camped on the west bank of the Firehole River in the bend east from Castle Geyser ("The Wonders of the Yellowstone," 121); Doane says it was a few hundred yards below Old Faithful and half a mile upstream from Castle Geyser.

crater. This had originally been a crack or fissure in the calcareous ledge[10] the seam of which could be traced by minute vents a distance of sixty feet, but was now closed up by deposits from the water to an opening seven feet long by three feet wide in the centre from which the steam escaped with a loud rushing sound. The hillock formed by the spring is forty feet in height, and its base covers about four acres.

Near the crater and as far as its eruptive waters reach the character of the deposit is very peculiar. Close around the opening are built up walls eight feet in height of spherical nodules from six inches to three feet in diameter. These in turn are covered on the surface with minute globules of calcareous stalagmite incrusted with a thin glazing of silica. The rock at a distance appears the color of ashes of roses, but near at hand shows a metallic gray with pink and yellow margins of the utmost delicacy; being constantly wet, the colors are brilliant beyond description.

Sloping gently from this rim of the crater in every direction, the rocks are full of cavities in successive terraces, forming little pools with margins of silica the color of silver, the cavities being of irregular shapes constantly full of hot water and precipitating delicate coral like beads of a bright saffron. These cavities are also fringed with rock around the edges in meshes as delicate as the finest lace.[11] Diminutive yellow columns rise from their depths, capped with small tablets of rock and resembling flowers growing in the water. Some of them are filled with oval pebbles of a brilliant white color, and others with a yellow frost work which builds up gradually in solid stalagmites.

Receding still farther from the crater the cavities become gradually larger and the water cooler, causing changes in the brilliant colorings and also in the formations of the deposits.

---

[10] Doane is wrong in calling this a calcareous ledge. Old Faithful's cone is built up of a mineral called geyserite, or silicious sinter, whose whitish-gray coloration is often mistaken for limestone. Geyserite belongs to the quartz mineral family.

[11] This marvelously beautiful and delicate natural stonework has long ago disappeared under the tread of tourists and the vandalism of "collectors." There are remote places in Yellowstone Park where it may still be found, but those who know the location do not reveal it for fear of its destruction.

These become calcareous spar of a white or slate color and occasionally variegated. The water of the geyser is colorless, tasteless and without odor. The deposits are apparently as delicate as the down on a butterfly's wing both in texture and colorings, yet are firm and solid beneath the tread.

Those who have seen stage representations of Aladdin's Cave and the Home of the Dragon Fly, as produced in a first class theatre, can form an idea of the wonderful coloring, but not of the intricate frost work of this fairy like yet solid mound of rock growing up amid clouds of steam and showers of boiling water. One instinctively touches the hot ledges with his hands and sounds with a stick the depths of the cavities in the slope, in utter doubt of the evidence of his own eyes. The beauty of the scene takes away one's breath. It is overpowering, transcending the visions of Mosoleum's [Moslem's] Paradise; the earth affords not its equal, it is the most lovely inanimate object in existence. The period of this geyser is fifty minutes. First an increased rush of steam comes forth followed instantly by a rising jet of water which attains by increased impulsions to the height of one hundred and twenty-five feet, escaping with a wild hissing sound while great volumes of steam rise up to an altitude of five hundred feet from the crater. Rainbows play around the tremendous fountains, the waters which fall about the basin in showers of brilliants, then rush steaming down the slopes to the river. After a continuous action for a space of five minutes the jet lowers convulsively by degrees, the waters finally disappear and only a current of steam pours forth from the crater. When we consider that it plays through an aperture 7 x 3 feet in measurement, an idea can be formed of the vast quantity of water ejected by this great natural fountain. In the neighborhood of this are several old geysers choked up by their own deposits to small simmering craters with their outside slopes decomposed and shelly.

BLACK SAND BASIN

Following the edge of the valley southward, we passed hot

springs of various sizes from three to fifty feet in diameter, with craters built up in rounded knolls from three to forty feet above the general level. All these were of clear water without sulphur vents; most of them had periodical turns of violence during which they threw off immense columns of steam and water in jets from the center of their basins to heights varying from three to fifty feet. Many of these springs gave evidence of having been once geysers of the first class, but their waters in such cases had burst out from excess of pressure in large springs at the bases of the old craters where they were building up anew.

Large swampy places in the hollows were formed of a greasy calcareous slime covered with turf growing evergreen from the warm water below. In many localities there were large groups of standing trees in these marshes, dead, and denuded of bark to the height of three feet, their bare trunks being of a snowy whiteness and fast turning to stone. These were always found in places where hot water flowed down at some period from geysers above. They presented with their deadened tops and bare and whitewashed stumps a very singular appearance.

No sulphur springs, no sulphur deposits are found in the valley [;] but few mud springs are seen and these are small in dimensions.

Along the margin of the stream [12] coming in from the south, are swampy flats from which many partially submerged craters project. These boil violently and flow quantities of hot water, but do not throw jets.

SUNSET LAKE

Near the mouth of the stream and on the west side is a lake of Bluestone water, a hundred feet in diameter with steam evolving from its waters which flow over a low rim in every direction down the slopes depositing a yellow bed which is now many feet in thickness. Below this on the margin of the stream is a spring 30 feet in diameter boiling with great fury and flowing a

[12] Iron Creek.

large stream into the creek.

On the opposite side at a distance of fifty yards, a fissure in the strata becomes visible six feet in width and of unknown depth. It is bridged in most places with rock, but has frequent steam vents and runs a large stream of hot water from west to east with a rapid current. This stream can be traced for a distance of three hundred yards, the rush of its subterranean waters being distinctly audible from under ground.

RAINBOW, EMERALD, AND GREEN POOLS

In the angle of the woods at the mouth of the creek are several large bluestone springs, some flowing, other quiessent. Whole trees fallen in the craters of these are incrusted with a white calcareous deposit, and gradually turn to stone. Leaves, pine cones, grass appears, [13] and twigs are also thus incrusted in the most delicate manner.

In these springs are calcareous deposits in the shape of mushrooms with tops spreading out at the surface of the water. [14] These are often fifteen feet in diameter and supported by stems ten feet high and two feet thick, all of solid rock.

There are two cones on the opposite bank, 40 to 50 feet in height, with small springs in their summits. [15]

The space in the angle between the streams is partially filled with a slimy marsh.

CASTLE GEYSER

Along both banks of the Fire Hole river are the greatest of the geysers. Our camp was a few hundred yards below the first

[13] As written and crossed out in Doane's manuscript. The Senate version had changed this word to read grasshoppers, which is probably correct. Perhaps the word had been misspelled by the scrivener and Doane had corrected it trying to make sense. Peterson said in 1900 that they had found petrified grasshoppers and had taken two bunches as curiosities. (Haines, *The Valley of the Upper Yellowstone,* 40)

[14] Modified slightly, Black Sand Opal Pool seems to fit this description.

[15] Reference is no doubt being made to Whistle and Spouter Geysers. Whistle's cone would rise about twenty feet above Iron Creek.

Castle Geyser cone, sketched by Trumbull during the 1870 expedition.

Castle Geyser cone. Moran woodcut modeled on Trumbull's sketch; used
to illustrate Langford's second *Scribner's* article, June 1871.

Castle Geyser. Moran watercolor, 1872. Courtesy Thomas Gilcrease Institute, Tulsa, Oklahoma.

crater described, and the most beautiful of them all.

Near the bank of the river and a half a mile below camp, rose on the farther margin of a marshy lake the Castle crater, the largest formation in the valley. The calcareous knoll on which it stands is 40 feet in height and covers several acres. The crater is built up from its center with irregular walls of spherical nodules in forms of wondrous beauty to a castellated turret 40 feet in height and 200 feet in circumference at the base. The outer rim at its summit is formed in embrasures between large nodules of rock of the tint of ashes of roses and in the center is a crater three feet in diameter bordered and lined with a frost work of saffron. From a distance it strongly resembles an old feudal tower partially in ruins.

This great crater is continually pouring forth steam, the condensation of which keeps the outside walls constantly wet and dripping. The deposit is silver grey in color, and the structure is wonderful in its massiveness, completion, and exquisite tracery of outline. At the base of the turret lies a large pine log, covered with a nodular and brilliant incrustation to the depth of several inches. The wood of this log is also petrified. The waters of this geyser have burst out in a new place, near the foot of the old crater flowing a large stream, boiling violently and diminishing the action of the great vent; yet we saw the latter on one occasion throw water to the perpendicular height of sixty feet with the escape of heavy volumes of steam.[16] It had doubtless been when intact the greatest fountain of them all.

CRESTED POOL

Near by and on the same hillock is a bluestone spring with an indented marginal basin 25 feet in diameter; this stands level full. Its interior lining is of a silver tint and the water in its perpendicular shaft appears to be of unfathomable depth.

[16] Tortoise Shell Spring.

GIANT GEYSER

A few hundred yards farther down the stream is a crater of flinty rock in shape resembling a huge shattered horn, broken off half way from its base. It is twelve feet in height, with a solid base; its sides have a curvelinear slope, ragged edges, and its cavity or nozzle is 7 feet in diameter.

During its quiescent state the boiling water can be seen in its chambers at a depth of forty feet. The action of the steam and water together producing a loud rumbling sound. Near and acting in concert with it are half a dozen smaller craters from two to eight feet in height constantly full of water and boiling violently from 2 to 6 feet into the air.[17] This great geyser played several times while we were in the valley, on one occasion throwing constantly for over three hours a stream of water 7 feet in diameter from 90 to 200 feet perpendicularly. While playing it doubled the size of the Fire Hole River, running at its maximum about 2,500 inches of water.

GROTTO GEYSER

Two hundred yards below this is a grotto formation similar in structure to the turreted spring; this is twenty feet in altitude, 40 feet in outside diameter, and has side apertures large enough for a man to crawl into; these lead to cavernous craters on the interior. A large and singular pillar of stone stands in the middle of the vent. Several of the party crawled through the interior when it was quiet, but an hour afterward it was throwing a column of water 6 feet in diameter to the height of 60 feet. Near it were several large vents[18] in which water boiled to the height of 6 feet constantly, and large streams of water ran from these down the banks into the river.

Still farther below and on the opposite bank of the stream

[17] Mastiff, Catfish, Bijou.
[18] One of these is Rocket Geyser.

Giant Geyser cone, sketched by Trumbull during the 1870 expedition.

Giant Geyser cone. Moran woodcut modeled on Trumbull's sketch; used to illustrate Langford's second *Scribner's* article, June 1871.

Grotto Geyser cone, 1871. W. H. Jackson photo. *Courtesy U.S.G.S.*

Grotto Geyser cone. Woodcut illustration for Langford's second *Scribner's* article, June 1871.

Fan Geyser. Woodcut illustration for Langford's second *Scribner's* article.

are two small craters,[19] with apertures two feet each in diameter; these two are connected, one throwing steam and the
other, water, and also alternating with another small crater
below. First the stream would rush from the upper crater roaring violently, then this would suddenly cease to be followed by
a fan like jet of water rising from the lower crater to the height
of over forty feet, often playing for perhaps two minutes; then
this would suddenly stop flowing and the steam would rush
forth again for a time. Occasionally the small crater threw a
transverse stream, sometimes alternating with either of the
others and thus they played on for hours, after which all would
subside to a gentle bubbling.

All along both banks of the river are small craters and spouts
built up in every conceivable shape; all were active except the
geysers, and each entirely independent of the others. Several
streams of water poured out in cascades from round holes in the
rocky bank of the river and a number of little geysers played
from six to forty feet at intervals.

GEYSER HILL

Opposite camp on the other side of the river is a high ledge of
stalagmite sloping from the base of the mountain down to the
river; numerous small knolls are scattered over its surface, the
craters of boiling springs from 15 to 25 feet in diameter. Some
of these throw water the height of three and four feet.

GIANTESS GEYSER

In the summit of this bank of rock is the grand geyser of the
world, a well in the strata 20 x 25 feet in diametric measurements, the perceptible elevation of the rim being but a few
inches, and when quiet having a visible depth of a hundred feet.

19 Fan and Mortar Geysers. The Washburn-Doane party named Fan Geyser.
(Langford, *Discovery*, 170)

The edge of the basin is bounded by a heavy fringe of rock and stalagmite in solid layers is deposited by the overflowing waters. When an eruption is about to occur, the basin gradually fills with boiling water to within a few feet of the surface, then suddenly with heavy concussions immense clouds of steam rise to the height of five hundred feet. The whole great body of water 20 x 25 feet ascends in one gigantic column to the height of ninety feet, and from its apex five great jets shoot up radiating slightly from each other to the unparalleled altitude of two hundred and fifty feet from the ground. The earth trembles under the descending deluge from this vast fountain, a thousand hissing sounds are heard in the air, rainbows encircle the summits of the jets with a halo of celestial glory. The falling water plows up and bears away the shelly strata, a seething flood pours down the slope and into the river. It is the grandest, the most majestic, and most terrible fountain in the world. After playing thus for twenty minutes it gradually subsides, the water lowering into the crater out of sight, the steam ceases to escape and all is quiet.

This grand geyser played three times in the afternoon but appears to be irregular in its periods as we did not see it in eruption again while in the valley. Its waters are of a deep ultramarine color, clear and beautiful. The waving to and fro of the gigantic fountain when its jets are at their highest, and in a bright sunlight affords a spectacle of wonder of which any description can give but a feeble idea.

Our whole party were wild with enthusiasm. Many declared it was three hundred feet in height but I have kept in the figures as set down above within the limits of absolute certainty.

We were led to believe by indications on the rocks that some of these geysers do occasionally play to an altitude of 500 feet, but this we did not see. [20]

[20] George D. Marler, Yellowstone Park naturalist who is more familiar with today's geysers than anyone else, gives maximum height of the Giantess, of which Doane is speaking, as 200 feet, and gives heights for the Grand Geyser at 200 feet, Beehive 200-219 feet, and the Giant over 200 feet. There are estimates of some eruptions of the Giant to 250 feet. The greatest of all Yellowstone geysers was Excelsior Geyser which ceased its eruptions in 1888 and was estimated to have

Giantess Geyser. Moran woodcut illustration for Langford's second *Scribner's* article, June 1871.

Above on the slope of the mountain is another great geyser which has lately broken out. It has deadened the timber on a wide space and for half a mile between its crater and the river. It must run a perfect torrent of water at its periods of eruption.

I have now described seven of the largest geysers seen in the Fire Hole basin and the description falls far short of the reality; to do justice to the subject would require a volume. The geysers of Iceland sink to insignificance beside them; they are above the reach of comparison.

We could not distinguish on every occasion the geysers from the other hot springs except by seeing them play and doubtless there are many besides in the valley of great size which we saw when quiet and classed as boiling springs. They all vary in times, force, deposits, and colors of water.

The number of springs of all kinds in the valley is not less than fifteen hundred and with the exception of the Bluestone Springs scarcely any two are exactly alike. Taken as an aggregate the Fire Hole basin surpasses all other great wonders of the continent. It produces an effect on the mind of the beholder utterly staggering and overpowering.

During the night we were several times awakened by the rush of steam and the hissing of the waters as the restless geysers spouted forth in the darkness; a constant rumbling as of machinery in labor filled the air, which was damp and warm throughout the night.

BEEHIVE GEYSER

Monday, September 19, twenty-ninth day. This morning we were awakened by a fearful hissing sound accompanied by the rush of falling water, and looking out saw on the other side of the stream a small crater, three feet in height, and with an opening of twenty-six inches in diameter which had scarcely

reached a height of 300 feet, sometimes playing for an hour and a half.

It was unusual that the Washburn-Doane party saw so many geysers in action. Giantess rarely erupts.

been noticed on the previous day, and was now playing a perpendicular jet to the height of two hundred and nineteen feet with great clouds of steam escaping, and causing the ground to tremble as the heavy body of water fell with tremendous splashes upon the shelly strata below.[21] Huge masses of the rocks were torn from their places and borne away into the river channel; it played thus steadily for ten minutes giving us time to obtain an accurate measurement by triangulation which resulted as above stated; this crater gave no notice of being a geyser. Its appearance and size were altogether insignificant compared with others. We were more than ever convinced that continued observation would develop the knowledge of geysers in greater numbers and of perhaps greater projectile force than any we had seen.

Our rations were becoming scarce however and seven days had been comparatively lost in searching for Mr. Everts.

We sent the train in advance at 9 o'clock and waited all the forenoon at the grand geyser in hopes of witnessing another eruption. The waters rose gradually until the great crater was nearly filled but did not play, and we were forced to leave without witnessing a repetition of the phenomena.

Doane indicated the various geysers and features on the Firehole River but did not emphasize the nomenclature. Trumbull, in his articles for the *Overland Monthly,* quite clearly locates and gives the reasons for the names of the various geysers, as follows:

[Trumbull] *The following day we traveled northwest, and soon reached the Fire Hole river. After passing by a fine cascade — which we stopped but a short time to examine — we forded the river, and camped about noon in the midst of the most wonderful geysers yet discovered in any country.... We remained two days in this wonderful basin. The most prominent*

---

21 The Washburn group named Beehive Geyser because it resembled an old-fashioned straw beehive with the top cut off. (Langford, *Discovery,* 173) An eruption of Beehive often follows that of Giantess.

geysers which we saw in operation we named as follows:

"Old Faithful" was the first geyser we saw throwing up a column of water. It was named on account of its almost constant action. It did not intermit for more than an hour at any time during our stay. . . . All around it were found pebbles and small stones, which, when broken open, proved to be simply pieces of wood, thoroughly incrusted, and perfectly hard and smooth on the outside, having the appearance of an ordinary stone. [22]

About the crater of "The Castle" was the largest cone, or mass of incrustations, in the basin. . . . We called it "The Castle," on account of its size and commanding appearance. . . . The water did not retain the shape of a column, like that thrown out by "Old Faithful," but rather splashed up and slopped over. This geyser did not appear to be doing its best, but only spouted a little in a patronizing way, thinking to surprise us novices sufficiently without any undue exertion on its part. . . .

"The Giant" discharged a column of water [which] played as if through an immense hose. We thought it deserved to be called "The Giant," as it threw out more water than any other geyser which we saw in operation. . . .

"The Grotto" has two craters, connected on the surface by the incrustations which surround them. We did not ascertain whether there was any subterranean connection between them. We did not observe both craters discharge at the same time, but one began when the other ceased. . . .

. . . .just at the edge of the timber, we found a mound in the true shape of a cone. . . . This geyser did not appear to have discharged for some time. The ground was quite dry all around, and a number of incrusted pine twigs, leaves, and cones were found, which retained their shape perfectly, but were hard, smooth, and white as alabaster. At that point, much ballast was obtained for the pack animals. [23]

[22] The relentless hand of the souvenir collector has forever swept away these marvels from public observation.

[23] Souvenir collecting was already in progress.

Crossing the river, we named the "Fantail" geyser from the fact that it discharged two streams from its vent which spread out very much like a fan.

One of the most remarkable geysers was "The Giantess". . . . When in action, "The Giantess" became a fountain with five jets, shooting the spray to a height of two hundred feet. . . . It burst forth just before sunset, and the last rays of light gave prismatic tints to the glistening drops. . . . The clouds of steam . . . became a golden fleece lit up by wreaths of rainbows. . . . "The Giantess" was by far the most beautiful sight we saw in the geyser basin.

"The Beehive" — named from the shape of its mound — was quite small, but threw its water higher than any other geyser which we saw. . . .

We were probably very fortunate in the time of our visit, for those we left behind to search for Mr. Everts came by these geysers several days later, and saw but two in operation: "The Fantail," and a smaller one near it. They were, however, short of provisions, and remained in the vicinity of the geysers but a few hours. [24]

[Washburn] *Geysers were spouting in such size and number as to startle all, and are beyond description. Enormous columns of hot water and steam were thrown into the air with a velocity of noise truly amazing. We classified and named some of them according to size.*

No. 1. The Giant, 7 by 10 feet, throwing a solid column of water from 80 to 120 feet high.

No. 2. The Giantess, 20 by 30, throwing a solid column and jets from 150 to 200 feet high.

No. 3. Old Faithful, 7 by 8, irregular in shape, a solid column each hour 75 feet high.

No. 4. Bee Hive, 24 by 15 inches, stream measured 219 feet.

No. 5. Fan Tail, irregular shape, throwing a double stream 60 feet high.

No. 6 is a beautiful arched spray, called by us the Grotto,

[24] Trumbull, "Yellowstone Expedition," 492.

with several apertures, through which, when quiet, one can easily pass, but when in action each making so many vents for the water and steam. . . .

Standing and looking down into the steam and vapor of the crater of the Giantess, with the sun upon your back, the shadow is surrounded by a beautiful rainbow, and by getting the proper angle, the rainbow, surrounding only the head, gives that halo so many painters have vainly tried to give in paintings of the Savior. Standing near the fountain when in motion, and the sun shining, the scene is grandly magnificent; each of the broken atoms of water shining like so many brilliants, while myriads of rainbows are dancing attendance. No wonder, then, that our usually staid and sober companions threw up their hats and shouted with ecstasy at the sight. [25]

Hedges' notes are even briefer. Speaking of Old Faithful, for example:

[Hedges] Soon came in sight of great geyser, crossed creek little above in bad place, lost one of my gloves — my packhorse went in all over — all rushed up side of geyser — beautiful sides in little ridges, near top worn loose stones — drove down near bank in center of geyser district and camped. . . . [26]

Langford's account adds a bit more information.

[Langford] When we left Yellowstone lake two days ago, the desire for home had superceded all thought of further explorations. Five days of rapid travel would . . . bring us . . . within twenty-five miles of Virginia City. . . . We had within a distance of fifty miles seen what we believed to be the greatest wonders on the continent. . . . Judge, then, of our astonishment on entering this basin, to see at no great distance before us an immense body of sparkling water, projected suddenly and with terrific force into the air to the height of over one hundred feet.

[25] Washburn, *Helena Daily Herald*, September 28, 1870.
[26] Hedges, "Journal," 390.

We had found a real geyser. . . . The one I have just described General Washburn has named "Old Faithful," because of the regularity of its eruptions, the intervals between which being from sixty to sixty-five minutes, the column of water being thrown at each eruption to the height of from eighty to one hundred feet. [27]

---

[27] Langford, *Discovery*, 168, 170.

Although the party studied Old Faithful for only twenty hours, they were amazingly accurate and prophetic: Old Faithful's average eruption intervals are 66 $^3/_{10}$ minutes, the shortest interval being thirty-three minutes, and the longest recorded interval ninety-five minutes. See G. D. Marler, *The Story of Old Faithful,* 35.

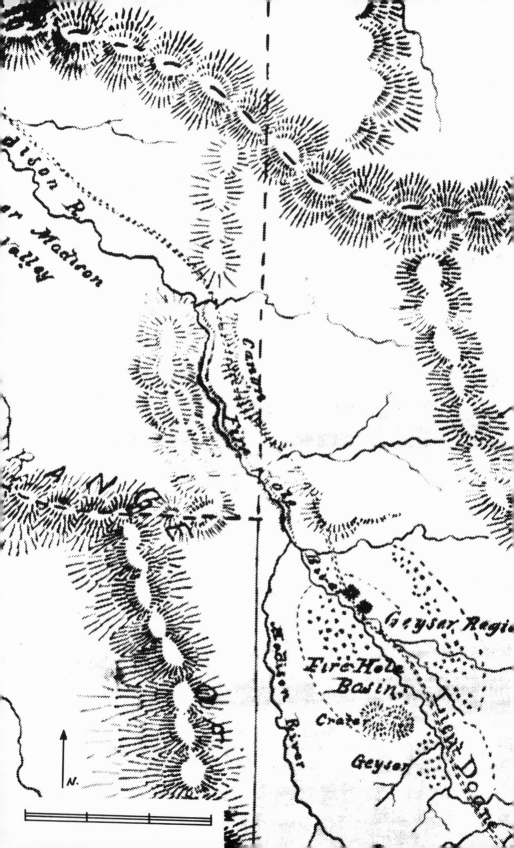

CHAPTER 14

OLD FAITHFUL TO MADISON JUNCTION

On September 19 the party follows what is now the Grand Loop Road route north down the Firehole River, discovering the further wonders of the Midway and Lower Geyser Basins. The national park idea is discussed at Madison Junction camp on September 19.

MIDWAY GEYSER BASIN AND GRAND PRISMATIC SPRING

Moving down the stream on the north side past springs and small geysers of every variety for a distance of three miles, we then traversed a valley five miles in length, swampy in many places, and in others much obstructed by fallen timber.

Thermal springs were scattered along the whole route, but none large enough to be remarkable here.

In eight miles we came to an enormous Bluestone spring nearly circular in form, 450 yards in circumference, and of unfathomable depth, boiling hot, and with clouds of steam evolving from its surface.[1] It has built up a hill fifty feet above the general level and covering about a hundred acres with a calcareous bed.

The margin of the great basin is bounded by a rim thirty feet back from the brink of the crater and elevated a few inches; the waters overflow in every direction keeping the long slopes constantly wet.

[1] Grand Prismatic Spring.

The deposits are of variegated colors, a circumstance not before remarked in any springs of this class;[2] the water boils up slightly in many places far out in the river but steadily and with no indication of violent or periodic action; the steam arising is evolved from the surface of the water, and does not escape through it from beneath.

The margin of this lake is a hundred and fifty yards from the river, which has cut away its deposit to a bluff bank, forty feet in height at that distance. Between this bluff and the basin, but at a lower level by twenty feet is a geyser with a basin 50 feet in diameter and playing a strong jet from the center to the height of 20 feet. Just beyond this and at a different level still are several smaller geysers and a bluestone spring seventy feet in diameter. Flowing from these latter over the bank into the river are five streams of boiling water, either one large enough to run an ordinary grist mill.[3] These steaming cataracts are among the most beautiful we have witnessed on the trip.

Below the great basin and at a distance from the bank are two more Bluestone springs respectively seventy-five and a hundred feet in diameter;[4] these do not flow.

Here the valley opens out to several miles in width, being of triangular shape and about twelve miles in length. The Madison river[5] comes in from the south along the west side of this valley joining the Fire Hole river at its northwest angle. In this large valley has formerly been a repetition of Fire Hole basin, but on a much larger scale. On the south side are two hills[6] of calcareous deposit having gigantic, but extinct craters on their summits. These hills are for the most part bare on the slopes, but are in some places grown up with pine timber and are eight hundred feet in height. Some of the fragments of the crater walls are 50 feet in altitude.

The south side, between the forks of the rivers contains innumerable extinct craters of great size and a few small ones in

2 Every color but violet.
3 Four only now; one has dried up.
4 Opal and Turquoise Pools.
5 Actually Fairy Creek.
6 Twin Buttes, with more pine timber now than Doane describes.

operation, but with a low grade of action.

LOWER GEYSER BASIN

On the north side of the Fire Hole river the valley slopes gradually from the bluffs to the river a space of three miles in width and is a calcareous swamp with the summits of extinct craters projecting by hundreds above its surface. This great marsh has been deposited by waters from a vast series of geysers and springs along the foothill range; though much decreased in action many of these are still in operation and for miles the swamp is yet flooded with their waters. These we passed at a distance and without visiting, but saw their clear fountains and stream jets playing on the side hill as we threaded the swamp.[7] The amount of water flowing down from this system is enormous and it was with the utmost difficulty that we found a passage through the slimy morass. Along the banks of the Fire Hole river were seen numerous stream jets and in the center of the valley is quite a range of hills now grown up with timber but which were formerly craters of immense geysers.[8] Around their bases are ponds of tepid water, and the deposit of the great marsh rises high up on their slopes.

Near the lower end of the valley a large stream comes into the Fire Hole from the north just above its junction with the Madison. This stream runs through a deep and beautiful valley in the range, and judging from the color and deposits from its waters has large systems of thermal springs somewhere on the line of its course.[9] The Madison comes in a mile below in a stream fifty yards wide and two feet deep, a mountain torrent

[7] They saw Fountain Geyser, named by Hayden in 1871. (Langford, *Discovery,* 177*n.*)

[8] Around Nez Perce Creek.

[9] The Gibbon River. Doane is right. Ten miles above Madison Junction is the Gibbon Geyser Basin, and 1.7 miles above that is Norris Geyser Basin. The Gibbon River was named for General John Gibbon who in 1872, while touring the Park, tried to ascend the North Fork of the Madison, but gave up the attempt. (Chittenden, *Yellowstone National Park,* 1903 ed., 130) Later, Doane marched in Gibbon's column in the Sioux (Custer) campaign in 1876.

running on a bed of solid lava and having its source in Madison lake[10] about forty miles above.

The whole valley has a singularly ruinous and melancholy aspect. The few groups still in activity and the thousands of extinct and broken craters attest the grandeur of its former phenomena; an air of desolation settles upon the landscape which renders it almost painful to contemplate.

Following down the river bank through a deep cañon of volcanic rocks in many places broken in huge fragments we presently came to rapids having a fall of perhaps 40 feet in a half mile.[11]

At this point the channel narrows to one hundred and fifty feet and is shut in by perpendicular rocks. We were obliged to scale the ridges above and follow down the stream on its summit through dense timber and steep ravines with considerable difficulty. In three miles we reached a level bottom on the river at the junction of a large creek coming in from the northeast. Camped at the junction; distance, 18 miles. Barometer, 23.50; thermometer, 38° [43°]; elevation, 6,594 feet.

THE NATIONAL PARK IDEA
by the editors

The party camped at Madison Junction where the Gibbon and Firehole Rivers combine to form the Madison. Doane makes no mention of a campfire discussion on the national park idea, but Langford says in his diary on September 20, 1870:

[Langford] *Last night, and also this morning in camp, the entire party had a rather unusual discussion. The proposition*

[10] Again, the Senate document differs from Doane's manuscript and reads Henry's Lake (see Chapter 12, note 21). Henry's Lake is on the Snake River (Henry's Fork) drainage and is not the source of the Madison. However, one drainage source of the Madison (Horn Creek) extends within four miles north northwest of Henry's Lake. Doane's map had clearly shown Henry's Lake draining into Henry's Fork.

[11] Firehole Canyon and Firehole Falls, one mile south of Madison Junction.

was made by some member that we utilize the result of our exploration by taking up quarter sections of land at the most prominent points of interest, and a general discussion followed. One member of our party suggested that if there could be secured by pre-emption a good title to two or three quarter sections of land opposite the lower fall of the Yellowstone and extending down the river along the cañon, they would eventually become a source of great profit to the owners. Another member of the party thought that it would be more desirable to take up a quarter section of land at the Upper Geyser Basin, for the reason that that locality could be more easily reached by tourists and pleasure seekers. A third suggestion was that each member of the party pre-empt a claim, and in order that no one should have an advantage over the others, the whole should be thrown into a common pool for the benefit of the entire party.

Mr. Hedges then said that he did not approve of any of these plans – that there ought to be no private ownership of any portion of that region, but that the whole of it ought to be set apart as a great National Park, and that each one of us ought to make an effort to have this accomplished. His suggestion met with an instantaneous and favorable response from all – except one – of the members of our party, and each hour since the matter was first broached, our enthusiasm has increased. It has been the main theme of our conversation to-day as we journeyed. I lay awake half of last night thinking about it; – and if my wakefulness deprived my bed-fellow (Hedges) of any sleep, he has only himself and his disturbing National Park proposition to answer for it.

Our purpose to create a park can only be accomplished by untiring work and concerted action in a warfare against the incredulity and unbelief of our National legislators when our proposal shall be presented for their approval. Nevertheless, I believe we can win the battle.

I do not know of any portion of our country where a national park can be established furnishing to visitors more wonderful attractions than here. These wonders are so different from anything we have ever seen – they are so various, so extensive — that the feeling in my mind from the moment they began to appear until we left them has been one of intense surprise and of incredulity. Every day spent in surveying them has revealed to me some new beauty, and now that I have left them, I begin to feel a skepticism which clothes them in a memory clouded by doubt. [12]

Although Langford says Hedges suggested the national park, Hedges does not mention the incident in his diary, but merely states:

[Hedges] *Didn't sleep well last night — got to thinking of home and business, seems as if we were almost there.* [13]

However, Hedges added a footnote to his diary as published in August 1904:

[Hedges] *It was at the first camp after leaving the Lower Geyser Basin when all were speculating which point in the region we had been through would become most notable, when I first suggested uniting all our efforts to get it made a national park, little dreaming such a thing were possible.* [14]

Hedges' first public mention of this idea is in his article on "Yellowstone Lake" in the *Helena Daily Herald* of November 9, 1870:

[Hedges] *Hence the propriety that the Territorial lines be so readjusted that Montana should embrace all that lake region west of the Wind River Range, a matter in which we hope our citizens will soon move to accomplish,* as well as to secure its future appropriation to the public use. [emphasis added by editors]

[12] Langford, *Discovery*, 179.
[13] Hedges, "Journal," 370.
[14] Ibid.

It must be noted that Hedges had taken part in an earlier discussion of the national park idea in 1865, when Hedges, Acting Governor Meagher of Montana, and Territorial Judge H. L. Hosmer, among others, had been told of the Yellowstone wonders at old St. Peter's Mission near the mouth of Sun River by Father Kuppens, a young Belgian priest who had just visited the area that spring of 1865.[15] The 1865 discussion had come at a time when the federal government had, only a year earlier, granted the Yosemite Valley to the state of California "for public use, resort and recreation."

Folsom and Cooke had publicly suggested the national park idea in the manuscript of their article which was published in the July 1870 issue of *The Western Monthly,* but this portion was cut out by the editors.[16] Folsom had mentioned it again to General Washburn on the eve of the General's departure with the Washburn-Doane Expedition.[17]

Washburn's notes of the expedition do not mention the national park idea.[18]

But the idea was not entirely new by any of these persons. A national park in the West, with Indians in their native life and the country in its undisturbed naturalness had been suggested by George Catlin in 1832:

> What a splendid contemplation too, when one . . . imagines them as they *might* in future be seen, (by some great protecting policy of government) preserved in their pristine beauty and wildness, in a *magnifi-*

---

[15] See Part II, Chapter 1; also Hedges, "Account of a Trip to Fort Benton in October, 1865," *Rocky Mountain Magazine,* Vol. I, No. 3, 155; Cook, Folsom, Peterson, *The Valley of the Upper Yellowstone,* xxviii.

[16] Chittenden, *Yellowstone National Park,* 1964 ed., 80n.

[17] Langford, *Discovery,* 38.

[18] *Helena Daily Herald,* September 27 and 28, 1870.

Madison Junction, where the September 19, 1870 campfire discussion of a Yellowstone National Park took place. National Park Mountain in background. Photo taken in the 1880's or 1890's.

> *cent park,* where the world could see for
> ages to come. . . . A *nation's Park,* contain-
> ing man and beast, in all the wild and fresh-
> ness of their nature's beauty![19] [Catlin's
> italics and parentheses]

After their return from the expedition, members of
the Washburn-Doane party launched efforts toward
the establishment of a national park. These efforts
and the resultant creation of Yellowstone National
Park, on March 1, 1872, are discussed further in "The
Trail Widens," Appendix to Part II of this book.

National Park Mountain (7,500 feet), southwest of
Madison Junction, was later named to commemorate
the 1870 discussion at Madison Junction.

[19] George Catlin, *North American Indians,* I, 261-262.

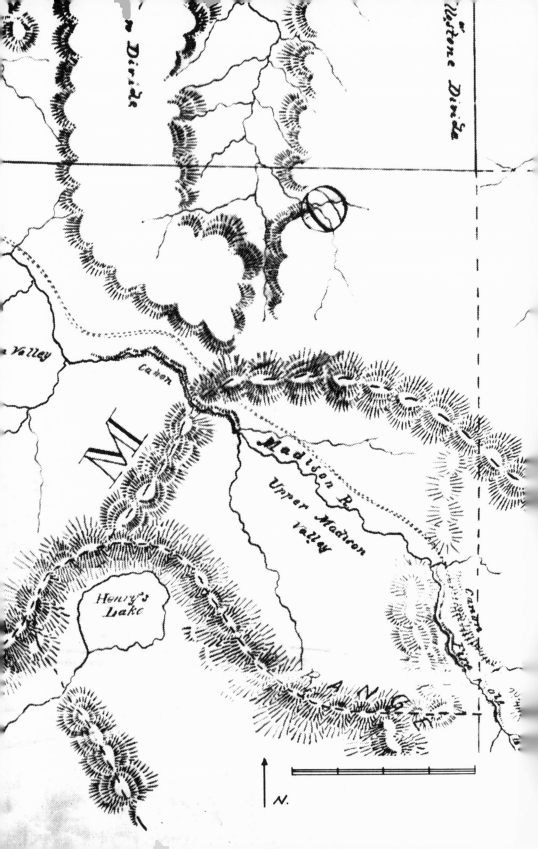

CHAPTER 15

DOWN THE MADISON RIVER TO VIRGINIA CITY

The party goes west down the Madison, through the Upper Madison
Basin. They turn north near West Yellowstone. Madison Canyon is
described, followed by descriptions of the Middle and Lower Madison
Valleys. On September 23, Doane heads for Fort Ellis, leaving the main
party on its way to Helena.

Tuesday, September 20, thirtieth day. We now thought ourselves clear of the geysers but in the morning were surprised to
see a graceful column of steam ascending to the height of three
hundred feet on the opposite side of the creek and in the elbow
of a mountain range.

We did not visit this group, but forded the Madison twice just
below camp and followed down its right bank.[1]

The river is here shut in by a canon of high lava mountains
rising with a perpendicular front of from one thousand to two
thousand feet. The bare rocks stand out in impassable walls
seamed with fissures and scarred by storms of centuries. Huge
fragments in many places overhang the narrow path. In others
the summits of the wall are composed of trachyte, overlaid with
masses of basaltic columns of immense height.[2]

---

1 Terrace Spring, one half mile up the Gibbon River.

2 Today's Park traveler follows Doane's route and description by driving west
from Madison Junction, through Madison Canyon, to West Yellowstone. Rock debris,
from old as well as recent earthquakes, almost blocks the highway traveler as it did
Doane's party.

Often the grassy narrow shelf on the margin of the stream is covered with débris, and we were frequently obliged to take to the river which runs on a ledge of lava full of deep cavities and strewn with large boulders. After threading our way thus for twelve miles through the grandest vistas of volcanic mountain scenery, the ranges suddenly fell away to the right and left and we entered upon a great plateau heavily timbered and sloping to the west. This was the upper valley of the Madison[3] and is within the limits of the great basin.

We passed rapidly down this uniform slope for ten miles all the way through timber, in many places deadened by fire, coming in on the river bank in the center of the valley and thence followed down to an open district in the middle of which rise two hills of considerable altitude.[4]

Mr. Langford and myself ascended to the summit of the highest of these and obtained a full view of the surrounding country.

The valley is nearly circular about twenty miles in diameter with the Madison running from south to north through its center.[5] The land slopes gradually to the river from east and west.

Two large streams head in the east and west points skirting the margin of the valley through rolling prairie lands, and joining the Madison near the north point.[6]

The land is open all around the edges of the valley but its central portions are heavily timbered, a circumstance very unusual in this country. The timber is wholly pine, the valley being above the region of cottonwood. The river bottom is much lower than the slopes which terminate in bluffs on both sides of the stream. The formation is débris washed down from the mountains and covered by a deep loamy soil. In the narrow

[3] Now called Madison Valley.

[4] They are now in Montana. The two buttes are called Horse Butte. Take U.S. Highway 191 north from West Yellowstone to drive through the Madison Valley Doane now describes.

[5] Madison Valley is about fifteen miles in diameter with the Madison running in a northwesterly direction through its center.

[6] Cougar Creek (northeast) and either Denny Creek or South Fork Madison River (west and southwest).

bottoms are numerous small lakes swarming with water fowl. The river channel is extremely crooked and full of islands and the woods abound with game of various sorts.

THE BANNOCK TRAIL

The great Bannock trail crosses the valley from west to east, from the snake river to the head waters of the Gallatin.[7] We should have skirted the foothills on the east side and thus have avoided the timber, but were traveling by the compass and could not see the lay of the country on account of the dense forest. We camped three miles north of the two hills near the junction of one of the two streams and eight miles from the head of the cañon through which the river flows out of the valley. Distance, 27 miles. Barometer, 23.60 [23.50]; thermometer, 32° [38°]; elevation, 6,434 feet.

HORSE THIEVES

This district has a bad reputation as being a place of rendezvous for the bands of horse thieves and road agents which infest the territory. Its dense forests[,] moderate climate, enormous range, and abundance of game rendering it a pleasant and secure retreat for lawless men.

[7] This great Indian highway was the only feasible route for the Bannocks to reach Crow country without invading other Indian territory to the north (in Montana) or to the south (Wyoming). It extended from Henry's Lake across the Gallatin Range of the Park, following down Indian Creek and the Gardner River to Mammoth Hot Springs, where it was joined by another coming up the valley of the Gardner. Between Mount Holmes and Bell's Peak was a pass through which the hostile Bannocks entered the Park in 1878. There is also another pass north of Quadrant Mountain and still a third south of Mount Holmes.

From the Gardner the trail led across the plateau to the ford above Tower Falls and then up the Lamar Valley, closely paralleling the present day highway to Soda Butte. One fork there paralleled today's Cooke City Highway, the other fork followed the long divide between Cache and Calfee Creeks and down Timber Creek to Clark's Fork, finally reaching the Big Horn valley by way of the Shoshone River. See Chittenden, *Yellowstone National Park,* 1964 ed., 12; Norris, *Annual Report of the Superintendent for 1880,* 9; W. F. Replogle, *Yellowstone's Bannock Indian Trails.*

About the rustling element in the Yellowstone area:

[Langford] *Mr. Hauser and Mr. Stickney all through the day were a few miles in advance of the rest of the party, and just below the mouth of the cañon they met two men who manifested some alarm at the sight of them. They had a supply of provisions packed on riding saddles and were walking beside their horses. Mr. Hauser told them that they would meet a large party up the cañon, but we did not see them, and they evidently cached themselves as we went by. The Upper Madison in this vicinity is said to be a rendezvous for horse thieves.*[8]

According to Hedges, Langford and Doane came upon three horses which they caught and used during the rest of the journey. The horses were said to be those of the Murphy-Edmonson gang of outlaws. This was their area of operation.[9]

Horse and cattle rustlers found big money in the systematic robbery of the large herds then on the open range. Men like "Teton" Jackson, Ed Harrington, and Bob Tarter worked both sides of the Divide and found high meadows in and near Yellowstone ideal for their crisscross plan of shipment — stolen Wyoming and Montana stock were slipped through to the Utah market; coming back, Idaho goods found their way into Cheyenne, and so on.

MADISON CANYON

Wednesday, September 21, thirty-first day. We moved at 9:30 a.m. down the river traveling for eight miles through a constantly narrowing arm of the valley thickly grown up with sage brush. We then entered a cañon extending for ten miles, very crooked with a general trend to the northwest and break-

[8] Langford, *Discovery,* 181.
[9] Hedges, "Journal," 391.

ing through a high volcanic range heavily timbered in places. [10]
The trail was easy and the bottom of the cañon quite hilly;
heavy masses of débris having fallen from the lava summits on
either side. The walls of the cañon are steep but seldom perpendicular, and numerous ravines, the channels of small streams
come in laterally.

Numbers of large springs gush out high up on the mountain
sides, forming cascades which tumble down the rocks, glittering
in the sunlight like ribbons of silver.

This range forms a section of the outer rim of the great basin,
and its summits are above the altitude of the drift.

The river channel falls rapidly throughout the whole length
of the cañon, and debouches at its outlet in the middle valley of
the Madison where we came once more into Montana scenery —
a broad valley of bare sloping ridges flat on their summits and
composed of modified drift with sparsely timbered mountains
beyond the limit of vision. The river here turns sharply to the
north.

Following the slope to the great range on the right, we
traveled over foot hills of drift. [11] Numerous streams come
down from the range through deep ravines worn in the slopes.
The summits of the peaks are Russia Granite [12] and some of the
lower ones are ground smooth by the drift current. The ground
descends with great rapidity, and in ten miles we came to a
series of bluffs, falling away northward into another and much
lower terrace of the valley.

The lateral streams from the range now became larger and ran
over beds of cobbles and boulders of every variety of granite.
The feldspathic and Russian being most frequently found.

Surface lava cropped out on the hill slopes but the whole
lower valley is one mass of modified drift. We camped in a deep
wooded ravine by the side of a clear mountain torrent sheltered
completely from a cold wind storm which had chilled us all the

---

10 This is the now famous Madison Canyon where the great earthquake of August
17, 1959, occurred, and filled Hebgen Lake.
11 The Madison Range.
12 A colloquial or obsolete term, unknown today in geology.

afternoon. Distance, 26 miles. Barometer, 23.70 [23.60]; thermometer, 40° [32°]; elevation, 6,382 feet.

The night was clear and cold, ice froze to the depth of one and one half inches on still water, by morning.

Thursday, September 22, thirty-second day. We started at 8 o'clock, climbing the steep slopes of the ravine and following the table lands for several miles. The valley widened constantly and the huge granite peaks grew higher and higher as we descended to a lower level. After following the slopes for six miles we went down to the river bank and there found numerous prospect holes in the drift and wagon tracks showing a near approach to settlements.

In twenty four miles the valley again fell off in steep bluffs of drift cobble stones, and we came to a lower terrace on which occasional herds of stock were seen grazing.[13] Cottonwood timber now appeared in the place of the pines, the valley widened to twelve miles, the bottom or lowest terrace along the river being a bed of washed granite boulders lightly covered with earth for the most part, but in places bare rocks for the space of hundreds of acres.

The stream ran bank full, over a bed of the same formation. The lava no longer appeared in the valley, though huge masses cropped out from the lateral ranges.

The granite peaks here tower above on the right to the height of over three thousand feet, their bald summits glistening in the sunlight, reflected from the red granite and the masses of snow. We camped on the river bank in sight of the upper settlements of the Madison. Distance, 30 [38] miles; Bar. 25.00, Ther. 38°, Elevation 4,937 feet.

Friday, September 23, thirty-third day. We moved down the river crossing two miles below camp at a point[14] nine miles distant from Virginia City, and striking the road to Sterling

[13] They were following what is now Montana State Highway 1 along the Madison north to Ennis, Montana.
[14] Near Ennis, Montana. Sterling was near Norris, Montana.

which follows the valley for ten miles. The river then bends to the northeast through a deep gorge in the hills which bound the valley on the north.

The level portions of this valley are well settled with numerous large farms near the head of the cañon, and along the borders of a district overflowed at some seasons of the year. All crops are here irrigated and small grains produce abundantly.

At the point where the road leaves the valley[15] for Sterling, I separated from the Helena party taking a near cut over the hilly range to the Madison bridge, at the crossing of the Virginia City and Gallatin Valley road. This road passes over ridges burrowed in every direction after quartz, and through ravines with arastras and quartz mills on their streams. I halted for the night at the bridge on the Madison. Distance, 35 miles.

In the cañon of the Lower Madison are found large numbers of small petrifactions of great beauty. These are brought down by the current from the volcanic regions above and are highly prized for settings of jewelry.

[15] Near McAlister, Montana.

A typical ranch house in the country south of Bozeman and Fort Ellis, 1872. This is the territory Doane traveled in returning to Fort Ellis after leaving the Washburn party. W. H. Jackson photo. *Courtesy U.S.G.S.*

CHAPTER 16

END OF THE EXPEDITION

Doane describes the Gallatin Valley. More about Everts. Summary of
the Washburn-Doane Expedition.

Saturday, September 24, thirty-fourth day. I started for Fort
Ellis at 9 a.m. The road is passable for stages and leads over
rolling hills eastward to the Gallatin Valley, which is about
sixteen miles across from east to west and thirty miles in length.
The west or main branch of the Gallatin river rising in the north
rim of the great Yellowstone basin flows northward through
this valley. Its bottom lands are grown up with cottonwood,
and its waters afford irrigation to fertile farms which already
support a population of over two thousand. This valley is regarded as the finest settled portion of Montana. It is superior in
all natural resources to many of the most valuable districts east,
and resembles in many respects the Cumberland Valley in
Pennsylvania, with the exception that nature works on a
grander scale in the wilds of the West than elsewhere. The
mountains are higher, the scenery more picturesque, and the air
and waters clearer than any found east of the Missouri.

The formation of the Gallatin Valley is of modified drift,
falling successively to the lowest point. Wood and grasses are
abundant and stock maintain themselves at large in good condition, without being fed at all during the winter.

I arrived at Fort Ellis in the afternoon; distance, 35½ miles.

Privates Moore and Williamson returned on the second of October. They had gone back on the trail to our second camp on the south side of the lake, thence struck the head of Snake river and followed down the stream for a distance of twenty-five miles from the Yellowstone lake. They found game plentiful and tame, and had no difficulty in obtaining an abundant supply. After an ineffectual search of five days they followed our trail, arriving without accident at the above date.

> Upon the return of the balance of the party, the news of Everts' loss was wired all over the country. On October 6, in the *Helena Daily Herald,* "Judge" Robert Lawrence (a Helena lawyer, not a judge) offered a reward of $600 to which others contributed, for the recovery of Everts. As a result of this, Jack Baronett and George A. Prichett, two experienced and old mountaineers, were provided with thirty days' provisions and dispatched in search of him. They announced their purpose to remain until the deep snows of winter drove them back unless they succeeded in finding the lost man before that. They found him October 16, which was thirty-seven days from the time he was lost.[1]

Mr. Everts was found on the tenth [sic] of October by two men from the Yellowstone Agency. On the first day of his absence he had left his horse standing unfastened with all his arms and equipments strapped upon his saddle; the animal became frightened, ran away into the woods and he was left without even a pocket knife as a means of defense. Being very nearsighted, and totally unused to traveling in a wild country without guides, he became completely bewildered.

He wandered down to the Snake river lake,[2] where he remained twelve days, sleeping near the hot springs to keep from

---

[1] Cramton, *Early History of Yellowstone National Park,* 16.
[2] Heart Lake.

freezing at night and climbing to the summits each day in the endeavor to trace out his proper course[.] [H]ere he subsisted upon thistle roots boiled in the springs, and was kept up a tree the greater part of one night by a California lion.

After gathering and cooking a supply of thistle roots he managed to strike the southwest point of the lake, and followed around the north side to the Yellowstone, finally reaching our camp opposite the Grand Cañon. He was twelve days out before he thought to kindle a fire by using the lenses of his field glass, but afterward carried a burning brand with him in all his wanderings. Herds of game passed by him during the night on many occasions when he was on the verge of starvation. In addition to a tolerable supply of thistle roots, he had nothing for over thirty days but a handful of minnows and a couple of snow birds. Twice he went five days without food and three days without water in that country which is a network of streams and springs. He was found on the verge of the great plateau above the mouth of Gardiner's river.[3] A heavy snow storm had set in and extinguished his fire, his supply of thistle roots was exhausted, he was partially deranged and perishing with cold.

A large lion was killed near him on the trail which he said had followed him at a short distance for several days previously.

It was a miraculous escape considering the utter helplessness of the man, lost in a forest wilderness, and with the storms of winter at hand.

[Everts] *Groping along the side of the hill, I became sud-denly sensible of a sharp reflection, as of burnished steel. Look-ing up, through half-closed eyes, two rough but kindly faces met my gaze.*
"Are you Mr. Everts?"
"Yes. All that is left of him."

[3] Everts was found about two-thirds of a mile south of the Tower Junction-Mammoth Hot Springs road, 9.9 miles west of Tower Junction, 8.3 miles east of Mammoth Hot Springs in the Blacktail Deer Creek valley, east branch. On this sum-mit is the Baronett-Everts Cairn.

Everts being rescued by Baronett and Prichett. Woodcut illustration for Everts' *Scribner's* article, November 1871.

"We have come for you."
"Who sent you?"
"Judge Lawrence and other friends."
"God bless him, and them, and you! I am saved!"[4]

Thus the Yellowstone Expedition closed. We saw many strange and wonderful phenomena, many things which would require volumes for adequate description, and which in future geography will be classed among the wonders of the earth; yet we only followed up the Yellowstone river, passed around two sides of the lake, and down one branch of the Madison to the main stream. We did not explore one-third of the great basin. The district will be in easy reach of travel if the N. P. Rail Road comes by way of the lower Yellowstone Valley.[5] The difficulties of the journey amount to but little after the various routes had been laid down correctly. From the 1st of June to the 1st of October the climate is very mild, considering the location.

As a country for sight seers, it is without parallel. As a field for scientific research it promises great results, in the branches of Geology, Mineralogy, Botany, Zoology, and Ornithology.

It is probably the greatest laboratory that nature furnishes on the surface of the globe.

In one special and important particular a thorough survey of this region would be of use. It is the apex of the greatest water shed in the northwest territories, and such a survey would locate correctly the sources of a large number of streams including the Missouri, Yellowstone, Big Horn, and Snake rivers. The existing maps are all far from correct in the bearings of all these rivers near their sources, the Upper Missouri being located several miles west of its true position, and too much space being left between the heads of all these great streams, thereby shortening all their channels.

By correctly locating their sources the labor of tracing their channels would be greatly simplified, as the successive trends of

[4] Everts, "Thirty-seven Days of Peril," 16.
[5] The Northern Pacific followed this route more than a decade later.

the streams could then be worked up from either of two known points — the head or the mouth.

Accompanying this report are appended a table of Meteorological Observations taken at different points along the route, a geological profile of the country traversed, and a general map of the district.[6] This latter has been compiled from our observations, together with those of a surveyor who went around by the north side of the lake last year.[7] It connects on the west side with lines of territorial survey as a base and is believed to be as correct as a map of so large a district can be made in the absence of actual measurements of the ground traversed.

Very Respectfully
Your Obt. Servant
G. C. Doane
2d Lieut. 2d Cavalry

---

[6] See "The Maps," in Appendix to Part II.
[7] David E. Folsom of the Folsom-Cook-Peterson Expedition.

APPENDIX TO PART II

by the editors

YELLOWSTONE EXPEDITION OF 1870.

METEOROLOGICAL OBSERVATIONS OF THE YELLOWSTONE EXPEDITION.

Date.	Station.	Aneroid barometer.	Thermometer.	Altitude.*	Remarks.
1870.			°	Feet.	Worked by Burt's tables.
Aug. 22	Fort Ellis, Montana Terr..	25.20	62	....	Morning.
Aug. 22	.....do..............	25.25	92	4,911	Noon; mean of 2 observ'ns; altitude.
Aug. 22	Bozeman Divide	24.10	70	6,140	Noon.
Aug. 23	Trail Camp	24.30	54	5,803	Morning.
Aug. 23	Butler's Ranch	25.10	40	4,837	Evening, stormy weather.
Aug. 24	.....do..............	25.10	40	4,837	Morning, stormy weather.
Aug. 25	Yellowstone Cañon	25.10	40	4,837	Morning.
Aug. 25	Gardiner's River..........	24.80	77	5,383	Evening.
Aug. 26	.....do..............	24.80	49	5,215	Morning.
Aug. 26	Crossing Divide...........	23.10	72	7,331	Noon.
Aug. 27	Antelope Creek...........	23.80	57	6,367	Morning.
Aug. 27	Hot Spring Creek........	23.60	60	....	Evening.
Aug. 28	.....do................	23.70	46	....	Morning.
Aug. 29	.....do................	23.70	45	6,546	Morning; mean of 3 obs'ns; altitude.
Aug. 29	High Mountain South	21.60	65	9,113	Noon.
Aug. 29	Washburn's Peak.........	20.80	50	9,966	Do.
Aug. 30	Camp Jordan	23.00	50	7,270	Morning.
Aug. 31	Near Falls................	22.60	46	....	Do.
Aug. 31	.....do................	22.70	58	....	Evening.
Sept. 1	.....do................	22.50	32	7,697	Morning; mean of 3 obs'ns; altitude.
Sept. 1	Mud Springs..............	22.75	60	....	Evening.
Sept. 2	.....do...........	22.60	32	....	Morning.
Sept. 3	.....do................	22.60	32	7,487	Morning; mean of 3 obs'ns; altitude.
Sept. 4	Yellowstone Lake	22.60	58	....	Morning.
Sept. 5	.....do................	22.50	44	....	Do.
Sept. 6	.....do................	22.40	38	....	Do.
Sept. 7	.....do................	22.50	32	....	Do.
Sept. 7	Langford's Peak..........	20.35	65	10,327	Noon.
Sept. 8	Yellowstone Lake	22.50	32	....	Morning.
Sept. 9	.....do	22.60	45	....	Do.
Sept. 10	.....do................	22.50	44	....	Do.
Sept. 11	.....do................	22.60	55	....	Do.
Sept. 12	.....do................	22.60	55	....	Do.
Sept. 13	.....do................	22.40	40	....	Morning, rainy and snowing.
Sept. 14	.....do................	22.50	36	....	Morning, snowing hard.
Sept. 15	.....do................	22.60	44	....	Morning, rainy.
Sept. 16	.....do................	22.70	44	....	Morning.
Sept. 17	.....do................	22.65	50	7,714 3-5	Morning.‡
Sept. 18	Snow Camp...............	22.70	40	7,535	Morning, rainy.
Sept. 19	Firehole Basin...........	23.50	43	6,626	Morning, clear.
Sept. 20	Madison River............	23.50	38	6,594	Morning.
Sept. 21	Madison Cañon	23.60	32	6,434	Do.
Sept. 22	Madison River...........	23.70	40	6,382	Do.
Sept. 23	Madison Settlements......	25.00	38	4,937	Do.
Sept. 24	Madison Bridge..........	....	....	....	No observations.

* Altitudes calculated from an ocean-level barometer, 30 inches; thermometer, 60°.
† Fort Ellis, Montana Territory, latitude, 45° 45'; longitude, 110° 53' west.
‡ Rainy. Mean of 15 observations. Altitude.

These altitudes all fall short, as the Aneroid barometer does not indicate with accuracy above 5,000 feet.

G. C. DOANE,
Second Lieutenant Second Cavalry.

APPENDIX A

METEOROLOGICAL OBSERVATIONS CHART

On page 208 of this volume is a photograph which shows Doane's original handwritten journal open to the Meteorological Observations chart page. The purpose of that photograph is to show the overall format of the book in which the journal was written; therefore, the chart is hardly readable.

On the facing page here is reproduced the chart which appeared in the Senate printing of Doane's journal. Though the reproduction is only fair, it does allow for a summary view of the meteorological observations made by the Washburn-Doane Expedition and for a comparison of the differences which sometimes appear between the figures in Doane's handwritten text and in the Senate's printed version. (cf. page 232, note 1)

VOL. IV. JULY, 1870. No. 19.

THE

WESTERN MONTHLY

DEVOTED TO

LITERATURE, BIOGRAPHY,

AND

The Interests of the West.

CONTENTS:

CHICAGO:

THE WESTERN MONTHLY COMPANY,

Tribune Building.

S. C. GRIGGS & COMPANY, CHICAGO:

AGENTS FOR THE TRADE.

APPENDIX B

THE WESTERN MONTHLY

Even though, as Langford says, the July 1870 issue of *The Western Monthly* had "some of the most interesting portions" cut out of the Folsom-Cook article, it was still the first article about mysterious Yellowstone to be published in a magazine with some national circulation.[1] But it hardly caused a ripple in public opinion. Why? Perhaps the watered-down content editorially imposed upon the article made it, albeit more believable, less stimulating. Also, there was not the follow-up which came in the wake of the Washburn-Doane Expedition: many articles written by the party members, lectures given by Langford and others, persuasive influence exerted on Washington politicians. Furthermore, the distribution of the July issue is a

[1] *The Western Monthly,* "Devoted to Literature, Biography, and The Interests of the West," as its subtitle ran, was a significant magazine in the early 1870's. Its subscription list totaled 9,000; although this was comparable to a magazine such as *The Overland Monthly,* it was considerably below the 40,000 circulation of *Scribner's Monthly* in 1871 and far below the 100,000-300,000 mass circulation figures reached in the late 1870's and early 1880's by such publications as *Ladies' Home Journal, Frank Leslie's Popular Monthly, Police Gazette, Scribner's* itself, and at least two dozen others.

As one example of some national attention which *The Western Monthly* commanded, in early 1871, at the height of his popularity as editor of *The Overland Monthly,* Bret Harte was offered the editorship of *The Western Monthly,* which had just changed its name to *The Lakeside Monthly.* Harte came to Chicago from California and seriously considered the offer, but traveled on to New York City.

Frank Luther Mott says of *The Western Monthly*: "It remains to this day [1938] the most important general literary magazine of a consistently high class ever published in Chicago." (*A History of American Magazines 1865-1885,* 416)

story in itself. Langford tells it as follows:

> The office of the Western Monthly was destroyed by
> fire before the copies of the magazine containing Mr.
> Folsom's article were distributed, and the single copy
> which Mr. Folsom possessed and which he presented
> to the Historical Society of Montana met a like fate
> in the great Helena fire [January 1874]. The copy
> which I possessed and which I afterwards presented
> to that Society is doubtless the only original copy
> now [1905] in existence; and, for the purpose of
> preserving the history of the initial step which even-
> tuated in the creation of the Yellowstone National
> Park, I re-published, in the year 1894, 500 copies of
> Mr. Folsom's narrative. . .[2]

This story has been passed along for many, many years, but it
harbors a slight but significant inaccuracy. A fire did in fact
completely destroy the printing offices of *The Western Monthly*
on September 4, 1870,[3] but the July issue was not consumed
"before the copies . . . were distributed." In the fall of 1870,
The Western Monthly sent to its subscribers a note telling about
the fire and its consequences. The note, after specifying the
place and date of the fire, then announced:

> The October No. of the Magazine was at that time
> nearly completed, and . . . was entirely destroyed. . . .
> It was apparent that it would be necessary to forego
> entirely the re-publication of the October No. . . . but
> the November No. appears in its usual dress . . .

In other words, the July issue did in fact go out to the regular
subscribers; it was the October issue which was destroyed prior
to distribution. It is quite likely, however, that all *extra* copies

---

[2] Langford, *Discovery,* 23-24.

[3] Not to be confused with the great Chicago Fire, which occurred one year and
one month later.

of the July issue were destroyed. This would help explain the scarcity of that issue, and certainly it would explain the almost total lack of distribution of the magazine in Montana.

Langford speaks of *one* existing copy. Actually there are more — but not many more — known to exist at present. The Library of Congress has an original copy. The Historical Society of Montana has the copy given them by Langford. In addition, among public and university libraries and historical societies, there are at least eleven more copies.[4]

However, later publications of the Folsom-Cook account made their story somewhat more available than if it had been confined to the less than a dozen publicly stored copies. Under Folsom's name, the Cook *Western Monthly* article was republished in 1894 by Langford, as *The Folsom-Cook Explorations of the Upper Yellowstone in the year 1869*; Langford added a preface. Ten years later, under the same title, the account, with Langford's preface, was republished by the Historical Society of Montana in Volume V of their *Contributions*. Expanded, and in different format, the article's material was most recently included in the book edited by Aubrey L. Haines, *The Valley of the Upper Yellowstone: An Exploration of the Headwaters of the Yellowstone River in the Year 1869, As Recorded by Charles W. Cook, David E. Folsom, and William Peterson.* Haines incorporated into his excellent 1965 book not only the above-mentioned accounts but also reminiscences of Peterson and additional writings by Cook, thus giving us the definitive first-hand story of the 1869 expedition.

Finally, there is the question of the authorship of the *Western Monthly* article. The magazine attributed it to Cook; Langford, in his 1894 republication, attributed it to Folsom. Haines refers to it as "The account prepared by David E. Folsom from his and Charles W. Cook's notes following their return to civilization . . ."[5] In 1922, Cook himself wrote:

---

[4] *Union List of Serials*, 3d ed., 2345. In addition to the institutions listed therein as having a complete set of volume IV, Northwestern University Library and the American Antiquarian Society also have the July issue.

[5] Haines, *The Valley of the Upper Yellowstone*, ix.

Soon after my return from the trip of 1869, I received a letter from Mr. Clark, a friend whom I had met the previous year, stating that he had read that an expedition to the source of the Yellowstone and Madison rivers had been contemplated, and, supposing of course that I was with it, wanted to know what we had discovered. I at once answered this letter, giving him some idea of our trip and discoveries. He at once replied and asked for a writeup of all details. I then took the matter up with Mr. Folsom and, as we had not much to do that winter at the "Ditch Company," we prepared an amplified diary by working over both the diaries made on the trip, and combining them into one. . . . Mr. Folsom then added to this diary a preliminary statement, and I forwarded the same to Mr. Clark. He wrote back at once asking my permission to have it published to which request we gave our consent. Later I received a letter from Mr. Clark stating that he had made an effort to have our amplified diary published in the *New York Tribune,* and also in *Scribner's* or *Harper's* magazines, but both refused to consider it for the reason that "they had a reputation that they could not risk with such unreliable material." Finally, he secured its publication in the *Western Monthly Magazine* . . . and received, as a compensation, the sum of $18.00. The condition in which this amplified diary appeared in the June [sic] number of the *Western Monthly Magazine* was neither the fault of Mr. Folsom nor myself, as the editor cut out portions of the diary which destroyed its continuity, so far as giving a reliable description of our trip and the regions explored.

In the original article, I alone, was credited with writing the article, but later, when a reprint was made of it by N. P. Langford, he credited it to D. E. Folsom, neither of which was correct. We did not sign the diary sent to Mr. Clark, and, as he did not know

Mr. Folsom but had carried on the correspondence with me, he had it credited to me; but the actual facts are as above outlined.[6]

[6] C. W. Cook, "Preliminary Statement to the Cook-Folsom Diary," *Haynes Bulletin,* December 1922, 7.

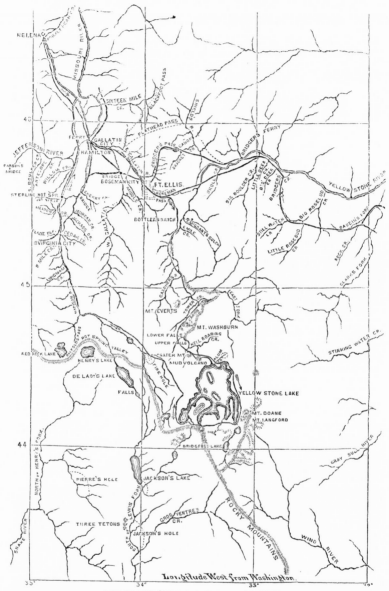

MAP OF THE UPPER YELLOWSTONE COUNTRY.

APPENDIX C

THE MAPS

The maps of the Washburn-Doane Expedition brought new intelligence about one of the then unmapped spaces of the West – the region now called Yellowstone National Park. Both Lieutenant Doane and General Washburn carefully prepared maps of the area.

In the concluding paragraphs of Doane's 1870 journal, he refers to appending "a general map of the district." This map was not published with the Senate printing of Doane's journal and it lay buried in confidential army files for almost ninety years. Carl I. Wheat says, "One would not know from the report of Doane's survey in *Wheeler Report,* vol. I, p. 637, that Doane prepared a map."[1]

Washburn's carefully drawn map also disappeared for many years. But Washburn's map was copied (with some errors, and with some insignificant format changes such as the lettering used, etc.) for Langford's *Scribner's Monthly* article; in this way the information was made public. Also, Walter deLacy, who was a draftsman in Washburn's office, used the information and maps from the Washburn-Doane Expedition to correct later issues of his famous and widely published maps of the 1870's, including an 1874 "second edition corrected & improved," now

[1] Wheat, *Mapping the Transmississippi West,* Vol. V, Part 2, 293*n*13.

with the Historical Society of Montana,[2] and another which Bancroft used in his *History of Washington, Idaho and Montana* (p. 633).

In their early researches the editors unearthed the Doane map in the National Archives and it has since been available there to other researchers.[3] Wheat published it in his monumental work, *Mapping the Transmississippi West* (1963), and called it "a pioneer map of great interest."[4] A portion of it was published in Aubrey L. Haines' *The Valley of the Upper Yellowstone* (1965).

The editors located the original tracing (or at least *an* original tracing, on engineer's linen) of the Washburn map among the archives at Mammoth Hot Springs, Yellowstone Park, and reproduce it in this volume,[5] for the first time as far as is known. The editors believe that the Washburn map was included with some of Langford's papers which his nephew Langford Smith sent to Yellowstone National Park in July, 1929.[6] It came to light when the editors were searching for Langford's original manuscript of his 1872 climb of the Grand Teton, which they also found there.

[2] Ibid., 276.

[3] "Map of the Route of the Yellowstone Expedition, September 1870." Record Group 77, Q329 No. 30. Records of the Office of the Chief of Engineers. National Archives. The original manuscript map is 24½" x 31½". It is reproduced in the present volume as a foldout map, approximately half size. The lighter blue color, indicating water features, has been added for this edition; the slightly darker blue line indicates the route traveled by the party.

[4] Wheat, *Mapping the Transmississippi West,* Vol. V, Part 2, 294.

[5] It is the foldout map which carries the handwritten legend in upper right corner, "Route of Washburn Party 1870 . . ." Note that this map shows the old Bozeman Trail and the old Bridger Trail east of Fort Ellis. The original manuscript map was 12¾" x 17¾".

In order to more faithfully reflect the original Washburn map, the reproduction presented herein has been changed slightly from the tracing discovered by the editors. On the tracing, in the upper left corner, the words "Helena," "Missouri River," and "Prickly Pear Creek" had obviously been added or altered, presumably at a later date: the lettering was clearly larger and in a different hand. These words have been re-lettered to match the rest of the original map. Also, the words "Rocky Mountains" and the markings indicating this range have been re-traced simply to darken them, because they had faded so as to be almost illegible.

[6] Langford says: "Soon after the return of our party to Helena, General Washburn, then surveyor-general of Montana, made in his office for the Interior Department at Washington, a map of the Yellowstone region, a copy of which he gave to me." (*Discovery,* 126n)

It is interesting to compare the Doane and Washburn maps with each other and with the actual terrain.

Both maps show the *Henry's Lake* drainage correctly, as they also do *Delusion Lake* and the arms of *Yellowstone Lake.*

Both err in showing the *Heart Lake* drainage coming in below rather than above Jackson Lake. Doane shows Heart Lake with a peninsula on the south rather than the north side and has it about four times out of scale. Washburn has Heart Lake in better scale but with no peninsula at all. Neither names it.

Both the Doane and Washburn maps show two lakes between Yellowstone Lake and the Firehole basin where only one lake actually exists, illustrating the usual difficulties of early map makers trying to synchronize information from two divergent sources – in this case their own observations and those of Walter deLacy. As was often the case, each map maker gave a fairly accurate representation of the geography of the area he traveled, but the map scales differed and there were no common points to tie them together.

Both Doane and Washburn actually saw *Shoshone Lake* west of West Thumb,[7] but both mistakenly mapped it as draining into the Firehole River instead of the Snake River where it actually flows. There is no such lake on the Firehole drainage. They did not actually see the drainage and the low hydrographic divide by the route they traveled and they made a bad guess as to the direction of outflow, having mistakenly heard about a "Madison Lake" flowing into the Firehole and Madison Rivers. On the Washburn map this lake is unnamed; on the Doane map it is called Madison Lake. Doane maps it about the actual distance from West Thumb as Shoshone Lake and has it about the shape of the east half of Shoshone Lake, but scales it about three times too large.

But having done this on the Firehold drainage, Doane and Washburn then had to account for the lake which deLacy had seen and mapped on the Snake River drainage and had named for himself. So they added a second lake to their maps, not

---

[7] See Part II this book, Chapter 13, note 4.

realizing it was the same lake they had seen. Washburn called it De Lacy's Lake and Doane left it unnamed.[8]

Like a schoolboy writing one spelling of a word over the other on an examination in hopes the teacher will credit him with the right one, Washburn fudges on the drainage of his De Lacy's Lake so that it could be construed as flowing into the Snake River or the Firehole River or both.

Neither Doane, Washburn, nor for that matter deLacy (who insisted the lake be named for himself as discoverer) shows the large half of Shoshone Lake extending west of the narrows, as it was hidden from their view.[9]

Below De Lacy's Lake, Washburn shows *Lewis Lake,* unnamed, with the falls north of it instead of south as they should be. Neither De Lacy's Lake nor Lewis Lake is in good scale on Washburn's map. Doane's map does not show Lewis Lake at all.

Washburn shows another lake next to the word "Firehole" on that drainage. This presumably is the Grand Prismatic Spring.[10]

Washburn also shows *Red Rock Lake* (actually there are several lakes there), but scales it too far east. Doane does not try to show it; correctly scaled it would be off the left margin of his map.

Both the Washburn and Doane maps show and name *Bridger's Lake.* The editors have not located any previous mapping of it although Doane himself said that he had seen it on an earlier map.

Mount Washburn is shown correctly on both maps if one accepts the middle of the printed words "Mount Washburn" as the location on the Washburn map. (The woodcut map in Langford's *Scribner's* article took a point east of the printed words as the location and put it on the wrong side of the Yellowstone River.)

---

[8] On the reproduction of Doane's map in this present volume, this unnamed lake, which is actually Shoshone Lake, has not been colored blue.

[9] Shoshone Lake, rather than Yellowstone Lake, may be the lake shown as "Lake Eustis" on William Clark's 1814 map. See discussion in Bonney, *Guide to Wyoming Mountains,* 1965 ed., 26-27.

[10] See Part II this book, Chapter 14, note 1.

Washburn designates *Mount Everts.* Doane calls it Great Plateau. The location on either map is approximately the same as designated on today's maps.

Remarkably, Doane shows (unnamed on his map) a creek known today as *Surprise Creek* originating on one of the south peninsulas of Yellowstone Lake and flowing into the Snake River drainage just south of Heart Lake. Washburn does not show any drainage from that point.

Doane, by recording the distances of the daily marches, enabled observations by his party and by others to be checked according to scale. This also tied in the entire Yellowstone region to a scale. Doane also gives better indication of the mountain ridges than Washburn or most prior maps.

Both the Doane and Washburn maps have longitude fairly accurate. For example, each shows the longitude of the west shore of West Thumb with only a few seconds error. Doane reckoned longitude from Greenwich and Washburn from Washington.

The chapter-opening map sections used in Part II of this book are taken from Doane's map. To facilitate the use of these section maps, two small additions have been made: a North compass direction arrow and a scale of distance have been added at the bottom of each map; in each case, one scale unit equals three miles. The route traveled by the party is marked by double dotted lines; this is on Doane's original.

On July 21, 1871, Mammoth Hot Springs became the first feature to be photographed in what would become Yellowstone National Park. W. H. Jackson photo. *Courtesy U.S.G.S.*

APPENDIX D

THE ILLUSTRATIONS

As much as there was to photograph and paint in Yellowstone, the Washburn-Doane Expedition had with it neither photographer nor professional artist. As Langford says:

> It is much to be regretted that our expedition was not accompanied by an expert photographer; but at the time of our departure from Helena, no one skilled in the art could be found with whom the hazards of the journey did not outweigh any seeming advantage or compensation which the undertaking promised.[1]

One must not be too critical of any reluctant Montana artist in the summer of 1870. After all, how was a photographer or painter to know then that he could make his reputation on Yellowstone alone.

The first pictures of Yellowstone to receive wide national exposure were the more than two dozen engraving illustrations accompanying Langford's two *Scribner's Monthly* articles in May and June of 1871. Langford was fortunate to have *Scribner's* publish his articles because they were committed to a program of numerous and fine illustrations for the magazine,[2]

[1] Langford, *Discovery,* 184.

[2] In the first issue (November 1870) of *Scribner's Monthly, An Illustrated Magazine For The People,* the editor, Dr. Josiah Gilbert Holland, promised "to

partly in an attempt to outdo a chief competitor, *Harper's.*

THOMAS MORAN

How could an illustrator in New York City, an artist who had never seen Yellowstone, accurately portray the mysteries of the region in 1871? Three sources were used: the artist's own imagination, Langford's descriptions, and actual sketches made by two members of the Washburn-Doane party. While without professional artists, the expedition did have its amateurs. One of Doane's men, Private Moore, made sketches of various Yellowstone scenes. Also, Trumbull did some sketches. Langford sent a number of Moore's and Trumbull's drawings to *Scribner's* along with his article, but the magazine editor found them too crude for direct reproduction. Major responsibility for illustrating the Langford articles was turned over to Thomas Moran, who had been doing wood engravings for *Scribner's* since their first issue. His "Crater of the Castle Geyser" and "Crater of the Giant Geyser," for example, were faithfully copied from Trumbull's drawings and embellished with figures and background landscape. This can be seen in the juxtaposed illustrations reproduced in this volume; see pages 347 and 351. Moran's version of the "Upper Falls of the Yellowstone," for example, followed Private Moore's sketch; see pages 271, 272.

Accuracy was sacrificed when Moran had to rely too much on his imagination. Obviously the awesomeness and drama of the Grand Canyon of the Yellowstone had been communicated to him from Langford's manuscript. This Moran captured in his engraving "The Great Canon of the Yellowstone," but it was

furnish the finest illustrations procurable at home and abroad. . . . The feature of illustrations has been adopted to meet a thoroughly pronounced popular demand for the pictorial representation of life and truth. . . ." (page 106) Toward the end of his career and his life, June 1881, Holland reflected: "I suppose that if anyone were asked what, more than anything else, had contributed to the success of the magazine, he would answer: its superb engravings, and the era it introduced of improved illustrative art." Frank Luther Mott agrees: "There can be no doubt that the success which came to *Scribner's* was due in large measure to the quality and quantity of its illustration." (*A History of American Magazines 1865-1885,* 466)

THE GREAT CAÑON OF THE YELLOWSTONE

Moran woodcut.
1871.

hardly recognizable as the same geographical area. As Wallace Stegner says: "The chasm appears about four feet wide and four miles deep."[3]

Moran redeemed this with his "Grand Canyon of the Yellowstone" oil painting which became one of his most famous works – for that matter, one of the most famous paintings of the American West.

As a result of Moran's assignment to Langford's article in the spring of 1871, he was inspired to visit Yellowstone himself. When he learned that Langford would accompany Hayden's survey to Yellowstone that very summer, he made plans to personally finance and make the trip through Yellowstone with the Hayden party. Though Langford did not go with the 1871 expedition, Moran did and returned with a portfolio bulging with sketches and an imagination bulging with ideas.

"In finding the Yellowstone, Moran had found himself as artist; and, as Hayden observed, his reputation was now made."[4] Moran himself, reflecting some years later, said:

> I have wandered over a good part of the Territories and have seen much of the varied scenery of the Far West, but that of Yellowstone retains its hold upon my imagination with a vividness of yesterday.[5]

The public had always been skeptical about the reports of Yellowstone marvels. National magazines had rejected as fiction the Folsom-Cook article on their 1869 expedition. Langford's *Scribner's* articles had evoked letters to the editor protesting the magazine's running such fabrications as a true story. Illustrations by Moran and others helped, but paintings and etchings could lie just as well as the written word. Even *seeing* Yellowstone with one's own eyes did not necessarily bring instant and

[3] Wallace Stegner, *Beyond the Hundredth Meridian: John Wesley Powell and the Second Opening of the West*, 178.
[4] Thurman Wilkins, *Thomas Moran: Artist of the Mountains*, 71.
[5] Ibid., 65.

easy truth. During the 1870 expedition, Doane had pleaded that "it was with difficulty we could believe the evidence of our senses." Washburn and Langford had even gotten up early one morning to retrace their steps and see *again* the sights which were so "at war with all former experience" that Langford felt "as if my own senses might have deceived me." He even suspected his own earlier diary entries might have been exaggerated, but "No! they are not!" he confirmed after re-visiting the site.

WILLIAM HENRY JACKSON

Perhaps the best proof of the fact would be the photograph. This Hayden provided for in his 1871 expedition. Hayden had met the Nebraska photographer, William Henry Jackson, in 1869. In July 1870, Hayden went to Jackson's Omaha studio to sound him out about joining that year's survey team. Jackson showed Hayden his 1869 portfolio of photographs taken along the Northern Pacific Railroad line.

> "You can make a picture like this?" he [Hayden] cried, bringing his hand down on a view of rock formations near the Green River Station, "I wouldn't have believed it. Why I could classify the strata from this."
> "I can do better . . . with better equipment."
> "We leave Cheyenne next week." Hayden turned suddenly, his eyes snapping with eagerness. "You must come. I can give you nothing but your keep and your kit, but you understand my purpose, and you can make it yours."[6]

And Jackson did. By 1871, Jackson had become a permanent and salaried member of the Hayden Survey staff.

In addition to Moran and Jackson, the Hayden Yellowstone

6 Clarence S. Jackson, *Picture Maker of the Old West: William H. Jackson,* 82.

Survey of 1871 had another painter and another photographer. The artist Henry W. Elliott had accompanied Hayden previously and had provided fine paintings and sketches. Besides Jackson

> there had been two other photographers in the Yellowstone that season. One of them was Crissman [with Hayden], whose pictures never passed the confines of a purely local market. The second man was the expert T. J. Hine of Chicago, who had been attached to the Barlow-Heap party. Hine got back to Chicago just in time to have every single negative destroyed in the terrible fire of 1871. And so the fact that my pictures were the only ones to be published that year is something for which I have to thank Mrs. O'Leary's cow.[7]

J. Crissman was a local Bozeman, Montana photographer whose camera blew off a cliff during the 1871 Yellowstone trip; Jackson loaned him one for the remainder of the journey.

Portable wet-plate camera equipment supplied a traveling photographer such as Jackson in the 1870's, but "portable" hardly had the same meaning then as it does in the 1970's.

At least one mule for packing and preferably one man as a helper was the minimum needed by a photographer. On his 1871 trip, Jackson took three cameras: an 8 x 10 box plus lens, a 6½ x 8½ box plus lens, and a stereo — "with its pair of brass-barreled Willard lenses, it looked like a young cannon." In addition to the cameras and a small darkroom tent, there were the chemicals and various apparatus. This was similar to the list Jackson compiled for his 1870 trip with Hayden:

2 Tripods
10 lbs. Collodion
36 oz. Silver nitrate
2 quarts Alcohol

[7] William H. Jackson, *Time Exposure: The Autobiography of William Henry Jackson*, 202-203.

10 lbs. Iron sulfate [developer]
Package of filters
1½ lbs. Potassium cyanide [fixer]
3 yds. Canton flannel
1 Box Rottenstone [cleaner for glass plates]
3 Negative boxes
6 oz. Nitric acid
1 quart Varnish
Developing and fixing trays
Dozen and a half bottles of various sizes
Scales and weights
Glass for negatives, 400 pieces[8]

Jackson had to manufacture each negative in his darkroom tent immediately before using it, by floating a wet sensitizing solution on a glass plate.

My invariable practice was to keep it [the darkroom tent, his "dark box"] in the shade, then, after carefully focussing my camera, return to the box, sensitize a plate, hurry back to the camera while it was still moist, slip the plate into position, and make the exposure.[9] Next step was to return to the dark box and immediately develop the plate. Then I would go through the entire process once more from a new position. Under average conditions a "round trip" might use up three-quarters of an hour.

[8] Robert Taft, *Photography and the American Scene: A Social History, 1839-1889,* 309.
[9] "No shutters were employed, all exposures were by cap. In my landscape work I usually stopped down to about F/32 with an average exposure on a bright, clear day of 10 to 15 seconds (5 seconds in absence of near foliage) – more or less according to the condition of the collodion and the silver bath. . . . On a well lighted subject at F/8 'instantaneous' exposures could be made with the primitive drop shutter." (Jackson quoted in Taft, *Photography and the American Scene,* 310) "By this time I had rigged up my first gadget for 'speed' work – a drop shutter, actuated by a rubber band, that enabled me to shoot action at high noon with a one-tenth second exposure. . . . When speed was no consideration I always stopped my lens down to get maximum depth and definition." (Jackson, *Time Exposure,* 197)

But many conditions were not "average" in Yellowstone.

> We proceeded to Tower Creek. At the point [Tower
> Falls] where that stream drops into the gorge the
> view is magnificent — but recording it on a glass plate
> from the bed beneath turned out to be my biggest
> photographic problem of the year.[10]

The basic problem was that Jackson could not get his heavy
dark box close enough to his camera. Finally he resorted to
climbing and falling abilities and to sheer determination.

> After setting up and focussing my camera at the
> bottom of the gorge, I would prepare a plate, back
> the holder with wet blotting paper, then slip and slide
> and tumble down to my camera and make the ex-
> posure. After taking my picture, I had to climb to the
> top carrying the exposed plate wrapped up in a moist
> towel. With Dixon [George B. Dixon of Philadelphia]
> to help, cleaning and washing the plates, I succeeded
> in repeating the procedure four or five times. The end
> of the day found us exhausted but very proud.[11]

One of Jackson's Tower Falls photographs is reproduced in this
volume; see page 252. A number of other Jackson photographs
are reproduced as examples of the excellent visual images of
Yellowstone available to the American public in the 1870's.

A large selection of woodcut illustrations of this period are
also used for a similar reason — to give the reader some idea of
an important picture medium popular a hundred years ago.

THE 1870 PARTY

The photographs of the civilian members of the 1870 Washburn party used in this volume are taken from the 1905 edition

[10] Ibid., 199.
[11] Ibid.

of Langford's *The Discovery of Yellowstone Park, 1870.* Each photograph does not necessarily portray the man as he looked in 1870, because they were taken at various times. Langford's book did not include photographs of Trumbull or Smith and the editors have been unable to locate any elsewhere.

THE BELKNAP TOUR 1875

One is tempted to wonder if Doane himself might have made some sketches during the 1870 Yellowstone expedition, along with Trumbull and Moore. Five years after that expedition, Doane guided Secretary of War Belknap through Yellowstone Park and presumably made at least one sketch of that trip. Belknap wrote Doane a letter on December 9, 1875, thanking Doane for "Yours of November 23 [Doane's letter] ... together with a package containing a negative." Belknap then adds:

> Your mule sketch has been turned over to another Artist, and I should not be surprized if we had it in the book, and in an improved state.[12]

"The book" was probably William E. Strong's *A Trip to the Yellowstone Park,* an account of the 1875 tour; Doane's "mule sketch" might have been the model for the illustration which did appear in Strong's book showing two men "Throwing the Diamond Hitch" on a pack mule or for the illustration picturing Doane's mule litter carrying the ill General Marcy — "Leaving the Mud Volcano"; see page 49. However, there is no evidence to document this latter speculation, and certainly there is no evidence whatever to support any speculation about Doane's sketching on the 1870 expedition.

The mule litter illustration does suggest a perhaps more fruitful assumption about another matter. Doane's use of mule

[12] Doane Summary, National Archives.

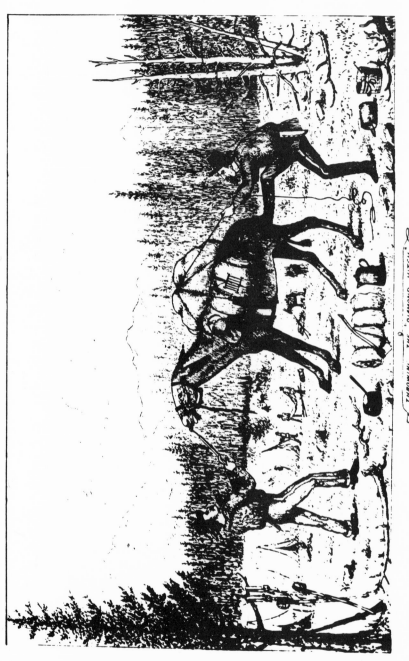

THROWING THE 'DIAMOND HITCH

Illustration from Strong's book, *A Trip to the Yellowstone National Park.*

litters appears rather prominently in his biography. For example, Strong dwells on the whole episode of Marcy and Doane's litter, the skepticism on the part of the party members, and the actual success of the litter. Also, Rodenbough and Haskins, in their account of the Custer massacre, single Doane out for his "fertile genius" in employing the mule litter for Reno's wounded.[13] General Alfred Terry, commander of the Department of Dakota, wrote his divisional headquarters in Chicago on October 7, 1877: "[T]he wounded men of the 7th Cavalry were carried to the Big Horn River in mule litters constructed by 1st Lieutenant G. C. Doane, 2d Cavalry. These litters answered their purpose admirably and I think that a knowledge of the manner in which they were constructed would be of great value to at least every medical officer of the Army. At my request Lieutenant Doane has prepared a detailed report upon the method of construction used by him." But Doane himself never takes credit for this device, and rightly so, for it was by no means original with Doane. An interesting irony of Doane's 1875 use of the litter with Marcy is that Doane had surely read Marcy's 1859 book, *The Prairie Traveler,* which fully described and illustrated just such a horse/mule litter.[14]

In any case, the illustrations of the Belknap tour used in this present volume are taken from the 1876 edition of Strong's book.

[13] See Part I this book, Chapter 4, note 8.
[14] Randolph B. Marcy, *The Prairie Traveler: A Handbook for Overland Expeditions,* 150-153.

TE :MS OF SUBSCRIPTION

The Helena Daily Herald.

Vol. 7. Helena, Montana, Monday, September 26, 1870. No. 48

Helena Daily Herald.

D. W. FISK, Publisher and Proprietor.

R. E. FISK, Editor.

MONDAY, SEPTEMBER 26, 1870.

The Pioneer Daily of Montana.

The best Advertising Medium in the New Northwest.

THE YELLOWSTONE EXPEDITION.

Interesting Data of the Trip, from Notes Furnished by Hon. N. P. Langford.

THE TERRITORIAL FAIR.

FIRST DAY.

TELEGRAMS.

SPECIALLY REPORTED FOR THE HERALD BY THE WESTERN UNION COMPANY'S TELEGRAPH COMPANY.

THE WAR!

Bismarck's Demands as the Conditions of Peace.

The French Provisional Government will not Accede to the Conditions.

The French Claim Success in the Recent Engagements.

The Defense of Strasbourg Still Continued.

Marseilles and Toulon Preparing for a Vigorous Defense.

Paris Prepared to Make a Heroic Resistance.

The Revolutionary Uprising of the Reds Denied.

Bazaine Reported Ready to Capitulate on Conditions.

FRANCE.

ENGLAND.

PRUSSIA.

SPAIN.

APPENDIX E

THE TRAIL WIDENS

1870 EXPEDITION

The return of the tired and jaded explorers, as they came in separately, was as newsworthy an event to the citizens of Montana as the return of astronauts from the moon in our time. Langford went directly to Virginia City on September 22; "the intelligence of my arrival in Virginia City, and of the loss of Mr. Everts from our party, had been telegraphed to Helena from Virginia City, and on my arrival I was besieged by many of the friends of Mr. Everts for information." Langford had to refuse invitations to visit people at their homes and tell them of the trip because of his "present delapidated condition;" he goes on to tell that "Jake Smith is the only one of our party who has returned with a garment fit to wear in the society of ladies."[1] Stickney, Trumbull, Hauser, and Washburn arrived in Helena September 25 and Langford on the twenty-seventh. Smith, Hedges, and the pack train came into Helena on September 27. Doane arrived back at Fort Ellis on September 24. Gillette and Privates Moore and Williamson were back at Fort Ellis on October 2, still with no word of Everts.

[1] Langford, *Discovery,* 183.

Helena Daily Herald.

D. W. FISK, Publisher and Proprietor.

R. E. FISK, Editor.

MONDAY, SEPTEMBER 26, 1870.

The Pioneer Daily of Montana.

The best Advertising Medium in the New Northwest.

THE YELLOWSTONE EXPEDITION.

Interesting Data of the Trip, from Notes Furnished by Hon. N. P. Langford.

The party left Bozeman on the 22nd of August, reaching the Yellowstone on the 24th, and traveling up that river until the 27th, when they reached the Lower Fall creek, where they remained in camp one day. On this creek is the Lower Fall, a beautiful cascade 115 feet high. The Indian trail crosses the Yellowstone at this point to the east side, but the party kept upon the west side of the river, near the base of Mt. Washburn, a peak 10,570 feet in height, passing the Hell-broth Springs on the 29th, and on the 30th camping opposite the Great Falls of the Yellowstone, on Cascade creek. Nearly two days were spent in examining the Falls and their surroundings. Mr. Langford suspended a weight perpendicularly from the rock adjoining the Falls, 491 feet to the bottom of the canon, and deducting from this the distance from the top of the rock to the surface of the water above the Fall, found it to be 350 feet in height. The Upper Fall, half a mile further up the stream, is 115 feet high. A day and a half more brought the party to the Hot Sulphur and Mud Springs, sixty to seventy-five in number, of diameters varying from two to seventy feet. From scores of craters on the side of the mountain adjoining these springs, issue hot vapors, the edges of the craters being incrusted with pure sulphur. Six miles further on is the first geyser, which throws a column of water twenty feet in diamater to the height of thirty to thirty-five feet. Near by is a volcano, which throws up mud from the bottom of its crater to the height of thirty feet or more, with explosions resembling distant discharges of cannon, the pulsations occurring at intervals of five seconds, and the explosions shaking the ground for a

occupied by the party two days before Mr. Everts was lost, but could discover no trace of him—the trail made by the thirty-seven horses belonging to the party being in many places entirely obliterated. Messrs. Trumbull and Smith followed the shore of the lake, and General Washburne and Mr. Langford traveled south to the head waters of Snake river, but neither party could find any trace of the lost man. While in camp on the lake, snow fell to the depth of two feet. An inventory of provisions was then taken, and on the 17th, eight days after the loss of Mr. Everts, most of the party started for the Madison, with sufficient supplies to carry them home, leaving Mr. Gillette and Messrs. More and Williamson, of the 2nd cavalry, with the balance of the provisions to prosecute the search.

It was the opinion of all the members of the party, when Mr. Langford left them on the Madison, that if Mr. Everts had not then been heard from in Virginia or Helena, he had been shot by Indians. The only route that he could have taken that would not have brought him to Virginia or Helena a week since, is that leading by the "Three Tetons" to Eagle Rock Bridge, which point he could have reached several days ago ; and had he done so, would undoubtedly have telegraphed his friends here.

It is the intention of Mr. Langford to prepare for publication, as soon as practicable, a detailed report of the journey to and from this most interesting portion of our country, where, in a space so circumscribed, are presented at once the wonders of Iceland, Italy, and South America.

THE TERRITORIAL FAIR.
FIRST DAY.

The first exhibition of the Montana Mineral and Agricultural Association commenced this morning under more favorable auspices than any previous one. The weather was warm as a Summer's day, the roads in excellent condition and everything about the Fair grounds in the most complete and systematic order. About 10 o'clock we rode down and took a brief stroll inside of the enclosure, and were not a little surprised to see everything so perfectly arranged. The

LADIES' DEPARTMENT,

or Floral Hall, is handsomely decorated with evergreens and flags. It is much larger than the old hall and far more convenient. The ladies who have charge of this department are Mrs. Ashley, Mrs. Gilbert, Miss Nellie Lathrop, Miss May Chumasero and Miss Irvine of Deer Lodge. They preside with much dignity and grace, and entertain their visitors with that courtesy, po-

On September 26, 1870, the *Helena Herald* published the first of a series of reports on the Washburn-Doane Expedition under the heading: "The Yellowstone Expedition – Interesting Data of the Trip, from notes Furnished by Hon. N. P. Langford." It also announced Mr. Langford's intention to prepare for publication a detailed report of "this most interesting portion of the country, where ... are presented at once the wonders of Iceland, Italy, and South America."

The following day, September 27, the *Helena Herald* carried a two-column article signed by H.D.W., headed: "The Yellowstone Expedition. Explorations in a New and Wonderful Country. Description of the Great Falls of the Yellowstone, Volcanic Eruptions, Spouting Geysers, etc., from the Notes of Hon. H. D. Washburn, Surveyor General of Montana." September 28 brought the second installment by Washburn, which included the naming of Old Faithful and other geysers.

All copies and extra editions of the *Helena Herald* were immediately sold out and a special reprinting of the above articles was released in the issue of September 30, 1870.

In the *Herald* for October 8 appears a full-column letter by Hedges about Mount Everts, its climb and its naming, in which he pays high tribute to Everts, thought dead. Hedges followed this on October 15 with an article, "The Great Falls of the Yellowstone – A Graphic Picture of Their Grandeur and Beauty;" on October 19, "Hell Broth Spring;" on October 24, "Sulphur Mountain and Mud Volcano;" and on November 9, "Yellowstone Lake."

These well written and highly interesting accounts were immediately copied generally by the national press, as testified to in the *Helena Herald* of October 1, which stated: "Our exchanges, East and West, are just now reaching us, containing copious extracts from the Herald's Yellowstone reports. These contributions ... have proved, as we rightly predicted, of unusual interest, not alone to Montanans but to the reading public throughout the country."

One Washington, D.C. correspondent wrote a letter to the *Herald* of November 14, 1870, telling how the graphic descriptions and the news of the recovery of Everts "sent a thrill of sympathetic joy through the entire community."

On October 16, Baronett and Prichett had found Everts. Concerning the expedition itself Everts wrote:

> A desire to visit this remarkable region, of which, during several years' residence in Montana, I had often heard the most marvelous accounts, led me to unite in the expedition of August last. The general character of the stupendous scenery of the Rocky Mountains prepared my mind for giving credit to all the strange stories told of the Yellowstone, and I felt quite as certain of the existence of the physical phenomena of that country, on the morning that our company started from Helena, as when I afterwards beheld it. I engaged in the enterprise with enthusiasm, feeling that all the hardships and exposures of a month's horseback travel through an unexplored region would be more than compensated by the grandeur and novelty of the natural objects with which it was crowded. Of course, the idea of being lost in it, without any of the ordinary means of subsistence, and the wandering for days and weeks, in a famishing condition, alone, in an unfrequented wilderness, formed no part of my comtemplation. . . .

> My heartfelt thanks are due to the members of the Expedition, all of whom devoted seven, and some of them twelve days to the search for me before they left Yellowstone Lake; and to Judge Lawrence, of Helena, and the friends who cooperated with him in the offer of reward which sent Baronet and Prichette to my rescue.

> My narrative is finished. In the course of events the time is not far distant when the wonders of the Yellowstone will be made accessible to all lovers of

sublimity, grandeur, and novelty in natural scenery, and its majestic waters become the abode of civilization and refinement; and when that arrives, I hope, in happier mood and under more auspicious circumstances, to revisit scenes fraught for me with such thrilling interest; to ramble along the glowing beach of Bessie Lake; to sit down amid the hot springs under the shade of Mount Everts; to thread unscarred the mazy forests, retrace the dreary journey to the Madison Range, and with enraptured fancy gaze upon the mingled glories and terrors of the great falls and marvelous canon, and to enjoy, in happy contrast with the trials they recall, their power to delight, elevate, and overwhelm the mind with wondrous and majestic beauty.[2]

Gillette had been kidded during the trip about romancing Bessie, the daughter of Truman Everts. However, she married another. Everts himself lived a long and vigorous life to the age of eighty-five years and had a son when he was seventy-six.

YELLOWSTONE NATIONAL PARK

The Washburn-Doane Expedition had hardly returned to civilization before Harry Norton and another printer named Brown rushed from Deer Lodge, Montana, into the Firehole Basin and cut a large number of poles, intending to return in the spring and fence in a tract of land containing the principal geysers. By 1871 Jim McCartney had started commercialism with his improvements at Mammoth Hot Springs.[3] If the campfire idea of September 19 were going to prove fruitful, action would have to come soon and meaningfully.

The newspaper publicity helped to alert public opinion. The

2 Everts, "Thirty-seven Days of Peril," 1, 17.
3 Langford, *Discovery*, 38, 40.

articles in various magazines by the party members were influential. Langford gave several lectures on Yellowstone, including one at Lincoln Hall in Washington, D. C. on January 19, 1871 and one at Cooper Union in New York on January 21, 1871.[4]

On March 3, 1871, the Committee on Territories ordered Doane's journal printed as *Senate Executive Document No. 51.* Hayden said of it: "For graphic description and thrilling interest, it has not been surpassed by any official report made to our government since the times of Lewis and Clark."[5]

As a direct result of the 1870 expedition, the U. S. Geological Survey changed its program under Hayden in order to give attention in 1871 to the new wonderland;[6] and the military sent Captains John W. Barlow and D. P. Heap of the Army Engineer Corps into Yellowstone that same summer of 1871.

On December 18, 1871, the bill to create Yellowstone National Park was introduced simultaneously in both Houses of Congress. The speed with which it was enacted is surprising to any student of federal legislation. Langford, Everts, and Hauser were in Washington urging its passage. Hayden, at the Interior Department, was doing likewise. Walter Trumbull was clerk of the Senate Committee on Judiciary, of which his father, Senator Lyman Trumbull of Illinois, was chairman. Congressman William H. Clagett from Montana and other Washington lawmakers worked hard for the bill. Four hundred copies of Langford's *Scribner's* article were distributed among the Congress-

---

[4] Advertisement in the *Washington Star,* January 17, 1871; and news story in the *New York Herald,* January 23, 1871. The Twelfth Annual Report of the Cooper Union, May 31, 1871, lists Langford as having delivered the fourth of the "Free Saturday Lectures" given in the Great Hall for 1871. This would have been January 28, whereas the *New York Herald* reported on the lecture the previous week. Fred H. Graves, Head Librarian at The Cooper Union for the Advancement of Science and Art, comments: "From previous work in these old records we would not be surprised to find that the lecture in question may have been transferred to some other day of the week and the listing in the Annual report not corrected to show the change. It is my opinion that the newspaper is more likely to have reported the actual date of delivery." (letter, October 1, 1969)

[5] Langford, *Discovery,* 34.

[6] Hayden continued his surveys in Yellowstone in 1872 and 1878. During the nine-year period of the Hayden Surveys, half of their time was spent in Wyoming.

8TH.—NUMBER OF PERSONS

Who have availed themselves of the privilege of free consultation with the Professors of Science, on matters relating to industrial pursuits.

Prof. Charles S. Stone, Industrial Chemistry, -   207
Prof. George W. Plympton, Mechanics,   -   -   114

    321

9TH.—FREE SATURDAY LECTURES

For the people in the Great Hall, commencing Jan. 7th, 1871, and ending April 29th, 1871, by the following named gentlemen :

A. J. MUNDELLA, ESQ., M. P., on "Strikes, Arbitration and Labor questions in Great Britain."

Prof. E. L. YOUMANS, M. D. on "The Dynamics of Life."

Major J. W. POWELL, on "The Great Cañon of the Colorado."

Hon. N. P. LANGFORD, on "The Upper Waters of the Yellowstone River."

ARTHUR GILMAN, Esq., on "Traits of Yankee Humor."

Dr. A. J. EBELL, on "The Microscope and its Revelations."

Dr. A. J. EBELL, on "The Anatomy and Natural History of Insectians."

Prof. W. D. GUNNING, on "The last Glacial Epoch in America."

P. B. WIGHT, ESQ., on "Architecture in its Practical Relation to the needs of the Present Day."

Prof. S. E. FROBISHER, Readings.

R. W. RAYMOND, ESQ., Ph. D. on "Darwin's Hypothesis of the Origin of Species."

JAMES B. HODGSKIN, ESQ., on "Work, Weather and Wealth."

Prof. THOS. EGGLESTON, on "The Manufacture of Iron.

Prof. J. C. ZACHOS, on "Shakespeare."

Dr. C. F. CHANDLER, on "Illuminating Gas."

Prof. BENJAMIN SILLIMAN, 2 lectures on "The Atmosphere, with Reference to Respiration and Ventilation."

Prof. CHAS. DAVIES, LL. D. on "The Metric System with Reference to its Introduction and Use in the United States."

The Twelfth Annual Report of the Cooper Union, page 8, listing Langford as one of the 1871 "Free Saturday Lectures" speakers. *Courtesy Cooper Union.*

men, and each was personally interviewed.

But some Senators and Representatives understandably shared that persistent skepticism about Yellowstone. What made Yellowstone so special? Surely this 3,578-square-mile area 2,000 miles from Washington could not be so literally fantastic as to merit the almost unprecedented legislation being called for.

What about influencing the people with Jackson's photographs? Hayden had already distributed hundreds of the photographs and the stereoscope slides, but how was a "mass" circulation of Jackson's Yellowstone work to be effected? Photo-engraving and ten-cent picture magazines were still unknown; but an astonishing number of people bought finished photographs to hang on their walls, or to view through stereoscopes.[7]

But time was too short to wait for the public to be flooded with Jackson photographs and respond with a grass roots support urging their Congressmen to create Yellowstone National Park. Better to go directly to the lawmakers themselves.

Therefore, on the desks of all Senators and members of the House appeared "handsomely bound folio volumes of the photographs, neatly captioned, and bearing the name of the recipient in gold."[8]

The bill was passed by the Senate on January 30, 1872 and went to the House where it passed on February 27, 1872.[9] It was promptly signed by President Grant and became law on March 1, 1872. N. P. Langford became the first superintendent

[7] Jackson, *Time Exposure,* 196. Jackson's 1869 Northern Pacific photographic tour had been "launched largely on the strength of one order. . . . [We] got an order for ten thousand stereographs of scenes along the train route. . . . On the train I unexpectedly drummed up a neat piece of business. The 'news booster' bought all the Indian pictures I had with me and placed an order for a thousand stereos of Weber Canyon." (Ibid., 176, 177)

[8] Jackson, *Picture Maker,* 145. From among the photographs which Clarence Jackson indicates were chosen by the lobbyists to be included in the folio, four have been reproduced in this volume: Tower Falls (page 252), Grand Canyon of the Yellowstone (page 278), Grotto Geyser (page 352), Mammoth Hot Springs (page 404).

[9] The vote was 115 ayes and sixty-five nays, with sixty not voting. The pro and con count by party was as follows: For, ninety-seven Republicans, fifteen Democrats, three others. Against, fifty-two Democrats, eleven Republicans, two others.

SCRIBNER'S MONTHLY.

VOL. II.   MAY, 1871.   No. 1.

meeting with several gentlemen who expressed like curiosity, we determined to make the journey in the months of August and September.

The Yellowstone and Columbia, the first flowing into the Missouri and the last into the Pacific, divided from each other by the Rocky Mountains, have their sources within a few miles of each other. Both rise in the mountains which separate Idaho from the new Territory of Wyoming, but the headwaters of the Yellowstone are only accessible from Montana. The mountains surrounding the basin from which they flow are very lofty, covered with pines, and on the southeastern side present to the traveler a precipitous wall of rock, several thousand feet in height. This barrier prevented Captain Reynolds from visiting the headwaters of the Yellowstone while prosecuting an expedition planned by the Government and placed under his command, for the purpose of exploring that river, in 1859.

The source of the Yellowstone is in a

I HAD indulged, for several years, a great curiosity to see the wonders of the upper valley of the Yellowstone. The stories told by trappers and mountaineers of the natural phenomena of that region were so strange and marvelous that, as long ago as 1866, I first contemplated the possibility of organizing an expedition for the express purpose of exploring it. During the past year,

VOL. II.—1

Opening page of Langford's first *Scribner's* article.

of the first national park.

The legislation provided that Yellowstone be "dedicated and set apart as a public park or pleasuring ground for the benefit and enjoyment of the people." There was to be no "wanton destruction of fish and game — and the capture or destruction for the purpose of merchandise or profit." Also assured was "the preservation from injury or spoilation of all timber, mineral deposits, natural curiosities or wonders within said park and ... retention in their natural condition."[10] Hayden rhapsodized:

> That our legislators, at a time when the public opinion is so strong against appropriating the public domain for any purpose however laudable, should reserve for the benefit and instruction of the people a tract 3,578 square miles, is an act that should cause universal joy throughout the land. This noble deed may be regarded as a tribute from our legislators to science.[11]

But universal joy did not reign. Voices of commercialism protested in that early day as they do today against preservation of parts of our great national heritage as wilderness areas. The *Helena Gazette,* for example, editorialized in 1872:

> In our opinion the effect of the measure will be to keep this country in wilderness and shut out for many years the travel that would seek that curious region if good roads were opened through it and hotels built therein. We regard the passage of the act

[10] The continuous protection offered by this auspicious act is repeatedly illustrated. Note a recent example: In discussing the relatively new process of tapping into hot springs and geyser systems for the development of geothermal electric power in the United States, Lawrence Lessing reminds himself and his readers of Yellowstone's inviolability: "Elsewhere in California and twelve other western states — *excluding Yellowstone National Park, which cannot be commercially exploited* — there are roughly 86 million acres that may have geothermal resources." [italics added] ("Power from the Earth's Own Heat," *Fortune,* June 1969)

[11] Jackson, *Picture Maker,* 143.

as a great blow struck at the prosperity of the towns of Bozeman and Virginia City which might normally look for considerable travel to this section if it were thrown open to a curious but comfort loving public.

The debate continues. And in the meantime the people continue to enjoy the pleasuring ground. In the year 1969, there were more than 2,000,000 visitors to Yellowstone National Park.

Doane himself said:

In future, when the park shall have been made accessible to the pleasure-seekers of the world; when silvery laughter shall echo through its forest glades, instead of the melancholy voices of panthers; when bright eyes shall view its wonders, and gentle hearts be stirred by its attractions; when its clear waters shall reflect the forms of youthful loveliness and grace, it will be a satisfaction not to be derived from wealth nor honors to have been in some degree concerned in the discovery and development of a new source of pleasure and instruction for the human race.[12]

[12] Rodenbough, *From Everglade to Cañon*, 419.

PART III

THE SNAKE RIVER EXPLORATION OF 1876-1877

INTRODUCTION TO PART III

by the editors

CHAPTER 1

KNOWLEDGE OF SNAKE RIVER PRIOR TO 1876

What would Doane learn by exploration of the Snake River in 1876?

At that time the geography of the Snake River was fairly well known from its headwaters in Yellowstone Park to the Portneuf River near present-day Pocatello, Idaho and from the mouth of the Box Canyon above Lewiston, Idaho to the point where the Snake River entered the Columbia River.

But between the Portneuf River and Lewiston was a stretch of more than half of the thousand-mile river. This section was virtually unknown.

ASTORIANS

Doane had read Washington Irving's *Astoria.* The Astorians in their westward journey had embarked at Henry's Fork of the Snake River on October 18, 1811, and one or more parties of this expedition had followed the Snake River to its mouth. But their report was of a fight for survival rather than of geography. They conveyed little knowledge of the thousand miles of river except its desolation and that it flowed into the Columbia. Doane knew that the Astoria-bound travelers had lost two of their best canoeman and all of their boats in various rapids of the Snake, and ended up traveling hundreds of miles on foot, half-starving on the meat of a few horses some Indians reluctantly traded to them.

FUR TRADERS

Fur traders from the Hudson's Bay Company and North West Company had ventured into the Snake River country and were acquainted with portions of it. Donald McKenzie was first in 1819-20. None of his records is known to exist, but his trip is mentioned in Alexander Ross' *Fur Hunters of the Far West,* first published in London in 1855; the book contained a map of the Snake River, but it was partial and inaccurate. McKenzie was followed by Finian McDonald in 1823, Alexander Ross in 1824, and Peter Skeen Ogden in 1825. These trips were commercial and the British took pains not to enlighten the competing Americans about fur values on the Snake River or how to travel there. It is certain that the information – scanty, inaccurate, and incomplete as it was – would not be available to Doane, the U. S. Army, or other Americans.[1]

Also, David E. Jackson, Jedediah Smith, and William A. Sublette were in the area in 1829-30. Whatever knowledge this partnership had of the Snake River flowing through the rich beaver meadows of the Jackson Hole and adjacent country was kept largely a trade secret.

Osborne Russell and Warren E. Ferris were learning the Snake River in the 1830's, but their stories were not published until the twentieth century. Neither had the account of the gold-seeking Walter deLacy party of 1863 been widely available; it was not published until 1876, and then in a limited-circulation state historical journal.

---

[1] William Kittson's map was with Ogden's journals of 1825 when they were finally published in London in 1950. It states; "The Snake River from Portneufs is put down rather by guesswork and I think it is much too far to the north in this part." For Snake River the map shows "Henry's Fork," "Middle Fork" (swinging east of "Trois Tetons"), and "Salt Fork," and states that "Snake enters Columbia nine miles above Fort Nez Perce." *Hudson's Bay Society,* XIII, 255, 209*n* 1.

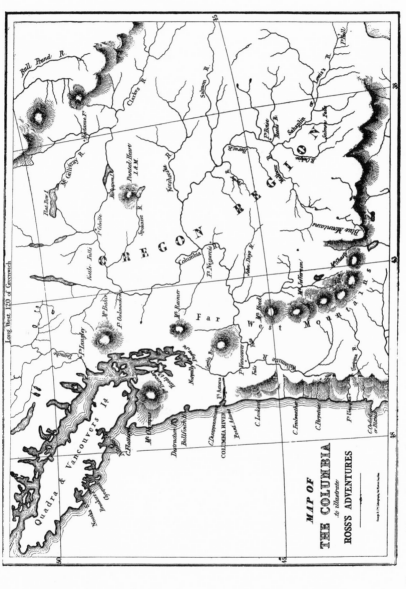

Map used to illustrate Alexander Ross' 1849 publication, *Adventures of the First Settlers on the Oregon or Columbia River: Being a Narrative of the Expedition Fitted Out by John Jacob Astor. Courtesy Yale University Library.*

CAPTAIN BONNEVILLE

Doane did have available an additional Washington Irving account, *The Adventures of Captain Bonneville* (especially Chapters 29-36), which was relevant for knowledge of the area.

Captain B. L. E. Bonneville had made a trip by horseback through the Snake River country for the express purpose of exploring it. With three companions he left his winter base camp on the Portneuf River on Christmas Day, 1833, and arrived March 4, 1834 at the Hudson's Bay Company's Fort Walla Walla on the Columbia below the mouth of the Snake. Bonneville returned to his encampment on the Portneuf May 12, two months later than he had expected, to find it had vanished.

Washington Irving bought Bonneville's journals and may be the only one who saw them, as they have not since been found. They were an important source for Irving's *Captain Bonneville,* which at the time was the most complete information on that part of the Snake River.

Doane must indeed have been tantalized by Irving's grandiloquent phrases and stirred by an ambition to translate them into factual and scientific observation.

> [T]hrough this vast and singular defile, Snake River is upwards of three hundred yards wide, and as clear as spring water. Sometimes it steals along with a tranquil and noiseless course; at other times, for miles and miles it dashes on in a thousand rapids, wild and beautiful to the eye, and lulling the ear with the soft tumult of plashing waters. . . .
>
> "The grandeur and . . . views presented on every side," says Captain Bonneville, "beggar both the pencil and the pen. Nothing we had ever gazed upon in any other region could for a moment compare in wild majesty and impressive sternness with the series of scenes which here at every turn astonished our senses and filled us with awe and delight."
>
> Indeed, from all that we can gather from the jour-

nal before us, and the accounts of other travelers, who passed through these regions in the memorable enterprise of Astoria, we are inclined to think that Snake River must be one of the most remarkable for varied and striking scenery of all the rivers of this continent. From its headwaters in the Rocky Mountains, to its junction with the Columbia, its windings are upward of six hundred miles through every variety of landscape. Rising in a volcanic region, amid extinguished craters and mountains awful with the traces of ancient fires, it makes it way through great plains of lava and sandy deserts, penetrates vast sierras or mountainous chains, broken into romantic and often frightful precipices, and crowned with eternal snows; and at other times careers through green and smiling meadows and wide landscapes of Italian grace and beauty. Wildness and sublimity, however, appear to be its prevailing characteristics.[2]

Certainly both *Astoria* and *Captain Bonneville* forewarned Doane of the possibility of suffering and starvation. Bonneville and his men had struggled through deep snow, seemingly impassable terrain, ice, cold, and starvation; toward the end of their westward journey they were three days without food; they shot one of their mules and lived three more days on the soup from the bones, drying the flesh and conserving it as long as they could do without it.

LAWMAKERS

In 1805, from present-day Lewiston, Idaho, Lewis and Clark had more or less followed the course of the lower Snake River 154 miles westward to the Columbia River. Lewiston itself had been incorporated in 1861 and when Idaho became a territory on March 3, 1863, Lewiston was its first capital. Oregon had

---

[2] Washington Irving, *The Adventures of Captain Bonneville,* 216, 245.

become a state on February 14, 1859. The boundary between Oregon-Washington and Idaho followed the Snake River for 250 miles or so. In truth the lawmakers knew where the boundary started down the river and where it ended, but they knew practically nothing of the region in between. The river was a definite boundary marker without a definite survey.

SURVEYORS AND SETTLERS

The Hayden Surveys of 1872 had mapped and had straightened out knowledge of the geography of the Snake River from its Yellowstone headwaters to the mouth of the Blackfoot River.[3]

Old historic Fort Hall had been established on the Snake River by Nathaniel J. Wyeth in 1834 near present-day Pocatello, Idaho. Now in 1876, 200 miles of the Snake River valley above the fort were occupied by scattered settlers and ranchers and could hardly be called unknown.

If Doane failed to travel beyond Fort Hall his exploration would add little to the knowledge of the Snake River.

[3] F. V. Hayden, *Sixth Annual Report of the U.S. Geological Survey of the Territories.* This Report as published in 1873 carried a map (between pp. 254-55) of the country between the Grand Canyon of the Yellowstone and Fort Hall, Idaho; this map was "reduced from the Preliminary Map after Surveys by . . . Snake River Expedition." This is the map the editors have used to illustrate Doane's Snake River Expedition.

CHAPTER 2

WHAT DOANE COULD DISCOVER IN 1876

POSSIBILITIES

The Snake is a larger river than the Columbia to which it is tributary. It drains 109,000 square miles including western Wyoming, all of Idaho except the north and extreme south-eastern corner, the northwest corner of Utah, the northeast corner of Nevada, eastern Oregon, and the southeast corner of Washington. The basin of the river extends 450 miles in length and an equal width. It is fed by fifty-six rivers, seventeen of which are regarded as major tributaries, and by seventy-four large creeks.

Would Doane's portable boat of one inch planks carried by packhorse and assembled with screws survive the need of constant repair? Would it plunge over American Falls as the unsuspecting canoes of the American Fur Company had done nearly half a century before? How would Doane make the portages of Twin Falls' 180 feet, Shoshone Falls' 212 feet, Dry Creek Falls, Pillar Falls, and Auger Falls with its twists and spirals.

How would he navigate the 200-mile gorge below the Astorian's disastrous "Caldron Linn" (below present-day Milner Dam)? Would Doane "discover" and write up in his characteristic factual, scientific manner Hell's Canyon of the Snake River between today's Weiser and Lewiston, Idaho? This canyon has an average depth of 5,500 feet for fifty miles. Its deepest point occurs as it passes He Devil Peak of the Seven Devil Mountains. Here its walls reach ten miles from rim to rim and drop 7,900 feet. This canyon is greater in magnitude than the Grand Canyon of the Colorado whose width is four to eighteen miles with a depth of 5,650 feet at Bright Angel Point, seven miles from the river. The Snake River in this section narrows to less than a hundred feet and drops almost thirteen feet to the mile.

From Brush Creek past the mouth of Deep Creek there is a stretch of four miles of perpendicular walls rising 2,000 feet to a bench and then reaching high and sheer to a second shelf. Modern boats must portage the Steamboat, Deep, Hells, and worse yet the Granite Creek rapids.

Would Doane solve some of the problems of the Snake River's ancient geology as he did those of Yellowstone Park? Would he determine that one of the earlier volcanic lavas flowed a great stream of molten rock from Idaho across Hell's Canyon and then across Oregon to the sea. Would he realize this lava flow backed up the Snake River over the plains to the region of Yellowstone Park and formed an immense lake which undoubtedly flowed back into the ancient Lake Bonneville, the immense natural lake of which today's Great Salt Lake is a remnant; and that these backed up waters of Snake River, aided by melting glaciers, eventually broke over and out through the lava flow to create Hell's Canyon?

What would Doane's conjecture be as to the source of The Thousand Springs which gush 5,000 cubic feet of water per second from the walls of Snake River canyon (about thirty-seven miles west of Twin Falls), whose origin today is still a matter of guesswork but is believed to be the outlets of the Lost River and other streams. From the mouth of Henry's Fork to the Malade River, a distance of 200 miles, he would not find a single tributary reaching Snake River by surface travel. All the streams disappear into the volcanic terrain before reaching the Snake River.

Would Doane discover on the Snake River near today's Nampa, Idaho, the largest single Indian pictograph known — a stone on which is carved a great map which roughly includes not only the Snake River valley but also Jackson Lake in western Wyoming and a few areas adjacent to both. If he explored and reached this point on the Snake River, would he recognize this great pictograph as a map of the stream he had traveled?

Would Doane make these discoveries, or would his expedition, like the Astorians, become preoccupied with survival?

And what would be the final effect of his having gone over Major Brisbin's head and against Brisbin's strenuous objections to the entire expedition?

RESULT

Oldtimers say it was poor judgment to attempt a mid-winter expedition through Yellowstone National Park and the Jackson Hole country. Major James S. Brisbin evidently thought so, too.

However, winter was the only time Doane was not involved in Indian warfare. As soon as he could get back to Fort Ellis from the Sioux fight in which Custer died, he started on this expedition. He had no more than returned from the near-disastrous expedition than he was campaigning again, this time against the Nez Perces.

Doane and his soldiers were hardened to travel in mid-winter as no other soldiers have been. In the Piegan campaign they marched thirteen days in snow and 40° below zero weather without losing a man. Compare this with Napoleon in Russia in 1812 and the loss and disintegration of his entire Grand Army of 650,000, or the thousands of Russian soldiers lost against the Finns in the winter of 1939-40, or our own 10,000 American soldiers of World War II, frozen and trench-footed, put completely out of action as winter casualties of 1944-45.

Armchair historians, controverting John Colter's 1807 route, have supported their pet theory with opinions that no man could ever travel through this country in winter. Doane did it.

It appears Doane used his contacts with Department Commander General Alfred H. Terry the summer of the Custer disaster to arrange for the trip. Telegraphic orders for the expedition from Terry were timed for Doane's return arrival at Fort Ellis.

If Doane had followed his experience of transport by pack horse he could have reached Fort Hall, Idaho, in half the time and would have been that much nearer to completing his exploration of the river below Fort Hall. He could have built his boat at Fort Hall. Better still, if he had traveled to Fort Hall via Virginia City and the stage road he would have reached it even quicker.

But there would have been too much of a problem of army protocol in starting his exploration at Fort Hall. General Terry in the Department of Dakota could easily order Doane to leave Fort Ellis and embark upon Snake River waters within the jurisdiction of that department, whereas he could hardly give Doane orders to perform a military task beginning at Fort Hall which was in the Department of the Platte.

Doane was determined to learn the navigability of the entire Snake River, as well as its geography. Perhaps the frustration of his old dream of steaming up the Zambesi River and down the Nile in Africa in a dismantleable launch led him to take a twenty-two-foot long, screw-together boat for the trip, packing it through country hardly fit for a horse, guiding it over rocks, rapids, and hazards of every sort, and trying to keep it in repair. But the delay and the struggle finally wrecked both boat and expedition, and nearly cost the men their lives.

CHAPTER 3

WRITINGS OF THE 1876 PARTY

DOANE'S JOURNAL

Doane's 1876 journal reflects the same careful and scientific observations which characterized his 1870 Yellowstone journal. But now one finds an added dimension. Doane is much freer in expressing his own feelings and his own opinions, not only reactions to events of the journey itself but also to the world outside the Snake River. He takes out after misleading popularizers of science and he is clearly less than enthusiastic about certain army personnel and policies. Doane now seems quite comfortable with human interest stories, with light touches — even with a caustic wit. Note how he handles their meals of otter and an old army horse, or how he characterizes his own men or religious literature. This hint of cynical humor becomes even more pronounced by 1880 when he writes his Arctic exploration report.

How do we account for this shift in Doane's style? Some years of association with the sage-brush pungency of frontier humor probably contributed to it. Furthermore, by 1876, particularly as a result of his Yellowstone Park trips and of his role in the Indian campaigns, Doane had become intimately acquainted with top government officials and top commanders in the army. Any awe he might have had of them had worn off. This and his genuine friendship with them simply gave him a freedom and a confidence in expressing criticism. Shortly after the 1876 expedition, his independent commands gave him even less constrictions.

OTHER WRITINGS

Unlike the 1870 expedition, the 1876 trip did not produce a host of diaries. For one thing, the members in 1876 were more concerned with sheer survival than was the 1870 party. For another, though certainly it was a close-knit group, Doane's men were soldiers under the command of an officer, not individual professional men some of whom made their living writing reports and journalistic stories.

In any case, Sergeant Fred E. Server did keep a daily diary beginning Wednesday, October 11, 1876, and ending February 2, 1877, running from about thirty to sixty words a day, about 4,000 words total. He gives the day of the week, the month, the time they left camp, usually a short comment on the weather such as "Weather fine" or "Clouded up about 4 P.M. and commenced to snow," and the distance traveled each day.

Doane used this diary in preparing his own journal and it does not add anything to Doane's journal itself.

In addition, there were letters from two of Doane's party, Private C. B. Davis on December 18, 1876 and Private William White on December 19, both written from the Caribou mining district in Idaho to two army friends back at Fort Ellis.

The editors have not located any other writings or diaries of any of the other members of the party.

CHAPTER 4

THE STORY OF DOANE'S ORIGINAL 1876 JOURNAL

This official report was ordered by Commander of the Department of Dakota, Brigadier Alfred H. Terry. It was originally intended that Doane would go to San Francisco to prepare the report. However, after the expedition had nearly ended in disaster before reaching Fort Hall, Idaho, Major James H. Brisbin succeeded in having Doane ordered back to Fort Ellis, Montana.

When Doane finished the report is not known. References in the entries of October 11 and January 3 to railroads which were not built until several years later and a reference to Norris' log bridges in the October 16 entry, indicate later writing or revision after he had been transferred from Fort Ellis.

On October 15, 1930, Junior Park Naturalist Newell Joyner interviewed Doane's widow, Mrs. Mary L. Doane, at Bozeman, Montana. At this time Mrs. Doane gave to the National Park Service six photographs of old Fort Ellis. She also loaned to the Park Service her husband's original handwritten report on the Snake River Expedition. The report is written on 122 loose sheets of paper: 8 by 12 inches, ruled with light blue lines, and held together with two metal staples or brads. It is written in Doane's own hand with an average of 250 words per page.

The National Park Service made typewritten and mimeographed copies of this Snake River journal; also, abstracts from it were published in *Yellowstone Nature Notes* for September-

Lodge - was constructed of Army Wagon Covers Cut - in proper form Ed fourteen feet - in diameter. This weighed but thirty pounds. and sheltered the entire Party.

On the evening of October 10th ~~1876~~. All Preparations were Completed - for an Expedition never attempted before. in the Winter time - And never accomplished Since. The enlisted force was of picked men Selected for special Qualifications In addition to those enumerated in the previous order - Privates Morgan Osborn G. Troop - the Carpenter who built the Little boat And John M. Ward of L. Troop A teamster Ed Packer - were taken along to bring back extra Mules Ed the wagon - from whatever point might - be selected en route.

October 11th 1876 - We moved out - from Fort - Ellis - with eight - mules in the wagon team And the other two carrying the boat - material. The men were all furnished with horses - an extra being led for the teamster. We took the Trail Creek road. Jogging along in that Splendid Sunshine of a Montana Autumn. through Rock Canon - where the Northern Pacific Track now runs - Over foot-hills. since burrowed with Coal mines - and over the Yellowstone divide - to a favorite Camping Place. by an icy spring ~~which this~~ which

A page from Doane's 1876 journal, in his own handwriting. *Courtesy M. G. Burlingame.*

October 1935. But distribution in both these forms was very limited and availability today in libraries is extremely rare. Therefore, this present publication of the complete official report now makes it available to a wide public for the first time.

It is fortunate indeed that Mrs. Doane had permitted and arranged with the National Park Service to make exact copies and distribute them. Years later, at Montana State University, the original 1876 journal was put away by one of its history professors in connection with a project on which he was then writing, but which soon became dormant. Today this original manuscript of Doane's is buried and unavailable for research. Hopefully, some day it will emerge and be placed in the Special Collections Library at Montana State University where it belongs.

Note on Format

The editors have provided chapter titles and subheadings for each chapter, in both cases using present-day nomenclature and spelling. In the text itself, spellings have been left as Doane had them—e.g., Gardiners river, Jackson's Lake, cañon, Boteler for Bottler, etc. Also, the paragraphing of the Doane text follows the National Park Service mimeographed version which was copied from the original manuscript.

Doane's original manuscript introduced each new day's entry with the notation, e.g., "October 11th 1876" or "Oct. 12" or simply "14." The editors have standardized and supplemented these notations to read, e.g., **Tuesday, October 17, seventh day.**

The summary paragraphs introducing each chapter (5-17) are by the editors.

The text of the Doane manuscript is set with a maximum line width.

> The editors' comments, interspersed throughout
> Chapters 5-17, are set with a shorter line width, as
> per this paragraph.

For explanation of the chapter-opening map sections, see Appendix to Part III, A, "The Maps."

DOANE'S JOURNAL

CHAPTER 5

PREPARATION AND START

Orders from General Terry on October 4, 1876 and Captain Ball on
October 7, 1876 launch the expedition. A boat is built and dis-
assembled, to be packed on two mules. Doane describes his men and
equipment as "an arctic outfit." By October 10 they are ready to leave.

ORDERS

Saint Paul, Minn.
Oct. 4th, 1876

To the
    Commanding Officer
    Fort Ellis, M.T.

Under authority received from the Lieut-General,[1] 1st Lieut.
G. C. Doane, 2d Cavalry is ordered to make exploration of
Snake River from Yellowstone Lake to Columbia River. He will
be furnished a mounted detail of one non-commissioned officer
and five men of the 2d Cavalry. The pack animals, 60 days
rations for party, and the necessary camp equipage. You will
cause also a small boat to be built by the quartermaster for
Lieut. Doane's use, under his directions. Lieut. Doane will send

_____
[1] The "Lieutenant General" was Phil H. Sheridan, commanding the Army Division of Missouri, with headquarters at Chicago.

back his Detachment from mouth of Snake River to Fort Ellis, and will himself return to his post via San Francisco, California, remaining at the latter place, long enough to make his report.

By command of Gen. Terry
Edw. Smith
Capt. of A.D.C.

(Special Order No. 142 – Extract)

Headquarters, Fort Ellis, M.T.
October 7, 1867

II. 1st Lieut. G. C. Doane, 2d Cavalry is hereby relieved from duty at his post and will comply with telegraphic instructions from Headquarters, Department of Dakota, Saint Paul, Minn. Date Oct. 4th, 1876.

III. The following named enlisted men are hereby detailed for detached service mounted, and will report to 1st. Lieut. G. C. Doane, 2d Cavalry for duty.

Sergeant, Fred Server, Company "G" 2d Cavalry
Private, F. R. Applegate, Company "G" 2d Cavalry
Private, Daniel Starr, Company "F" 2d Cavalry
Private, William White, Company "F" 2d Cavalry
Private, John B. Warren, Company "R" 2d Cavalry
Private, C. R. Davis, Company "L" 2d Cavalry

They will be furnished with sixty (60) days rations.

IV. The Post Quartermaster is hereby directed to furnish 1st. Lieut. G. C. Doane, 2d Cavalry with the pack animals, camp equipage and boat, necessary, to enable him to carry out the telegraphic instructions from Headquarters, Department of Dakota, St. Paul, Minn., dated October 4, 1876.

By order of Captain Ball
Chas. B. Schofield
2nd. Lieut. 2nd Cavalry
Post Adjutant

EQUIPMENT

As I had previous notice that the expedition would be ordered, partial preparation had been already made. Ration boxes were prepared for ten packs and a boat was built – a double ender – twenty-two feet long, forty-six inches beam and twenty-six inches deep. Flat-bottomed on transverse section, but curved strongly fore and aft. Capacity two tons. It was built entirely of inch plank, and put together with screws, then taken apart again and the lumber lashed in two equal bundles which were slung like the side-bars of a litter. The whole forming an easy load for two pack mules.

All the mules at Fort Ellis were thoroughly trained pack animals, having been used in numerous trips through the National Park since my first exploration of 1870 – Report published (Senate Ex. Doc. 51, 41st Congress, 3d Session.) I arranged for a six mule wagon to transport stores as far as the wagon road extended.

For shelter an Indian lodge was constructed of army wagon covers cut in proper form and fourteen feet in diameter.[2] This weighed but thirty pounds and sheltered the entire party.[3]

In the posts of Montana we had then no aparejos, but instead a vile substitute, called a McClellan pack saddle.[4] It is worked with the diamond hitch in the same manner but is a mule killer and liable to burst asunder at any time. Ours were braced with angle irons as well as they could be, and answered quite well, with a triple allowance of blankets.

Our outfit was an arctic one, omitting the stereotyped religious literature. We had buffalo coats and moccasins, rubber

[2] The tepee lasted throughout the trip and helped to save their lives.
[3] The following two paragraphs have been transposed by the editors from the diary entry of October 16.
[4] See Preface this book, note 3, for description of the aparejo.
The McClellan saddle (with modifications), originally intended to be usable either as a pack or riding saddle, was hated by individual troopers for seventy-five years.
The last official act which the editor performed after the end of World War II (in Quartermaster General's Office, U.S. Army) was to have declared surplus all of the McClellan riding saddles which the army then had on hand. There were 50,000 of them, many in original crates which had been shipped to France and back in World War I. Some of them dated back to Doane's day.

boots and overshoes, heavy underclothing, and plenty of robes and blankets. The detachment carried carbines only. Pistols are worthless in the mountains. In fact they are worthless anywhere in the field. I carried a 12 pound Sharpes Buffalo Rifle, with globe sight on the stock and chambered for long range cartridges. (Our provisions did not include pemmican, Biltongue, lime-juice or any other of the orthodox food preparations, but consisted of plain American rations, with some added commissaries, and an abundance of tea and tobacco. Matches were packed on every animal, and each individual carries several boxes constantly. Each man had a good hunting knife, not the crossed hilted and murderous looking kind but a short one intended for cutting up game. Our cooking apparatus included two fry pans, two Dutch ovens, four camp kettles, and some mess pans.) We had plenty of axes and each man carried a hatchet on his saddle. To put together the boat required only a saw, a screw driver and a gimlet, and we had a sack of oakum, with which to calk the seams.

Before starting, there had been no solemnities, but each man's personal outfit was complete, arranged with a view to meet all possible contingencies without delay. I had duplicate note books, one of which Sergeant Server carried and from his, the only one left, I take my notes for this report. Of instruments, I carried a prismatic compass, Aneroid Barometer, max and min thermometers and a long tape measure. None of these were provided by a generous government, but all were purchased by myself – as usual in such cases.

On the evening of October 10th, all preparations were complete for an expedition never attempted before in the winter time, and never accomplished since.[5]

PERSONNEL

The enlisted force was of picked men selected for special qualifications. In addition to those enumerated in the previous

[5] Still true in 1970.

order, Private Morgan Osborn "G" Troop, the carpenter who built the little boat, and John L. Ward of "L" Troop, a teamster and packer, were taken along to bring back extra mules and the wagon from whatever point might be selected en route.

Of the men[6] who composed my party, **Sergeant Fred Server**[7] was a Philadelphian of good family — a wild boy — who had settled down to a splendid daring soldier, an expert horseman, a good shot, a man of perfect physique and iron constitution.

Private F. R. Applegate was a small wiry Marylander, used to hard knocks, thoroughly at home anywhere, full of expedients, and know-all about managing small water craft.

Private Daniel Starr[7] was a man of powerful voice and massive form, had served on a war vessel, could turn his hand to any work. A man of infinite jest and humor, and reckless beyond all conception. He was already a celebrity in Montana on account of his uproarious hilarity, daring and wild adventures. He ran the first boat on the Yellowstone Lake in 1871,[8] had piloted several parties through the Park, and was always a volunteer in anything which promised a new field and a basis of new stories of the most ludicrous and most exaggerated character.

Private William White was a quiet solemn young fellow, useful in any service, full of romantic ideas, sober, reserved. A man of fearless disposition.

Private John B. Warren was an Englishman, very set in ideas,

[6] This characterization of his eight men is in Doane's diary under date of October 25, but is transposed here so the reader can become acquainted with the men at the beginning.

[7] Both Sergeant Server and Private Starr went east with Doane for the Arctic expedition of 1880. However, the Secretary of War denied their applications for discharge when the expedition's backing was shifted from government to private sponsorship. The two men then returned to Montana while Doane continued with the expedition. See Part I this book, "Arctic Exploration: 1880."

[8] This was the F. V. Hayden survey party of 1871, which arrived at Yellowstone Lake on July 28, 1871 (See Part I this book, Chapter 3, *Yellowstone* section). Hayden says, "We had brought up the framework of a boat twelve feet long and three-and-one-half feet wide, which we covered with stout ducking well-tarred." They launched it July 29, claiming it to be the first recorded boat on Yellowstone Lake. It was named the "Anna" for the daughter of Senator H. L. Dawes who had been instrumental in getting the appropriations for Hayden's 1871 expedition to Yellowstone. The flimsy craft did not compare with Doane's twenty-two foot boat of one-inch planks.

an older man than the others. A man of intelligence, a most indefatigable fisherman and an all around utility man.

Private C. B. Davis was a born cook. He lived for his stomach alone and knew how to prepare food for its pacification. He saw no value in anything that was not edible, talked, thought and dreamed of good things to eat but came out strongly over a camp fire. With a dishcloth in one hand and "something dead" in the other, he smiled beamingly into the yawning interior of an open Dutch bake oven, and inhaled with unspeakable delight, the fragrant aroma of a steaming coffee pot. The above named formed the regular detail for the expedition.

The others, **Private Morgan Osborn**, a carpenter, was a careful, sober man, not used to the mountains, faithful and honest and therefore useful.

Private John L. Ward was a hardy vigorous man, good on a trail, in a boat, or on a wheel mule, a packer and a woodsman.

They were all enthusiastic on the subject of the present expedition, and were reliable intrepid men.

CHAPTER 6

FORT ELLIS TO GARDNER RIVER CROSSING

Doane describes the beauty of Trail Creek Road and the geology of the Yellowstone Valley.[1] At Bottler's Ranch he tells of the wonders of the mountains to the east, now known as the Absaroka and Beartooth ranges.

Doane waits October 13 and 14 at Bottler's for mail and forgotten articles from Fort Ellis. The rest of the party starts on. On the fourteenth, the wagon tips over in Yankee Jim Canyon, is abandoned, and the outfit is loaded on the pack animals. Doane joins the party on the fifteenth; they camp near present-day Gardiner. Warren and the mail finally catch up with them.

THE TRAIL CREEK ROAD

Wednesday, October 11, first day. We moved out from Fort Ellis, with eight mules in the wagon team and the other two carrying the boat material. The men were all furnished with horses an extra being led for the teamster. We took the Trail Creek road jogging along in the splendid sunshine of a Montana autumn, through Rock Cañon, where the Northern Pacific track now runs,[2] over foothills, since burrowed with coal mines, and over the Yellowstone divide to a favorite camping place by an ice spring which gushes from a mass of volcanic breccia and is

---

[1] The route taken is the same as in 1870. Doane is more familiar with the way, describes the country in detail rather than the road itself which he detailed earlier.

[2] The Northern Pacific was constructed through Rock Creek Canyon to Bozeman in 1883, indicating Doane had written or edited the manuscript since that date.

sheltered by a thicket of mountain aspen.[3]

The elevation of the divide is six thousand feet,[4] carboniferous limestones upheaved and cut through on the ridges by volcanic rocks form picturesque groups on either side, and the descending trail leads through a lovely little valley opening out on the broad expanse of the second basin of the Yellowstone. Dark green masses of young pines, interspersed with long reaches of yellow mountain grasses fully ripened for the winter range, give to the mountain sides a rich variety of coloring heightened now by the red and gold of autumn colorings unsurpassed in any land.

The night was frosty and the morning sun came to view from behind the summit of the mighty peaks whose glaciers form the sources of the Boulder. Distance 18 m.

UP THE YELLOWSTONE VALLEY

Thursday, October 12, second day. Today the road descended several miles, then turned southward into the valley of the Yellowstone, over long slopes of terminal moraines, where the Grand Glacier of the Yellowstone Cañon during the ice period made its farthest advance down the channel. Here are several townships of land covered to an unknown depth with boulders of Gneiss, jammed and striated by an irresistable force which has left them in long, wave-like ridges covering the expanse of the valley. Huge masses carried on the surface of the ice flow and dropped by its receding front stand at intervals on the surface, rough and uncut, as they fall from the cañon walls above. Many of these are as large as a good sized horse. All of them are of coarse grained Gneiss, and easily traced to the mountains whence derived.

---

[3] The editors did not locate this spring. Floyd Bottler and others living in the Yellowstone Valley knew nothing about it. They recalled that Barnette Allen had his establishment, "Mountain House," about 1.5 miles down from the divide where travelers usually stopped. "Ice spring" may have been Doane's way of saying "cool spring."

[4] Elevation is now reckoned at 6,011 feet.

Above the moraines and after crossing two splendid mountain torrents, the road turns shortly down a steep slope into the old glacier channel, the fertile valley now of the wild and winding Yellowstone. The river here runs in a deep channel with banks of heaped up boulders. It is a hundred yards wide and unfordable. Its waters are of crystal clearness and alive with trout. Venerable mountain cedars line its banks clinging to the rocky soil where no other trees would find sustenance.

Farther up, the banks become lower and of alluvial soil, the channel widens, groups of islands appear, grown up with groves of cottonwood and fringed with willows, formerly favorite retreats of elk in their breeding season, but now inhabited by pioneer settlers who safely dwell where the savages roamed at will but seven years before,[5] and where buffalo skulls are strewn by thousands – mementos of a wild and romantic past.

CAMP AT BOTTLER'S RANCH

We camped at Botelers Ranch, a half way station between Fort Ellis and the Park, distance 17 m. elevation, 4837 ft. At this point a basaltic flow forms a terrace a mile in width reaching from the foothills on the right to the margin of the river bottom which is two miles wide. The basalt terrace terminates in a wall of Columns from thirty to one hundred feet high, and parallel with the river's course. Several mountain rivulets fall at intervals from this wall and at its foot are groups of ice cold springs.

THE ABSAROKA AND BEARTOOTH RANGES [6]

The bottom land in front is fenced and cultivated. The river is bordered by a heavy growth of Cottonwood, and beyond it

[5] The east side of the Yellowstone Valley was included in lands which the Crows gave up by treaty of May 7, 1868. (C. C. Royce, "Indian Land Cessions in the United States," *Bureau of American Ethnology,* XVIII, Pt. 2, 786, 848, maps, Nos. 39 and 40)

[6] F. V. Hayden calls these the "Snowy or Yellowstone Range," in *Preliminary Report of the U.S. Geological Survey of Montana,* 1.

the bottom land extends some distance then slopes gradually upward on a long talus of drift to the foot of a grand mountain, Emigrant Peak, whose snowy summit reaches an elevation of 10,000 feet.[7] This dazzling cone is the highest of the range bounding the valley on the eastern side.[8] A more alpine group this continent cannot show. They fill the whole immense space between the Park and the Lower Yellowstone, and eastward as far as Clarke's Fork, a compact mass of mountains, next to impassable in any direction, cut through in places by cañons thousands of feet in depth which terminate in precipitous walls. Baby glaciers nestle in lofty peaks hidden away among surrounding peaks. Plateaus 11,000 feet in altitude glisten afar with snow that never melts away and a central group of icy spires, visible from a distance of two hundred miles, are yet untrodden by human footsteps, walled in by precipices, capped with sheets of glacial neve.[9]

THE BOULDER RIVER [10]

Here find their sources, the wild Boulder, with its trough-like cañon, 2000 feet deep and forty miles long running straight into the mountains, its wondrous natural bridge of sixty foot span and forty feet in width. Its subterranean well three hundred feet in depth, its cascade and side channel cut in solid rock for a mile, and its tunnel two thousand feet in length terminating in a mighty spring by which the whole summer flow of the river escapes from the rocky wall. Here are chambers and labarynthium passages which honeycomb the cañon wall for half a mile

[7] 10,969 feet.

[8] In the area Doane is discussing, Mount Cowan (11,206 feet), fourteen miles northeast of Emigrant Peak, is higher. Granite Peak (12,850 feet), farther east in the Beartooth Range, is the highest point in Montana.

[9] This "untrodden" area is preserved today in the Beartooth Primitive Area of Custer National Forest.

[10] Going west to east, the Boulder and Stillwater Rivers are southern branches of the Yellowstone, with sources in the Absaroka Range. Continuing east, also southern branches of the Yellowstone, are Rosebud and Rock Creeks and Clark's Fork, all heading in the Beartooth Range.

where one can roam about all day long through passages in solid rock, water worn and smoothed by the wear of floods through centuries. Many of these tunnels lead to the river bed, others to openings hundreds of feet above in the rocky walls. A whole army could here lie concealed in a fortress at once acceptable and impregnable. [11]

THE STILLWATER AND BUFFALO JUMP

Farther east comes the beautiful Stillwater issuing from a mighty and closed cañon and bordered by a basaltic terrace terminating in sheer walls above the stream. Here was once a buffalo trap. The Indians drove the great herds slowly to the table land in rear and having closed in on the side toward the valley, stampeded and rushed them over the precipice. Their bones lie at the foot of the rock cliffs in a long windrow of bleaching thousands. [12]

[11] The Natural Bridge, a spectacular phenomenon and local tourist attraction for many years, is located on the Boulder River approximately eight miles southwest of McLeod, Montana, in Section 26, T3S, R12E.

According to Joe T. Helle, District Ranger, Big Timber, Montana, in 1964, the 300-foot deep subterranean well is no doubt the "Glory Hole" where the river sinks to its subterranean channels under the falls and comes out in the river channel approximately 0.5 miles downstream. During high water in the spring the majority of the water flows over the Natural Bridge and cascades over the falls, which is about ninety-five feet, a beautiful sight.

As to the chambers and labyrinthine passages which Doane refers to, Mr. Helle has not personally seen these, but feels confident that in a limestone formation of this type the area no doubt has these tunnels and caves. (Letter dated November 25, 1964, O. H. Bonney Collection)

According to Thomas G. Ellis, District Ranger (1969), the Forest Service is planning a recreation development around this natural phenomenon as soon as funds are available.

[12] This buffalo jump is on the Walter Keogh Ranch near Nye, Montana. It is No. 24ST401 of the National Archeology Sites.

According to Stuart W. Conner, Billings, Montana, this jump, instead of the more common V-shaped rock lines, has parallel rock lines winding down a hill. The nearby buffalo wallow is unusual. When the Indians were moving a herd to its destruction, the bison were routed through the fifty-yard-wide course, making turns first left then right into the drive lane and over the sixty-foot cliff. They landed on the steep talus slope and rolled about a hundred feet. ("Unusual Characteristics of the Keogh Buffalo Jump")

SPRINGS ON THE ARAPAHOE TRAIL

Still farther east on the Arapahoe trail is a wonderful group of springs, which in summer ebb and flow twice daily, having sources in melting snow forty miles away.[13] One of these bursts out a hundred feet above the trail in a jet the size of a barrel projected horizontally twenty feet from a hole in the rock, and falling in a splendid cascade. Six hours afterward, not a drop will flow, and a man can crawl into the tunnel some distance without finding water.

This group of intermittent springs furnishes water for a stream which dries up and flows alternately every six hours — This alternation being due to the sun's daily energy, split in effect by the distance from the source of different springs which thus flow at different times. There are several streams in the world which flow daily and are dry at night but none like this which flows every six hours night and day during the summer months. In winter it is dry, excepting that some water comes to its channel from its cañon walls.

ROSEBUD CREEK

The Rosebud[14] comes next with its hidden lakelet, shadowed by a granite wall three thousand feet in height[15] and

[13] The old Arapahoe Trail, according to Clarence G. Rich, Nye, Montana (his mother was Mary Lee Doane's sister), started from the Yellowstone River near Livingston, went ESE across the mountains passing near the Natural Bridge, present-day Anderson Springs, Nye, and Dean, Montana, to Red Lodge. (Letter dated December 10, 1964 to Mrs. Mary Anna Herron, O. H. Bonney Collection)

The editors have found no one today who seems to know of the intermittent springs. Neither Mr. Rich nor William H. Wilson, who covered the region with the U.S. Geological Survey, could identify them in the general location given by Doane.

Perhaps these have dried up or have been taken into the irrigation systems. Hank Rate, District Ranger in the area, thought it might have been due to the forest fires which destroyed the timber and soil mantle between 1890 and 1910, leaving practically no surface water in the burned area. (Letter dated October 14, 1964, O. H. Bonney Collection)

[14] This Rosebud Creek is not to be confused with the more historic Rosebud Creek 130 miles east, which heads in the Big Horn Range.

[15] Ranger Hank Rate thinks Doane refers to East Rosebud Lake. The walls above the lake are 3,800 feet high. There is one vertical granite wall 1,600 feet high just

beyond this is Clarke's Fork breaking through the mountain wall in a cut four thousand feet in depth, to escape from a "Garden of the Gods" which will be described hereafter.[16] Besides these are hundreds of smaller streams with their cañons and their waterfalls and all of them teeming with beautiful trout.

BOTTLER'S RANCH

Botelers Ranch House is at the foot of the basaltic bluff, by a group of crystal springs, the united waters of which form a rippling brook swarming with fat and lazy trout which are daily fed and so tame that one can catch them with the hands. Opposite and below the "Emigrant Gulch" comes in from behind the Peak of the name in a tremendous cañon, terminating in a long rocky slope. This is a placer stream and has been worked for years.[17] The fertile, peaceful valley in front, and the mighty wall of mountains beyond furnish a landscape of grandeur indescribable.

We were wakened the next morning by the racket of a barrel churn run by a little overshot water wheel, and breakfasted on two pound trout, flanked by hot biscuits with butter thumped into rich consistency by our tormentor of the early dawn, washed down in draughts of the richest milk the world produces, so rich that the U.S. Geological Survey are reputed to have drunk one hundred thousand dollars worth since 1870. (Their supply camp was usually kept at Botelers.)

Friday, October 13, third day. Started the transportation on up the river and remained at Botelers with one man. The road follows the river bottom six miles and then rises past a column

above East Rosebud Lake. This is visible for many miles out onto the prairie and is known as the "Foot of the Sleeping Giant." (Letter dated October 14, 1964, O. H. Bonney Collection)

[16] Doane does not describe these later.

[17] William Ludlow says ". . . the owners [are] taking out $10 to $25 per man . . . [the] net profit on each laborer being $5 to $15 per day." (*Report of a Reconnaissance from Carroll, Montana Territory, on the Upper Missouri, to the Yellowstone National Park, and Return, made in the Summer of 1875*)

of amygdaloid which overhangs the river flowing three hundred feet below, a side cut from this point leads to the valley beyond.[18] It is a dangerous road as an upset wagon inevitably lands in the river and is lost.

To the right rises a precipitous and weathered out wall of Breccia, in beautiful forms and brilliant colorings. Across the river are bluffs of Talcose material and the mountain range closes in on the stream.

WAGON WRECK IN YANKEE JIM CANYON

The valley on the right extends five miles further crossed by the channels of two fine creeks and then enters the 2nd cañon of the Yellowstone.[19] Here is abundant evidence of glacial action. The walls of the cañon are ground off smoothly, projecting points are rounded and striated. The river bed is a mass of huge boulders and here is a terminal moraine of a second and receding period, with its huge deposits of blocks of Gneiss, gorging the cañon to an unknown depth. The wagon road winds among these masses and over a projecting spur, high above the river thence descends over boulders to the level of the stream. It is a bad place for a long team and in one place the swing animals have to be detached or pulled at right angles up the bank in order to give a wagon room to make the turn.

Here our wagon came to grief, an unruly wheeler failed to pull at the right time, and the heavy vehicle cramped and went over crushing a hind wheel and reducing the body to something

[18] This point may be seen directly west of the Yellowstone crossing, 10.7 miles south of Emigrant on U.S. Highway 89.

[19] This immense canyon of the lower Yellowstone is known today as Yankee Jim Canyon, named for Yankee Jim (James George) whose foresight chose this narrow canyon, the only available pass in the area, in which to build his twenty-seven mile toll road. The old road can be seen high above the railroad (south).

Following the reports of the 1870 party of the wonders of the Yellowstone, development of access to the region progressed rapidly. By 1875, the old trail had become a road. See Ludlow for the description of the road, its tolls, and its bridges. (*Reconnaissance 1875*)

Rudyard Kipling visited Yellowstone Park in 1889 and described Yankee Jim in *American Notes,* 126.

Yankee Jim's toll gate on his road to Yellowstone Park, c 1881. He charged in terms of size of the traveling unit, e.g., up to $25 toll for an eight-horse team with trailers. He later sold his road to the Northern Pacific Railroad for a large sum and comfortably retired. F. Jay Haynes photo.

resembling kindling wood. The stores were too securely packed to be much damaged, and pine timber was plentiful. The wagon was righted, a drag pole put in place of the broken wheel, and the mules all packed with the property to the foot of the hill, the empty wagon dragged down and the party went into camp. Distance 15 m.

At this point in the early days there was no road nor trail, a passage was effected by climbing over the rocks and holding up the animals by side lariats, lest one should stumble and roll into the river two hundred feet below, in which case it would not be worth while to go after it.

The walls of the cañon are massive Gneiss, rising several hundred feet on the right and several thousand feet on the left bank of the river where a spur of the mountain comes in with a steep slope to the stream. Since the period of glacial action which must have kept the channel clear, the impending walls on either side have weathered off enormous masses and these form slopes to the margin of the river which is here alternate pools and rapids and a notable place for fishing. Private Osborn caught over fifty pounds that evening while camp was being pitched.

Saturday, October 14, fourth day. Remained in camp to repair damages and refit. Sergt. Server and Ward came back to Botelers to see if I wanted another wagon. Sent them back in the evening with instructions to abandon the wagon there and get the cargoes lashed for the packs, giving the animals a rest.

Sunday, October 15, fifth day. I had delayed at Botelers expecting Pvt. Warren to catch up from Ft. Ellis with some necessary articles. As he did not come I went on to camp in the afternoon. Found the packs all prepared for a start. We cached the wagon draft outfit and Linchpins so that the broken wagon would not be disturbed.

Monday, October 16, sixth day. Started at 8 A.M. The road follows the river in a narrow valley a couple of miles then crops a spur several hundred feet in height, formed of crumbling volcanic materials. On the summit of this ridge in depressions are two little ponds.

Descending into the river valley once more we come to a

succession of broken dikes, then pass a projecting spur and reach an open desolate little valley, the bounding wall of which is on the right, the Devil's Slide, or Cinnabar Mountain.

The coal measures of this mountain were discovered by me in 1870 and are mentioned in my report of that year. Neither the Engineer Parties of the following years nor the Geological Survey reported or found this coal though both had my report to guide them to what they did discover. These mines now produce the best cooking coal in Montana, and in unlimited quantities. The valley here is fertile but waterless. It is even now being made productive and quite well settled, being outside the Park limits.

At Gardiner's river the old trail crosses one of Norris' monumental log bridges[20] just above where this splendid torrent joins the Yellowstone, and we camped at the foot of the Great Plateau,[21] by a small spring and at the foot of the Black Cañon of the Yellowstone.[22] At this time there was no town of "Gardiner," but two men lived at the Mammoth Springs, and no one in the rest of that vast region. Opposite camp is a lofty mass of Basalt and on a shelf half way up its side is a large bed of pure white marble. An extraordinary deposit and in an unusual locality. Above this is Bear Gulch, a placer mining district which yields some gold, but being gorged with enormous granite boulders, the expense of removal renders the business but slightly profitable.[23]

During the afternoon such of the men as desired visited the Mammoth Springs four miles up Gardiner's river, and in the evening Private Warren arrived from Fort Ellis bringing mails, the last to be received for months. The Packs all worked well, and the party was now beyond wagon roads. Distance 15 miles,

---

[20] P. W. Norris, second Park superintendent, 1877-1882, said nothing was done about roads in the Park until 1877, when Congress allotted $15,000 to commence the work. Therefore, Doane's 1876 party could not have crossed one of Norris' monumental log bridges. Again this shows Doane is up-dating his report.

[21] Mount Everts.

[22] Black Canyon is the third canyon of the Yellowstone.

[23] Early prospectors traveling up the Yellowstone first discovered gold here. (J. E. Haynes, *Haynes Official Guide: Yellowstone National Park,* 1961 ed., 162)

elevation, 5200 ft.[24]

During the night a cold blast blew up the valley and a sleet storm came on after dark.

[24] Three paragraphs were transposed from here to Chapter 5, *Equipment* section.

CHAPTER 7

GARDNER RIVER CROSSING TO TOWER FALLS

On October 17, the party abandons one mule, then crosses the great
summit plateau of Mount Everts, and camps. On the eighteenth, they
reach Tower Falls, which Doane describes. On October 19 and 20,
Sergeant Server, with a half-loaded train, goes ahead up Mount Washburn, and returns.

Tuesday, October 17, seventh day. The morning broke chilly
and the air filled with frosty mist. One mule, a queer old slab-
sided one was down, paralyzed across the kidneys. Here was an
emergency. It was unable to stand alone when lifted to its feet,
and would starve to death in a few days if we left it. But one
remedy was available and that was a severe one. We heated
kettles of water so that it boiled violently and scalded the
animal along. the spine. The first kettlefull brought him to his
feet, without other assistance, and a few cupsfull from a second
restored his nerves enough so that he kicked vigorously at his
kind physicians, and refused further treatment. He was fearfully
scalded but restored, and returned to Fort Ellis next spring of
his own volition, got entirely well and survived all of his comrades of the pack train several years.

The saddle outfit was cached in some bushes, the load distributed among the saddle horses, and we moved up the steep
trail which leads to the summit of the great plateau. Very
slippery travelling. Skirted the ponds of the table land and

camped near the foot of the plateau on the farther side. Weather gloomy and threatening during the day. As we have not cut lodge poles [for the tepee], a shelter is improvised with pine boughs. Camp in a narrow ravine well sheltered with fine grass. Distance 15 m. elevation of plateau 7,300 ft. Of camp 6,300. Owing to the murkiness of the atmosphere we missed the grand views of the "Hellroaring River" cascades, the Cañon Fall of the Yellowstone and the terrible depths of the Black Cañon itself.

CAMP AT TOWER FALLS

Wednesday, October 18, eighth day. Snow fell heavily from 9 A.M. During the day and night we traveled under great difficulties and camped at the crossing of Tower Creek just above its falls. Distance six miles. Elevation 6,500 ft. A steep hill leads to the crossing. This was very slippery and most of the animals slid or rolled down into the creek. One of the boat bundles burst its lashings and several packs were badly wet. Busy all night gathering wood and keeping things dry.

TOWER CREEK AND BASIN [1]

Tower Creek is a rushing torrent about fifty feet wide and barely fordable. It heads in a basin flanked by Mount Washburn and the peaks in front of the Mammoth Springs.[2] This basin is filled with a forest of young pines growing thick as hair.

The Tower Creek basin is not over fifteen miles in diameter, yet it furnishes a minimum of flow of not less than 10,000 inches of water over Tower Falls. These are without question the most beautiful in the Park. I doubt whether they can be

[1] The following three paragraphs are transposed from October 19 entry, in order to make the proper sequence.

[2] All these peaks are part of the Washburn Range. Looking ESE from Mammoth Hot Springs they are (north to south): Prospect Peak (9,525 feet), Folsom Peak (9,326 feet), Cook Peak (9,742 feet), and Observation Peak (9,397 feet).

equalled in the world. The water falls 156 feet and spires of amygdaloid basalt rise above it in strange forms to the height of fifty to one hundred more. A black wall of basaltic columns flanks it, and a few hundred yards below the splendid wall of the Grand Cañon, opposite the junction of Tower Creek with the Yellowstone, gleams through the pine foliage of the open forest. It is most thoroughly hidden from distant view, and is a wonder among wonders, when seen.

Half a mile above it on the creek is the "Devil's Den," where the stream issues from its impassable cañon into a black walled cavern of basaltic columns, overshadowed by forest trees whose foliage meets overhead. From the mouth of Tower Creek the Grand Cañon of the Yellowstone makes a splendid curve around the base of Mount Washburn.

DOANE'S 1874 EXPLORATION OF THE BASIN

In 1874 I made an attempt to traverse this [Tower Creek] basin by going down from a depression in its mountain rim and striking the junction of its two principal water channels.[3] I had with me one man and two light packs thoroughly trained to follow. On entering the dense forest, we found the pines about six inches in diameter on an average, and free from low limbs. The ground was cushioned with pine needles and entirely free from undergrowth. No living thing was seen nor heard. We had the advantage of going down hill which aids materially in squeezing through between the young trees, most of the time it was impossible to ride, so we walked dragging our horses after us and followed by the packs. These would get stuck fast every five minutes which circumstance we partially remedied by fastening poles to their necks and to the saddles, which enabled

[3] The two principal water channels are upper Tower Creek and Carnelian Creek. The basin lies below, parallel, and northwest of today's Loop Road between Tower Falls and Canyon Village, unseen from the road because of the dense evergreen forest. The "depression" Doane descended drops approximately at the junction of the Mount Washburn turnoff, 10.6 miles north of Canyon Village, 8.6 miles south of Tower Junction.

the animals to pull through in most cases, as the poles would slip on the standing trees.

The ground was grown with mosses under the pine needles forming a springy cushion on which the animals left no trail. A diminuitive whortleberry, the plant not being over six inches high and bearing berries the size of No. 2 shot was the only growth seen excepting the mosses. In many places detours had to be made in order to get through, and with all the dodging possible, it was still necessary to chop trees continually.

We had about five miles to go to reach the center of the basin and started at it. It took us twelve hours of constant labor to get there. It had now become dark and darkness in such a forest means something. We were still struggling onward when the sound of trickling water came to our ears as if from far below. A yawning blackness appeared in front with a streak of starlight through the mass of foliage above. I stopped in time [but my mule] disappeared rolling down some distance then lodged against something, grunted loudly and seemed unhappy.

We had fixed the forks of Tower Creek, exactly where I had intended, and were in a fix. The stream runs in a channel of solid rock, the walls of which are three hundred feet in height and generally not over fifteen feet apart at the brink of the chasm. Our mule had lodged against a huge boulder which had fallen into the gorge, and been caught between the walls at a depth of about thirty feet.

We found a bare space of rock on which to build a fire and lighted several candles. These gave us light enough to get lariats on the mule and after removing his load, we helped him out successfully — being a mule he was of course unhurt. There was nothing left to do but to tie up the animals and wait for morning light. It being midsummer, the air was pleasantly warm. We needed no bedding.

To get water was the question. I lowered a lighted candle into the gulf of the main channel as far as all our ropes would allow without getting in sight of water, though we could hear it rushing far below. Next tried the west fork, with better results, as the light went out at about 200 ft. below. We next found the channel of a side cut, and I sent the man down with a rope around his waist, which I paid out to him from a turn around a tree. In a few minutes he came back with a small kettle full of water, having found a spring about half way down. We made coffee, ate supper and were soon asleep.

Next morning it was late before there was light enough to see distinctly. We did not wait for breakfast, but after looking in vain for a place where a bridge could be built of the slender material at hand, were forced to give over the idea of going on through the basin, and followed up the west fork. In this we were successful, excepting that there were numerous short lateral gorges to be gone around. These were closed at the upper ends and generally contained springs below the brink.

In one of them however, my horse came to grief. At its head was a spring, on the surface of the ground. The animals were very thirsty and mine stepped in this with his head down and went out of sight in a black ooze, thinly covered with green moss. As it was almost in a fluid state he scrambled out on the other side. Fortunately I was on foot and did not share his fate. Here we halted for breakfast and watered the animals with a camp kettle.

While there, had a narrow escape. Our fire caught on a small pine which started to burn like a torch. I wrapped a blanket around the flaming tree till my companion could get water and extinguish the fire. Had it burned three feet higher the flames would have caught in the mass of resinous foliage which burns like a gas jet, and there would have been no escape. We would have been enveloped in a sea of fire in five minutes.

Late in the afternoon we reached the summit of the mountain toward Mammoth Springs, coming out in an open space where there were thousands of Elk horns. There are many such places in the Park, where these animals have gone for centuries to drop their horns in the early winter. In this open space we found great flocks of sage hens, and at the lower edge of it a pool of water, with fine grass. All these were duly appreciated and enjoyed.

Thursday, October 19, ninth day. Morning clear and cold.

Snow 18 inches deep. A brilliant and dazzling sunshine. We could not move all the property at once as the next march involved climbing the long slope of Mt. Washburn. I sent the Sergeant with the train half loaded, with instructions to break the trail to the summit, get the loads under cover and return next day. Kept two men with me. These filled the camp with trout from the Yellowstone, and washed all the available soiled clothing in the boiling springs near by.

During the day the weather changed to snow and sleet by turns and during the night it snowed heavily.

Friday, October 20, tenth day. Continued to snow. The Sergeant came in during the afternoon, having made a successful trip.

CHAPTER 8

TOWER FALLS TO YELLOWSTONE LAKE

On October 21, the party relays the loads over Mount Washburn in a heavy snowstorm to a camp near present-day Canyon Village. The next day, on route to camp at Lake Junction, they startle an elk herd. The men put their boat together on October 24 and 25, patch up a canoe they find, and thoroughly enjoy the work, scenery, fishing, hunting, and wildlife. The boat is launched October 26.

ACROSS MOUNT WASHBURN

Saturday, October 21, eleventh day. Made an early start for Mount Washburn with the rest of the property. Abandoned a mule. This left us eight. Snow fell heavily all day, but the weather was warmer. We climbed the long slope and reached the gap[1] at 2 P.M. Elevation 9200 ft. Rested for an hour. The men at the summit of Mt. Washburn had put up the lodge and dinner was ready when we arrived. This was the highest point to be crossed and I was terribly uneasy lest we should find it blocked with snow as a depth of 30 feet is not unusual in February.

As we passed the great divide it was an inexpressible relief. Beyond and at our feet now lay the Great Basin of the Yellowstone, with its dark forests, its open spaces all wintry white, and its steam columns shooting upward in every direction. It was

1 There is a gap on the trail one mile north of the summit, at Doane's elevation.

like coming suddenly upon the confines of the unknown, so differently did the snow landscape appear in the summertime. To us it was an enchanted land, the portals of which had just been safely passed, and we struck the downward trail full of enthusiasm, reached the open basin of Crystal Spring Creek, the lowest point in the Great Basin, and camped in snow two feet in depth.[2] Distance 18 m. Elevation 7250 ft.

Sunday, October 22, twelfth day. Laid over with four men. Sent Sergeant with the train back to the summit after balance of property, which he brought in safely in the afternoon. During the day it continued to snow very hard but cleared during the night. Hunted in vicinity of camp but found nothing.

Men went down to the Grand Canyon and Falls. As it was snowing continuously, the game was all hidden away in the forest.

Monday, October 23, thirteenth day. The animals had been pawing snow all night to get at the grass, and were leg weary. Left camp in a glaring sunshine and uncomfortably warm. Taking light loads and leaving a man with balance of the plunder to keep off the bears as these animals are affected with a childish curiosity in relation to government rations.

TWO THOUSAND ELK

I started in advance of the party on the Lake trail,[3] and was riding along slowly with my eyes shaded when my horse shied violently, with a snort, and stood trembling. I jerked away the shade and saw that I had ridden close up to a herd of at least two thousand elk.[4] They had been lying in the snow, and had all sprung up together frightening my horse. In a minute the great herd was out of sight, crashing through the forest. The old bulls screaming their strange fog-horn cry. It was a magnificent

[2] Cascade Creek, near Canyon Village.
[3] Doane was following the same route as today's Canyon-Lake road.
[4] This report, long before man's interference, helps to refute some modern notions that Yellowstone Park itself will not support large game herds this late in the year.

sight as the bulls were in full growth of horns, and the calves all large enough to run freely with the herd. No game animal has the majestic presence of a bull elk when he is not frightened, and in herds they manuever with a wonderful precision breaking by file at a long swinging trot and coming into line right-left or front to gaze at some object of apprehension with a celerity and absence of confusion truly remarkable. In chasing them on horseback the first effect is to break them from a trot into a gallop, when they move more slowly and soon tire. In deep snow, when the herd breaks the trail for the horse to follow in, there is no difficulty in catching them.

I remember a chase in the Yellowstone Valley one winter day when two of us killed seventeen elk in less than an hour. Two large wagon loads of meat. On this occasion I did not shoot, as we had a long march to make and it would have caused delay, but watched them till lost to view and rode on. This sign of abundant game was exceedingly favorable and gave a confidence which nothing else could have inspired.

From the camping place it is seven miles to Crater Hills. There I killed a deer and had it ready to tie on the packs when they came up. Six miles farther are the mud volcano springs. By the time we reached there the snow was nearly melted. Camped at Yellowstone Lake where the river makes its exit.[5] Distance 20 m. Elevation 7850 ft. At this point the grass is fine and there is an open glade of several hundred acres. There was no ice on the lake or river, but small ponds were frozen over.

WINTER EFFECTS ON THERMAL SPRINGS

Tuesday, October 24, fourteenth day. Sergeant and two men went back with the train after the rest of the stuff. Clear day. So far we have noticed no variation in the thermal spring action

[5] This was an ancient campground for Indians, fur trappers, and those who followed, down to the present-day visitor-hordes. Jim Bridger's outfit camped here August 18, 1836 and August 3, 1837. (Osborne Russell, *Journal of a Trapper, 1834-1843,* 1955 ed., 44, 62)

which might be traced to change of temperature of the atmosphere. All varieties of springs, fumerolles, mud puffs and geysers act the same as in mid summer. This was to be expected. Nothing excepting humidity develops and influence, this only on the show of vapor.[6] At the Great Falls, the volume of spray is more than doubled. At the Seven or Crater Hills, a dense cloud overhangs the whole group. At the Mud Volcano group the steam columns rose a thousand feet, and floating away, hung over the low hills in fleecy clouds of frozen moisture.

CAMP AT LAKE JUNCTION

We put in the day preparing the outfit for the double transportation by land and water. The boat material was found to be in perfect order. The boards were laid out on the snow to absorb moisture, so that they would readily bend to their place. The frame was set up and screwed together. We carried oakum with us, but gathered pitch from the forest, which produces it in abundance.

In the afternoon we cut and peeled lodge poles and sewed the lodge seams. That night we put up the "Teeps" and found it perfect. Worked until late in the night and retired to rest feeling that all was well so far.

A BULL MOOSE STAMPEDES THE STOCK

During the night the stock stampeded and ran in close to the camp fire. A strange threatening voice was heard in the dense forest nearby, a noise I had never heard before. A loud roaring sound terminating abruptly, and followed by a crash, after which the roaring was repeated. Applegate gathered his belt and carbine and I the big rifle, and while the others quieted the

---

[6] This sentence should probably read: "Nothing excepting increased humidity develops, and this influences the show of vapor."

stock we moved out in the direction from which the sound came. It receded as we advanced, and shortly, with a continued crashing, the animal retreated out of hearing into the timber. We soon came upon its trail and I sent back for a lantern. It was an old bull moose. It had pawed up quite a space and barked a couple of young trees with its horns thus producing the crashing sound we had first noticed. In accounts of Moose hunting, read previously I had never seen it stated that a moose gave any call whatever. These in the Park have voices, unquestionably and use them with the utmost freedom.

Toward morning we were again roused by a flock of swans circling over us with their wild and splendid notes, harmonized to a glorious symphony. In the morning I shot and wounded a large wolverine but did not stop him, and Starr while prowling along the river bank below camp shot a goose and found a small plank canoe in which he proceeded to paddle out into the lake and open a fusilade on a large flock of Pelican, knocking over several of them before breakfast.

Wednesday, October 25, fifteenth day. In camp on the lake. A glorious day. We worked on the boat and refitting the pack outfits. Sergeant Server came in with the balance of the property and a mule left at the Mud Volcano two days before. We calked and painted the little boat by firelight.

That evening, the moon was in full and rising high above the lake and mountain, its soft light bathed the splendid landscape in floods of silver. The mighty ranges of the great divide were sharply outlined in cold gleaming white.[7] Below their ragged summits dark green forest masses filled the spaces to the margin of the water. At intervals, steam jets played along the shore and the deep valley of the Upper Yellowstone reached the farthest limit of vision in the foreground. On the left front appeared a group of ghostly hills of chalky luster by the banks of Pelican Creek,[8] and beyond there a winding valley constantly rising as it receded with glittering channels, from thermal springs threading its long green slopes. On the right front loomed up the

[7] Absaroka Range.
[8] Sulphur Hills.

yellow flank of Mount Sheridan,[9] seemingly ready to burst forth with sulphurous flames; and flooding the space between lay the glorious lake with its rippling moonlit waters. Its long sand beaches and deeply indented shores, its rocky islands of splendid coloring, its cliffs and inlets and its still lagoons. A picture indescribable, unequalled and alone.

From the distant marshes on the newborn Yellowstone, came the sound of fluttering cries of restless waterfowl. From the echoing forest beyond; the mountain lions screaming and moaning at intervals while we put the finishing touches on our little vessel. Starr and Applegate, both expert boatmen paddled the little canoe far out on the sparkling waters and sang Crow Indian war songs, as the work went on. The horses and mules having stuffed themselves with luxuriant mountain grasses, came up and stood meditatively with their noses over the camp fires in thorough contentment. It was a night and a scene to be remembered — a touch of nature vibrating into infinity.

Thursday, October 26, sixteenth day. Launched the boat and found her to work well. Riding on an even keel and rising to the waves in fine style. Having found a small grindstone cached on the beach, it was set up and all the tools freshly ground, an operation much needed. So many trout were caught that the camp was full of them the next day when we left. Killed a deer and two geese. Murdered a lot of pelicans.

VISIT TO STEVENSON'S ISLAND

Starr, Applegate, Ward and myself went out to Stevenson Island in the new boat. Saw fresh bear tracks on the island which is two miles from the shore. We felt sure that the bear must be on the island, but could not find him. Found two beautiful springs of water gushing from the rock near the shore.

Another glorious night. Mountain lions in chorus beyond the river, and a pack of wolves howling far down the lake shore.

[9] Captain J. W. Barlow named Mount Sheridan after Lieutenant General P. H. Sheridan, the distinguished soldier and friend of the Park.

CHAPTER 9

LAKE JUNCTION TO WEST THUMB

Doane follows practically the same route as the Loop Highway of today between Lake Junction and West Thumb.[1] On October 27 the boat is swamped and the party camps early. Doane goes ahead to break trail and set up camp east of today's Grant Village campground. He discusses the water level and winter conditions of Yellowstone Lake, and has his say about the destructive tourist and about the lethargic policy of specimen collecting by many museums and universities.

Friday, October 27, seventeenth day. Loaded the boat carefully and found it carried everything excepting the saddle outfits on the animals. As the beach is continuous and sandy for many miles we put a harnessed mule on the end of a tow-line, with one man in the boat to steer her off shore, and towed down the beach at a trot. Left a broken down mule and pulled out briskly.[2]

THE BOAT IS SWAMPED

The beach of the Yellowstone Lake, encloses numerous lagoons formed by the influx of small streams of water. These

[1] While he does not say it, the geography, distance, and time make it apparent Doane is following the west shore. Doane's trail distances here vary only about 10% from today's official distances. (O. H. and L. Bonney, *Guide to the Wyoming Mountains and Wilderness Areas*) Toward the end of the journey, Doane tends to overestimate distances.

[2] The third mule to be abandoned.

fill and overflow, bursting the barriers and draining into the Lake, which then washes up land and closes the bar again. We passed two of these breaks, but the channels were fordable. At 12 miles we came to a rocky promontory and the tow-line was taken in.[3] Two men rowed around the point and coming close to the shore, a wave struck the little vessel under the lee quarter, and swamped her instantly. The water was shallow and everything was saved in a few minutes. This forced us to camp at once. Distance 15 m.

Worked hard all the afternoon and half the night keeping up fires in a circle to dry out the baggage. In the morning found that the waves had knocked loose the calking in the bottom of the boat, obliging us to go over all the work again. We had some oakum left and pitch was plentiful.

THE PACK TRAIN PUSHES AHEAD

I was very uneasy on account of the snow in sight on the Continental Divide in front of us, and decided to leave Starr, Applegate and Ward, to recall the boat, while the rest of us with all the property on the packs should push on, cross the divide, break a trail and return with mules and horses to the lake shore to meet the party with the boat.

CAMP NEAR WEST THUMB

Saturday, October 28, eighteenth day. Traveled through fallen timber several miles, then along the lake shore to lower end of southwest arm where the foothills come on the shore. Skirted around to the east side past the great group of silicate springs, and camped at the foot of the Great Divide at the nearest point opposite Heart Lake.[4] Weather cloudy and threatening in the forenoon. Light snow fall during the afternoon and

3 Probably Rock Point.
4 This camp was southeast of West Thumb and east of Grant Village campground.

night. As we did not have the boat to carry, the seven remaining mules brought everything through very easily. Distance 25 m.

Sunday, October 29, nineteenth day. Waited until 11 A.M. before starting in hopes that the men with the boat might come, in meantime examined the group of springs before referred to. These are all silicate excepting the mud groups, but none of them are geysers as far as known. They have deposited a great ledge of geyserite on the margin of the Lake and this ledge has been cut into by its waves to a depth of several feet. As the surface of the Ledge is being built up by surface deposition, continually, its present level is higher than any former one.

The bed of geyserite runs far out into the gradually deepening water. It could not have been deposited under water, and its surface bears marks of erosion as far out as it can be seen. The beach line of the Lake, has therefore gradually encroached on the land, and in so doing has risen at a rate which has carved by the surf action a gradual slope.

Either the lake is increasing in size or the shore at this point is quite rapidly sinking. Many indications at other points indicate the former result. All along the shore and out in the lake are large craters shattered and broken up by the waves and by ice action. One crater cone still active stands in front of the main group, pouring a stream of boiling water into the cold surrounding lake.[5] It is here that anglers catch the trout and cook them on the hook.

All the inflowing streams have deep back water channels, and there are marshes along the shore being eaten away by the waves. These marshes are strongly protected by willow growths, and naturally should encroach upon the shore line. Such is not found to be the case.

The rise of the water has been very gradual through a long period of time. It has apparently reached its culmination, the river current being strong enough and its volume heavy enough to have begun to cut out its channel of exit enough to keep the lake at its present level. The annual rise and fall of its surface is

[5] Fishing Cone at West Thumb.

less than two feet, as the heavy body of ice formed in winter melts slowly. The same is true of the winter snow, which is mostly absorbed and drains off very gradually.

WINTER CONDITIONS ON YELLOWSTONE LAKE

Floods in the park region are impossible. Above 9000 feet of elevation there is a growth of moss everywhere. Iceland or Reindeer moss grows on the trees in beautiful yellow festoons. The Lake seldom freezes over entirely, but occasionally in January and February is solidly covered, excepting where hot springs empty into it. It has no capacity for producing ice gorges, as the outflow is very gentle and in an obstructed channel. There is never any lake ice in the river below the upper fall. The concussion on the lower projecting ledge is so tremendous as to pulverize anything which passes the brink. Consequently the lower fall during winter flows over gigantic pilastors of ice which also forms a huge bank at the foot of the cascade bridging the river and reaching upward sometimes two hundred feet. This winter obstruction causes the water to cut the walls of the cañon laterally and scoop out the wide basin into which it descends perpendicularly during the summer months.

The lower Fall is receding perceptibly. The upper one shows no sign of so doing. In a few centuries there will be but one. It is a well established fact that the volume of all streams forming the Missouri River is increasing. With such increase their erosive capacity increases.

THE GRAND CANYON

The Grand Cañon of the Yellowstone is deepening and will continue to do so for thousands of years. It receives no sedimentary deposits, the waters are always clear and the bottom of the channel is of hot spring deposits, a friable material. Its lateral cañons, of which there are several, below where it breaks through Mount Washburn, all present similar characteristics, are full of thermal springs and run back but short distances.

SPECIMEN RIDGE

One of them, the largest, heads in "Specimen Mountain,"[6] a great plateau which falls off to the valley of the East Fork.[7] The surface of this plateau to an unknown depth, but certainly to a depth of three hundred feet is formed of petrified forests, layer upon layer, overflowed and bedded in silicate deposits. The amethystic and other specimens are common. Their abundance is little known. If each tourist should carry off a ton weight of them, it would take a thousand years to properly open the quarries. The same remark may be made in relation to concretionary deposits. There is enough of obsidian in sight, in the Park region, to cover the whole of New England, one foot in depth. Enough sulphur is being sublimated from vapor daily there to supply the world's daily consumption without drawing on the vast brimstone basins containing billions of tons of the yellow crystals.

THE PUBLIC AND GEOLOGICAL SAMPLES

The refreshing stupidity of the average tourist, who desires to break off and deface spring and geyser formations which are fresh, but soon fade and crumble is quite equalled by those who cover up coal veins and fail to intelligently open to the public the unequalled wonders underground. Vast deposits of delicate silicates and magnesian lime formations which are stainless in color, perfect in formation and delicately intricate beyond

---

[6] Specimen Ridge can be seen from the Northeast Entrance Road between Tower Junction and Soda Butte. It lies south of Lamar River. Exposed on Specimen Ridge are petrified upright trees and stumps of twenty or twenty-one successive generations' cycles. See Haynes, *Guide*, 1961 ed., 155, citing Charles B. Read.

[7] Now known as the Lamar River.

description – these are to be obtained under the surface and below frost action in the "dead formations" where the thermal action has long since ceased.

Every museum, every cabinet, every educational institution in the world should be supplied with these specimens which illustrate the most obscure branch of geological science, metamorphism. If there was any money to be made in such work, syndicates would find cogent reasons for opening up these treasures to the world, and the benevolence of such a measure would soon grow to public policy, if not necessity. But a proposition to enter upon such a work for the purpose of investigation, development for the enlargement of the field of human knowledge, and human enjoyment, however earnestly, and strenuously urged, and frequently renewed, falls flat as the rattling of a measure of corn upon the auditory nerves of a dead mule.

CHAPTER 10

WEST THUMB TO HEART LAKE

With the pack train Doane crosses the Continental Divide to Heart Lake, then returns to Yellowstone Lake for the overdue boat and its crew. The boat is hauled over the Divide. Doane sends two men and five animals back to Fort Ellis.

At 11 o'clock A.M. [October 29] we pulled out up the slope of the Continental Divide in a heavy and blinding snow storm. The way is through a tangled forest which opens out a little on nearing the summit. The snow was two feet deep and the declivity in places quite steep. The elevation of the divide above the Lake is about two thousand feet, at the point of crossing.[1] Farther north[2] there is a small stream which heads in a group of springs on a peninsula projecting into the Lake. This stream is Snake River water.[3] The elevation of its source above the Lake cannot be over 100 feet.[4] Our party of 1870 camped at this spring, and I followed down its rivulet far enough to satisfy myself at the time that it flowed into Snake River and was liable to be its longest branch. The discovery by Dr. Hayden afterward that Madison (now Shoshone) Lake emptied into the

[1] The Divide is not more than 8,000 feet elevation here; the lake is 7,733 feet.
[2] Doane means east.
[3] Doane is referring to Surprise Creek; his 1870 map and his diary for September 9, 1870 so indicate. See U.S. Geological Survey topographic map, Yellowstone National Park, Wyoming, 1961.
[4] The head of Surprise Creek is about 8,000 feet; Yellowstone Lake is 7,733 feet.

Snake or rather is the Snake River, gave him properly the credit of locating the true source of that stream. Before that discovery it was believed that Shoshone Lake was the source of the Madison.[5]

The weather grew rapidly colder as we climbed the divide. The snow flakes assuming the fanciful forms of crystalization which indicated temperature far below zero.

HIBERNATION HABITS OF THE GRIZZLY

When near the summit we started up a fine large grizzly bear which bounded away over fallen logs before a shot could be fired at him. This recalls the subject of hibernation of these animals. The males do not hibernate at all. The females always do when enceinte and until three weeks after the cubs are born, but at no other times. No one has ever killed a she bear that was not barren. These remarks apply to all of the genus, to polar bears as well as others.[6]

On the top of the ridge we were obliged to halt and build a fire as both the animals and ourselves were loaded with snow and ice. The trail was very heavy and unsatisfactory. I was sure we were travelling too far. After resting an hour we proceeded, till long after dark, when we reached the first hot spring basin[7]

[5] See Part II this book, Chapter 12, note 21.

[6] According to John J. Craighead, who with his brother Frank, has been studying the habits of grizzlies in Yellowstone Park for years: "Both the male and female grizzly bears hibernate and this is true of all North American bears. The grizzlies generally go into hibernation in the Yellowstone area about the first week in November and come out of hibernation about the last of April." (Letter, August 6, 1964, O. H. Bonney Collection)

Strangely, all the bears go into hibernation the same day, the date varying from year to year, usually in connection with a blowing snowstorm which covers their tracks to the hibernation dens. The bears have dug their dens and lined them with evergreen boughs earlier in the fall.

[7] "This small but important geyser basin contains the Deluge, Spike and Rustic Geysers, and the Fissure Group of springs. The Rustic is remarkable in having about it a cordon of logs, evidently placed there by the Indians or white men many years ago. The logs are competely incrusted with the deposits of the springs." (Chittenden, *Yellowstone National Park*, 1903 ed., 308)

However, when the editors last visited the area in 1962, these logs were not readily visible.

a mile from Heart Lake. Driving out a large herd of Elk resting there, we went into camp. Animals very tired, and ourselves likewise. In the basin the grass was very fine. We built a great fire of seasoned pines and spent most of the night in drying out. Distance 15 m. Elevation 7000 ft.

Monday, October 30, twentieth day. I was not at all satisfied with our route of the previous day. We had come entirely too far, and had struck too much fallen timber. Started back in the morning to the lake with extra horses and mules to meet the boat. Weather clear. I made a new trail, and reached the Lake in ten miles, at exactly the spot where we had left it on the preceding day, all the way through the forest and without crossing our former trail or seeing it, also without looking at a compass, an instrument I never use in travelling near summit of divide.

ANXIETY FOR AN OVERDUE BOAT

Sent the stock down to the hot spring group on the shore to graze and built a watchfire on a bluff to serve as a beacon to those in the boat, which had not arrived at dark. That was their third day and I was consumed with anxiety. A cold wintry blast was driving down the Lake in a direction at right angles to their course. The waves were running high and on the opposite shore we could see the surf flying against the rocks covering them with glittering masses of ice. It was growing colder every minute, and the night was intensely dark. A driving sleet began to fall. This was dangerous as it adhered to whatever it touched.

Our apprehensions were almost beyond endurance. I knew those men would start that night no matter what perils might be encountered. They had twenty miles to come, in an egg shell boat which had never been tried in rough water. Nothing could live in that icy flood half an hour, if cast overboard. The wind and cold were both increasing constantly. Hour after hour passed. I followed the beach a couple of miles, but finding no traces returned. The Sergeant went in the other direction with like result.

THE ORDEAL OF ICY WATERS

We were standing together on the shore despairing when suddenly there was borne to us on the driving blast the sound of boisterous and double-jointed profanity. The voice was Starr's and we knew that the daring invincible men were safe and successful. We ran to meet them and helped them beach and unload the few articles the boat contained. The oars were coated an inch thick and the boat was half full of solid ice. When the three men came in front of the camp fire, they were a sight to behold. Their hair and beards were frozen to their caps and overcoats and they were sheeted with glistening ice from head to foot.

The boat had nearly filled three different times, but Applegate, who steered, threw her bow to the waves and held her while the others bailed her out. They found that she would not bear the cross sea, so they kept her head to the wind, and forced her to make leeway by pulling stronger on the opposite side and working the steering oar to correspond. Thus they battled with the storm hour after hour until they had drifted twenty miles and reached the other shore. We changed clothing with them and after giving them a warm supper made them go at once to bed. The rest of the night we put in drying their clothes, as they soundly slept.

Tuesday, October 31, twenty-first day. The storm was over and the sun came out brightly. During the forenoon we brought the boat down in front of camp and dug the ice out of her with axes. Then threw in hot ashes to dry her out inside and cut and fitted slipper poles under her for runners. This took much time, and we were not ready to start till 3 P.M. One of our mules in trying to avoid being caught fell into a mud puff and had to be dragged out having most of the hair on his legs and stomach scalded loose by the soft hot mud. We dragged him into the lake, the cold waters of which washed off the mud, and set most of the hair again. He dodged mud holes for some time afterward.

We hitched two mules tandem to drag the boat over the

snow, and had her guarded with dragging side poles to glance on the timber in passing. All worked well, excepting that she was often wedged between small trees, one of which had to be cut down in order to let her pass. This made the most favorable progress slow. We followed our last made trail over the divide, and at 9 o'clock at night left her on the Pacific slope of the Rocky Mountains, and went on with the tired stock into camp. We found the work severely telling on the mules on account of the depth of the snow.

Wednesday, November 1, twenty-second day. Sent fresh animals back by Sergeant Server after the boat with instructions not to overwork them. They dragged about four miles and returned to camp which we moved down to the upper end of Heart Lake, and at the foot of Mount Sheridan.

WARD AND OSBORN RETURN TO FORT ELLIS

Thursday, November 2, twenty-third day. I did not need the extra men or animals any longer, so started Ward and Osborn back to Fort Ellis, with their horses and the three poorest mules. They were given 10 days rations and were to pick up the mules and property left at different points on the way. They did not want to take the rations, but I insisted in their doing so. Sergeant Server and the boat party went with them to the Divide and saw them start down on the eastern slope in safety. This left us seven horses and four pack mules. Eight animals less than we started with.

The Sergeant's party brought the boat to the last slope.[8]

Ward and Osborn had a severe experience. They got along nicely as far as the lower end of the Lake, found the mule and property left there and went on to the Mud Volcano. Then took a side trip to the Geyser basin, forty miles, and back to the Grand Cañon, forty more. Here they were caught in a heavy snow storm and delayed several days. Killed two elk. When the

---

[8] This sentence is transposed. It originally followed Doane's story of Ward and Osborn's experience.

Lower Falls of the Yellowstone, winter and summer, 1880's. F. Jay Haynes photo, from his 1887 book, *Yellowstone National Park: Photo-Gravures From Nature.*

weather cleared it took them two days to reach Mount Washburn camping place, climbing through deep snow. They now had two horses and four mules. In passing the slope of Mount Washburn after crossing the divide an avalanche swept two mules packed with their bedding, down into the basin of Tower Creek. They went on to Tower Falls, and picked up the mule left there. As they could not sleep on account of the increasing cold, they overcrowded the animals and reached Mammoth Springs with their horses and one mule only. Here they were safe and thence proceeded at leisure to Fort Ellis arriving several days later, very much fatigued but uninjured.

CHAPTER 11

HEART LAKE TO SOUTH ENTRANCE

After lengthy repairs the boat is again launched, November 5. The men cross Heart Lake and camp at its outlet; the pack train goes via the west shore. More difficulties with boat transportation. Doane ponders the scarcity of game. More boat problems. It has already cost the party at least a week of travel time in freezing weather. The animals carry all supplies; the boat is empty and a burden.

BOAT REPAIRS

Friday, November 3, twenty-fourth day. Weather clear and cold, 20°. The Sergeant went back and brought in the boat. Severe labor as the snow had crusted heavily and it was like dragging over sand. Animals much fatigued. We found that the cold had shrunken the boards and opened all the seams. Put the boat on stocks and re-calked her. Slow work, as we had to gather pitch from the trees in the deep snow. Kept a bed of coals under her till thoroughly dried out so the pitch would adhere and put everything in complete order. Also stripped her bottom with split poles of green pine so she would slide over rocks in shallow water. Put up the Lodge for the first time since leaving the first camp on the Yellowstone Lake, and found it in perfect order.

Moved camp to where boat was, on the shore of Heart Lake,

Distance 1 mile. Elevation 7400. One of the men caught a live duck.

Saturday, November 4, twenty-fifth day. In camp at work. Snowed hard all day. Caught a large porcupine and had it baked for supper. It was very fat and resembled in taste young pork with a faint flavor of pine.

Sunday, November 5, twenty-sixth day. In camp. Finished repairs on the boat and launched her on Heart Lake. I went around to the lower [south] end of the Lake to find its outlet without success.

HEART LAKE GEYSERS AND HOT SPRINGS

The upper end of the Lake received a large body of hot water from the flank of Mount Sheridan, which slopes down sharply to the water's edge. On the shore there are several small geysers. Most of these flow continuously or nearly so. One of them is a beauty.[1] Its jet is but two inches in diameter and thrown to fifteen feet in height with continuous impulsions at intervals of two seconds. It plays for hours then is quiescent for a while. Its little crater is lined with pearly silica in gem-like forms, and pines are growing all around it. These in cold weather are loaded with ice condensed from the steam puffs of the little geyser.

Farther up on the yellow slope of the great mountain are several large groups of silicate springs. These are very violent in discharge but do not play. Steaming wells of boiling water rush down the mountain side and join into quite a creek before the Lake is reached. The thermal action in the Snake River basin shows well defined characteristics, differing greatly from those evidenced on the other side of the divide. The springs are all much smaller, but the flow of water is far greater. The normal temperature is much higher in consequence, and the crater formations are entirely different. The flow of water into this lake keeps the upper end of it free from ice.

[1] Probably Rustic Geyser, which today erupts at intervals of twenty-six to ninety minutes, one to four minutes duration, maximum height of thirty feet.

MOUNT SHERIDAN

Mount Sheridan, though near the southern boundary of the Park, is in the center of the region of thermal and other phenomena. It is central to Wonderland, and the youngest of the mountains in that region. Its lava flows are on the surface everywhere and filling the Yellowstone and Snake River Lake basins down as far as the Grand Tetons. These belong to another period and an older one.

Mount Sheridan is so recent that it has no glacier channels. No cañons and its talus of weathered rock is still surfaced on a natural slope. It is a fragment of an old crater rounded off by frost action into a quite regular cone, 10,400 feet in altitude above the sea.[2] Its slopes are mostly bare and of dull reddish yellow color. It apparently needs only to be kindled well in order to burst forth in lava flows again. Being open to the wind from both slopes of the Divide, but little snow remains on its flanks.

It lacks the variety of vistas for which Mount Washburn is celebrated. It is insignificant besides the mighty Tetons, but it is the apex of the watershed of this continent. Its melting snows and boiling waters reach the Gulf of Mexico, and the Columbia.

Heart Lake is about seven miles long. Its depth is unknown. On the east side is an extensive marsh full of Beaver dams and trenches. It receives but little water excepting hot water, unless from springs under its surface, of which there must be many as its outflow is fully eight times its visible inflow.

CROSSING HEART LAKE[3]

Monday, November 6, twenty-seventh day. We loaded all the property in the boat and headed her across the lake. The

---

[2] Latest U.S. Geological Survey elevation is 10,308 feet. It is an old volcano, as Doane states. It is not the apex of the watershed as Doane states in the next paragraph; its waters reach only the Columbia River. (Doane described his crossing of the Divide in his October 29 entry; see Chapter 10.) Triple Divide Peak, whose waters flow to the Mississippi, Colorado, and Columbia Rivers, is sixty miles southeast. See also Part III, Chapter 13, note 8 regarding Two Ocean Creek.

[3] See Part II, Chapter 12, note 8 for more on Heart Lake.

Sergeant took the animals around by the west shore. I kept the instruments in the boat. Took bearings of our course at intervals or estimated distances, and kept a system of triangulation running by means of the highest summits in range, intending to plot in the course traveled by the intersection of lines by bearings taken with points located with reference to two known stations. This kept me quite busy as we seldom ran a course over a mile in length and I had to constantly be on the watch to get my located points. The weather was cold, being below zero at noon.

At the lower end of the lake we struck a field of solid ice covered with several inches of snow. Dragged the boat out and putting on the tandem mules, pulled her on the ice about three miles, to the outlet which was open, but flowed a stream only about fifteen feet wide and six inches deep.[4] Not one quarter as large as we had hoped to find it. The cause was so much water locked up in ice as to diminish the outflow. Distance 12m.

THE STRUGGLE DOWN HEART RIVER

Tuesday, November 7, twenty-eighth day. Started the loaded boat in the stream but had to unload her and pack the animals with the property. The stream led into a small cañon immediately and descended over granite ledges half a mile with a fall of two hundred feet or more in that distance. The water merely trickled over this wide granite slope, and the boat we dragged over it by hand. Hard and slow work. Came out in a little valley marshy in the summer time, and camped. Distance 3 m. Weather fine.

Wednesday, November 8, twenty-ninth day. Clear cold day. 23°. Worked very hard all day dragging the boat over rocks in a channel where she would not float at any point.[5] Used a mule

---

[4] Heart River, at the southeast corner of Heart Lake.

[5] In 1947, without knowledge then of Doane's 1876 exploration, a party consisting of Ernest Guild, Orrin Bonney, and Roger Bonney reconnoitered the feasibility of packing a foldboat to Heart Lake, and navigating it across Heart Lake, down Heart River and Snake River to Jackson Lake. They scrambled the entire length of the Heart River on foot and discovered it unnavigable at any season or time.

part of the time and wore out the bottom of the boat as well as ourselves making three miles. Abandoned one horse and one mule.[6] Left the boat at sundown and went on to camp. Distance 6 m.

Thursday, November 9, thirtieth day. Went back after the boat and dragged it to camp during the day. The Sergeant took all the heavier stuff three miles below to the head of a cañon and returned.

The basin through which we have been travelling since leaving the lake is mostly timbered, but contains large spaces of crossed foothills. The valleys are marshy and grownup with willows. There has been a great deal of work done along all the water courses by Beaver. The country is very rough being a mass of converging ridges descending from the great divide which curves around between the Upper Yellowstone above the Lake and the Snake River basin in which we are travelling.

Friday, November 10, thirty-first day. Worked the boat down to the head of the cañon which proved to be a deep cut in ferruginous sandstones of a fine quality. Meantime the packs moved through the canons and established camp. The boat did not get in. 9 m. Snowed during the night. 20 below zero. Crossed the junction of Barlow Creek, which is the stream heading between two arms of the Yellowstone Lake.[7] It is not so drawn on any of the maps.

Saturday, November 11, thirty-second day. Cleared in the morning. The boat runs a little faster since the junction of Barlow Creek. We can now walk alongside in the water and keep it going by lifting over the larger boulders. Empty, it only draws four inches.

6 This leaves them six horses and three mules.

7 Doane is wrong. Barlow Creek (present-day Upper Snake River) does not head between the arms of Yellowstone Lake. It flows from the southeast, coming from the western slopes of Two Ocean Plateau and meandering through Fox Park south of Yellowstone Park. (See also Surprise Creek, previous chapter, note 3)

Concerning the name, Chittenden says: "Following the Washburn Expedition [1870] came those of 1871. Captain Barlow was the only member of his party who succeeded in leaving his name in the Park. For several years it designated the upper course of Snake River, but was later transferred to a neighboring mountain, Barlow Peak (9,622), in order that the true name of the river might apply to its source." (*Yellowstone National Park*, 1903 ed., 128)

Meantime the pack train moved on. Water constantly improving in volume. Beautiful scenery in the Red Cañon, small streams and cascades numerous. Jumped the boat sideways over a fall of 12 feet without injury as she fell on a shelving bottom and slid downward into water deep enough to float her at once. It is now so cold that we do not mind ordinary leakage. A cup full of water inside the boat mends the leak by freezing when poured in, thus keeping out the water of the stream. Commenced snowing about 4 P.M. and continued during the night. 9 m.

Sunday, November 12, thirty-third day. Stopped snowing in the morning and cleared up warm. We worked at the boat continually but could not get it into camp the previous night. Worked all day and passed the mouth of Coulter's creek, which doubled the size of the little river.[8] Meanwhile the train moved on the stream and camped. 12 m.

Passed a hot spring system on the banks of the stream.[9] Nothing remarkable excepting the number of small hot springs all flowing constantly and all depositing geyserite. The intervening spaces being of a curious fungoid growth, mossy vegetable substance, which was silicified at the roots as it grew. 10 miles.

Monday, November 13, thirty-fourth day. Worked at the boat all day. The quantity of water is sufficient but the channel in places is packed with boulders, and passes into another cañon, and the river is joined by a small stream from the right. Several ancient spring deposits were passed and some small groups of living ones. The boat still far behind the pack train which I sent in advance to find a hot spring basin large enough to afford the stock abundant grazing. The train moved to a large hot spring group, where the streams from Shoshone and Lewis Lake comes in.[10] 18 m. Weather moderated a little.

Tuesday, November 14, thirty-fifth day. Worked the boat

[8] Named by the 1872 Hayden Survey for their botanist, John M. Coulter. (Bonney, *Guide to Wyoming Mountains,* 428)

[9] These are the Snake River hot springs near the mouth of Red Creek.

[10] Lewis River joins the Snake River just northeast of the South Entrance of Yellowstone Park.

without reaching camp. Snow falling all day and night.

Wednesday, November 15, thirty-sixth day. Snowing hard and a strong wind blowing up the river. Toward evening turned warm and rained for about an hour. Did not reach camp. We are all getting worn out by the excessive labor with the boat.

Thursday, November 16, thirty-seventh day. Heavy snow during the day and night. We worked in a dark and crooked cañon of folded beds, mostly volcanic. Passed out of it into a worse one of strange looking limestones. Hot spring craters of curious forms seen at intervals.

Friday, November 17, thirty-eight day. Weather cleared. Worked the boat down to a group of springs just above camp in another Cañon.

AT SOUTH ENTRANCE

Saturday, November 18, thirty-ninth day. Reached camp in the forenoon with all the calking melted out of the seams and all the ice thawed out of the interior of the boat by the floods of boiling water passed through in the river channel just above. Took her out of the water and put her on the stocks to be dried out and thoroughly repaired.

Her bottom was a sight to behold. The green pine planks were literally shivered by pounding on the rocks. The tough stripping of the seams, two inches or more in thickness was torn away. Two of the heaviest planks were worn through in the waist of the vessel, and three holes were found in her sides. The stern was so bruised and stove that we had to hew out a new one. We took out the seats, floor and bulkheads, and this gave us lumber enough to put on a new bottom. Mended the holes with tin and leather. Recalked her, using candles and pitch mixed for the filling. Split young pines and put a heavy strip on each seam and made her stronger than ever. This occupied the 19th which was a stormy day, and the 20th, which was clear long enough to enable us to finish the boat. [11]

[11] The boat has lost them another week of travel time (ten days versus three for the pack train), a total loss now of seventeen days.

When it is remembered that the wood had to be dry before the pitch would adhere, and that we were obliged to keep a bed of coals under the boat constantly to effect this, on ground saturated with snow water and with the snow falling most of the time, it can be realized that the labor was of the most fatiguing description. Half of the party worked while the others cared for the animals and slept.

Warren here came out as an invaluable member of the party. He kept the camp full of trout and we fared sumptuously.

THE LEWIS RIVER

The stream from Shoshone Lake is the true Snake River and not the one we are on. It is twice as large as this one, and should be mapped as the main stream. It is not quite as long as the Barlow Creek branch, however. It comes in through a gloomy cañon of volcanic rocks. Numerous steam columns are seen along its course. I should have been glad to have followed it back to the Lakes, but the animals were too far gone, and we had not rations enough left to allow such a venture. [12]

The group of springs below which we are camped, was of more than ordinary interest and flowed a vast quantity of water into the river. [13] Most of the strongest springs were in the bed of the stream, all of them were Snake River Geysers. That is, they flowed continuously from small craters. One jet was four feet in height and six inches in diameter; a boiling fountain, without impulsions. Its crater was built up in a bell shaped cone three feet in height. The temperature of these springs was constant, and their water discharge very great. Nearby were several wells in the rock, of great size and full of tepid water.

Behind the hills in every direction here, as at other points

[12] The Lewis River is larger than the Upper Snake River. The highway follows its west bank ten miles, from the crossing below Lewis Falls (a mile south of Lewis Lake) to South Entrance of Yellowstone Park. Doane would have found difficulty exploring its "gloomy cañon," — five miles of roaring cascades and vertical walls 700 to 800 feet high, rapids, and one fall of fifty feet.

[13] These are east of South Entrance checking station, across the Snake River.

were steam columns and clouds of vapor which indicate that presence of ponds or lakes not frozen over. There are beds of strange limestones, very ancient and signs of coal, in regular carboniferous beds. These show grandly among the Tetons below.[14]

From this point we feel sure of plenty of water and will start with a partial load in the boat. The strain on the animals has been terrible as they have had to double trip the route almost continually, which means three times the distance of actual progress. We have had but little depth of snow, and this while favorable in one sense has been detrimental in another, as it has allowed the game to run high on the mountains, where we had not time to go. Had there been deeper snow, the water supply would have been greater, the game would have been forced down to the valleys and we would not have been obliged to use the animals so constantly.

The problem was to get where the boat could carry the property and make distance before the animals gave out. Also to get to settlements before rations were exhausted. I know we had the formidable "Mad River Cañon" of the old trappers between us and human habitations.[15] With plenty of large game in range, this would have caused no uneasiness, but we were descending daily and leaving the game behind.

I spend many an hour over this problem studying all the chances, and endeavoring to be prepared to act instantly in any possible emergency that might arise.

At sundown a black ousel or water canary lit on a rock near camp and sang for an hour, the most wonderful flood of melody I ever heard any bird pour forth. Its notes were similar

[14] There is no coal in the Tetons. He may be referring to the huge diorite (black) dikes of Mount Moran and the Middle Teton. There is coal in the Gros Ventre Range region east of the Tetons and Jackson's Hole.

[15] "Mad River" was the name given to the canyon below the mouth of the Hoback River by the French Canadian voyageurs with Wilson Price Hunt's party of Astorians in 1811. These experienced canoemen took one look at the canyon and shook their heads – they considered it unnavigable. (Washington Irving, *Astoria,* 149)

Mad River Canyon lies between the mouth of Hoback River (junction of U.S. Highways 187-189 with 26-89) and Alpine, Idaho (junction of U.S. Highways 26 and 89).

to those of a canary, but many times louder. These birds are solitary in habit, do not sing in the summer time, frequent water falls, and are scarce. This one was evidently not migrating, but entirely at home. It was the size of an ordinary blackbird. [16]

[16] This chunky, slate-colored bird loves the rushing mountain streams. From a precarious perch on a slippery, mid-stream rock, he bobs energetically until he spots a choice bit in the water and makes his dive. The bird sings year round.

The Teton country which the Doane party was nearing as they came toward Jackson Lake. Grand Teton on right. Thomas Moran woodcut, 1879.

CHAPTER 12

SOUTH ENTRANCE TO JACKSON LAKE OUTLET

At last the boat ride becomes exciting with more water in the stream. Better time is made, though not as good as the pack train.[1] On November 24 the party starts a seven-day struggle through the tangle of downfall, forest, and rock slides along the west and south shores of Jackson Lake to its outlet – still today the toughest bushwhacking in Wyoming.

During the night a mountain lion prowled around the camp causing the horses to snort occasionally. In the morning we found his tracks in the snow within three feet of a poor old mule. He had gone round and round the mule, packing the snow to a trail and had crouched twice to spring, but had not ventured to do so. Evidently was afraid of the halter, or suspicious of the frightfully sore back of the intended victim. We were obliged to leave this animal knee deep in rank grass growing from a hot water marsh, but with a prospect of grim companionship.[2]

[1] From South Entrance, modern highways will carry one along the Snake River for the balance of Doane's trip (though not by his exact trail or route). See Bonney, *Guide to Grand Teton National Park and Jackson's Hole,* Trips 2, 5, 6e, 8a, 8b, or 11.

From South Entrance of Yellowstone Park take U.S. Highways 89-287 south, passing Jackson Lake Lodge junction (from there it is a short trip south to Jackson Lake Dam and back); and continuing east to Moran junction. Then follow U.S. Highway 26 south through Jackson to Hoback Junction. Take the right (west) fork, U.S. 26, through Snake River Canyon to Alpine junction; then go north along U.S. 26 through Swan Valley. Total: 120.7 miles.

[2] Six horses and two mules left.

TO JACKSON LAKE

Tuesday, November 21, forty-second day. Weather fine. Half loaded the boat and took Starr, Applegate and White with me. Sergeant Server, Warren and Davis went with the animals. This division of labor we proposed to maintain until varied by circumstances. We turned the head of the little craft into the new powerful stream. Applegate steered and Starr got astride the bow. He and White had spike poles with which to push her off rocks and guide her into deep channels. I kept the course and noted the altitude, temperature and characteristics of the country traversed.

As we proceeded the stream coursed rapidly and soon we were shooting along between sheer walls two hundred feet in height.[3] All was lovely. Starr had just begun to sing one of his favorite missionary hymns, something about "the Gospel ship is sailing now," when the river made a sudden turn to the left with a boiling eddy, and the boat crashed head on against the overhanging wall of rock, smashing all the lodge poles and compelling the boisterous singer to turn a somersault backward to save himself from being instantly killed. The gallant little craft bore the shock without bursting, and we went downstream foremost a short distance onto a shelfing rock where an examination developed the fact that nothing was damaged excepting twenty-two fine lodge poles.

As we proceeded the cañon grew deeper. Huge rocks had fallen in heaps in the channel. We were obliged to hold back constantly, with the spike poles and sometimes to go to shore and let the boat down with a check line in rear. Worked hard all day and did not get to camp. The train made 8 m. Clear magnificient night. An old Moose screamed at us during darkness just after night fall, but made off before the moon arose, so we failed to get a shot at him. 8 m. Temp. 20°.

Wednesday, November 22, forty-third day. Brought the boat into camp before breakfast and started early. Cañon soon

[3] Traveling south from South Entrance to Flagg Ranch (two miles) the Snake River is east of U.S. 89-287. The "walls" are mainly on the east bank.

opened out into a marshy valley.[4] Water therefore good. Flocks of swans circled over us in the morning. No other waterfowl seen for several days previously and none at all afterward. Weather threatening snow. Passed several groves of bitter cottonwood, or aspen. This was a disappointment as we had calculated on finding the ordinary kind at this elevation for forage, its bark being good feed for stock.[5] The valley widened and became more marshy as we went on. Reached camp at sundown. 15 m. Stock badly used up. Snow during the night.

Thursday, November 23, forty-fourth day. Snowed heavily all day, but cleared in the evening. The valley opened out more and more. We soon came to slack water and a deep channel. Hundreds of otter were seen. These growled at us in passing from their holes in the bank, not being accustomed to boats. We shot several. When the sky cleared we were under the shadow of a mighty curve of bare rock, the upper end of the Teton Range. An hour after, we ran out into Jackson's Lake,[6] and passed the train just as a mule fell under a log across the trail, struggled a moment and died.[7] Camped on the lake shore three miles from the inlet.[8] Distance 12 m. Clear, cold night.

[4] Two miles south of today's Snake River bridge at Flagg Ranch, the river flows through marshy country to Jackson Lake. The highway (U.S. 89) remains east of the river down to Hoback Junction.

[5] The aspen is *Populus tremuloides.* The bitter or narrowleaf cottonwood is *Populus angustifolia.* Apparently Doane was trying to find the Western broadleaf (heart-shaped) cottonwood *Populus sargentii,* known to the early trappers and Indians as the sweet cottonwood. It was used as horse fodder and food for man.

T. B. Marquis says: "Cottonwood . . . was one of the food delicacies enjoyed by the Crows. When the spring sap flowed upward, it produced this toothsome dessert. The outer bark of the tree was pulled off, then the peeled surface was scraped. The yield was a mucilaginous or jellylike froth that tasted like ice cream. The bigger the tree, the better the taste and the greater the results." (*Memoirs of a White Crow Indian,* 160)

[6] The former inlet, before the dam, was about five miles south of the present inlet, now 6.5 miles south of South Entrance.

[7] Six horses and one mule left.

[8] This camp, near the mouth of Waterfalls Canyon, is 3.75 airline miles east of the peak now called Doane Peak (11,354 feet). Grand Teton National Park personnel named this peak which became official in 1938. See Part II, Chapter 11, note 18 about the other mountain in Wyoming named for Doane.

BUSHWHACKING ALONG JACKSON LAKE

Friday, November 24, forty-fifth day. Followed the lake shore under the shadow of the great range. Snow storm in the morning and clear during the afternoon and night. Terrible severe travelling for the train, climbing over rocks and through tangled forests of pine, aspen and other varieties of timber. Passed the termini of several avalanche channels. Abandoned one horse.[9] Distance 10 m.

We were too near the mountains to get a full view, but above us rose the huge masses of glistening granites too steep to retain much snow. Their sides were seamed with glacial channels, now those of avalanches, which carry on the work of erosion. The lake shore is bordered by a mighty talus of great fragments intermingled with tree trunks, some of these are seven feet in diameter, crushed and broken by the irresistable force. These masses of debris encroach upon the lake from year to year, and the silt from the long marshy valley above is rapidly filling up its basin.

On the opposite shore are extensive Beaver Swamps, and great area of marsh, now frozen.[10] At the upper end of the range we saw our last steam column, rising from a small group at the north foot of the mountains.[11] At this point there is a low pass leading through to Beulah lakes and Fall River and to the Henry's fork of the Snake.[12] This country beyond the Tetons is a wild and beautiful district and a valuable one, of great extent.[13] It is susceptible of bearing a large population. At this time it was a favorite rendezvous for bands of des-

[9] Five horses and one mule left.

[10] The swamps lie between Jackson Lake Lodge and the lake. They can be seen today from the great west window of the lodge.

[11] There is a group at Huckleberry Hot Springs (turn off on Grassy Lake road, 0.2 miles north of Flagg Ranch, 2.5 miles south of South Entrance Yellowstone Park – follow signs). There were also hot springs near the north end of Jackson Lake, now covered by the lake since the dam was built in 1910.

[12] Doane is referring to Berry Creek trail over Conant Pass (Bonney, *Field Book The Teton Range,* Trail No. 1, 69), and to the lakes named by the 1872 Hayden Survey at the headwaters of Falls River, now called Beula (north) and Hering (south) Lakes.

[13] Pierre's Hole, now known as Teton Basin, in Idaho.

peradoes and thieves. [14]

OTTER MEAT FOR FOOD

The trout bite well and we have a good supply. Ate our last flour today. [15] Starr cooked one of the fine otter killed the day before. The flesh was nice looking. It was very fat and tempting. Baked in a dutch oven and fragrant with proper dressings we anticipated a feast, were helped bountifully and started with voracious appetites. The first mouthful went down, but did not remain. It came up without a struggle. Only Starr could hold it. The taste was delicately fishy, and not revolting at all, but the human stomach is evidently not intended for use as an Otter trap. Like Banquo's ghost, "It will not down." We did not try Otter again.

We were camped on a short promontory and beyond it is an incursing shore enclosing a small bay. [16] In the center of this bay are two little islands, rocky and well grown up with pines. The farther shore is a section of a long curve toward the east and bounds the lower end of the Lake Jackson. This shore is heavily timbered and very rocky. On the farther side and half enclosing the little bay, is a mass of debris. Huge rocks and crushed timber at the terminus of a great avalanche channel, formerly that of a glacier. This channel is three thousand feet deep and winds around the base of Mount Moran, on the northern side. [17] Its walls are of glistening granite and its declivity is very precipitous.

Saturday, November 25, forty-sixth day. Laid over, giving the stock a rest and repaired boat. Warren kept us well supplied with trout, which were in fine condition.

---

[14] This country and trail was the setting for the hanging of Steve in the climax of Owen Wister's *The Virginian,* Chapter 33. See *Bonney's Guide,* Trip 12, Jackson Hole Outlaws, 118.

[15] They had left Fort Ellis October 11 with "60 days rations." This is the forty-fifth day. Their rations will actually last only fifty days.

[16] Moran Bay.

[17] Moran Canyon.

FIRST GAME IN A MONTH

In the afternoon my attention was called to an object moving in the Lake. It proved to be a deer, swimming from the large island across to the opposite shore of the little bay. We had just finished the little boat, and catching up the big rifle, while the others pushed off, Starr and Applegate rowed out to intercept the deer. It saw us coming and turning to the left reached the shore about three hundred yards away, where it stopped, shivering on the bank. We stopped and let the boat settle to steadiness and I fired. The deer was badly hit, and stood still. I fired again, and it fell into the water dead. It was the first game we had killed for a long time and came in the nick of time.[18] After dragging it into the boat we found the two bullet holes about three inches apart and the last one had gone through the heart of the animal.

MORAN BAY ECHO

When the gun was fired first, the whole party turned out along the shore thinking that an avalanche was coming, and the noise of the second discharge had not ceased when we landed with the game. It was an echo. We spent hours testing it afterward, and surely nothing on earth can equal it.

The report of the big rifle was followed by a prolonged roar that seemed to eddy in the little bay in a vast volume of condensed thunder, then charged up the great glacier channel in a hollow deep growl giving consecutive reports which bounded from cliff to cliff and these re-echoed until far up the cañon came back a rattle of musketry as on a skirmish line, mingled with mournful waves of vibratory rumbling. These were succeeded by cracks and rustlings, and a moaning sign which slowly receded and died away far up along the heights. Time, one minute and 26 seconds.

[18] They had killed one deer on October 23 and another on October 26.

We tried our voices together, and the result was deafening and overwhelming. There were seven in the party, and we were answered back by a hoarse mob of voices in accumulating thousands from the great gorge, and these, a moment after retreating up the channel called to each other and back at us till the multiplied voices mingled in a harsh jargon of weird and wild receding volume of sound, ending in a long moaning sigh and a rustling as of falling leaves among the gleaming spires far away above us.

I then tried Starr's tremendous voice alone, and had him call, "Oh, Joe!" with a prolonged rising inflection on the first and an equally prolonged falling inflection on the second word, repeating it at intervals of 30 seconds. Experience had taught us that this call could be heard more distinctly and farther in the mountains than any other practiced. The sound of his voice at the first call had not ceased when a hundred exact repetitions were reflected to the little bay. Then a rush of hoarse exclamations followed up the gorge and the fusilade of calls on every rock and cliff answered "Oh, Joe!" And these sounds echoed and re-echoed a thousand times reaching higher and higher along the mighty walls, till faint goblin whispers from the cold icy shafts and the spectral hollows answered back in clicking notes and hisses, but distinctly always the words, "Oh, Joe!"

A full band of music playing here would give such a concert as the world has never heard. There is a weird unearthly volume and distinctness to the echo here, and a chasing afar off and returning of the sounds, unequalled and simply indescribable. We named this inlet Spirit Bay. The night was clear and frosty. A heavy snow storm in the morning.

Sunday, November 26, forty-seventh day. Followed the lake shore with the boat. The animals had a frightful day among the rocks and heavy timber. Weather cleared at noon. My horse was abandoned on the trail.[19] Passed in the rear of the large island and camped.[20] Train distance 10 m.

[19] Four horses and one mule left.
[20] Now known as Elk Island. It was formerly called Warren Island, U.S. Geological Survey, Grand Teton, Wyoming topographic map of 1901.

Monday, November 27, forty-eighth day. Snow in the forenoon and weather colder. 15°. The train travelled till dark to
make 15 m. Stopped the boat at a finely grassed meadow. We
are now moving directly away from the great range.
Tuesday, November 28, forty-ninth day. High wind and
heavy snow storm. The wind was blowing directly on shore, and
we made but 2 miles. Obliged to beach the boat and go into
camp on account of the waves.[21] Weather clearing in the
evening.

Here all the party were taken violently ill. Strange as it may
seem, the Deer had been overheated and eating its flesh gave all
of us an attack of cholera morbus.[22] As we had nothing in the
form of bread, we lived on baked beans for the time. I had an
abundance of proper medicines, so we made a business of getting well. In the meantime the stock were recuperating.
Wednesday, November 29, fiftieth day. Laid over. Snow as
usual in the morning. Temperature falling. 25°. Sergeant Server
and myself still unable to travel. White and Starr took a boat
load of the property down to the outlet of the lake and returned.[23] A magnificent night, but cold.

JACKSON LAKE[24]

Jackson's Lake is about ten miles in length and from three to
five in width.[25] On the side opposite the Tetons there are

21 Strong and violent winds often rush down out of the mountains here. They are
gusty and make navigation on the lake difficult.
22 In Doane's day diarrhea was called "Cholera morbus." The illness may have
resulted from drinking glacier water rather than as Doane suggests. Since November
24 they had been traveling along the flanks of Mount Moran, where Skillet Glacier
and Falling Ice Glacier (both much larger than they are now) pour out the principal
streams. This water is saturated with "rock flour" in suspension – in such quantity it
gives the streams a milky appearance. Rocks frozen in the glacier grind the "flour" as
the ice creaks, groans, and moves over the bedrock. Glacier water nearly always
causes diarrhea.
23 Jackson Lake Dam (1.3 miles south of Jackson Lake Lodge Junction), rebuilt
in 1910, now crosses the outlet of Jackson Lake, raising the level of the lake,
covering its shore contours, and flooding the old trapper trail which crossed north of
it.
24 This description of Jackson Lake has been transposed to this chapter rather
than where Doane had it – after leaving the lake.
25 Present-day Jackson Lake, with its outlet dammed, is from three to eight miles

marshes and Beaver swamps of great extent. A large island[26] almost divided the Lake into two bodies of water but there is a channel all around it of deep water. The water must be very deep in places, but the lake is filling up rapidly as the lands in its vicinity are highly susceptible of erosion, while the numerous avalanche channels from the great range empty directly into the lake their enormous masses of debris.

During the winter season, as long as the water is open the following phenomenon occurs daily. The afternoon being clear, great clouds of vapor rise. These during the night lie in heavy masses on the slopes of the range and are precipitated in a morning snow storm. The same is true of all the other lakes and ponds in this basin, though in most cases the snow does not fall on the spot where the vapor rises, as at Jackson's Lake, there being no mountains to hold the clouds in place during the night. We soon learned to locate lakes without going to them at all and found ourselves correct in all cases afterward. By this means we located lakes at the foot of several of the Teton cañons, also in other places in the basin.

wide, and sixteen miles long. Once in the past decade (1962) Jackson Lake waters were so low as to be within their original boundaries again.

[26] Elk Island.

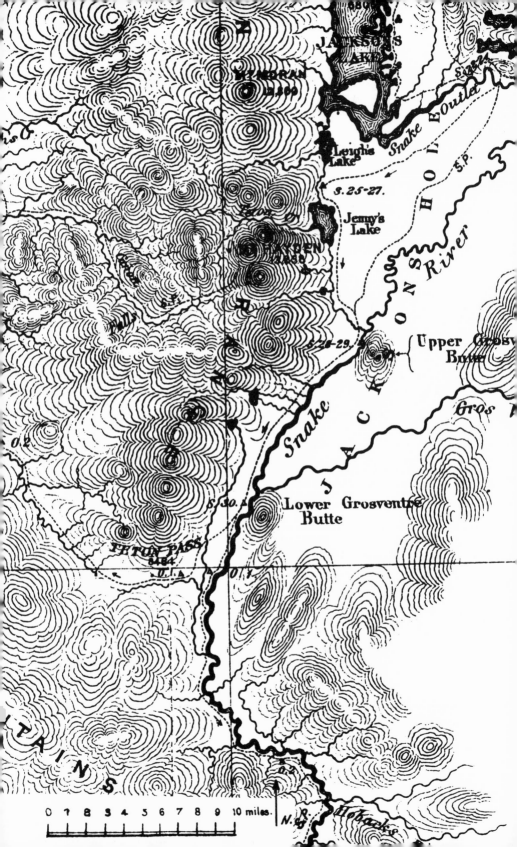

JACKSON'S LAKE

S. 25-27.

Leigh's Lake

Snake R. Outlet

JACKSON'S HOLE S.P.

Jenny's Lake

MORAN

Leigh L.

HAYDEN

S.P.

JACKSONS River

S. 28-29.

Upper Grosv.
Butte

Falls C.

Snake

Gros

S. 30.

Lower Grosventre
Butte

TETON PASS
8484

U T A H

0.2

MOUNTAINS

Hoback

0   1   2   3   4   5   6   7   8   9   10 miles.

N.

CHAPTER 13

JACKSON LAKE OUTLET TO HOBACK RIVER

On November 30 the snowstorm abates and the party moves to the outlet of Jackson Lake, loads the boat, and starts down the river. Camp that night is below the mouth of Spread Creek, just north of Snake River Overlook in today's Grand Teton Park. The following night the men camp at Blacktail Butte, almost on the site of present-day Teton Park headquarters at Moose, Wyoming. They eat the last bite of food, then go out to view the indescribable beauty of the Tetons. On December 6 the party camps near the old Indian and trapper' crossing of the Snake below present-day Wilson, Wyoming. They meet John Pierce, a trapper. Doane's boat reaches the mouth of the Hoback River on December 10.

Thursday, November 30, fifty-first day. Did not leave camp till after the snow storm was over. Sergeant not able to ride on horseback. Took him in the boat. At 3 o'clock we reached the outlet of the lake and found the river large enough to float the boat with everything we had in it.[1] Loaded the property left there the day before and started down the river, making good time as the channel is narrow and the current rapid. Passed over several curious beds of fine clay in the bed of the stream. A creek[2] from the left comes in eight miles below the Lake, and two miles below this point, Buffalo Creek.[3] A strong stream

[1] Today's visitors to Jackson's Hole may take a float trip on this part of the Snake River in rubber life rafts from Pacific Creek to Moose Village (Blacktail Butte).
[2] Pacific Creek, 3.2 miles east of Jackson Lake Lodge.
[3] Buffalo River, 0.2 miles south of Moran Junction.

heading in the Great Divide joins from the east side also.[4]
Camped below its junction.[5] Train distance, 19 miles. The boat
made about 30 miles.

On the trail which makes a large cut-off, Warren saw a large
herd of Elk but was unable to get one.[6]

Below the Lake and at the foot of the great range is a broad
valley about twenty miles in length.[7] This is formed of terminal
moraines, and lake terraces, modified by the changes of Snake
river from one channel to another. This valley is a sage brush
district, producing fine grass wherever sufficient water is afforded. It has an appearance of dilapidation, as well it might
with the terminals of about forty old glacier channels on its
western border.

TWO OCEAN PASS AND BRIDGER LAKE

Buffalo Creek heads on the summit of the great divide opposite the sources of the Upper Yellowstone. At one of its
initial springs is the best development of the "two-ocean" water
I have ever seen, though there are dozens of such on the great
divide.[8] This particular one is on the summit west of the little

[4] Spread Creek, which heads in the Mount Leidy Highlands. U.S. Highway
26-89-187 crosses this creek four miles south of Moran Junction.

[5] North of present day Snake River Overlook on U.S. Highway 26-89-187 in
Grand Teton National Park.

[6] Part of the Jackson Hole elk, ancestors of today's herd.

[7] Doane is describing Jackson's Hole between the Lake and north of the town of
Jackson. The twenty miles refers to airline distance. He logged about seventy-five
miles of river travel between these points from November 30 to December 5. A
packhorse train in good condition, traveling in a direct line along the trail, would
have taken only a day, not over two, instead of the six days it required with their
boat. The editor has run this stretch of the river in summer easily in two days; once
he loafed along for three days.

[8] "Two-ocean" water to which Doane refers is not on the drainage of Buffalo
Creek, as Doane calls it (Buffalo Fork of the Snake River is the proper name),
although one of the old trapper routes, still followed today, starts up the Buffalo
Fork and crosses over to Pacific Creek into which the two Two Ocean creeks flow.
Two Ocean Pass is SSW of Bridger Lake.
Compare this description of "two-ocean" water with Doane's 1870 description
which was wrong (Part II, Chapter 12, September 9 entry and note 9). In 1871, with
Hayden, Doane was near but not at Two Ocean Pass (See Part 1, Chapter 3, *Yellow-*

pond called Bridger Lake, on the upper Yellowstone.[9] (The existence of this lake, Hayden denies, but it is there all the same, and more, he has seen it for I showed it to him, from the summit, the same day we together found the spring I am about to describe.)

The Divide is a flat plateau slightly eroded by water channels finding their sources in ponds on the summit.[10] These only flow during the summer months and in July they are covered with ice every night. The ground is covered with a mossy sponge on the margin of these ponds and the diverging channels are full of the same vegetable growth. In some places it is two feet in depth and is of the nature of peat, precipitating black muck, filled with preserved vegetable fibre. One of these ponds is about a quarter of a mile in diameter and apparently of considerable depth.

The channel from it in August 1871, flowed about five hundred inches of water. This channel ran north a few hundred yards over a bed of mosses, then equally divided one branch running eastward and the other west. There was no trickling nor percolation about it. A surface flowing stream splits into two surface flowing rills of good volume and one of these goes to the Columbia and the other to the Gulf of Mexico.

Intricate and wonderful as the water system of this region is, mistakes have often occurred. They are not all corrected yet, nor will they be until a different spirit of interest is manifested in the development of the Park region.

The grand sweep of the Continental Divide is a splendid

---

stone section and note 5).

Two Ocean Pass is a relatively flat open meadow at the Continental Divide. Here, in the edge of timber, North Two Ocean Creek divides and forms a Y with one arm flowing to the Atlantic Ocean and another to the Pacific. South Two Ocean Creek from the opposite side of the meadow similarly divides and joins the same outlets to both oceans. Fish swim freely from one side of the Divide to the other. See Bonney, *Guide to Wyoming Mountains,* 1965 ed., 425.

9 Bridger Lake is 4.5 miles west of the southeast corner of Yellowstone Park, fourteen miles south of Yellowstone Lake inlet, and twenty-eight miles northeast of the mouth of Buffalo Fork. Doane correctly located and described it in 1870. The lake no doubt received its name because of the times Jim Bridger's men rendezvoused in the area. See Russell, *Journal of a Trapper,* 1921 ed., 46.

10 Two Ocean Plateau.

mountain curve, averaging 10,000 feet in elevation, [11] but in the presence of the Tetons it is dwarfed and loses its attractions. It is much older than the latter as might be expected. [12]

The Upper Yellowstone Basin includes the greater portion of the National Park. Its upper stream rises fifty miles south of the Park Limits, and interlaces with the Upper Snake along the Continental Divide, toward the sources of Wind River. In like manner the East Fork interlaces with the sources of the Stinking Water branch of the Bighorn. [13]

Friday, December 1, fifty-second day. Moved on down the river. Sergeant and myself still very weak. Camped opposite Gros Ventre Butte, [14] which is in the middle of the valley, and in front of Mount Hayden [15] and its mighty cañon. During the day Warren and White followed a herd of Elk till dark but did not get one. Light snow on the ground. Weather warm. At noon 65°. Distance 12 m.

The boat now carries all the property as the animals can carry no more. The River is a fine broad stream but the current is that of a mountain torrent and the channel divides so often that we counted over one hundred islands today. Occasionally therefore we came to shoal water by getting in the wrong chute and have to lift her over. The bed of the stream is entirely of coarse gravel and boulders, mostly of granite, and the banks are low.

Fishing good, but fresh fish is too thin a diet to subsist on alone. We now have no coffee, sugar, tea, bacon, and worst of all, no tobacco. Nothing but a few beans left. The game is scarce

[11] Doane is looking at the Mount Leidy Highlands and the Gros Ventre Range which border the east side of Jackson's Hole. The Continental Divide is farther east, but the Gros Ventre Range connects with it at Triple Divide Peak. The Continental Divide can be seen only by climbing a Teton summit, or driving up Teton Pass (Wyoming Highway 22).

[12] He is correct. It is older geologically.

[13] This paragraph has been transposed. It was originally the final paragraph in Doane's 1876 journal.

[14] Blacktail Butte. It is apparent that Doane has studied the maps and reports of the Hayden Surveys from the fact that he is trying to use correctly the names the Hayden party gave on their earlier trip through the valley. Hayden called present day Blacktail Butte the North Gros Ventre Butte. (Hayden, *Sixth Annual Report,* 261)

[15] This is the Grand Teton (13,766 feet). In 1872 the Hayden surveyors tried to name the peak after their boss. The name never took. Even Hayden himself referred to it as the Grand Teton. (Ibid., 256)

and shy. I cannot hunt and keep the observations at the same time. The boat can now go faster than the stock, but we cannot separate, with "Mad River" Canon in front of us.[16]

THE TETONS ON A MOONLIGHT NIGHT

A glorious night. Moon in the full, but empty stomachs. We are now far enough away from the lakes to be clear of the clouds of vapor and local snow storms. Our camp is about at a central point with reference to obtaining a view of the Tetons, and at a distance of fifteen miles from the nearest part of the range.[17]

The moonlight view was one of unspeakable grandeur. There are twenty-two summits in the line, all of them mighty mountains, with the gleaming spire of Mount Hayden rising in a pinnacle above all.[18] The whole range is of naked rocks in vast glittering masses, mostly coarse granites, but with some carboniferous and metamorphose rocks, the splendid colorings of these sheeted as they were with ice, contrasted finely with the snowy masses in all places where snow would lie, and with the sombre depths of the great avalanche channels and mighty cañons.

Of the latter the grandest is the Teton, which half surrounds Mount Hayden, is four thousand feet deep, where it comes out into the valley in front of us, has a splendid torrent of roaring cascades in its channel and a baby glacier still at its head.[19]

The wide valley in front seamed with rocky channels and heaped with moraines, is a grim ruinous landscape. There are no foothills to the Tetons. They rise suddenly in rugged majesty from the rock strewn plain. Masses of heavy forests appear on

[16] See Chapter 11, note 15.

[17] Doane is incorrect as to this distance. The Grand Teton is 7.5 airline miles to the northwest; Buck Mountain is about six airline miles WNW. No main peaks are nearer.

[18] Bonney, *Field Book The Teton Range,* lists about 165 summits in the Teton Range. The skyline points vary with the persons counting them.

[19] Teton Canyon, now called Cascade Canyon, with Schoolbook Glacier at its head.

the glacial débris and general field of vision is glittering glaciated rock. The soft light floods the great expanse of the valley, the winding silvery river and the resplendent deeply carved mountain walls. The vast masses of Neve on the upper ledges from their lofty resting places, shine coldly down and stray masses of clouds, white and fleecy, cast deep shadows over lake and terrace, forest and stream.

And later on when the moon had gone down in exaggerated volume behind the glorified spire of the Grand Teton, the stars succeeded with their myriad sparkling lights, and these blazed up the setting on the sharp cut edges of the great serrated wall like Indian signal fires in successive spectral flashes, rising and dying out by hundreds as the hours passed on. On the wide continent of North America there is no mountain group to compare in scenic splendor with the Great Tetons.[20]

LAST OF THE RATIONS

There was not a pound of food in camp. We ate the last beans for supper, before going out to make notes on the Teton view.

Saturday, December 2, fifty-third day. Laid over and hunted carefully until late in the afternoon for game excepting Warren who fished with a purpose. Our hunting was without avail. The animals were too weak to carry us far uphill, and the game was far up on the eastern foothills. We came back to camp tired and worn. Warren had caught sixteen magnificent trout, and we ate them all for supper.

Shot Warren's horse for food, selecting the poorest and weakest animal in the lot.[21] He had not a particle of fat on his carcass, and we had no salt or other seasoning. Drew the powder from a package of cartridges and used it. We had been using the same old coffee and tea grounds for two weeks and the decoctions derived therefrom had no power in them, no momentum. For tobacco we had smoked larb, red willow, and rosebush

---

[20] The editors agree with Doane.
[21] Three horses and one mule left for the six men and their outfit.

bark. All these gave a mockery and a delusion to our ceaseless cravings. We chewed pine gum continually, which helped a little.

We boned a quarter of the old horse, and boiled the meat nearly all night, cracking the bones as well, and endeavoring to extract a show of grease therefrom out of which to upholster a delicious and winsome gravy. The meat cooked to a watery spongy texture, but the gravy sauce was a dead failure. Horse meat may be very fine eating when smothered with French sauces, but the worn out U.S. Cavalry plug was never intended for food. The flesh tastes exactly as the perspiration of the animal smells. It is in addition tough and coarse grained. We ate it ravenously, stopping to rest occasionally our weary jaws. It went down and stayed, but did not taste good.

Weather turned colder toward morning. River running ice in cakes which screamed and crashed continually through the night.

Sunday, December 3, fifty-fourth day. Loaded up the plunder and three quarters of horse meat. Sergeant still too weak to ride, making four in the boat. River in narrow channel and with a swift current. Banks so high as to shut out the view. No accidents. Made easily 18 miles. Animals came in late over an easy trail. Weather fine.

Monday, December 4, fifty-fifth day. Weather colder, clouds of vapor rise from the rapids and submerged rocks near the surface are becoming massed with adhering ice. There is an ice foot on either bank several yards in width and on it the frost vegetation is wonderful, building up in crystaline forms of flowers and sprays and intricate geometrical forms. These are at first of extreme delicacy and fragile, but the spaces fill with water, and the whole is solidified. We saw this formation over a foot in depth, a miracle of nature's handiwork in strange forms of water.

The river channel today is very much broader with gravelly beds and low banks. It is much cut up by islands, and therefore shallower. We passed the mouth of a stream from the Tetons, the first one met with below the lake on that side.[22] Camped at the junction of Gros Ventre Creek,[23] a large stream from the Great Divide, having worked very hard all day, lifting the boat over riffles. The boat ran with tremendous speed on a sunken rock, and knocked a hole in her bottom also pitched Starr, who was sitting astride the bow, headlong into the roaring torrent. 19 miles.

Warren caught fifteen trout. Everything in the boat very wet. Spent the night in drying out and boiling more horse meat.

Tuesday, December 5, fifty-sixth day. Laid over to repair boat. Warren caught sixteen trout. White very ill from constant working in the water. No lumber left. Used canvas and leather, cut off the saddles. We do not calk the boat any more, but drag her out on the ice foot, chop the ice out of her and pour in a few cups full of water where the leaks are. This freezes solidly and keeps out the river water. Weather fine, not colder. 20° at sunrise and everything covered with ice from the clouds of vapor rising off the river.

Wednesday, December 6, fifty-seventh day. Same difficulty with the river. Numerous islands and shallow water in the chutes. Ran fourteen miles and had another hole knocked in the boat, forcing us to camp on an island in the middle of the river.[24] Mended the boat after supper and busy all night drying out.

Thursday, December 7, fifty-eighth day. River flowing over gravel bars and on a level with the valley. Channel often a mile wide with a dozen small streams, none of which would float the boat properly. Current swifter than before. We worked hard to make 8 miles. As the country was open the Sergeant and Davis went hunting, and Warren fishing.

---

[22] Possibly the creek from Stewart Draw. The party missed Cottonwood Creek (easy to do) in the intricacies of the Snake River's braided channels.
[23] Mouth of Gros Ventre River is about five miles NNW of Jackson, Wyoming.
[24] They are now on the Snake River south of Wilson, Wyoming.

JOHN PIERCE[25]

Sergeant found at the base of the range the cabin of an old trapper, John Pierce, who was greatly surprised to see anyone with animals at this time of the year in the Snake River Basin. He was evidently incredulous as to the boat, but gave them a substantial meal and some salt which improved our regal fare by somewhat smothering the sour perspiration taste of the old horse. He also sent word to me about the settlement below Mad River Cañon. River too shallow for fishing, but we had salt on our horse for supper.

Friday, December 8, fifty-ninth day. The old trapper came to our camp before we started bringing on his shoulder a quarter of fat elk, also a little flour. He was a gigantic rawboned and grisled old volunteer soldier. We gave him in return some clothing of which he was in need and a belt full of cartridges, as he had a big rifle with the same sized chamber as mine. While talking with him, Starr and Davis were busy and soon we had a meal. The elk meat all went, the balance of the flour was reserved for gravies.

The old trapper gave me explicit and correct information about the settlements below. He was trapping for fine furs only,

[25] Doane's mention of John Pierce is interesting. This is indeed an early and authentic record of a white or red man living in Jackson's Hole in the winter time.

Cora Nelson Barber (1884-1965) remembers seeing John Pierce when she was a child. The yellowness of his eyes and face from yellow jaundice, which caused his death, had impressed her. Mrs. Barber came to Jackson's Hole in 1888; she was the first white child to live there.

Pierce may have lived near the Miller homestead, now part of the National Elk Refuge. Further information about him in 1876-77 is gleaned from the diary of Beaver Dick Leigh, after whom Leigh Lake and Leigh Canyon of Grand Teton National Park are named. Leigh lived and trapped on the Idaho side, sometimes guiding excursions into Jackson's Hole – Hayden in 1872, for example. In his diary, courtesy of Mrs. Bill (Edith) Thompson of Midwest, Wyoming, Leigh tells about meeting Pierce on the Snake River below present-day Swan Valley, Idaho, on September 13, 1876. Six days later he again came across Pierce, sick and needing help. Pierce stayed with him until September 25, and then represented that he was starting for Montana. But it will be observed that actually Pierce circled back to Jackson's Hole, where the Doane party met him two months later. Evidently he did not want Leigh and the Idaho people to know his whereabouts, and was quite nervous about the motive of Doane's trip into the valley.

For other instances of nervousness, related or unrelated, compare Part II, Chapter 15, *Horse Thieves* section; Part III, Chapter 12, note 14; *Bonney's Guide,* 118.

mink, martin, fisher, and otter. Said it would not pay to go after beaver unless one had pack animals and these could not winter in the valley.

He told me that he had not believed the Sergeant's story about the boat at first, and throughout his visit was evidently completely puzzled as to what motives could have induced us to attempt such a trip in such a way and at such a season. I sent him home on horseback with Sergeant Server, who told me after returning that he had been given another "Holy meal." Meantime we worked on down the river with renewed strength among rocks and torturous channels. Worked till after dark and camped at the head of "Mad River Cañon."[26] 15 miles.

Saturday, December 9, sixtieth day. Weather still fine but cold. Entered the cañon which cuts through the Snake River Mountains in a constantly deepening gorge.[27] Passed the mouths of several small streams and one good sized one.[28] The channel is narrow and the water deep, boiling over boulders and swirling in numerous eddies.

The boat behaved well, glancing off the slippery boulders and spinning around in the whirlpools long enough for us to see what was ahead on the next turn, and to land with a tow line if necessary as it often was. With all four of us on the ice foot, holding the long line to let her down easily over rolling cascades and between huge overhanging rocks she danced like a duck through the boiling surges and came out securely into still waters below. Then one of the party would go down along the ice foot and catch her till he had drawn in and coiled the line, or taken a new stand for paying out, as the circumstances might require. We had a most exciting day and made 20 miles.[29]

[26] They are camped in South Park, the valley south of Jackson, Wyoming, through which U.S. Highways 26-89 and 187-189 pass, giving a fine view of the river. At the south end of South Park the numerous channels of the Snake are squeezed into a single defile by a Gros Ventre foothill (east) and Munger Mountain (west), with hardly enough space for the paralleling highway. Doane considers this the beginning of the "Mad River Cañon." See Chapter 11, note 15.

[27] Snake River Range is west, Gros Ventre Range is east.

[28] North to south, these are Game, Squaw, Porcupine and Horse Creeks.

[29] This was one of the rare occasions on which the boat made better time than the pack train.

The animals travelled on mountain sheep trails and got in late. Kept awake most of the night by the screaming of an ice gorge which passed down. Since leaving the lake we have been apprehensive of this and never leave the boat near the water. We hoped the gorge would move on slowly so that we could follow it with the boat in its back water but it did not wait for us.

Sunday, December 10, sixty-first day. Found the river in bad order. The gorge had torn away the icefoot and ice was massed in the eddies grinding and crunching in a very ominous way. The boat being lighter than the ice cakes and a double ender slid over and between the fragments in fine style. We passed several small streams, one of them coming in from the right was a stairway of ice encrusted cascades for a thousand feet.[30]

---

[30] Doane struggled three-and-a-half days boating this stretch of river which modern experts do in a day.

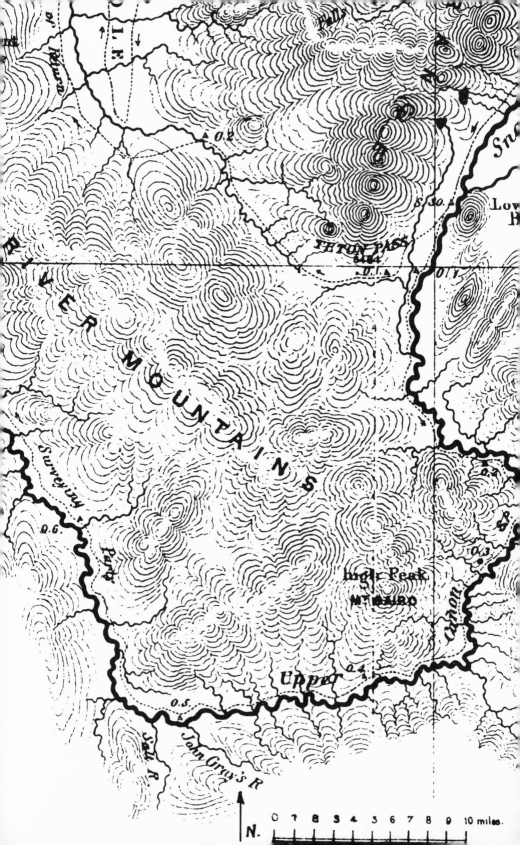

CHAPTER 14

HOBACK TO KEENAN CITY

The week of December 10 is filled with the struggle to stay alive. On the eleventh the party shoots White's horse for food. For three-and-a-half days of the ordeal the men have nothing to eat. The boat overturns on December 12 and guns, instruments, and notebooks are lost. Server and Warren go ahead with the animals to the "settlements" to bring back rations. The two men become lost. On the fifteenth, Doane beaches the boat and his party starts out on foot, in below-zero weather, for the "settlements." On the seventeenth they reach a miner's cabin. Server and Warren come in about the same time.

In the afternoon we passed the mouth of a deep valley coming in on the left, Hoback's River mentioned in Irving's Astoria.[1] Here the Sergeant's party ran onto a fine fat cow, wild as a deer. They tried to get it but their worn out horses could not run fast enough and their shots failed to hit. Had we killed that cow, many mishaps might have been avoided and many dangers escaped.

After passing the [Hoback] valley, the cañon deepened more suddenly with soft walls of metamorphic rocks, showing near the river bed many folds. In this vicinity there have been concentric circles of pressures producing strangely confusing results.

[1] Wilson Price Hunt named the river for his guide, fur trapper John Hoback, who helped guide the Astorians to Jackson's Hole. (Irving, Astoria, 149)

DOANE ON CONTEMPORARY CONTROVERSIES

A patent geologist would dispose of them all in a few lines of scientific verbiage, but a student who really desires to get things as they are and not to draw unlimited returns in conjecture from a few bald and undigested observations would have to study and observe for months before announcing conclusions. I have met some of these "Engine turned scientists" whose published works are distributed by the ton, through the franks of well intentioned congressmen, and all expenses paid by the government; who are household gods of science in the minds of simple country folk, to whom the U.S.I.D.[2] branch is a guarantee of truth as it is of honesty in an Indian agent until caught out. These lofty titled volumes rest side by side in many a quiet homestead and in many a modest city residence with the soul absorbing old patent office report, having the tear-bedewed portrait of Farmer Jones' sow for a frontespiece, and both are regarded with and are entitled to equal reverence.

These worthies never particularize. All is in glittering generalities. All mountains are to them of about the same elevation until otherwise proved by someone else. All rivers have identical characteristics and all thermal springs must be produced in a prescribed manner in accordance with a conjectural siphon, the patent of which has run out long ago. They will take one observation of effects and fill a volume with conjectural causes, or one on causes and get out a second volume on effects.

The work of such men has degraded the Park district as far as it could be degraded in the estimation of the world at large. Beardless cubs who never before saw a spring that did not have a gourd [on a peg beside it] have written of the falls, cañons, and geysers in an easy familiar way as if all these things were familiar to them from childhood, and nothing new nor strange. The grandest productions of nature's handiwork actuated by unlimited forces only set them to work the old siphon gotten up a few hundred years ago to show timid old women that there was no danger of water running out of the spout of a teakettle

2 United States Interior Department.

by rising above its own level in the body of the vessel.[3]

There are a few small groups of thermal springs in the cañon, but none of noticeable characteristics.[4] Camped on a shelf of rock above a great pool in the river, which at this point is solidly frozen over. The ice gorge had expended its force before reaching here. Dragged the boat out and around a corner, and made her fast with two lines. Carried the property up on the shelf. 15 miles. Sergeant and party did not get in till next morning, having been obliged to sleep by a campfire without bedding and go without food 24 hours. A cold night.

Monday, December 11, sixty-second day. Cañon deeper and wilder. River still frozen pools and boiling rapids.[5] We dragged the boat over the ice empty then sledded the property loaded at each rapid and let her down with ropes. Very cold in the shaded chasm.

Otter, fat and sleek, played around us on the ice and snarled at us from holes in the wall, all day long, safe from molestation in their fishy unpalatableness. We had no time to shoot for sport, no transportation for pelts and no desire for any game not edible. All day and as late at night as we could see to labor, we toiled on to make 6 miles. Tied up as before.

Meantime the Sergeant's party had gone on expecting we would make distance as before. They had to return hunting for us on the way and had a terrible time among the rocks and snowdrifts. No food left but a handful of flour.[6] Shot White's horse, and feasted.[7]

It was now evident that we were not going to run the cañon

---

[3] See Appendix to Part III for clarification of this section.

[4] For example, Astoria Mineral Springs, 2.3 miles southwest of Hoback Junction.

[5] For a description and location of some of the rapids, see *Bonney's Guide,* Trip 2. Doane was five days on a stretch of river that the editor and his son, Roger Bonney, ran in about eight hours. However, it also ended in near disaster.

[6] This was some of the flour which John Pierce gave them December 8; their original supply was finished on December 1.

[7] Two horses and one mule left.

with the boat, but must tug away slowly. We were about 42 miles from the first settlement, if our information was correct, but the Cañon if very crooked as it had been so far might double that distance. I desired to get the boat through if we had to risk everything in order to do so. This Cañon was the terrible obstacle and we were more than half way through it. Apparently the worst had been gone through with. All the men agreed to this with enthusiasm.

We gathered together all the money in the possession of the party, and arranged for Sergeant Server, the most active and youngest of the party, and Warren, who could be of no assistance to those remaining, as his stomach had begun to give way, to go on next day with the two horses and one mule remaining and bring us back rations.

Tuesday, December 12, sixty-third day. Sergeant's outfit was packed separately before moving in the morning. They took guns, bedding, an axe, a slab of horse meat, a pack outfit on the mule, and travelled along parallel with us. This arrangement left five with the boat, Starr, White, Applegate, Davis and myself. After dragging over ice twice and shooting two rapids the boat was able to carry three of us.

Starr and Davis walked along the bank with the tow line. I signalled to them to hold her and she swung in to the ice foot above a tremendous rapid. As she touched the bank her bow slid upward on a rock and she filled to within two inches of her gunwale while we were jumping out on the ice. We caught and held her level just in time. Unloaded and baled out the water. We spread the lodge canvas over her to keep out the waves and let her drop over the rapid sideways, successfully. Repeated this twice and coming to smoother water, let her drag the tow line while we held her, following along the ice foot.

CAPSIZE!

The River was becoming better, the ice foot more uniform and the channel free from frozen pools when all of a sudden the boat touched the margin, turned under it, and the next instant was dancing end over end in the swift bold current. All of the horse meat, all the property, arms, instruments and note books were in the roaring stream. A few hundred yards below there was a narrow place where the ice foot almost touched the middle of the river. We ran thither and caught whatever floated. The clothing bags, valise, bedding, bundles, and the lodge were saved. All else, excepting one hind quarter of the old horse meat went to the bottom and was seen no more. All the rubber boots were gone excepting mine. The warm clothing all floated and was saved. We dragged in the boat by the tow line and pulled her out of the water and far up on a ledge of rock. 6 miles.

Started the Sergeant and Warren at once on their way down the river. The rest of us dried out the property and rested until morning.

Wednesday, December 13, sixty-fourth day. Last night was bitterly cold, and we slept by a roaring fire on a ledge of rock. We were camped at a place where several dead pines had fallen in a mass of broken up fire wood and dried out what was left of our sadly diminished outfit with less trouble than usual. We had our sheath knives left, and matches. Cooked our horse meat on sticks, Indian fashion. Started early and worked over frozen pools and open rapids, all day without accident. Toward evening had a fine open river. Pulled the boat out as usual at night. Seven miles. A cold night as usual. Cañon very deep and the descent rapid.

Thursday, December 14, sixty-fifth day. Moved on as before. Frozen pools and rapids. Hundreds of otter played around us on the ice. The boat is becoming ice bound and we have no axes or hatchets with which to chip out the rapidly accumulating ice. She floats all right but is cranky.

After working hard all day we came to an open space with two rapids. Passed them both successfully but the boat was filled as it came to the bank. We bailed her out and went on. Travelled as long as we could see, all of us walking on the ice foot excepting Applegate, who remained in the boat to balance her and keep her off the rocks and away from the ice foot.

Camped in a pocket in the cañon and pulled the boat into what we thought a place secure from ice gorges. We had eaten our last horse meat for breakfast, and had no food left. 6 miles. Dried out bedding as usual and all slept soundly.

AFOOT

Friday, December 15, sixty-sixth day. Morning intensely cold. Stowed away the bedding in rolls with the valise, high up among the rocks and started, unarmed, without food, and in an unknown wilderness to find settlements seven miles up on a stream which we had no positive assurance of being able to recognize when we came to its mouth.

We crossed the river on the ice and started down on the other side.[8] We soon came to a point in the Cañon where sheer walls rose from the water's edge hundreds of feet. Were obliged to double back and climb the face of the slope. Then worked along the brink of the precipice for a mile. We carried one lariat with which to help ourselves over dangerous places.

At one point the way led along the edge of an icy slope of a thousand feet down to the boiling river. A cut channel ran down the face of the cliff. Starr and White had crossed and I was next behind them. I was suddenly seized with dizziness and obliged to crawl up on the face of the bank till the feeling had passed away.[9] As nothing of this kind ever happened to me before, I was furious beyond measure and worked myself into a fever of provocation. My nerves finally became steady and I walked over the dangerous place as usual. Nothing like that feeling has ever come over me before, nor has since. I presume it was the effect of exertion without nourishment. We had tasted nothing since the previous morning.

A few miles below, the Cañon suddenly terminated, opening into a broad sage brush valley, just above the junction of John

---

[8] They walked along the south side. The ground they traveled from the point where they left their boat to McCoy Creek is now covered by the waters of Palisades Reservoir.

[9] See letters of Doane and White, next chapter.

Gray's River, a strong stream from the southwestward.[10] There
was an open channel from where we had left the boat and only
three rapids between there and the foot of the cañon.[11] This
we did not know till too late.

We waded through John Gray's River as it was not frozen
over.[12] It comes through a deep cañon and from the direction
of the sources of Green River which is the longest branch of the
True Colorado emptying into the Gulf of California. The lower
end of the Cañon of the Snake and of John Gray's Cañon are
both through upheaved limestones of the Carboniferous age.
These are broken up, folded and generally greatly displaced.
The timber growth shows signs of a more temperate zone. On
the banks of John Gray's River we had a meagre lunch of the
seed pods of rose bushes. These have a sub acid taste and serve
to stay hunger a little. There were still no sweet cottonwood
trees, and the bitter sweet inner bark of which would have given
us sustenance.[13] Only the Aspen which is bitter to the taste and
acrid.

A couple of miles farther on we waded Salt River, also from
the Southwest.[14] It is beautiful stream and has quite a valley. A
few miles above its junction there is a group of valuable brine

[10] This junction is 0.3 miles easterly from Alpine Junction, 22.7 miles westerly
from Hoback Junction. Named for trapper John Gray, a Rockaway Indian chief. The
name is also spelled Grey. Hayden mistakenly named this river after John Day, one of
the Astoria party. H. M. Chittendon raised a commotion and the name was changed
back to "Grays."

Historical Grays *River* is not to be confused with historical Grays *Creek,* about
twenty miles west, which drains what maps today call "Grays Lake," but is only a
vast marsh. Grays *Creek* has become Willow Creek (Doane so calls it).

See Russell, *Journal of a Trapper,* 1955 ed., 96, 106 for Grays River, Creek, and
Marsh; Alexander Ross, "Journal of Alexander Ross on Snake Country Expedition,
1824," *Oregon Historical Society Quarterly,* XIV, 366-388; P. S. Ogden, *Snake River
Journals, 1824-1826;* F. F. Victor, *River of the West* 103; H. M. Chittenden, *American Fur Trade of the Far West,* 783.

[11] The editor has run these; they were all easy for the modern boatman; they are
now submerged beneath the water of Palisades Reservoir.

[12] When the editor waded it after his boat spill, it was waist deep.

[13] See Part III, Chapter 12, note 5. They found no sweet cottonwood on the trip.
On November 22 they wanted it for horse fodder. Now they would welcome it as
food for themselves.

[14] This stream has been known as Salt River from the time of the earliest trappers
to the present. See Russell, *Journal of a Trapper,* 1921 ed., 98; W. A. Ferris, *Life in
the Rocky Mountains, 1830-35,* 47.

springs and a small establishment which formerly supplied Idaho and Montana with table salt.[15] We found a grove of Aspen about a clear spring which the Beaver had enclosed with a dam. Many of the trees were cut down and seasoned, affording an abundance of good fuel. We built a roaring fire and sat by it through the night. The wind blew down the valley, a cold chilling blast, and we stretched ourselves on platforms of small saplings, scorched on one side while the other was freezing. Hungry for food and craving tobacco. Davis talked all night long about good things to eat. 12 miles.[16]

Saturday, December 16, sixty-seventh day. We were moving at the break of day. Weather bitterly cold. Were obliged to build fires whenever we stopped to rest to prevent our feet from freezing. The snow was knee deep on level ground and crusted so that the leader on the trail had to break through at every footstep. We alternated at this labor. Could not make over a mile an hour.

About noon we reached an ice bound creek which empties into the Snake from the Southwest, the river channel having turned northward. This creek showed signs of placer washings and we followed it up.[17] As it was frozen, the walking was

[15] Doane is referring to the frontier salt factory called Oneida Salt Works which made a small fortune for Benjamin F. White and J. M. Stump at a time when other men were fruitlessly searching the rock gullies for gold. Game, trappers, and Indians were long acquainted with the bitter, clear waters of Salt Spring Valley, now called Stump Creek, a tributary of Salt River.

Today one can visit the Old Salt Works. From Auburn, Wyoming (seven miles northwest of Afton) drive south 0.5 mile, then turn west and drive along the Old Lander Trail into Idaho 3.5 miles to a road fork near the junction of Tygee and Stump Creeks. Take the right fork north 1.5 miles to the old buildings marking the Reed workings. (The salt crystals can be seen gleaming west of Stump Creek.)

To see the site where Stump and White launched their salt boiling careers continue north 2.6 miles. You will be disappointed. Mud flats have replaced the bustling activity of a century ago. The Lander Cutoff just west of Stump Creek has eroded into a mere trail, not accessible to auto travel.

See Hayden, *Fifth Annual Report,* 161; B. W. Clark, *Bonneville County in the Making*; Carpel, Leventhal, and Breger, *The Salt Resources of the Idaho-Wyoming Border.*

[16] Doane logs about forty-five miles through "Mad River Canyon." Today's road measures only twenty-three miles.

[17] McCoy Creek, named for F. M. McCoy, one of the discoverers of placer gold in this mining district. Server and Warren passed here on the thirteenth, traveling in two days with the horses the same distance it took Doane five days with the boat. Today,

easier. About 4 miles up it forks, and both branches showed the same signs of washings. How old these might be we could not tell, as the stream was locked fast in muddy ice. We took the left hand fork to avoid chances of having to go backward, in case it should prove to be the wrong one. It led up the slope of a mountain and terminated in a strange group of Beaver dams.

These animals had built up a reservoir including all the springs forming this creek, and it was at the head of a ravine. The retaining wall in front was over twenty feet high. An Aspen grove had furnished the timber. The structure was a wonderful one. It was braced and cross-tied with logs in a manner to excite astonishment. Hundreds of cords of timber were put into the embankment. It was also roofed over with a screen of small tree stems felled in such a manner as to cross each other over the center of the reservoir.

Darkness had just set in when we reached this point, and a moment's examination showed that we had taken the wrong fork. It was too late to retrace our steps, so we set fire to the dry timbers in front of the Dam, and remained there through the night. 15 miles.

We were sheltered from the wind, but the temperature went down very low, at least 35°. A thin film of vapor rose from the reservoir and condensed to a mist within radius of heat from the roaring flames of the great fire.

We slept a little but only to dream of bountifully set tables loaded with viands, all of which were abounding in fats and oils. What conversation there was turned entirely to matters pertaining to food. Davis talked incessantly on such subjects, giving all the minutest details of preparing roasts, gravies, meat pies, suet puddings, pork preparations, oil dressings, cream custards, and so on, until Starr finally choked him off with the Otter experience.

None of us felt the pangs of hunger physically. Our stomachs

to reach McCoy Creek and the Caribou Mining Region, take U.S. 89 south from Alpine, Wyoming, four miles, then turn west across Salt River. Drive north on a dirt road seven miles to the mouth of McCoy Creek on the southwest side of Palisades Reservoir, then continue west.

were cold and numb. We suffered less than for two days before, but there was a mental appetite, more active than ever. It was an agony to sleep. All the party evidenced the same mental conditions excepting Davis who was hungry clear through, sleeping or waking. One feeling we had in common. It can be found explained in Eugene Sue's description of the Wandering Jew. We were impatient of rest, and all felt a constant impulse to "go on, go on," continually. The men did not seem to court slumber, and Starr had an inexhaustible fund of his most mirth provoking stories which he never tired of telling. We listened, laughed and sang. Afterward we tried to catch a couple of Beaver which splashed within a few feet of us all night long. Had not a firearm in the party and here was the fattest of good meat almost under our hands, enough to have fed us for two days.

Sunday, December 17, sixty-eighth day. At last the first streaks of cold gray dawn appeared. We started. I had decided to skirt along the ridge we were on and bending to the right strike the other fork of the creek higher up. We tried to do so and headed one ravine, but came to an ice covered slope that we could not pass. Got some poles to steer ourselves with and slid down the slope about a thousand feet. A few minutes walk from its foot brought us back to where we had started up the hill the previous evening.

SURVIVAL

The sun came out brightly as we trudged slowly up the creek bed. After while we came to some bridge timbers among the drift. These showed old marks of wagon tires. Nothing recent yet. A couple of miles farther on we stopped to build a fire and warm outselves. Davis showed signs of undue restlessness. We had to call him back from climbing the hill sides several times.

While we were gathering wood for the fire, I found a section of sawed off timber blocks such as they use for the bottoms of flumes. It had been recently cut on one side with an axe. This satisfied me without further evidence that the mines above were not old placers, now deserted. The men were not so sanguine, but were cheerful, and we soon moved on again. In a couple of hours we came to an old flume. Shortly after Applegate declared he smelled the smoke of burning pine. In half an hour more we reached a miner's cabin and were safe. 18 miles.

We arrived at 3 P.M. having been 80 hours without food in a temperature from 10° to 40° below zero, and after previously enduring privations as before detailed. Two old miners occupied the cabin and they were both at home having returned from a little town above with a fresh stock of provisions. They at once produced some dry bread and made some weak tea, knowing well what to do. We had to force those things down. None of us felt at all hungry for anything but grease. After while they commenced cooking supper. Would not allow us to go near the fire.

About this time to our unspeakable delight, Sergeant Server and Warren also arrived. They had passed the mouth of the creek on the 13th and gone below to the next stream[18] which they had followed up fourteen miles without finding anything and returning to meet us had found our trail and followed it knowing that we had nothing to eat, while they had two horses and a mule with them.

Mr. Bailey[19] and his partner now gave us a bountiful supper of hot rolls, roast beef and other substantial fare, and we all ate heartily in spite of our previous resolutions not to do so. Cold dry bread had no charms, but hot and fatty food roused our stomachs to a realization that the season of famine was over. The change affected us severely. I had an attack of inflamation of the stomach which lasted me several hours. All of the men suffered more or less, excepting Starr who seemed to be unaffected.

[18] Probably Bear Creek.
[19] John Bailey.

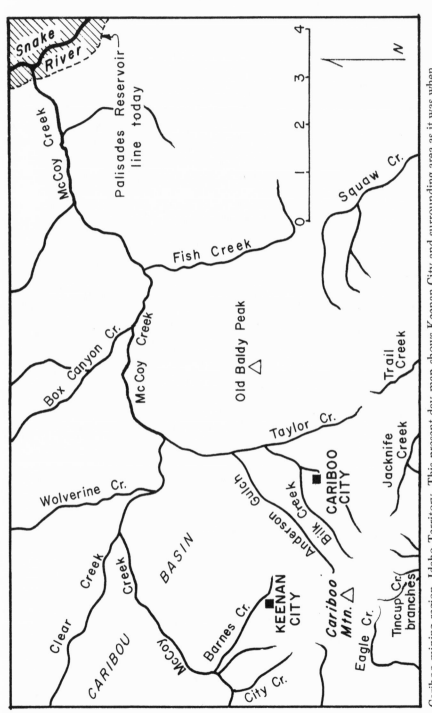

Cariboo mining region, Idaho Territory. This present-day map shows Keenan City and surrounding area as it was when Doane was there in 1876. See also page 581.

CHAPTER 15

KEENAN CITY

On December 18 the men move up to Keenan City, a once famous mining town, where they rest and recuperate until December 23. On the nineteenth they write letters and dispatch them by a stage line from Keenan City. The stage driver, having heard rumors that Doane and his men were A.W.O.L. from Fort Ellis, reports them to Fort Hall as fugitives. As a result, Captain Bainbridge, the commanding officer at Fort Hall, sends a squad of soldiers to capture rather than rescue them.

CARIBOU MINING DISTRICT

Monday, December 18, sixty-ninth day. We moved up to a little mining town, Keenan City, 5 miles.[1] All very weak and relaxed. It seemed as if all our physical forces were now concentrated on the assimilation of food, and the least exertion was fatiguing. Keenan City consisted of a store, saloon, post office, blacksmith shop, stable and a lot of miners cabins, many of them vacant. The stream we had followed up is called McCoy Creek, and the mining district is the long ago celebrated Caribou mines, now almost deserted.

The proprietor of the store, Mr. Hezekiah Moor, gave me a room and board.[2] The men moved into a comfortable cabin. I

---

[1] See editors' section on Keenan City at the end of this chapter.

[2] Correctly, Hezekiah D. Moore, also known as "Major" Moore. Storekeeping in the area lured him more than gold, but he finally acquired many placer claims, mostly on Iowa Bar and Bilk Gulch. However, the attractions of "Carriboo" held him

hired a Chinaman to cut wood for them and purchased such supplies as were to be had. Here we rested until December 23rd. For several days we were all very weak, and Warren was quite ill. After the fourth day we began to gain strength. The amount of beef and other food consumed by the party during this time was fabulous. On arrival I found my weight to be one hundred and twenty-six pounds. Usual weight one hundred and ninety. The others were similarly reduced.

The Caribou mining district is confined to several creek beds in this vicinity, all flowing into Snake River. At one time it contained thousands of miners, but had now settled down to three small camps of which Keenan City was the largest. The miners lived at home and worked during the placer season only, resting comfortably during the winter. The population included several families, all good people. It was an independent self sustaining little community hidden away in the mountains. There was no rough element present, and no roudyism, all were workers and producers.

The gold obtained was what is known as coarse gold.[3] The most attractive form in which it is found, as a man working "Three Dollar Diggings" is liable occasionally to pick up a nugget worth a week's labor, or even that of a year. No horses or cattle are kept in this region during the winter as the snow falls very deep and lies on the ground till very late in the spring. The mountains are of bare rock. Mostly metamorphic, and the level areas are the most barren of deserts. Lava beds of basalt. The general character of the Idaho mountains is above set forth, always excepting the Tetons.

---

too long. Others left their misfortunes, shouldered threadbare jackets, and slipped away down the mountain trail; or, with fortune smiling, carried off their riches to prosperity elsewhere. Moore stayed on, buying others off. By 1889 he was broke. His mercantile firm went to G. W. Gorton; the mining claims went to Arta D. Young. See Deed Records, Bonneville County, Idaho, Book A, 461; F. Whittemore and M. Christopherson, *Tosoiba*; Irene Shupe, *Caribou County.*

[3] Most accounts, other than Doane's, refer to it as "flour gold" which remains suspended in water and is difficult to recover. One analysis valued 1,000 of the minute particles (which the miners called "color") as worth one penny.

THE OLD FORTY-NINER

One character we met at Keenan City deserves a notice. He was the traditional forty-niner.[4] In most outside mining camps at least one is found. This one was in the last stages physically, an attenuated, wild-eyed skeleton, long haired and long-bearded, with stooping shoulders and hands like eagle's claws. His voice was weak and piping, and his footsteps slow and feeble, but the spirit of an invincible nature possessed him still. The old fellow looked upon me and my party as imposters, smarties, and swore that we had come up the river instead of down, until I happened to mention one day that my first experiences in California dated from May, 1849. The same evening the old man proposed to shoot anybody who should dare to insinuate that we had not done all we claimed to have accomplished, and ever so much more, and offered to stake all his quartz mines, placer mines, and prospects of various kinds, roughly estimated by himself to be worth a few millions, that we would get through all right, and without the slightest difficulty.

The old fellow sat in the store day after day, sometimes telling the wildest of Pacific Slope stories of hardships in the Sierra Nevada foothills, and of compensating revels in the San Francisco of long ago. Often [he sat] for hours without saying a word. He lived in an atmosphere of exaggeration in the memories of the rich placers of the Yuba, and the Stanislaus and the far away tinkling of Spanish guitars in Fandangos the dancers' wherein are now dust and ashes.

In the possession of mining property which he imagined contained fabulous riches, he looked with contempt upon the mere millionaire of civilization and derided the slow methods of ordinary accumulation, as beneath the merit of a passing notice. He belonged to a race soon to be extinct, whom the world fails to understand. Whose inner nature, Brett Harte, alone of all humanity has reached and struck the chords of. They have pros-

---

[4] Doane's characterization of the Forty-niner followed the last paragraph of this present chapter, but has been transposed by the editors for better continuity.

pected the lodes and placers of the whole earth, have quadrupled the volume of precious stones and precious metals, in the possession of mankind. The spirit of adventure which brought them together on the golden shores of the Pacific remains with them to the end. They may be weak as water when tempted but will face the music when in peril. They may fail physically — mentally they are self poised and daring to the last. To them there is nothing so insipid as a negative respectability. Nothing so detestable as a human soul with a dog collar on. They are the incarnation of independence of thought and speech. They are lions and not sheep.

Everyone was kind to and tolerant of the old forty-niner. He had a warm corner by the stove, and a warmer dose of Mormon "Coffin Tacks" whenever he chose to avail himself thereof. He was respected and protected also, like an old pocket piece, carried for luck. He was the "good medicine" of the camp. When I bade him good-bye, he charged me when we got to California to remember him to the boys. I did not get there till eight years afterward.

TELEGRAM AND LETTERS

Tuesday, December 19, seventieth day. On the 19th, I wrote to the Post Adjutant, Fort Ellis, reporting my arrival and sent a telegram by mail to the Post Adjutant, Fort Hall, asking him to wire the same to the commanding officer at Fort Ellis worded as follows. "19th to Commanding Officer, Fort Ellis, Montana. Arrived here yesterday. All well. Write today. Send mail to Fort Hall [signed] Doane."

There was a jerky stage line to Eagle Rock Bridge, so that our mail happened to go without delay. The driver of this stage had read the Montana papers and thereby "hangs a tale" which afterward unfolded to our advantage.

> Doane's letter, which he did not include in his journal, is of interest, and is included below; note that it was addressed to Fort Hall, not Fort Ellis.

Iowa Bar, Idaho Territory, December 19, 1876

To the Post Adj, Fort Hall

Sir: I have the honor to report my arrival here on yesterday under orders from Gen. Sheridan to make a survey of the Snake River basin from the Yellowstone Lake to Walla Walla. We have been from Ft Ellis since Oct. 11, got out of rations 20 days ago, have eaten up 2 horses and arrived at this camp 3 days and nights without food of any kind. I have 1 NCO and 5 men, 2 of them were crazy for 3 days. All are better now. We have come to the Yellowstone Lake with pack animals, crossing the divide at Mount Washburne 9500 feet of elevation in a snowstorm. Left lake Bessie or Heart Lake near head of Snake River Nov. 6th. Had a boat of 2 ton capacity which we launched on Yellowstone Lake, crossed to southwest end, had one shipwreck on lake, dragged her across the rocky mountains to Lake Bessie with pack mules and have dragged her over the rocky beds since to deep water. We have rebuilt her 4 times recaulked her 6 times and have passed through the grand canyon of the Snake River to within 6 miles of its terminus, swamped the boat at the grand rapids, lossing all our horse meat, my instruments and my CC and GE and struck out on foot to this camp at a venture and on a race for life. We have 3 horses left out of 15 animals. My men are worn out with fatigue and starvation. I will therefore remain here a few days and then resume the trip. Please expect to hear from me at the Bridge in 3 weeks at farthest. I will ask then a room for my men and the hospitality of your post for a short time preparatory to resuming my journey down the river. We get all needfull supplies here to last us to your post. I will expect to draw funds there to a limited amount also rations from Dec. 10 for 6 men. I request that the Commanding Officer may approve a requisition for my signature on arrival so that the AGS may set aside and hold in reserve as issued the December rations subject to our disposal. This is legitimate and I have had it done by order of Department Commander and Secretary of War several times. I am buying here of course to last to your post. Please do not send to meet us as we are past

all danger now. Be kind enough to send to Commanding Officer Fort Ellis M.T. the following telegram at once prepaid for me:
"Iowa Bar, Dec. 19, 1876 Arrived here yesterday all well write today. Send mail to Fort Hall Doane"
Would send money but do not know the rates. The people at Ellis will think we are lost until this is received. Sorry to trouble you this much. Starvation does not agree with good handwriting. Very respectfully

Your obedient servant
[signed] G. C. Doane, 1st Lt. 2nd Cav.

P.S. Please send telegram at once as the Fort Ellis people will be in a terrible state of anxiety. [signed] Doane.[5]

At least two other members of the Doane party wrote letters from Keenan City, Privates Davis and White; both wrote to army buddies back in Montana. Their letters follow, though of course neither letter was included in Doane's journal.

Kenon, Dec. 18, 1876

Friend Flanagan:
We have reached here today after a hard trip I can tell you. We got out of rations and lived on horse meat for 3 wks, and then we got all out of everything and got in the canyon and our boat upset and we lost everything but our bedding. Nothing to eat and only having 3 head of stock left. Doane then sent out 2 men for rations we having only 3 meals of horse left. And we got out of grub altogether and left our bedding and started out on foot for chuck and traveled 3 days and nights without any-

<hr>

[5] Doane to Post Adjutant, Fort Hall. U.S. Army Command, Department of Dakota, Box 20 for 1877, Letters Received from Adjutant General's Office, National Archives.

thing to eat and no blankets to sleep on. Doane nearly went crazy but we are all right now again. We got filled up pretty well. The coldest we had it was 15 below zero.[6] I want you to write to me as soon as you can, and direct to Fort Hall in care of Lt. Doane. I send my best wishes to all the boys. If there is any letters come for me when you write send them to me. I wont write any more to you this time so take care of yourself and I will do the same

From your ex-bunky [signed] C. R. Davis[7]

McCoy Creek, December 19, 1876

A B Conklin, Esquire
Dear Friend:

I have not got much time to write but thought I would give you a few items. We have had a great time since you last heard from me, but we have been very fortunate, not much snow this winter generally. There has been from 4 to 6 feet. We run short of rations and had to live on horse we killed Warren's which lasted us until we struck the canion where we had an accident lost all of our stuff but bedding and clothing, all of our rations of horse. Server and Warren started for rations but got lost so the rest of us started on foot, traveled 60 hours before we struck grub and you can judge we were hungry. We intend to go back to boat in a day or so and start down river Server and Warren reached ranch the same day we did but later. Lt. Doane will not let us do much until we get rested up. He bought all the cooking utensils he could find here and plenty of grub, butter, can fruit, pickles and everything he can find. We have got a ranch [range], plenty of wood but we pay a Chinaman $2 a day for chopping it. This is a mine country but does not do much in winter. We are about 90 miles from bridge by land and 150 by water. We don't expect to leave Hall before February. I hope

---

[6] In his December 17 entry, Doane refers to 40° below zero temperature. The discrepancy between Doane's and Davis' figures may simply be a difference of recollection. Winter temperatures of -40° are common in this area.

[7] Davis to Flanagan, National Archives.

will write as soon as you get this note and direct to Fort Hall. Tell all the boys how I am getting along and tell them I would like to hear from them. I will give you a full description when I get to Hall. I have not time now. The mail is ready to start. Give me all the news and tell me if you intend to stay out here when your time is up and give me your directions. Give my best regards to Doc Sarven, Cleland Shultes. I will close for the present. Don't fail to write as soon as you get this. I expect you all have had us froze up. Excuse this.

[signed] White[8]

KEENAN CITY
by the editors

This publication of Doane's 1876 journal again brings up the mystery of Keenan City and the fabulous Caribou Mining District of Idaho. Where was it? Who discovered the gold? How much was really taken out – fifty million? sixty million? or two-and-a-half million? Who got rich and who lost their shirts? Was the name of the town Caribou City, Keenan City, or Iowa Bar, or were there three towns? Was gold the only treasure on the mountain? Did they get it all?

Doane himself, out "to explore," seemed to have first learned from John Pierce on December 7, 1876, that this part of the country was already in "settlements."

The editors made many inquiries, but could find no one who seemed to have the facts about the Keenan City area. In 1964, we decided to find out for ourselves the truth about the "Carriboo" treasure. We hunted up all the old mining reports we could find, rummaged through dusty files of local histories in eastern Idaho, and even checked postal and other old records in Washington, D.C.

Then we drove our Travelall from Palisades Reser-

8 White to Conklin, Ibid.

voir in eastern Idaho up McCoy Creek, jeep-trailed as
far as we could, and tramped up Barnes Creek to
where rumors said the old mining camp had once
sprawled on the side of Caribou Mountain.

Where cabins once gophered into the hill we found
only eroded platforms of soil, covered with long
grasses and blue flowers, scattered with a few rocks
which once levelled up the foundation logs.

Earthen ditches tighten their coil around the
mountain everywhere; some still flowed water. Once
they squeezed every precious trickle from the hillside – from every spring and seep, every ravine and
stream.

In those days water rights on the Carriboo were
more valuable than mining rights.

Where the Forest Service now locates Caribou City
(they spell it thus), a few square nails hide in the
embedding earth, along with bits of melted glass
covered with dried mud – the town burned to the
ground in 1885. Visitors must use their imagination
as to where the famous three-story hotel "Green
House" once stood, filled with the sounds of a
vibrant, rollicking populace.

There are cabin ruins about the mountain, rotted
logs spiked together with rusting nails; but we found
they were round nails – manufactured after
1880 – thus establishing they were not from the
original dwellings.

Only a few oldtimers knew that the name
"Caribou" originated not from the shaggy animals of
the North, but from a stubble-faced prospecting
Canadian, Jesse "Carriboo" Fairchild, who found the
first gold there in 1870.

Jesse Fairchild had drifted into Idaho from British
Columbia with such tall tales of gold in the Caribou
there that they tagged him "Carriboo." Then the
Idaho mountain where he found more gold was nick-

named "Carriboo." The area became the "Carriboo" Mining District, and one of the settlements "Carriboo" City.

On September 17, 1881, a giant gray grizzly bear mauled "Carriboo" Fairchild. He died a week later of blood poisoning.

The original and legal name of his mountain, Pisgah,[9] survives to this day only in deeds and legal descriptions. After his death, no one ever called it anything but "Carriboo." Even the Forest Service took the name for their great Caribou National Forest in Idaho — only changing the spelling to "Caribou."

The first town in the Carriboo District was named Keenan City after John Keenan. Located on Barnes Creek, a tributary of McCoy Creek, by the end of 1870 Keenan City had a population of 500, with a Chinatown suburb of 300-400. All supplies had to be freighted by horse and oxteam from Corinne, Utah, on the Union Pacific Railroad — over 150 miles to the south.

Then there were Iowa Bar and Carriboo City, in addition to Keenan City. All three were official post offices at one time or another. William Clemens, cousin of Mark Twain, came in 1870, staked out the placer claims closest to Carriboo City, and became its first postmaster in 1883. In 1888 he sold out to John P. Scarff of Chicago for $25,000.

Doane's report says that he and his party were at "Keenan City," which is correct. His letter of December 19 from "Iowa Bar" is also correct, as that was the post office at that time.

Most of the Carriboo "flour gold" floated out of the sluice boxes and was never recovered. Even Thomas A. Edison once tried his genius on this problem, but failed. Yet the first ten years yielded about

---

[9] Pisgah was the mountain which Moses ascended just before his death and from which he viewed the Promised Land.

two million dollars worth, recovered mostly by placer washings, according to the late Barzilla W. Clark, governor of Idaho.

The lure of gold in men's eyes may have obscured a more valuable treasure on Caribou Mountain — that of copper or iron, or both.

A mining report says that the district was visited by Charles H. Wetsell, a mining engineer and Princeton graduate. Wetsell said, "Anyone who will drive a tunnel through Caribou Mountain at the lowest possible level, say around six thousand feet, will develop the greatest copper deposit in the United States, far superior to Butte."

In 1943, with World War II on and copper scarce, someone had the inspiration to look over the old dump of discarded rock at the district's Monte Cristo mine, hand-pick from it, and haul away twelve carloads of previously discarded copper ore.

In 1876, the U.S. Geological Survey reported a twenty foot wide vein of magnetic ore on the western side of the mountain, but no one appears to have bothered to look for it since.

Today, on the north slope of Caribou Mountain, one will find a weathered sign pointing out a rocky trail which leads up to the Monte Cristo mine, the last vain effort to capture the elusive gold. But if anyone ever recovers the fortune in gold which may still lie buried on the old scarred mountain, they will have to invent a better way to do it.

Maybe its copper and magnetic ore will one day make someone rich; more likely the mountain will only bring more heartaches and frustration in fruitless search for fortune.[10]

[10] See H. H. Bancroft, *History of Idaho, Montana and Wyoming*, XXXI, 533, 535, describing the Caribou Mining District; John Codman, *The Mormon Country*; Edith Lovell, *Captain Bonneville's County*; F. Whittemore and M. Christopherson, *Tosoiba*; A. R. Schultz, *Gold Development in Central Uinta County, Wyoming*; "Caribou Area," MSS.

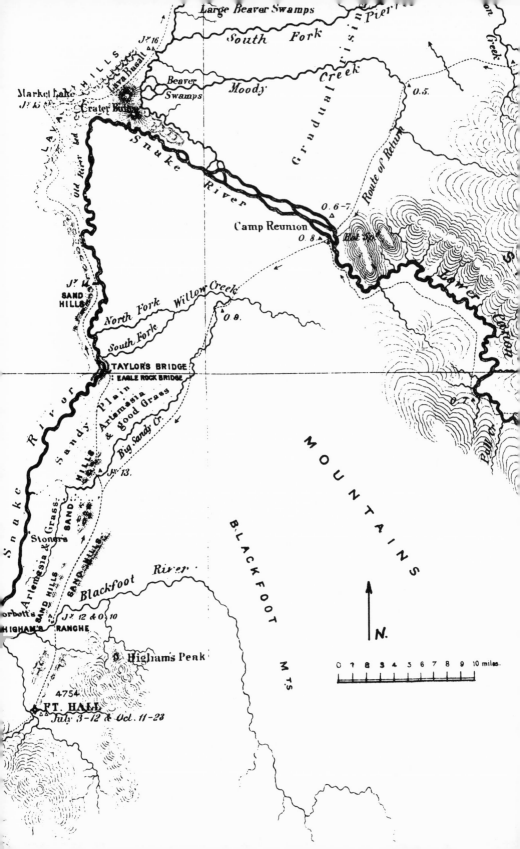

CHAPTER 16

KEENAN CITY TO FORT HALL

The party leaves Keenan City on December 23, reaches the Snake River on the twenty-fifth, and stays in an abandoned cabin until the twenty-ninth. On December 26 the party meets the army squad from Fort Hall. The lieutenant in charge doesn't know whether to rescue or arrest them. On the twenty-eighth Sergeant Server returns to report the boat destroyed. They pack up and start for Fort Hall, reaching there January 4.

Friday, December 22, seventy-third day. On the 22nd the weather grew threatening. We had gotten horse sleds ready to haul our rations and bedding on, intending to follow the river down to Fort Hall on foot, giving the three animals nothing to do but draw the little sledges. There to get fresh animals, return after the little boat and resume the survey. Our bills were all made up and property packaged, for a start next day.

Saturday, December 23, seventy-fourth day. Took the trail down the McCoy creek to Mr. Baileys. Sleds worked well. Clouded in the afternoon. 5 miles. Snowed occasionally during the night. Party all in good spirits but not very strong.

Sunday, December 24, seventy-fifth day. Moved on down the creek. Snowed hard until evening making it heavy travelling. Camped on the creek. 7 miles.

Monday, December 25, seventy-sixth day. Worked on down the creek. Sleds kept breaking causing delays as the runners were not high enough to keep the bedding rolls from catching in drifts and bushes. Reached a vacant cabin at the mouth of the creek and on Snake River, late in the evening. It had a good chimney and there was fine grass in the river bottom. 8 miles. Cloudy and snowing occasionally during the day.

ARREST/RESCUE SQUAD FROM FORT HALL

Tuesday, December 26, seventy-seventh day. Laid over to rest the animals and rebuilt sleds. Clear and pleasant night after snowing all day. Cold. About 9 P.M. we heard voices down in the river bottom, among our stock. On listening soon found that a party of troops had just gone into camp there. I hailed them and received unsatisfactory replies, but on giving my name and some particulars, an officer came up to the cabin and gave us the pleasing information that a party had been sent from Fort Hall after us.

It was Lieutenant Joseph Hall, 14th Infantry with four men and a good little pack train. I shall never forget the puzzled expression on the face of this officer when he first met me. He conversed in monosyllables for a couple of minutes and then told us that he had been sent to arrest a party of deserters, half a dozen in number which had been advertised for in the Montana papers, as having left Fort Ellis and were supposed to have gone through the Park and down Snake River. $30 each for apprehension and capture. The stage driver before spoken of had read the papers it seems and denounced us to the Post Commander at Fort Hall.[1] We first had a hearty laugh over the joke and he then placed himself and party at my disposal. We sat by the fire and talked nearly all night. He was Post Adjutant at Fort Hall, and evidently knew something more than he felt at liberty to tell me, but he denounced Major Jas. S. Brisbin, 2d Cavalry, my Post Commander in unmeasured terms, and told me that I was being made a victim of infamous treachery. This was a revelation but not a surprise_____[2]

[1] See Doane's December 19 entry.
[2] Several words after surprise were crossed out in the original.

Wednesday, December 27, seventy-eighth day. Sent Sergeant and four men with the fresh animals up the river after the boat and bedding left there on the 15th. Our worn out animals are making the best of their opportunities in the long dry grass.

BOAT DISCOVERED SMASHED

Thursday, December 28, seventy-ninth day. The Sergeant and party returned with the frozen packages, but not the boat. Reported that it was only fifteen miles by the trail on the other side of the river, and that the boat had been crushed into splinters by an ice gorge which had piled up in masses twenty feet high. This was a bitter disappointment as they found the river open all the way down, and we so found it afterward below. Here was another strange occurrence. In exploring as in hunting there is an element of chance which cannot be provided against. No foresight will avail, no calculations will detect, no energy will overcome. Caution might prevent, but with caution no results will be obtained. Risks must be taken, and there is such an element in human affairs as fortune, good or bad.

I decided at once to make all possible speed to Fort Hall, there refit and returning bring lumber to rebuild the boat on the ground where it had been lost, and continue on to Eagle Rock Bridge[3] on the Snake River, previously going back far enough beyond Jackson's Lake to take a renewal of the system of triangulations and notes, lost in the river when the boat capsized. At Eagle Rock Bridge it would be necessary to rebuild the boat again in a different form and much larger, to run the heavy rapids of the lower rivers to Astoria, at the mouth of the Great Columbia. The hardships and greater dangers we had already passed. With food for one day more we would have made the passage of Mad River Cañon despite the loss of all our weapons, instruments and tools. We had run all the rapids but two, and these were easier than many others safely passed above. All the party enthusiastically endorsed this plan.

[3] Now known as Idaho Falls.

Friday, December 29, eightieth day. We packed everything on the train and rode by turns on the few saddle animals, following down Snake River in a sage brush valley with snow two feet deep.[4] There were many ravines to cross and the foothills soon closed in so that the trail was somewhat difficult. Presently the River made a curve to the north and west into a Cañon of Basalt with sheer walls continually increasing in altitude. We kept on the terrace. Camped in a pine grove. Clothing thoroughly saturated. Dried out by a roaring fire as usual. 12 miles.

Saturday, December 30, eighty-first day. Followed the river over foothill trails and crossed quite a steep divide which ran in to the Basalt Canon. This was very fatiguing on account of the snow which made it all but impossible to climb any steep declivities. I endeavored to keep notes on the courses of the River, but found it impracticable as the Basalt terrace was full of trap holes concealed by the snow. It was like travelling across the surface of a glacier. Abandoned the effort after the first day. Camped on a small creek about a half mile from the river. Eleven miles.

Sunday, December 31, eighty-second day. Today was Sunday and the last of the year. We moved on parallel with the river which is here a basaltic cañon about 100 feet deep with a rapid but steady current and free from ice. Numerous islands were seen where the more solid masses of rock have withstood the fierce erosive power of flood waters in the spring of each year. We made a cut off to cross a bend in the stream and got entangled in a mass of rugged foothills and cañons coming in long after dark to the little valley of Sulphur Creek.[5] Camped at the mouth of the stream. Distance 15 miles.

4 Now under the Palisades water. Main highway U.S. 26 follows the Palisades shore and Snake River shore along their northeast bank, crossing to the southwest bank at Swan Valley and joining Doane's route, which has been completely on the southwest side.

5 Now known as Falls Creek. To reach the area Doane is now going to describe, turn southeast from U.S. 26 at the southwest end of Snake River bridge (at the north end of Swan Valley – forty-two miles east of Idaho Falls, sixty-four miles west of Jackson, Wyoming). Drive south 0.5 mile to Falls Creek and Falls Creek Falls, next described by Doane, a beautiful sight.

FALLS CREEK

The valley of Sulphur Creek is a calcareous marsh. The stream runs in a deep narrow ditch with banks cut as if by human labor. On each bank is a ridge as if the contents of the ditch were thrown out on either side forming an embankment. This is thickly set with willows. The valley has therefore no drainage by the creek channel. Its surface is covered with rank grass and rushes, and has a tropical look. The water of the Creek falls over a bluff about thirty feet into the Snake River valley, and deposits on the brink of the fall a stone dam which rises continually in a massive wall of limestone. It is a solid and beautiful structure curtained in front with long fringes of Stalagmite and festooned with thousands of growing stalactites, like icicles from a roof.

A circle of springs at the base of the Little Rock Mountains, north east of Fort Benton, Montana shows similar deposits. These springs however, are hot. Along each channel for miles are dams deposited at intervals of a hundred yards or so by the water. These were during winter favorite watering places for buffalo. I have gathered water cress from the channel of these springs when the temperature was -45°.

The train came in very late and we had supper just as the new year made its advent. Our camp was on the brink of the bluff overlooking the grim basalt covered plain, and the dark chasm through which the river runs. The night was cold and still. A grove of stunted pines gave us shelter and dry fuel was abundant. A large Beaver house was built at the edge of the beautiful waterfall. This we set fire to and welcomed the new year with a salute and three rousing cheers. Our animals are doing nicely as the fresh ones carry all the loads, and the members of the party walk or rather wade through the deep snow.

Monday, January 1, eighty-third day. In the morning I sent Sergt. Server up the Creek to look for springs as the valley was a very short one.[6] He found the source of the stream in six

6 It is possible to drive up Falls Creek on a good dirt, dry weather road. Mineral Springs are about three miles up.

gypsum springs. Four of them were in a basin about one hundred yards in diameter and ran in subterranean channels for about fifty yards, the other two were on a side hill above the others and have craters about four feet high. The water of all tasted of sulphur and was warm.

The peculiarity of the underground channels can be seen at the Soda Springs on Bear River, Utah,[7] and at other points less known in the Snake River basin, also in the Blue Mountains, beyond Boise. It is never seen in springs depositing geyserite or magnesian combinations, but only in calcareous deposits;[8] whether sulphurited or carbonetted, there is usually a sort of well in the rock several feet in depth, at the bottom of which the spring is seen, bubbling violently, while the water escapes in a rock lined channel, generally about four feet below the surface of the ground. This peculiarity is worthy of note as it gives a means of detecting in a general way the chemical held in solution by the water. We made a forced march. Passed the mouths of three small creeks and got away from the foot hills as the Snake River Valley widened out greatly. The train did not get in till 10 P.M. 20 miles. Camped on the river in a willow thicket, with an abundance of drift wood for fuel, and long dry grass for the stock.

The landscape here is a dreary one. Grim mountains on the opposite side, but of no great height. Shut out the view of the great ranges behind. In the west is a barren ragged looking divide and the valley is of basaltic lava beds overflown with dunes of yellow sand. A striking and important feature of Snake River Valley is that the "back country" at the foot of the ranges on both sides is everywhere lower than the banks of the stream. All waters coming to the river meander long distances before disappearing in a fissure or a Cañon which conveys them to the river. This will be again referred to and this feature is noticeable at every point below the foot of Mad River Cañon, where the stream issues from the mountains on a level with Salt

[7] At Soda Springs, Idaho.
[8] The calcium is softer and more soluble; the outlet channel erodes more rapidly and cuts deeper.

River Valley.

Tuesday, January 2, eighty-fourth day. Move diagonally away from the river over sandy plain. Weather clear in the valley but heavy snow clouds shut out a view of the mountains. I followed the river bank while the rest of the party took a straight course.[9] The basalt cañon deepens rapidly to four hundred feet. Islands of some size were passed. Some of these are grown up with cottonwood and covered with drift. Most of them are of boulders, with which the channel is gorged. The cañon walls are perpendicular in most places, and the chasm is from one quarter to a mile in width. In many places the sand dunes have blown up in wave like ridges almost covering the lava, which is full of hummocks where the crust has been lifted at a central point with radiating fissures extending sometimes several hundred yards. Probably due to water underneath the flow which has generated steam and blown up the semi-fluted mass.

Camped at Highams ranch, the uppermost one in the valley, on Birch Creek — a small stream flowing with a sluggish current through the sandy plain.[10] 18 miles.

Wednesday, January 3, eighty-fifth day. Made a straight course to Bucks Ranch on Willow Creek.[11] About ten miles and thence to Eagle Rock Bridge,[12] where the Utah Northern R.R. now crosses the Snake on its way to Butte City, Montana.[13] 22 miles.

Weather very cold and windy. Snow mostly blown away. In taking this course we cut off a great angular bend of the Snake River and leave the junction of Henry's Fork ten miles to the right of us. The point of junction is plainly marked by two

[9] The main party headed northwest, cutting across Antelope Flat, just like to-day's U.S. 26 does.

[10] Charles Higham and his family "moved the headquarters of their cattle operations from Lincoln Valley to Birch Creek in the present [town of] Poplar in 1876." (Edith Lovell, *Captain Bonneville's County*, 185)

[11] Orville Buck.

[12] The bridge was built in the spring of 1865 by Matt Taylor (Oneida Road, Bridge and Ferry Company). The Andersons (see note 19) later acquired an interest in it. Eagle Rock became Idaho Falls in 1899.

[13] Since the Utah and Northern Railroad sent its first train across this bridge on June 12, 1879, Doane must have written this portion of his journal at least two-and-a-half years after his visit here.

crater hills, very prominent land marks.[14] These craters have filled the old channel by which Henry's Fork joined the Snake and have forced it to run up stream, as it were, parallel to the Snake several miles before joining the latter.

Below the mouth of Henry's Fork, the river bed rises and opposite Market lake[15] it overflows enormously at high water. This is on the east side. On the West there is no overflow to amount to anything. Below Henry's Fork junction no stream enters the Snake by a surface channel for a distance of over three hundred miles. All of them are lost in fissures in the lava, and come out into the river basin in great springs gushing from the black basaltic walls.

Willow Creek has three mouths, two of them are a couple of miles apart, reaching Snake River ten miles from the point of separation.[16] The third one runs forty miles below and sometimes empties into the Blackfoot and sometimes sinks in the land.[17] The lower courses of most of the small streams entering the Snake on both sides are but little known, owing to the impassable nature of the lava fields with their innumerable fissures and hummocks. It is impossible with certainty to connect any inflowing spring in the Cañon with any particular stream in the back country. It is even uncertain whether the River itself contains all the water flow of the great valley. As there are great springs which boil up in its bed, others may flow in deeper subterraneans a thousand feet below and appear at a distance of hundreds of miles farther down.

These are matters of great interest and are uninvestigated and unknown today. At Eagle Rock the stream is shut in by massive walls and rushes through a gorge about ninety feet wide. A better locality for a bridge could not well be imagined but it caused a railroad to be built in the wrong place.[18]

[14] Menan Buttes.

[15] Now Roberts, Idaho. Market Lake received its name from an expression of early settlers, "Let's go to market" when they wanted to hunt the abundant waterfowl in the locality.

[16] At Idaho Falls.

[17] Now Sand Creek.

[18] The Union Pacific, successor to the Utah and Northern Railroad, finally con-

The road should follow up the west side of the river, cross at the mouth of Henry's Fork, follow Henry's Fork to Henry's Lake and thence down the Madison. It would then draw on fertile and extensive districts at the western base of the Tetons and would absolutely command the resources of the Great Snake River basin of the future. Distance 22 miles. We found mail matter at the Bridge Station and were hospitably entertained by Mr. Anderson, the proprietor of the establishment there.[19]

Thursday, January 4, eighty-sixth day. Weather very cold. Started for Fort Hall, having sent to the commanding officer on the previous evening the following telegram:

Eagle Rock, Idaho
Jan. 3rd, 1877

Commanding Officer
Fort Hall.
Camp here tonight. Do not send team. Will be there tomorrow.
[signed] Doane, Lieut.

We had travelled about half way when we met ambulances which had been most kindly sent to bring us. Arrived at the post at 2 P.M. Considerably worn down by the long tramp of eighty-six days, but all in good health and spirits. Dist. 28 mi.

---

structed a line on the west side of the river, very much as Doane had proposed. Its main line then ran from Ashton, Idaho, up the valley of Henry's Fork, across Reas Pass and down the Madison to West Yellowstone.

[19] John C. Anderson was one of the original stockholders in *The Idaho Falls Times*, founded in 1890 by R. C. Bonney, the editor's father. Anderson had a brother, Robert, also prominent in business here after 1882, who was part owner of the bridge at an earlier date. For the Anderson story and that of the bridge, see Clark, *Bonneville County in the Making*; Lovell, *Captain Bonneville's County*.

Fort Hall, I. T., 1849. Drawing made during Col. W. W. Loring's expedition to Oregon. Maj. Osborne Cross, quartermaster, says of this Fort Hall in his journal entry for August 8, 1849: "a trading establishment of the Hudson's Bay Company. . . . It is built of clay, and much in the form of Fort Laramie, having a large sally port. . . . There is a blockhouse at one of the angles." *Courtesy Denver Public Library Western Collection.*

Fort Hall, I. T. *Courtesy Denver Public Library Western Collection.*

FORT HALL
by the editors

There have been several Fort Halls.

Doane's Fort Hall references were to the military post by that name which was established May 27, 1870, by Captain J. E. Putnam and a company of the 12th Infantry. On the east side of Lincoln Creek (now known as Fort Hall Creek), a tributary of the Blackfoot River, it was about nine miles southeast of Blackfoot, Idaho.

At the time of Doane's stay there, Fort Hall was under the command of Captain A. H. Bainbridge, 14th Infantry.[20]

The army relinquished this fort to the Indian Service for school purposes April 26, 1883. The Caribou National Forest map shows it to be on Section 24, T3S, R36E.

This military post was about forty miles northeast of the historic old Fort Hall of fur trade and Oregon Trail days, which had been established by Nathaniel J. Wyeth in 1834 on the banks of the Snake River near the mouth of the Portneuf. This was sold in 1837 to the Hudson's Bay Company for $8,179.94; it was abandoned in 1855. Built largely of cottonwood logs, it was demolished by a flood in 1863. Retracing the Oregon Trail in 1906, Ezra Meeker believed it was on the section line between Sections 5 and 6, T5S, R33E, Boise meridian. Nathaniel J. Wyeth locates the fort on the east bank of the Snake River at latitude 43° 14' N.[21] Fremont more accurately gives the lati-

[20] There is an interesting reference to Captain Bainbridge in Hayden's 1877 report: "This peak, which was variously known by the names Caribou Mountain and Mount Pisgah, was rechristened by Mr. Bechler [topographer of the Hayden Survey] Mount Bainbridge, in honor of Captain Bainbridge, commandant at Fort Hall." (Orestes St. John, *Eleventh Annual Report of U.S. Geological and Geographical Survey of the Territories, 1877,* 360)

[21] *The Correspondence and Journals of Captain Nathaniel J. Wyeth, 1831-1836,* 226.

Fort Hall, I. T., 1871. This is the Fort Hall where Doane was in January 1877. W. H. Jackson photo. *Courtesy Yellowstone National Park.*

tude as 43° 1' 30" (longitude was not reliable until advent of telegraph).

Neither of these forts should be confused with the site temporarily occupied by Lieutenant C. H. Walker in 1865, or with Cantonment Loring which the army established in 1849 about five miles above old Fort Hall for the purpose of guarding the Oregon Trail.

Today's Fort Hall Post Office and Indian Agency are at still a different location on Ross Creek, eleven miles north of Pocatello, Idaho, on U.S. Highway 191.

Maj. James S. Brisbin. *Courtesy Montana Historical Society.*

CHAPTER 17

END OF THE EXPEDITION

Doane brings his report to a conclusion with copies of the military dispatches that were exchanged. They show that Brisbin, the commanding officer at Fort Ellis, was not sympathetic to Doane's mid-winter expedition. He succeeded in having Doane ordered back to Fort Ellis from Fort Hall, thus ending the expedition before Doane had little more than covered the ground already explored and mapped by the Hayden Survey of 1872.

Doane, Applegate, Starr, Warren, and Davis travel by stagecoach from Fort Hall via Virginia City, Montana, to Fort Ellis, arriving there January 20.

Server and White, with the remaining two horses, one mule, and baggage, leave Fort Hall on January 12. Captain A. H. Bainbridge, commander, furnishes them a wagon from Fort Hall. They travel through the coldest of winter and deep snows to arrive at Fort Ellis February 2.

Rather than encumber the reader with a confused detail of certified military telegrams and orders out of sequence as Doane did in his original journal, the editors have arranged them in chronological order and have quoted and summarized the first five telegrams.[1]

COMMUNIQUES

On December 17, 1876, Major Brisbin wired Fort Hall for information:

[1] Doane's journal introduces these telegrams with these words: "The Post Adjutant . . . handed me the following telegrams, showing an interest in the success of the expedition somewhat unexpected and remarkable, excepting as taken in a sinister sense . . . These it will be seen were none of them to me or for me."

Lieut. Doane and his party exploring Snake River. They were to get rations at your Post. Enquire of hunters and answer as soon as possible.

Captain A. H. Bainbridge, commander at Fort Hall, telegraphed back on December 19:

Is Lieut. Doane exploring . . . Henry's Fork, the north Fork of the Snake, or the Snake, and known in this country as south Fork of Snake?

Brisbin replied December 20:

Doane and party left Heart Lake November third . . . to explore south Fork of Snake River. Have they passed the bridge [at Idaho Falls], and is river now frozen over?

Bainbridge replied on December 21 that Doane had not passed the bridge and that the Snake River was not frozen over below junction of Henry's Fork. On December 26 Brisbin resumed his inquiries to Fort Hall:

Do you hear anything of Doane? How far up the River can you get information?

[Doane's journal continues] As will be seen from the following telegram, the wording of which shows that the Commanding Officer, Fort Hall did not believe in the authenticity of my dispatch, as Lieut. Hall and party were sent to arrest deserters.

Fort Hall, Idaho, Dec. 27th, 1876

To Commanding Officer, Fort Ellis, Montana
The following was received today in a letter to Post Adjutant of this post, purporting to be from Lieut. Doane.
"Iowa Bar, Idaho, Dec. 19th, 1876
To Commanding Officer, Fort Ellis, Mont.
Arrived here yesterday. All well. Write today. Send mail to Fort Hall. [Sig.] Doane."
Have sent an officer with four men to look for Doane. Expect them back tomorrow.

Bainbridge.

Captain A. H. Bainbridge, 14th Infantry, the Commanding Officer of Fort Hall received us [January 4th] with the greatest kindness, and everything possible was done for the comfort of myself and party, by all at the post. I at once sent the following telegram.

Fort Hall, Idaho, Jan'y 4th, 1877

To Commanding Officer, Fort Ellis, Montana
Arrived here today. All Well. Boat crushed by an ice gorge in cañon while absent. Relieved from here. Send mail here. Send mail here until otherwise notified. Will refit and proceed at leisure.

Doane.

To this no reply was received, neither was there any to my letter of 19th December from Keenan City, nor my dispatch which was sent from Fort Hall on the 27th December.

My letter from Keenan City of Dec. 19th was received at Fort Ellis on Dec. 28th and we received mail from the Post at Eagle Rock Bridge, but found none at Fort Hall from Ft. Ellis.

In the meantime [our] party at Keenan City was believed [by Fort Hall] to be a lot of deserters – why? . . . Lieut. Hall explained to me why, when he met me at the mouth of McCoy Creek.

We put in time at Fort Hall preparing to get together materials for another boat, intending to renew the expedition from Mad River Cañon. Meantime I had made one of my Centennial Tents for Captain Bainbridge.[2]

While so engaged on the 8th of January, the following telegram came [from the Adjutant General in Chicago dated January 6, 1877, to the Commanding Officer of Fort Hall]:

You will direct Lieut. Doane, Second Cavalry with his escort to rejoin his proper station Fort Ellis, as soon as practicable . . .

---

[2] See Part I, Chapter 6, *Centennial Tent* section for details on Doane's tent.

This was the result. I simply note here an extract from Sergeant Server's journal (the only one left us when the boat capsized). "Lt. Doane was very mad in consequence of our having to return, and so were all the men, but we tried to make the best of it."[3]

Over a year afterward I received the key to this mystery. And here it is. It will be observed that there is some little truth in it, and much that is false. And bear in mind that my letter and telegram from Keenan City were received on the 28th December, and that I had not yet been heard from at Eagle Rock or Fort Hall.

Fort Ellis, January 2, 1877

To Assistant Adjutant General
Saint Paul, Minn.
I hear Doane lost all his horses, seven and mules, three, his boat and camp equipage, even to blankets; lived three weeks on horse meat straight; the last three days, before reaching the settlement, his party being without food of any kind. I recommend that he be ordered to his post for duty with his company.

[signed] Brisbin

This appeal was made to General A. H. Terry, the kindest hearted of men, who believed it, and forwarded [it for] approval to General Sheridan.

I knew that an appeal would be useless as it would (before reaching authorities able to give a decision – [crossed out in original]) pass through Headquarters at Fort Ellis, and therefore I sent the following [to Brisbin on January 9]:

Ordered back by General Sheridan. Send team with forage to meet me on stage road. Also large tent and stove. Twenty rations for teamster. Answer. [Sgd] Doane.

---

[3] This was not the complete quotation. Server had continued, "Applegate got 1 gal. of whisky to have a good time with. Had quite a time at night."

Brisbin wired the next day:

Please forward Lieut. Doane and his men to Ellis by stage. In consequence of movement of troops to Flat Head I have no wagon I can send to meet him.

Herein was a statement which we interpreted to mean that the Flatheads had broken out. Afterward I was amazed to find out that the "movement of troops" meant a small detachment, and not a force. We had with us our clothing, bedding in great quantity and some other property. The enlisted men were only allowed a few pounds by stage, and would have been stripped of everything by complying with this order. We had also two horses and a mule which could not travel on stage time, a couple of hundred miles in the dead of winter. Captain Bainbridge evidently considered that this business had gone far enough. He directed an issue to me of a cart and harness, also such equipage as was necessary and with this outfit drawn by a mule and a horse tandem.

Sergeant Server and White, on the 12th of January started for Fort Ellis, with our baggage and the extra horse. He arrived there on February 2nd, bringing in all three of the animals. The journey involved crossing the Rocky Mountain divide during the coldest weather of the winter. It was a trip which consumed more time and involved greater hardships than would have been encountered had we prosecuted our survey to the mouth of the Snake, as expected. The benevolence of this change of orders did not come to the surface after we were once again subject to instructions from Fort Ellis.

The remaining five of the party reached Fort Ellis by stage on the 20th of January 1877. In December 1878 I was told by my commanding officer, Major Jas. S. Brisbin, that he had disapproved of the expedition from the beginning, and had worked to have me ordered back because I had not applied for the detail through him. I make no comment.

In April 1877 I was down the Yellowstone and in command of the Crow Indians, under direct orders from General Nelson

A. Miles, where an officer in obedience of orders was secure from a fire in the rear.

End of 1876 journal [4]

Although Major James S. Brisbin resented Doane's obtaining orders for the 1876 expedition without going through channels, and had Doane ordered back after disaster struck the expedition, yet he praised Doane in his annual report of Fort Ellis, September 1, 1876 to August 31, 1877. Concerning the expedition he also included this paragraph:

On the 27th of January 1877, Lt. Doane 2nd Cavalry reported back from an attempted exploration of the Snake River. He had been absent from the post since October 7th, and his expedition was a failure having lost his boat, a number of horses and mules, and came near starving to death in the mountains. The expedition started too late in the season, was ill-advised, and undertaken against my wishes in the matter. Still I was sorry to see it not succeed . . .[5]

The editors do not think there was anything sinister about the exchange of telegrams with Fort Hall. They indicate that the major was genuinely concerned with the whereabouts of his men. The editors think he would have ordered out a rescue party, if necessary. Surely Brisbin had not advertised for them as deserters or offered a reward. The stage driver, having heard the army was looking for the missing Doane

[4] The final paragraph of the 1876 report has been transposed to Chapter 13, end of November 30 entry.

[5] *Report* 1877, Secretary of War, Brisbin, 553.

and his party, doubtless got the facts garbled. In those days of the army on the frontier there were literally thousands of deserters. The army was always looking for them, and had probably put out some reward offers. Perhaps the stage driver assumed any missing army man was a deserter, and imagination had built up the tale by the time it reached Fort Hall. At any rate, the editors have found nothing to substantiate the idea that Brisbin was responsible for any advertisement or any reward offers.

NEWS TRAVELS SLOWLY
by the editors

In searching old newspapers for the supposed advertisement,[6] the editors came across several interesting items concerning the expedition (though not the advertisement). Compared with the speed of mass media in our own times, the pattern of these items illustrates two features often characteristic of the dissemination of news in those days: its slowness and its reliance upon exchanges which newspapers made with one another. For example, here is a story taken from an Oregon newspaper and printed in the April 21, 1877 edition of the *Idaho Statesman,* Boise City, Idaho Territory:

Exploring Snake River

Early last winter Lieut. Doane, of the second U.S. Cavalry, with headquarters in Dakota Territory, received orders from General Terry, department commander, to proceed with a small detachment of men down the Snake river. He was instructed to start at the extreme headwaters of Snake river and follow that rugged and torturous stream down as far as Lewiston, and make a complete map of the same, giving accurately and in detail its course. The party was to embark in a boat which was so con-

---

[6] See Chapter 16, Doane's December 26 entry.

structed that it could be separated into sections and thus be easily carried around the numerous portages which would have to be made, and descend as rapidly as the stream's course could be marked. As near as can be ascertained, Lieut. Doane and his party left sometime during December. Since leaving the post, nothing has been heard from this exploring party. Unless detained or overtaken by some disaster, the party should have arrived before now at Lewiston or points beyond that place. No uneasiness is felt yet for the safety and well being of the party, as it is quite probable that they were compelled to go into winter quarters before reaching their destination. The party may be expected to arrive at the point mentioned any time. The descent of this swift and turbulent stream from its source for 1,000 miles or more must be a passage fraught with constant danger and daring adventure. Lieut. Doane's account of the trip cannot fail to prove replete with thrilling interest. – Portland Oregonian.

If anybody in Idaho has seen or heard anything of this exploring party, we would be pleased to be informed of it.

These two items are also from the *Idaho Statesman:*

Thursday, May 3, 1877. Survey of Snake River. – Several months ago we noted the starting of an expedition under Lieut. Doane, U.S.A., to survey Snake river from its source to its mouth. The Lewiston Teller's statement that the party ought to have reached there some time ago, reminds us that several weeks ago a Montana exchange noted the return of the expedition in a dilapidated condition. – W.W. Union.

It is not surprising that the expedition failed. It was folly to attempt the descent of Snake river in the winter season, as the river is then very low and the rapids in their most unfavorable condition. With light boats in Summer the task of descending the river might be accomplished. The journey would open a rich field to scientific exploration.

Tuesday, June 12, 1877. – Although the explorers, Lewis and Clark, descended Snake river as early as 1804, very little is known of the stream; and it is hoped that Lieut. Doane will be permitted to complete his survey of the great river.

BRISBIN AND AN 1878 EXPEDITION
by the editors

As a final tribute to Doane's idea of exploring the Snake River and to its importance, the editors quote one more letter – found stuffed away in an old box of army records – signed by the original antagonist of the idea.

A year and a half after Major Brisbin ordered Doane to return to Fort Ellis, the major had come to realize that the Snake River should be explored, but he was not going to give Doane the honor of doing it. On June 2, 1878, Brisbin addressed a letter to Briga-dier General A. H. Terry in St. Paul:

I have the honor to respectfully ask the authority of the general commanding to send an officer and suitable detail to explore the Snake River, from the Yellowstone Lake to the Columbia River. This is a work that should I think by all means be done during the coming fall. That a river in the interior of the west should have remained unexplored so long is remark-able, and I trust the department commander will give his consent, to have the work done this year. I opposed the sending out an exploring party in 1876 because it was proposed too late in the year to make it successful. Lieut. Doane Second Cavalry contrary to my advice obtained over my head authority to start out in October and as a result lost his boat, got snowed up in the mountains and he and his entire party came near starving. I do not wish the general commanding to believe that because Lieut. Doane's and a previous expedition failed to make the exploration of Snake River it cannot be done for the sole cause of failure was the selection of an improper season for starting out.

I would respectively recommend that Second Lieut. E. J. McClernand or First Lieut. J. U. Robinson, Second Cavalry be authorized to make an exploration of Snake River. I would further recommend that the party be started out from this post to the Yellowstone Park not later than August 20th next and that it be furnished with two non com officers and 8 privates, 5 pack mules and 60 days rations, two boats instead of one as heretofor should I think be started so that if one boat swamps or gets disabled they will still have a boat left to go on with. The boats can be built by the quartermaster at Fort Ellis without cost or at but slight expense to the government.

I recommend that the detachment be sent back from the mouth of Snake River to Fort Ellis and that Lieut. McClernand or Lieut. Robinson himself return to this post via San Francisco, California, remaining at the latter place long enough to make up a report.

If the general commanding would authorize the hiring of two experienced citizens, water men, it would add to the safety and success of the expedition, but I desire this to be considered merely as a suggestion and not made a part of the above recommendation unless it shall be well pleasing in the sight of the general.

[Signed] James S. Brisbin, Major
Commanding Post[7]

The expedition requested by Brisbin was not ordered out, nor has the reply to his request been found.

It would remain for another generation to explore fully the Snake River and to discover the excitement of Hell's Canyon, the geologic puzzles, The Thousand Springs, and the great Indian pictograph.

[7] Letter 345 June 2, 1878, AAG St. Paul. National Archives.

APPENDIX TO PART III

by the editors

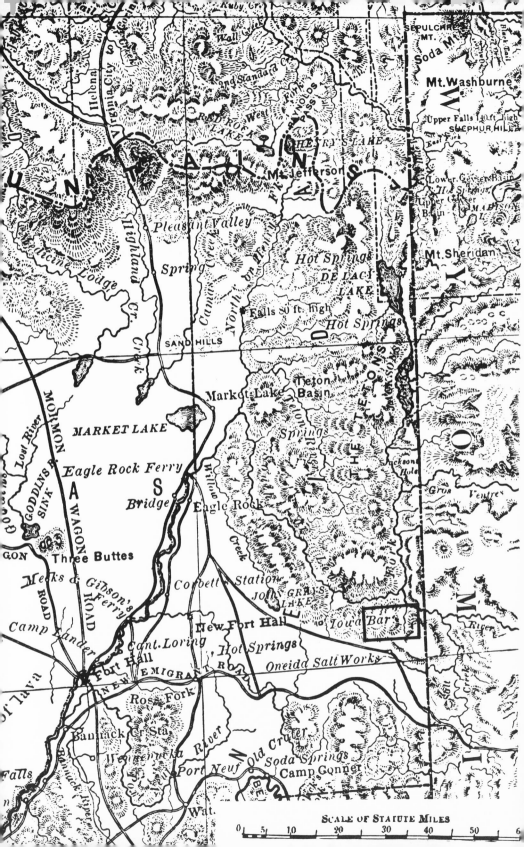

SCALE OF STATUTE MILES

0   5   10   20   30   40   50   6

APPENDIX A

THE MAPS

The map on the facing page is a segment of the Idaho Territory map from Rand, McNally & Company's *Business Atlas* of 1876. The map contains a number of topographical errors, but it does serve at least a dual function: it illustrates certain map knowledge of the area at the time Doane was making his Snake River Expedition and it gives some idea of locations referred to by Doane, either by name or by description, in Chapters 14-16 – e.g., Oneida Salt Works, Eagle Rock Bridge, Soda Springs, Willow Creek, etc. The small rectangle drawn in toward the lower right corner of the map has been added for this present volume to designate the area covered by the page 542 map, which details the location of Keenan City and Cariboo City.

Other than the page 542 map, which was drawn specifically for *Battle Drums and Geysers,* all other chapter-opening map sections used in Part III of this book are taken from the 1872 Hayden Survey map, "Sources of the Snake River . . . ," which is reproduced herein as a foldout map. To facilitate the use of these chapter-opening section maps, two small additions have been made: a North compass direction arrow and a scale of distance have been added at the bottom of each map. Because Doane's 1876 route from Fort Ellis to Yellowstone Lake was essentially the same as his 1870 route (except that in 1876 he went around the *west* side of the lake), section maps have been omitted until Chapter 10, when Doane leaves West Thumb and strikes south to Heart Lake. For Chapters 6-9, reference can be make to section maps in Part II.

The full foldout map is a reproduction of the 10"x10½" map published in F. V. Hayden's *Sixth Annual Report of the U.S. Geological Survey of the Territories.* The blue color, indicating water features, has been added for this edition. Carl Wheat says of this Hayden map: "In a very attractive way, it shows the country from Fort Hall to the Grand Canyon of the Yellowstone, and as far east as the upper Yellowstone River."[1]

---

[1] Wheat, *Mapping the Transmississippi West,* Vol. V, Part 2, 346.

APPENDIX B

DOANE ON CONTEMPORY CONTROVERSIES

What is Doane criticizing in the tirade which suddenly appears amid his December 10 journal entry? (see page 532) His discontent is directed toward "Engine turned scientists" who conjecture from a few bald and undigested observations, toward well-intentioned congressmen, toward lofty-titled volumes filled with glittering generalities, toward beardless cubs who do not know the difference between the thermal wonders of Yellowstone and an ordinary spring, and more. What does all this mean?

"Engine turned scientists" are what we today would label mass-produced or assembly-line scientists, or at least scientists made from the same mold. "Engine-turning" was the machine engraving of symmetrical patterns upon metals, as in the phrase from Charles Dickins: "A gold hunting-watch . . . engine-turned." A similar use, but with an additional twist which surely would have attracted Doane, was Oliver Wendell Holmes' judgment: "Your self-made man deserves more credit than the engine-turned article."

"Well intentioned congressmen" were frequently being criticized across the country for distributing government-funded publications too freely. In Montana itself, for example, the May 2, 1873 *Bozeman Avant Courier* newspaper carried this brief editorial:

> The Corinne[1] Reporter says about a ton and a half of public documents under the frank of Clagett await transportation at the stage office. What he is going to do with them in Montana is a mystery, as the Indians won't have them, and the Chinese get their books from home.

This comment is only a sample of many similar editorials. Doane likely did not have Congressional Delegate William H. Clagett in mind, because when Doane wrote his Snake River journal Clagett was no longer representing Montana in Washington; furthermore, Doane had favorable memories of Clagett, remembering Clagett's diligent efforts in behalf of the Yellowstone National Park bill in 1872.

Doane probably had specific persons and writings in mind to fit his epithets, but it would be speculative to attempt to pinpoint them. Resorting to some conjecture in an attempt to make sense of Doane's deeply felt, almost bitter complaints, perhaps the most fruitful approach is to recall two controversies current during the 1870's, controversies in which Doane must have taken a keen interest.

One had to do with geyser theories. There was in the 1870's and 1880's, precisely because of the discoveries in Yellowstone, a renewed interest – and a renewed controversy – among scientists about the origin and operation of geysers, and, for that matter, about whether the Yellowstone geysers were different from the Icelandic geysers with which scientists then were more familiar. In other words, review and revision of theories became common. And of course the Hayden Survey annual reports devoted careful attention to the matter. For example, for the *Twelfth Annual Report,* A. C. Peale contributed a summary of geyser theories current at the time, and even makes a teakettle comment.[2] It is impossible for us to determine which theory

---

[1] Corrine, in far north Utah Territory, was until the late 1870's an important stop on the Central Pacific Railroad. It was located where the transcontinental line crossed Bear River and also served as the southern terminus of the Montana Stage Line.

[2] "If water [is] . . . boiled in a kettle which has a lid and a spout, either the lid

Doane himself held to and which theories he dismissed; but it is certain that in his remarks about conjectural siphons, teakettles, and timid old ladies he was attacking some geyser theory.

Another field of controversy of the 1870's, far more fundamental and more complex than the geyser theory debates, was the struggle for control of federal government financed science. The decade witnessed the work and competition of the four major surveys: Powell, Wheeler, King, and Hayden; the congressional investigation in 1874 by the Townsend Committee of the rivalries and duplication of these various surveys; the basic clash between the War Department and the Interior Department over general Indian Policy and over exploration and survey policy; the 1875 Indian Ring scandal in the Interior Department; the decline of the army's influence in Western exploration; the establishment of the consolidating U.S. Geological Survey. This area of controversy was at the heart of Doane's own interests and experiences and his sharp phrases surely were directed toward this fray.

As an explorer, Doane sought support from any source. When the army did not back his Nile River project, he turned to the American Geographical Society; when the government withdrew its support from the Howgate Arctic Expedition, Doane took leave from the army and accepted command under civilian sponsorship. Nevertheless, Doane was an army man and basically he took an army point of view. Hayden, on the other hand, in the mid-1870's came to be identified with "Civilian Science." It seems safe to speculate that Doane's feelings toward Hayden were mixed.

True, Doane speaks favorably of Hayden more than once, and Hayden named a mountain after Doane and praised Doane's Yellowstone report highly. Yet Doane, as he watched Hayden's star rise after Hayden's 1871 Yellowstone Survey, probably felt that he could have done as well or even better than Hayden. After all, Doane had explored Yellowstone in 1870, had helped

will be blown off or the water will be forced out through the spout. . . . [This] exemplifies the theories which presuppose the existence of subterranean cavities with tubes at or near the surface." (Part 2, 421)

lay the groundwork for the 1871 Survey, and had assisted Hayden on that 1871 trip.

Do Doane's writings themselves give any indication of his competitive feeling toward Hayden? Only a couple of ambiguous hints. In the November 30 entry for his Snake River journal, Doane writes, perhaps with some irritation, about an incident then at least five years old: "The existence of this lake [Bridger Lake], Hayden denies, but it is there all the same, and more, he has seen it for I showed it to him. . . ." One cannot determine exactly what significance to attach to this statement. In Doane's 1874 Nile River proposal he suggests that his own African exploration "would solve a great problem in Science . . . [for] *one tenth* the cost of the Annual Explorations by Professor Hayden and others." The *one tenth* emphasis is Doane's and the phrase "and others" was an insert, presumably an afterthought by Doane. This could well be merely a straight statistical comparison which Doane employs to highlight the economy of his own exploration. Or it could harbor some discontent about the appropriations and assignments which came to Hayden but which seemed to elude Doane. Or it could also reflect the civilian-military science issue; Doane was writing just a few months after the Townsend congressional hearings when the army, in arguing its case, had made much of the fact that it could do exploration and survey jobs cheaper.

Doane brings up another facet of controversy with his clause, "the U.S.I.D. branch is a guarantee of truth as it is of honesty in an Indian agent until caught out," which emphasizes the well-known frauds and corruption of the Indian agents in the West.

Only the year before Doane's 1876 trip, O. C. Marsh, with cooperation from the army, had exposed the fraud of the Indian agent at the Sioux reservation in Nebraska, which, after investigation, led to the resignation of the Secretary of the Interior, Columbus Delano.

In summary, we can see that Doane, in this tirade which crops up in his journal, is making a brief and barbed contribution to discussions of contemporary interest to laymen, congressmen, and professional scientists.

ACKNOWLEDGMENTS

We wish to acknowledge with thanks the generosity of everyone who helped us in assemblying the material for this book. There is not space to name them all.

H. D. Hampton, working on his master's degree at Ohio State University and researching the period of the army administration of Yellowstone Park, came across a missing Doane file in the National Archives. This material, which he so kindly made available to us, was invaluable.

Aubrey L. Haines, historian of Yellowstone National Park, gave us considerable time, including many of his off-duty hours, in locating material in the Yellowstone Park Library. He made available his own research on the ascent of Mount Langford by Doane and Langford and on the peak first ascended by Everts. He found and furnished us with old photographs from the Park files. As one of the most reliable historians of the region, his suggestions have been most helpful.

Others in the National Park Service were very helpful to us. Lee L. Coleman, of Billings, Montana, now retired, reviewed carefully that portion of Doane's 1870 journal which dealt with the trip around Yellowstone Lake. He had studied that area thoroughly and had identified the September 19 campsite. Ranger George D. Marler perhaps knows more about today's Yellowstone geysers than anyone, and his assistance was valuable. We are grateful for the help of Lemuel A. Garrison (former superintendent of Yellowstone Park), Park Naturalist John M.

Good, and Ranger David Beal. To Newell Joyner (former junior park naturalist) and Chief Naturalist Merlin K. Potts (formerly at Grand Teton National Park) go much credit for preserving and making available to the public Doane's 1876 journal. Ranger Lowell Biddulph furnished much useful information about the Mud Volcano area.

Floyd Bottler, Livingston, Montana, told us many stories about his father Frederick Bottler, and the period about which this book is written. We have several hours of tape recordings of his stories.

Miss Minnie Paugh, Special Collections Librarian of Montana State University, has our great appreciation for her help in bringing to light the original manuscript of the 1870 Doane journal, and the typescript of Fred Server's 1876 journal.

Concerning the natural wonders in southern Montana mentioned by Doane in his 1876 journal, we have had correspondence with and helpful information from Stuart W. Conner of Billings, Montana, Forest District Rangers Joe T. Helle and Henry A. Rate, and Assistant State Geologist C. W. Wilson, Jr., of Laramie, Wyoming.

National Forest Ranger Station, Freedom Wyoming (Mrs. Beulah Croft) permitted us to copy excerpts from their manuscript history of Caribou National Forest.

Gilbert H. Doane, historian of the Doane Family Association of America, Inc., furnished us with information concerning the parents and lineage of Lieutenant Gustavus C. Doane.

We are grateful to the following persons for information furnished us: H. William Axford, University Librarian, Arizona State University; Earl M. Christensen; John T. Craighead (grizzlies); Mrs. Ethel M. (John) Crissman and Mrs. Elizabeth Will (1871 army uniform and centennial tent); Fritiof M. Fryxell (Mount Doane, Tetons, F. V. Hayden); Fred H. Graves, Head Librarian, The Cooper Union for the Advancement of Science and Art, New York; Mrs. Wayne Herron, niece of Mrs. Mary Lee (G. C.) Doane; Paul H. Love, district clerk, Virginia City, Montana; Mrs. Edith H. Lovell (Caribou district); Miss Harriett C. Meloy, Acting Librarian, Montana Historical Society, Helena;

Mrs. Edna Miner; James Penick, Jr., Department of History, Loyola University, Chicago; Clarence G. Rich, son of Mrs. Mary Lee Doane's sister; Verne Sexton, Bozeman Court House Historic Exhibit (photographs); Mrs. Harriet W. Smith, Librarian, Geology Library, University of Illinois, Urbána.

We spent much time working in the following libraries, all of whose personnel were most helpful: Bancroft Library, Berkeley; Northwestern University Library, Evanston; Denver Public Library; Fondren Library, Rice University, Houston; Fremont County Library, Lander, Wyoming; Grand Teton National Park Library, Moose, Wyoming; Houston Public Library; Idaho Falls Public Library; Idaho Historical Society, Boise; Library of Congress, Washington, D. C.; Livingston Public Library, Montana; Missouri Historical Society, St. Louis; Montana Historical Society, Helena; Montana State University Library, Bozeman; National Archives, Washington, D. C.; New Mexico Historical Society, Santa Fe; New York Public Library; Pocatello Public Library, Idaho; Teton County Library, Jackson, Wyoming; Society of California Pioneers, San Francisco; University of British Columbia, Vancouver; University of Oklahoma Library, Norman; University of Wyoming Library, Laramie; U. S. Geological Survey Library, Denver; Wyoming State Historical Department, Cheyenne; Yale University Library; Yellowstone Park Library, Mammouth Hot Springs.

We have also received useful material from the following: American Geographical Society, New York, Miss Nordis Felland, Librarian; Galesburg Public Library, Illinois, Mrs. Margaret Morris, Librarian; Gilcrease Institute, Tulsa Oklahoma, David Hunt, Curator of Art; Princeton University Library; University of the Pacific, Stockton, California, Ellen L. Deering, Registrar, and Mrs. Martha Seffer O'Bryon, Curator, The Stuart Library of Western Americana; Yazoo Library Association, Yazoo City, Mississippi, Mrs. M. P. Derden. The Bozeman Court House, Montana, has an interesting display of Doane memorabilia in their historical exhibit.

Grateful acknowledgment is also given to the following publishers for use of their material: Harcourt, Brace & World, Inc.,

The Pioneer Photographer, by William Henry Jackson; Harper &
Row, *The White Nile,* by Robert Taft; G. P. Putnam's Sons,
Time Exposure, by William Henry Jackson; Charles Scribner's
sons, *Picture Maker of the Old West,* by Clarence S. Jackson;
Charles E. Tuttle Co., Inc., *Jirah Isham Allen,* by Mary Allen
Phinney; University of Oklahoma Press, *Thomas Moran,* by
Thurman Wilkins.

We must add our thanks to Savoie Lottinville and the University of Oklahoma Press, who worked with us so long in the
planning and editing of this book and who then generously
released the work to us in order that an earlier publication date
could be effected; and to Durrett Wagner, editor of Swallow
Press, who personally has assisted so painstakenly in further
detailed editing and improvement of the book.

O.H.B. and L.B.

BIBLIOGRAPHY

MANUSCRIPTS

Barry J. Neilson. "The Route of John Colter." Yellowstone Park Library, Mammoth Hot Springs; Teton County Library, Jackson Wyoming.

Burlingame, Merrill G. "The Military-Indian Frontier in Montana, 1860-90." Ph.D. thesis, State University of Iowa, 1936. See also *General Histories and Reference Books.*

"Caribou Area." Unpublished manuscript, forty-seven pages, 1945. Freedom Ranger Station, Freedom, Wyoming.

Chittenden, Hiram M. "Echoes of Frontier Days." Yellowstone Park Library, Mammoth Hot Springs.

Conner, Stuart W. "Unusual Characteristics of the Keogh Buffalo Jump." Mimeographed. Billings, Montana.

Doane, Gustavus C. "Expedition from Fort Ellis, Montana, to Fort Hall, Idaho, October 11, 1876, to January 4, 1877." This ms. is printed in its entirety in Part III of this book, *Battle Drums and Geysers.* Original ms. is privately retained but probably will someday be at Montana State University, Bozeman, Montana. Mimeographed copy with National Park Service.

Doane, Gustavus C. "The report upon the so-called Yellowstone Expedition of 1870." This ms. is printed in its entirety in Part II of this book, *Battle Drums and Geysers.* Original ms. at Montana State University, Bozeman, Montana. See also *Government Documents: Congressional.*

Hamilton, James M. "History of Fort Ellis." Unpublished address. Yellowstone Park Library, Mammoth Hot Springs.

Hauser, Samuel T. Papers in archives of Montana Historical Society Library, Helena, Montana.

Langford, Nathaniel P. "A Frontier Tragedy." Yellowstone Park Library, Mammoth Hot Springs. Catalog 7492-7499, ACC 262.

Marler, George D. "Firehole Geyser Basin 1959," Vol. III of "Yellowstone

Geyser Observations and References" (manuscripts bound in three volumes). Yellowstone Park Library, Mammoth Hot Springs.

Server, Sergeant Fred. "Diary, 1876." Typescript of unpublished manuscript. Montana State University, Bozeman, Montana.

Voth, Hazel Hunt, and Russell, Dr. Carl P., eds. "Bibliography, Yellowstone National Park." 1940. National Park Service, Washington, D.C.

Weikert, Andrew J. "Journal of a Tour through Yellowstone National Park in August and September, 1877." Document 9787, W. 421. Yellowstone Park Library, Mammoth Hot Springs. See also *Periodicals.*

White, John G. "A Souvenir of Wyoming." Wyoming State Historical Department, Cheyenne.

GOVERNMENT DOCUMENTS: RECORDS

Bonneville County, Deed Records, Book A, Idaho Falls, Idaho.

Doane Army Records. Record Group No. 94, 2422 AGO 1876, Records of the War Department, Office of the Adjutant General, National Archives.

Doane Summary of Service, written by him February 16, 1889, at Presidio, San Francisco, California, with accompanying documents, National Archives. Microfilm copy in O. H. Bonney Collection.

Doane, Gustavus C., "Exploration of the Judith Basin." Report of February 19, 1874, to the Secretary of the Interior, Commissioner of Indian Affairs. Montana Historical Society Library, Helena, Montana.

_____. "Map of the Route of the Yellowstone Expedition Escort Commanded by Lieut. G. C. Doane, U.S.A. September 1870." Record Group 77, Q329-30, Records of the Office of the Chief of Engineers. National Archives.

_____. "Navigation of the Yellowstone." January 12, 1873. National Archives.

Fort Ellis Records. RG 98, 1867-1886, Records of the United States Army Commands, National Archives.

Fort Hall Records. RG 98, Records of the United States Army Commands, National Archives.

Fort Keogh Records. RG 98, Records of the United States Army Commands, National Archives.

Norris, P. W. Annual Report of the Superintendent of the Yellowstone National Park, 1877, 1878, 1879, 1880. Yellowstone Park Library, Mammoth Hot Springs.

United States Army. Annual Report, Department of Dakota, 1870. Adjutant General's Office, National Archives No. 1869.

GOVERNMENT DOCUMENTS: CONGRESSIONAL

Barlow, John Whitmey. *Indian Interference with the Northern Pacific Railroad.* 42 Cong., 3 sess., *Senate Exec. Doc. No. 16,* October 16, 1872.

_____. *Journey down the Yellowstone from Fort Ellis.* 42 Cong., 3 sess., *Senate Exec. Doc. No. 12,* GR 258, February 3, 1873.

Barlow, J. W., and Heap, D. P. *Report of a Reconnaissance of the Basin of the Upper Yellowstone in 1871.* 42 Cong., 2 sess., *Senate Exec. Doc. No. 66,* 1871.

Checklist of United States Public Documents 1789-1909. Vol. 1, Lists of Congressional and Departmental Publications. Third edition revised and enlarged. Washington, 1911.

Doane, Gustavus C. *Report upon the So-called Yellowstone Expedition of 1870.* 41 Cong., 3 sess., *Senate Exec. Doc. No. 51,* 1873. This is given in its entirety in Part II of this book.

Hayden, Ferdinand V. *Geological Survey of Wyoming and Montana* (Preliminary Report). 42 Cong., 2 sess., *House Exec. Doc. Nos. 325 and 326,* Vol. 1520, Parts 1 and 2.

Heitman, Francis B. *Historical Register and Dictionary of the United States Army 1789-1903.* 57 Cong., 2 sess., *House Doc. No. 446,* Vols. 96, 97.

Howard, O. O. to McDowell, October 1878. 45 Cong., 3 sess., *House Exec. Doc. No. 1* (Serial 1843), Part 2, 226.

Jones, W. A. *Report upon the reconnaissance of northwestern Wyoming, made in the summer of 1873.* 43 Cong., 1 sess., *House Exec. Doc. No. 285* (Serial 1615), Vol. 17, 256-290. No. 285 is Jones' Reconnaissance. One overall map and forty-nine trail maps. A revised edition of 121 additional pages, *Report upon the reconnaissance of northwestern Wyoming, including Yellowstone national park, made in the summer of 1873,* was published the following year.

Phillips, W. Hallett. 49 Cong., 1 sess., *Senate Exec. Doc. No. 51,* February 1, 1886.

Secretary of the Interior, *Annual Report 1886,* 49 Cong., 2 sess., *House Exec. Doc. No. 1,* Part 5, Vol. I.

Secretary of War, *Annual Report 1870,* 41 Cong., 2 sess., *Doc. No. 185,* Vol. 1418.

Secretary of War, *Annual Reports 1874-1892.* Each of the following reports are listed as *House Exec. Doc. No. 1,* Part II, with Congressional, Session, and Volume Nos. as follows:
1874, 43 Cong., 2 sess., Vol. 1635;
1875, 44 Cong., 1 sess., Vol. 1674;
1876, 44 Cong., 2 sess., Vol. 1742, contains reports of Sheridan, Terry, Gibbon, Crook, Reno, and Benteen on Sioux campaign;

1877, 45 Cong., 2 sess., Vol. 1794, contains reports of Gibbon, Howard, Gilbert, Sturgis, and Miles on Nez Perce battles of 1877;
1878, 45 Cong., 3 sess., Vol. 1843;
1879, 46 Cong., 2 sess., Vol. 1903;
1880, 46 Cong., 3 sess., Vol. 1952;
1881, 47 Cong., 1 sess., Vol. 2010;
1882, 47 Cong., 2 sess., Vol. 2091;
1883, 48 Cong., 1 sess., Vol. 2182;
1884, 48 Cong., 2 sess., Vol. 2277;
1885, 49 Cong., 1 sess., Vol. 2369;
1886, 49 Cong., 2 sess., Vol. 2461, map of Geronimo campaign;
1887, 50 Cong., 1 sess., Vol. 2533;
1888, 50 Cong., 2 sess., Vol. 2628;
1889, 51 Cong., 1 sess., Vol. 2715;
1890, 51 Cong., 2 sess., Vol. 2831;
1891, 52 Cong., 1 sess., Vol. 2921;
1892, 52 Cong., 2 sess., Vol. 3077.

Washburn, General H. D. "The Yellowstone Expedition," *Mining Statistics West of the Rocky Mountains,* March 21, 1871. 42 Cong., 1 sess., *House Exec. Doc. No. 10.*

GOVERNMENT DOCUMENTS: OTHER PUBLICATIONS

Carpel, Levanthal, and Breger. *The Salt Resources of the Idaho-Wyoming Border, with notes on Geology.* U.S.G.S. Bulletin 430. Washington, 1910.

Checklist of United States Public Documents 1789-1909. Vol. 1, Lists of Congressional and Departmental Publications. Third edition revised and enlarged. Washington, 1911.

Cramton, Louis C. *Early History of Yellowstone National Park and its Relation to National Park Policies.* U.S. Department of the Interior, Washington, 1932.

Hague, Arnold. *Geological History of the Yellowstone National Park.* Washington, 1928.

Haines, Aubrey L. *The Bannock Indian Trail.* Yellowstone Park, Wyoming: Yellowstone Library and Museum Association, 1964. See also Replogle.

Hayden, Ferdinand V., et al. *Fifth Annual Report. Preliminary Report of the U.S. Geological Survey of Montana and portions of adjacent territories.* Washington, 1872.

——————. *Sixth Annual Report of the U.S. Geological and Geographical Survey of the Territories for 1872.* Washington, 1873.

——————. *Twelfth Annual Report of the U.S. Geological and Geographical Survey of the Territories for 1878.* Washington, 1883.

Hodge, Frederick Webb, ed. *Handbook of American Indians North of Mexico.* 2 vols. Washington, 1912; Grosse Pointe, Michigan, 1968.

Ludlow, William. *Report of a Reconnaissance from Carroll, Montana Territory, on the Upper Missouri, to the Yellowstone National Park, and Return, Made in the Summer of 1875.* Washington, 1876.

Marler, George D. *The Story of Old Faithful.* Yellowstone Park, Wyoming, 1963.

Mattes, Merrill J. *Colter's Hell and Jackson's Hole.* Grand Teton Natural History Association and Yellowstone Library and Museum Association, 1962.

Mooney, James. "Calendar History of the Kiowa Indians," *Bureau of American Ethnology Annual Reports,* Vol. XVII, Part 1, 141. Washington, 1895-96. The map in this publication shows the distribution of the Indian tribes and locates sites of battles with the Indians.

Poore, B. P., compiled by. *A Descriptive Catalogue of The Government Publications of the United States, September 5, 1774-March 4, 1881.* Washington, 1885.

Replogle, Wayne F. *Yellowstone's Bannock Indian Trails.* Yellowstone Library and Museum Association, 1956. See also Haines.

A Report on Barracks and Hospitals with Descriptions of Military Posts. Circular No. 4, War Department, Surgeon General's Office. Washington, December 5, 1870. Information on Fort Ellis, Montana Territory, furnished by Surgeon P. C. Davis and Assistant Surgeon C. Ewen, U.S. Army.

Report of the Hygiene of the U.S. Army and Descriptions of Military Posts 1875. Circular No. 8, War Department, Surgeon General's Office. National Archives.

Royce, C. C. "Indian Land Cessions in the United States," *Bureau of American Ethnology Annual Reports,* Vol. XVIII, Part 2, 786, 848. Washington, 1896-97. An excellent reference for all of the treaties concerning Indian land cessions with the United States. It contains maps of each state showing original Indian boundaries.

Schultz, Alfred R. *Gold Development in Central Uinta County, Wyoming, and other points on the Snake River,* U.S. Geological Survey Bulletin 315. Washington, 1907.

United States Statutes at Large. 14 U.S. Stat. 428 and 15 U.S. Stat. 14 (Post Civil War, Reconstruction rights and disqualifications). 20 U.S. Stat. 150; 22 U.S. Stat. 118; 22 U.S. Stat. 456 (Army retirement, disability, and age). 22 U.S. Stat. 627 (Troops in Yellowstone Park). 25 U.S. Stat. (Indian Treaties).

The War of Rebellion. A Compilation of the Official Records of the Union and Confederate Armies and Navies. Four series, 128 vols. United States War Department. Washington, 1880-1901.

BIOGRAPHIES AND MEMOIRS

Bradley, Lieutenant James H. *The March of the Montana Column* (A Prelude to the Custer Disaster), ed. Edgar I. Stewart. Norman, 1961. See also *Periodicals.*

Catlin, George. *Letters and Notes on the Manners, Customs, and Condition of the North American Indians,* 2 vols., second edition, London, 1841.

Cody, William F. *Story of the Wild West.* Philadelphia, 1888.

Cook, Charles W. See Haines; see also *Periodicals.*

Dunraven, Earl of (Windham Thomas Wyndham-Quin, Fourth Earl of Dunraven). *Hunting in the Yellowstone.* Outing, 1917; New York, 1925. Reprinted from the original edition, *The Great Divide,* London, 1876. Republished as *The Great Divide: Travels in the Upper Yellowstone in the Summer of 1874,* with Introduction by Marshall Sprague. Lincoln, 1967.

Ferris, Warren A. *Life in the Rocky Mountains, 1830-35,* ed. Paul C. Phillips. Denver, 1940; Salt Lake City, 1940.

Folsom, Daniel E. See Haines; see also *Periodicals.*

Fremont, John Charles. *Narratives of Exploration and Adventure,* ed. Allan Nevins. New York, 1956.

──────. *Report of the Exploring Expedition to the Rocky Mountains in the Year 1842 and to Oregon and North California in 1843-44.* Washington, 1845.

Greely, A. W. *Three Years of Arctic Service: An Account of the Lady Franklin Bay Expedition of 1881-84.* 2 vols. New York, 1886.

Haines, Aubrey L., ed. *The Valley of the Upper Yellowstone: An Exploration of the Headwaters of the Yellowstone River in the Year 1869, as recorded by Charles W. Cook, Daniel E. Folsom, and William Peterson.* Norman, 1965. See also *Periodicals,* Folsom.

Jackson, Clarence S. *Picture Maker of the Old West, William H. Jackson.* New York, 1947.

Jackson, William H. *The Pioneer Photographer.* New York, 1929.

──────. *Time Exposure: The Autobiography of William Henry Jackson.* New York, 1940.

Johnson, Virginia. *The Unregimented General* (Nelson A. Miles). New York, 1962. Contains much of the personal correspondence of Miles to his wife during his campaigns.

Kipling, Rudyard. *American Notes.* New York, 1889.

Langford, Nathaniel P. *The Discovery of Yellowstone Park, 1870.* Second edition. St. Paul, 1923.

Marquis, Thomas B. *Memoirs of a White Crow Indian.* New York, 1928.

Miles, General Nelson A. *Personal Recollections and Observations* (and the story of his Indian Campaigns with comments on the Exploration, Development and Progress of our Great Western Empire). New York, 1897.

Ogden, Peter Skeen. *Snake River Journals, 1824-1826.* Hudson's Bay Record Society, XIII. London, 1950. See also *Periodicals.*

Peterson, William. See Haines.

Phinney, Mary Allen. *Jirah Isham Allen, Montana Pioneer.* Rutland, 1946.

Russell, Osborne. *Journal of a Trapper, 1834-1843.* Boise, 1921. Reprinted from the 1914 edition. Later reprinted, edited and with notes by Aubrey L. Haines. Portland, 1955; Lincoln, 1965.

Scott, Hugh Lenox. *Some Memories of a Soldier.* New York, 1928.

Strong, General William E. *A Trip to the Yellowstone National Park in July, August and September 1875.* Washington, 1876. Reprinted, ed. Richard A. Bartlett. Norman, 1968.

Stuart, Robert. *The Discovery of the Oregon Trail* (Narratives of Stuart's Overland Trip Eastward from Astoria in 1812-1813). ed. Philip Ashton Rollins. From the original manuscript in William Robertson Coe Collection in Yale University Americana Library. New York, 1935. Republished as *On the Oregon Trail: Robert Stuart's Journal of Discovery.* ed. Kenneth A. Spaulding. Stuart's account only; appendix with Hunt's journal not included. Norman, 1953.

Victor, Frances Fuller. *Eleven Years in the Rocky Mountains and Life on the Frontier.* Hartford, 1877. Story of Joe Meek.

_____. *River of the West.* Hartford, 1870. Stories of Joe Meek.

Vinton, Stallo. *John Colter, Discoverer of Yellowstone Park.* New York, 1926.

Wyeth, Nathaniel J. *The Correspondence and Journals of Captain Nathaniel J. Wyeth, 1831-36.* ed. F. G. Young. Eugene, 1899.

Wyndham-Quin, Windham Thomas (Fourth Earl of Dunraven). See Dunraven.

GENERAL HISTORIES AND REFERENCE BOOKS

Allen, E. T., and Day, A. L. *Hot Springs of the Yellowstone National Park.* Publication No. 466, 525 pages, The Carnegie Institution. Washington, 1935.

Bancroft, Hubert Howe. *History of California.* (The Works of Bancroft, Vol. VI) San Francisco, 1882-1890.

_____. *History of Washington, Idaho and Montana.* Ibid., Vol. XXXI.

Bartlett, Richard A. *Great Surveys of the American West.* Norman, 1962.

Beal, Merrill D. *The Story of Man in Yellowstone.* Caldwell, 1949. Revised edition. Yellowstone Park, Wyoming, 1960.

Bonney, Orrin H. and Lorraine G. *Guide to the Wyoming Mountains and Wilderness Areas.* Second revised edition. Denver, 1965.

_____. *Bonney's Guide to Grand Teton National Park and Jackson's Hole.* Revised edition. Houston, 1966.

_____. *Field Book The Wind River Range.* Revised edition. Houston, 1968.

_____. *Field Book The Teton Range and Gros Ventre Range.* Denver, 1963.

_____. *Field Book The Absaroka Range and Yellowstone Park.* Denver, 1963.

Brimlow, George F. *The Bannock Indian War of 1878.* Caldwell, 1938.

Brackett, L. P. *Our Western Empire.* San Francisco, 1881.

Brown, Mrs. Jennie Broughton. *Fort Hall on the Oregon Trail.* Caldwell, 1932.

Brown, Mark H. *The Flight of the Nez Perce.* New York, 1967.

Burlingame, Merrill G. *The Montana Frontier.* Helena, 1942. Most of this is from the excellent Ph.D. thesis of Burlingame. See *Manuscripts.*

_____, and Ross, Toole K. *History of Montana.* 3 vols. New York, 1957.

Cameron, Jenks. *The National Park Service: Its History, Activities and Organization.* New York, 1922.

Chittenden, Hiram M. *The Yellowstone National Park.* Cincinnati, 1895.

_____. Ibid., Cincinnati, 1903. Chittenden added much new material to this revision of the 1895 edition.

_____. Ibid., ed. Richard A. Bartlett. Norman, 1964. Some of the original omitted or rearranged.

_____. *American Fur Trade of the Far West.* 2 vols. New York, 1902.

Clark, Barzilla W. *Bonneville County in the Making.* Idaho Falls, 1941.

Codman, John. *The Mormon Country.* New York, 1874.

Crandall, Warren D., and Newell, Isaac D. *History of the Ram Fleet and the Mississippi Marine Brigade* (in the War for the Union on the Mississippi and its Tributaries.) St. Louis, 1907. 492 pages including photographs of the men available in 1907. This account is fairly complete, is authentic, without index or table of contents, and lacks readability.

Cullum, George W. *Biographical Register of the Officers and Graduates of the U.S. Military Academy.* Boston, 1891.

Garretson, Martin S. *The American Bison.* New York, 1938.

Graham, Colonel W. A. *The Custer Myth.* Harrisburg, 1953.

Guie, Heister D., and McWhorter, Lucullus V., eds. *Adventures in Geyser Land.* Caldwell, 1935.

Gunnison, Lieutenant J. W., *The Mormons, or Latter-Day Saints in the Valley of the Great Salt Lake.* Philadelphia, 1856.

Haynes, Jack Ellis. *Haynes Guide Yellowstone National Park,* 61st revised edition. Bozeman, 1961. The classic Haynes Guide to Yellowstone National Park was first published and illustrated by Frank Jay Haynes in 1890 and remained in print under the Haynes family until 1967, with revised editions almost annually, and sales sometimes reaching 25,000 a year. The text was authored by A. B. Guptell from 1890 to 1909, by Frank Jay Haynes from 1910 to 1915, and by the latter's son, Jack Ellis Haynes, from 1916. Joseph Joffe for many years assisted Jack Ellis Haynes in the preparation. Horace M. Albright, superintendent of the Park 1919 to 1929, had it designated as the official guide to Yellowstone National Park. After the death of Jack Ellis Haynes May 12, 1962, his widow Mrs. Isabel Haynes continued publication for about five years until she sold the Haynes' shops to Hamilton Brothers. The 1967 edition was the last published. Mrs. Haynes regarded this as the end of a historical era in contributions to the literature of Yellowstone Park and provided in writing that no more Haynes Guides would be published.

Predecessors of the Haynes guide books to Yellowstone Park included W. G. Norton, *The Wonders of Wonderland,* 1873; W. W. Wylie, *Yellowstone National Park or The Great American Wonderland,* 1882; Henry J. Winser, *The Yellowstone National Park, A Manual for Tourists,* 1883; Herman Haupt, Jr., *The Yellowstone National Park,* 1883; P. W. Norris, *Calumet of the Coteau,* 1883; John Hyde, *The Official Guide to Yellowstone National Park,* 1887-8. See also Richardson.

Hebard, Grace R., and Brininstool, E. A. *The Bozeman Trail.* Glendale, 1960.

Howard, Helen A., and McGrath, Dan L. *War Chief Joseph.* Lincoln, 1941.

Idaho. American Guide Series, Federal Writers Project. New York, 1937, 1950.

Irving, Washington. *Astoria.* 3 vols. London, 1836. Reprinted, ed. Edgeley W. Todd. Norman, 1964.

Lovell, Edith H. *Captain Bonneville's County.* Idaho Falls, 1963.

Madsen, Brigham D. *The Bannock of Idaho.* Caldwell, 1958,

Marcy, Randolph B. *The Prairie Traveler: A Hand-Book for Overland Expeditions. With Maps, Illustrations, and Itineraries of the Principal Routes Between the Mississippi and the Pacific.* New York, 1859. Reprinted. Williamstown, Massachusetts, 1968.

Marquis, Thomas B. *Custer on the Little Bighorn.* Albany, California, 1967.

Moorehead, Alan. *The White Nile.* New York, 1960.

Moran, Thomas, and Hayden, F. V. *Yellowstone National Park and the mountain regions and portions of Idaho, Colorado, and Utah.* Boston, 1876. 48 pages. Moran's paintings with an explanation by Hayden. There are only a few copies of this in existence. It is probably one of the finest examples of color lithography ever done.

Norris, P. W. *The Calumet of the Coteau.* Philadelphia, 1883. Contains the guide book to Yellowstone Park at that date.

Northrop, Henry Davenport. *Wonders of the Tropics or Explorations and Adventures of Henry M. Stanley.* Omaha, 1889.

Porter, Admiral David D. *The Naval History of the Civil War.* San Francisco and New York, 1886.

Raftery, John H. *The Story of Yellowstone.* Butte, 1912.

Richardson, James. *Wonders of the Yellowstone Region.* London, 1874; New York, 1889. This was probably the first handbook about Yellowstone Park. Essentially it was mainly quotations, information, and illustrations put together from the *Scribner's Monthly* articles by Langford in 1871; from Barlow, manuscript report of exploration; from Doane, official report of the Washburn-Doane Expedition; from Hayden, *Fifth Annual Report of the U.S. Geological Survey of the Territories;* and from Hayden, "More about the Yellowstone," *Scribner's Monthly,* February 1872.

Robertson, Frank G. *Fort Hall, Gateway to the Oregon Country.* New York, 1963.

Rodenbough, Theophilus F. *From Everglade to Cañon with the Second Dragoons (Second United States Cavalry), An authentic account of Service in Florida, Mexico, Virginia, and the Indian Country, Including the Personal Recollections of Prominent Officers. With an Appendix Containing Orders, Reports and Correspondence, Military Records, Etc., Etc., Etc. 1836-1875.* New York, 1875.

————, and Haskin, William L. *The Army of the United States: Historical Sketches of Staff and Line with Portraits of Generals-in-Chief.* New York, 1896. Reprinted, with additional material by Joseph P. Peters. New York, 1966.

Roe, Charles F. *Custer's Last Battle.* New York, 1927.

Ross, Toole K. See Burlingame.

Sanders, Helen F. *History of Montana.* Chicago, 1913.

Shupe, Irene, *Caribou County.* Colorado Springs, 1930.

Stewart, Edgar Irving. *Custer's Luck.* Norman, 1955.

Todd, A. L. *Abandoned: The Story of the Greely Arctic Expedition, 1881-1884.* New York, 1961.

Vestal, Stanley. *Sitting Bull.* Boston, 1932.

Westerners, The. *Great Western Indian Fights.* Potomac Corral, Washington, 1960.

Wheat, Carl I. *Mapping the Transmississippi West.* 5 vols. (6 books) San Francisco: The Institute of Historical Cartography, 1958.

Whitemore, Flora, and Christopherson, Mildred. *Tosoiba.* Soda Springs, 1958.

Wilkins, Thurman. *Thomas Moran: Artist of the Mountains.* Norman, 1966.

Withington, Mary C. *Western Americana Manuscripts in Yale University Library.* New Haven, 1952.

Wood, Catherine M. *Palomar from Tepee to Telescope.*

PERIODICALS

Bowman, Robert. "Reconstruction of Yazoo County," *Mississippi Historical Society,* Vol. VII.

Brackett, Colonel Albert G. "A Trip Through the Rocky Mountains," Historical Society of Montana, *Contributions,* Vol. VIII, 1917, 329-344.

Bradley, Lieutenant James H. "Yellowstone Expedition of 1874," Historical Society of Montana, *Contributions,* Vol. VIII, 105-126.

――――――. "Journal," Historical Society of Montana, *Contributions,* Vol. II, 140-228. Republished as Bradley, *The March of the Montana Column.* See *Biographies and Memoirs.*

――――――. "An Account of the Attempts to Build a Town at the Mouth of the Musselshell River," Historical Society of Montana, *Contributions,* Vol. II, 304-313.

Burlingame, Merrill G. "The Andrew Jackson Hunter Family – Mary Hunter Doane," *Montana Magazine of History,* Vol. I, No. 1, January, 1951. Beginning with the Spring issue of 1955, this periodical was called *Montana the Magazine of Western History.*

Clarke, Helen P. "Sketch of Malcolm Clarke," Historical Society of Montana, *Contributions,* Vol. II, 1896, 255-268.

Cook, Charles W. "The Valley of the Upper Yellowstone," *The Western Monthly,* July 1870. See also Folsom.

Cowan, Mrs. George F. "Reminiscences of Pioneer Life," Historical Society of Montana, *Contributions,* Vol. IV, 1903, 180.

deLacy, Walter W. "A Trip up the South Snake River in 1863," Historical Society of Montana, *Contributions,* Vol. I, 113.

Everts, Truman C. "Thirty-seven Days of Peril," *Scribner's Monthly,* November, 1871, 103. Reprinted in Historical Society of Montana, *Contributions,* Vol. V, 395-427.

Folsom, David E. "The Valley of the Upper Yellowstone," *The Western Monthly,* July 1870. Although Folsom and Cook authored this article, the by-line credited Charles W. Cook. Under Folsom's name, the article was later republished with a preface by N. P. Langford under the title:

——————. *The Folsom-Cook Explorations of the Upper Yellowstone in the year 1869.* St. Paul, 1894. Langford also presented a copy to the Montana Historical Society which republished it as:

——————. "The Folsom-Cook Explorations of the Upper Yellowstone in the Year 1869," Historical Society of Montana, *Contributions,* Vol. V.

Expanded, and in different format, the article's material was most recently included in the book edited by Aubrey L. Haines. See *Biographies and Memoirs.*

Forsyth, General G. A. "A Frontier Fight," *Harper's New Monthly Magazine,* June, 1895, 42-62.

Gibbon, Colonel John. "Last Summer's Expedition Against the Sioux," *American Catholic Quarterly Review,* Vol. II, April, October, 1877.

——————. "Hunting Sitting Bull," Ibid., Vol. II, October, 1877, 665-695.

Hayden, F. V. "More About the Yellowstone," *Scribner's Monthly,* February 1872.

Hedges, Cornelius. "Journal," Historical Society of Montana, *Contributions,* Vol. V, 1904, 370-394.

Hedges, Wyllys A. "Cornelius Hedges," Historical Society of Montana, *Contributions,* Vol. VII, 181-196.

Hughes, Colonel Robert P. "The Campaign against the Sioux in 1876," *Journal of the Military Service Institution,* Vol. XVII, No. LXXIX, January, 1896.

Hunt, Fred A. "A Purposeful Picnic," *The Pacific Monthly,* Vol. XIX; Part I, March 1908, 232; Part II, April 1908, 431; Part III, May 1908, 522. A photograph of Gustavus C. Doane is shown on page 530 of the May issue with a footnote to the effect that the photograph on page 440 of the April issue was not that of Gustavus C. Doane as shown in the caption but was the portrait of General George Crook. These articles were illustrated with an excellent collection of photographic portraits of both U.S. Army and Indian participants in the Custer fight of 1876. Photos are by Huffman, D. F. Barry, and Rhinehart.

Jackson, W. Turrentine. "The Washburn-Doane Expedition of 1870," *Montana the Magazine of Western History,* Vol. VII, No. 3, July, 1957, 36-51.

——————. "The Creation of Yellowstone National Park," *Montana the Magazine of Western History,* Ibid., 52-65.

Johnson, Walter W. "List of Officers of the Territory of Montana to 1876," Historical Society of Montana, *Contributions,* Vol. I, 326-333.

_____. "List of Officers of the Territory of Montana to 1890," Ibid., Vol. III, 359-361.

Kuppens, Father Francis Xavier. "The Origin of the Yellowstone National Park," *The Woodstock Letters,* Vol. XXVI, No. 3, 400-402.

Langford, Nathaniel P. "The Wonders of the Yellowstone," *Scribner's Monthly,* Vol. II, 1871, 1-17, 113-128.

_____. "The Ascent of Mount Hayden," *Scribner's Monthly,* Vol. VI, 1873, 129-157.

McClernand, Edward J. "With the Indians and Buffalo in Montana," *Cavalry Journal,* No. 36, January, April, 1927, 7-54.

McLemore, Clyde. "Fort Pease, The First Attempt at Settlement in Yellowstone Valley," *Montana Magazine of History,* Vol. II, No. 1, January, 1952.

Ogden, Peter Skeen. "Journal 1827-28." *Quarterly of the Oregon Historical Society,* Vol. II, 1910.

Quivey, Addison M. "The Yellowstone Expedition of 1874," Historical Society of Montana, *Contributions,* Vol. I, 268-284.

Ross, Alexander. "Journal of Alexander Ross on Snake Country Expedition, 1824." ed. T. C. Elliott. *Quarterly of the Oregon Historical Society,* Vol. XIV, 366-388.

Stewart, Edgar Irving. "Major Brisbin's Relief of Fort Pease," *Montana the Magazine of Western History,* Vol. VI, No. 3, Summer, 1956, 23-27.

Trumbull, Walter. "The Washburn Yellowstone Expedition," *Overland Monthly,* May and June, 1871.

Utley, Robert M. "Arizona Vanquished: Impressions and Reflections Concerning the Quality of Life on a Military Frontier," *The American West,* November 1969.

Weikert, Andrew J. "Journal of a Tour through Yellowstone National Park in August and September, 1877," Historical Society of Montana, *Contributions,* Vol. III, 153-174. See also *Manuscripts.*

Wesley, Edgar B. "A Still Larger View of the So-Called Yellowstone Expedition," *North Dakota Historical Quarterly,* Vol. V, 219-238.

Wheeler, William F. "The Late James Gemmell," Historical Society of Montana, *Contributions,* Vol. II, 1896, 331.

NEWSPAPERS

Boise City, *Idaho Statesman* and *Idaho Tri-Weekly Statesman,* April 21, May 3, 1877.

Great Falls, Montana, *Tribune,* August 21, 1924 (by C. W. Cook).

Helena, Montana, *Daily Herald* and *Herald:*

> "The Yellowstone Expedition," N. P. Langford, September 26, 1870.
>
> "The Yellowstone Expedition," H. D. Washburn, September 27 and 28, 1870.
>
> "The Yellowstone Expedition," Langford and Washburn, September 30, 1870.
>
> "The Yellowstone Expedition – Unprecedented Demand for the Herald," September 30, 1870.
>
> "Our Exchanges, East and West, are just now reaching us," October 1, 1870.
>
> "Mount Everts," Cornelius Hedges, October 8, 1870.
>
> "Great Falls of the Yellowstone," C. Hedges, October 15, 1870.
>
> "Hell Broth Springs," C. Hedges, October 19, 1870.
>
> "Sulphur Mountain and Mud Volcano," C. Hedges, October 24, 1870.
>
> "The Long Lost Found," October 21, 1870.
>
> "The Lost and Found," letter by S. W. Langhorn, October 28, 1870.
>
> "Letter of Thanks," T. C. Everts to Judge Lawrence, et al, October 28, 1870.
>
> Washington, D. C., Special Correspondent's Letter to the Helena Herald, November 14, 1870.
>
> "Yellowstone Lake," C. Hedges, November 9, 1870.
>
> "The Yellowstone Banquet," November 14, 1870.
>
> Notices re H. D. Washburn, December 3, 1870; January 28, 30, 1871.
>
> "The Hon. N. P. Langford is in Washington," January 16, 1872.
>
> "A National Park," January 31, 1872.
>
> "Our National Park," February 2, 1872.

Livingston, Montana, *Park County News,* November 23, 1923.

New York *Times,* "The Yellowstone," editorial, October 14, 1870.

Oregon Spectator for 1846.

Philadelphia, Pennsylvania, *Gazette,* September 27, 1827.

St. Louis, Missouri, *Niles Register* for 1846.

St. Louis, Missouri, *Republician* for 1846.

INDEX

Some items are not listed separately in alphabetical sequence, but are instead grouped under a category heading, e.g., Battles, Expeditions, Falls, Highways, Journals and writings, Maps, Pools, Roads, Springs.
Italic numeral refers to illustrative material.

534, 535, 538n, 549, 557, 559, 572, 573
Seven Devils Mountains, 440
Seven Hills. *See* Crater Hills
Seventh Cavalry, 53, 55, 71, 75, 414
Sheepeater Indians, 334
Sheridan, Col. Michael, 67
Sheridan, Gen. Phil H., 51, 62, 63, 67n, 75, 128, 451n, 480n, 547, 572
Sheridan, Mount, 309, 326, 328, 480, 493, 498, 499
Sheridan, Gen. R. H., 6, 8n, 30
Sherman, Gen. W. T., 46, 74, 82, 83, 84, 85, 107, 141, 187, 211
Sherman, Senator John, 46
Shields River, 224n
Shoshone Indians, 22n, 42, 219
Shoshone Geyser Basin, 175
Shoshone Lake, 174n, 177, 180, 198, 327n, 338, 339n, 401, 402, 489, 504
Shoshone River, 377n, 403n, 502
Shultes, Cleland, 550
Sierra Shoshone Range. *See* Absaroka Range
Signal Corps, U.S. Army, 109, 117n, 120, 121n
Sioux Indians, 17, 22n, 40, 42, 51, 59, 62, 76, 89, 141, 184, 219, 257, 441
Sitting Bull, 76, 86, 122, 141
Smith, Gen. Andrew J., 10
Smith, Capt. Edward, 452
Smith, Jacob, 189, 205, 207, 216, 221, 222, 237, 238, *239*, 240, 265, 269, 299n, 319, 327, 413, 417
Smith, Jedediah, 434
Smith, Langford, 400
Smith River, 184
Smithsonian Institution, 46, 132, 149-150, 211n
Smith, Theodor, 113
Snake Indians, 184
Snake River, 63, 94, 176, 177, 198, 199, 256, 263, 319, 320, 326,

327n, 328, 338, 339n, 387, 401, 402, 403, 433, 434n, 439, 451, 490, 501, 504, 519, 522, 525, 547, 558, 562, 570, 575, 576, 577; American Falls, 439; Auger Falls, 439; Basalt Canyon, 558, 561; Box Canyon, 433; Caldron Linn, 439; Canyon, 509n; Deep Rapids, 440; Dry Creek Falls, 439; geysers, 502n, 504; Granite Creek Rapids, 440; Hells Rapids, 439, 440, 578; Mad River Canyon, 505, 523, 527, 528, 534, 538n, 547, 557, 560, 571; Milner Dam, 439; Pillar Falls, 439; Shoshone Falls, 439; Steamboat Rapids, 440; Thousand Springs, 440; Twin Falls, 439
Snake River Range, 263n, 528
Society of California Pioneers, 3n, 133, 141
Soda Butte, 377n
Soda Springs, Ida., 560
Sour Creek. *See* Hellroaring River
South Park, Wyo., 528n
Spear, Col. Sam P., 7
Specimen Ridge, 485
Speke, John H., 45
Spike Geyser, 490n
Spirit Bay. *See* Moran Bay
Spouter Geyser, 346
Spread Creek, 520n
Spring Creek, 339
Springs, 172, 175, 181, 199, 216n, 247, 249, 257, 266n, 281, 287, 288, 289, 310, 331, 346, 365, 379, 428n, 477, 483, 503, 512n, 533, 560; Anderson, 462n; Arrowhead, 172n; Astoria Mineral, 533n; Beach, 301; Dragon Mouth, 180, 288n, 290; Fissure Group, 490n; Grand Prismatic, 365, 402; Heart Lake, 490; Hour, 175; Huckleberry Hot, 512n; ice, 457; Inkspot, 267; intermittent, 462; mineral, 559; Mud Pots, 288; Snake River, 502n, 504; Steamboat, 304; Sulphur, 287;

Bonney, Orrin H

Battle drums and geysers; the life and journals of Lt. Gustavus Cheyney Doane, soldier and explorer of the Yellowstone and Snake River regions [by] Orrin H. and Lorraine Bonney. [1st ed.] Chicago, Sage Books [1970]

xxv, 622 p. illus., facsims., maps (4 fold.), ports. 24 cm.

Includes Doane's journals of the Yellowstone exploration of 1870 and the Snake River exploration of 1876–1877.
Bibliography: p. [591]–604.

1. Doane, Gustavus Cheyney, 1840–1892.   2. Yellowstone River.
3. Snake River.   I. Bonney, Lorraine G., joint author.   II. Doane, Gustavus Cheyney, 1840–1892.   III. Title.

copy 2
F594.D627B6   917.8   70–91169
                                                                        MARC

Library of Congress   71 [7]